D1064396

MORRISON R. WAITE

The Triumph of Character

Chief Justice Morrison Remick Waite

MORRISON R. WAITE

The Triumph of Character

C. Peter Magrath

THE MACMILLAN COMPANY, NEW YORK
Collier-Macmillan Limited, London

The author is grateful to the following copyright holders for the use of their material: the Adams Manuscript Trust for permission to quote excerpts from the Diary of Charles Francis Adams; the Harvard University Press for permission to reprint letters from Thomas C. Cochran, *Railroad Leaders, 1845–1890, The Business Mind in Action* (1953), and Charles Fairman, *Mr. Justice Miller and the Supreme Court 1862–1890* (1939); the Louisiana State University Press for permission to reprint a letter from Louis Rubin, *Teach the Freeman*, Volume II (1959); the Yale University Press for the use of a photograph in Theodore Clarke Smith, *The Life and Letters of James Abram Garfield*, Volume II (1925); and the *Stanford Law Review* for permission to quote a passage appearing in Volume XL (1953).

First Printing

The Macmillan Company, New York
Collier-Macmillan Canada, Ltd., Toronto, Ontario
Divisions of The Crowell-Collier Publishing Company

Printed in the United States of America

Library of Congress catalog card number: 63-14340

Designed by N. Sylvester

To my father,

Laurence W. Magrath,

whose life also exemplifies character

ACKNOWLEDGMENTS

WHILE A BOOK'S AUTHOR IS ULTIMATELY RESPONSIBLE FOR THE ACCLAIM —or anger—which his handiwork evokes, it is nevertheless true that many persons and institutions assist in its preparation. My book is no exception: the authorship is solely mine, but others have given me aid and comfort.

I have a number of debts among my friends and teachers in the academic world which it is a pleasure to acknowledge. Walter F. Berns, Robert B. Dishman, Richard P. Longaker, Lawrence A. Parkus, Clinton Rossiter, David Spitz, and Alan F. Westin, each in his own helpful way, assisted me in my work. I think they know how thankful I am for their help.

In my searches for material on Morrison Remick Waite, three individuals in particular led me to those small but profitable "gold finds" which are the real rewards of historical research. The late Morison R. Waite of Cincinnati, a host as genial as his grandfather, the Chief Justice, made available to me both his papers and his entertaining recollections. Professor and Mrs. John B. Waite of Ann Arbor placed in my hands some of the oldest surviving material on Morrison Waite's early years. Mr. Watt P. Marchman of the Rutherford B. Hayes Library has earned my gratitude, as he has of so many other students of nineteenth century America, for his thorough responses to my requests; the Hayes Library, which he directs, has become an essential way station to a small army of researchers.

I am also grateful to the following persons for their various courtesies: Professor Harry Brown of Michigan State University; Professor Charles Fairman of Harvard University; Miss Grace I. Farwell of West Medway, Massachusetts; Mr. Robert E. Fessenden of the Oregon Historical Society; Mr. Justice Felix Frankfurter; Dr. Bess Glenn of the National Archives; Mr. Roland Gray, Jr., of Boston; Mr. Justice John M. Harlan; Miss Jane W. Hill of the Yale University Library; Mrs. Alice P. Hook of the Historical and Philosophical Society of Ohio; Professor Rayford W. Logan of Howard University; Mrs. Irene McCreery of the Toledo Public Library; Mr. David C. Mearns of the Manuscript Division, Library of Congress; Mr. Archie Motley of the Chicago Historical Society; Mrs. Walter Nelles; Mr. Stephen T. Riley of the Massachusetts Historical Society; Professor John P. Roche of Brandeis University; Mrs. Marion R. Small of the Maine Historical Society; Mrs. Pearl W. Von Allmen of the University of Louisville Law Library; and Mr. Conrad F. Weitzel of the Ohio Historical Society.

My study of Waite and his times, and the completion of this book, were materially aided by two financial grants, one from the Samuel S. Fels Foundation and the other from the American Council of Learned Societies.

Finally, I deeply appreciate the many efforts of my wife, Sandra; she was an unofficial—and first-rate—copy editor.

C. P. M.

CONTENTS

I can't write about my sensations as to the gown or otherwise. I will tell you all at some time. They were strange sometimes, but yet I seem to take to them naturally. *

* Morrison Waite to his wife,
commenting on his installation as Chief Justice of the United States.

MORRISON R. WAITE

The Triumph of Character

I

GRANT FINDS A CHIEF JUSTICE

The Miscast President. Spoilsmen in the Saddle.

Politico Conkling and the Chief Justiceship.

A Disdainful Refusal. Maneuvers and Intrigues.

A Scandalous Nomination. Attorney General Williams Withdraws.

"Rebel" Caleb Cushing. Justice Miller Overrules Cushing.

Morrison R. Waite of Toledo. Waite Nominated. Nation Relieved.

The Vagaries of Appointment in the Era of Grant.

SALMON PORTLAND CHASE, CHIEF JUSTICE OF THE UNITED STATES, died on May 7, 1873. Eight months later, January 21, 1874, the Senate confirmed Morrison Remick Waite of Ohio to succeed him as the nation's seventh Chief Justice. With a sigh of relief, Secretary of State Hamilton Fish picked up his pen and wrote, "We had '*a time*' over the Chief Justiceship. . . . It has been a hard parturition—I hope that what has been produced may prove successful." [1] From wise old Gideon Welles, the great diarist of the Lincoln Cabinet, came a similar sentiment. Waite, he allowed, would probably make a good judge. "It is a wonder," Welles told his son, "that Grant did not pick up some old acquaintance, who was a stage driver or bartender for the place. We may be thankful he has done so well." [2]

Fish and Welles had good reason to feel relieved, if not overjoyed, at Waite's elevation to the Supreme Court. For this was the Grant era. In politics the spoilsmen divided over offices rather than principles. In industry strong-willed men—Vanderbilt, Rockefeller, Carnegie—helped themselves to fortunes and in the process transformed America into the world's leading industrial nation. And everywhere, in politics, business, and society, there were disturbing signs of pervasive corruption: the Credit Mobilier scandal, which revealed shameless profiteering in the construction of the government-subsidized Union Pacific Railroad, the "Salary Grab" act of 1873

[1] Fish to Robert C. Schenck, Jan. 19, 1874, Letterbooks. Hamilton Fish Papers, Library of Congress (cited hereafter as L.C.).

[2] Gideon Welles to Edgar T. Welles, Jan. 22, 1874. Gideon Welles Papers, L.C.

which had Congress voting itself a tidy sum as a retroactive pay increase, the Whiskey Ring of distillers and federal revenue officers, who cheated the government of millions, and the Tweed Ring, which managed to bilk New York City of thirty million dollars. Less dramatic, but no less scandalous, was the squalor of the fast-growing urban slums that provided a stark contrast to the luxurious life of the wealthy. Earlier periods of scandal, concluded Henry Adams, were "relatively harmless" compared to the Grant era, which found "all the great active forces of society, in one dirty cesspool of vulgar corruption." [3]

When Ulysses S. Grant began his first term as President in 1869, he basked in the confidence of the vast majority of his fellow citizens. The great hero of the Union cause, the man who succeeded where others had failed in finally crushing Lee's Army would, it was widely believed, rise to even greater heights in the presidential chair. Unfortunately, the qualities which served General Grant so well in the Wilderness—a grasp of military strategy, stubbornness, and a fixed vision that Lee's forces had to be engaged—were useless to President Grant. Unskilled in the wiles of politics, he was easily manipulated by men like Roscoe Conkling, Ben Butler, or Matt Carpenter, who flattered his vanities and played on his weaknesses. Essentially without vision as to where he wanted to lead the country, Grant let his Administration drift. While unscrupulous adventurers fed at the public trough, millions of bewildered freedmen sought to adjust to a new way of life and the problem of an unreconstructed South cried for attention. And, though stubbornness and loyalty to subordinates had been an admirable quality when he pursued Lee through Virginia, it proved disastrous when, as President, he reappointed "Boss" Alexander Shepherd to another four-year term in Washington's city government after Shepherd had been exposed for corruption, and when he stuck by his private secretary, Orville Babcock, who was deeply implicated in the Whiskey Ring.[4]

[3] *The Education of Henry Adams* (New York: The Modern Library, 1931), pp. 271–272.

[4] A superb picture of Grant's Administration is given in Allan Nevins, *Hamilton Fish, The Inner History of the Grant Administration* (New York: Dodd, Mead and Company, 1936), cited hereafter as Nevins, *Fish*. See also, William B. Hesseltine, *Ulysses S. Grant* (New York: Dodd, Mead and Company, 1935).

The "hard parturition," as Hamilton Fish described the quest for a Chief Justice, was, in fact, a natural consequence of Grant's haphazard method of making appointments. From the outset they showed him to be a confused political amateur, groping along without any fixed principle or even a temporary plan.[5] When Henry Adams heard the announcement of Grant's first Cabinet, he suddenly realized that his intended future of government service had become a laughable "absurdity." With such a "miscarriage," he sadly concluded, "no thought of effectual reform could revive for at least one generation." [6] The President's casual attitude toward appointments was typified by the naming of Alexander T. Stewart, a New York department store owner who contributed heavily to Grant's campaign, as Secretary of the Treasury and Adolph E. Borie, an unknown but wealthy merchant who helped purchase a house in Philadelphia for the President, as Secretary of the Navy. To be sure, his first Cabinet included two men of caliber, Ebenezer Rockwood Hoar and Jacob D. Cox, but, for resisting the spoilsmen, both had been unceremoniously forced out of the Cabinet by 1870. Attorney General Hoar was replaced by the obscure Amos T. Akerman, Cox by Columbus Delano, who later resigned in disgrace because of corruption in his Interior Department. Only in Hamilton Fish, who became Secretary of State early in his first Administration, had Grant retained a man whose ability and unimpeachable integrity provided a dramatic contrast to the mediocrity and tawdriness that characterized the national administration.

However much the events that followed Salmon Chase's death in 1873 were typical of the Grant era, they remain unique in the history of the Supreme Court. Along with other public institutions of the day, the Court labored under a cloud of suspicion. Beginning with the *Dred Scott* decision of 1857, when the Court majority went out of its way to declare the Missouri Compromise unconstitutional, it declined in popular esteem. Throughout the Civil War the Court's Democratic members were suspected of favoring the rebel cause, with the Chief Justice, Roger Taney, an object of particular scorn for his part in the *Dred Scott* debacle. The pathetic spectacle of the aged

[5] Nevins, *Fish*, p. 108.
[6] *The Education of Henry Adams*, p. 262.

Chief Justice vainly resisting President Lincoln's suspension of the writ of habeas corpus marks one of the low points in the Court's prestige and authority.[7] After the war congressional fears that it would nullify the Reconstruction acts crystallized in an unprecedented curtailment of the Court's habeas corpus jurisdiction.[8] And, although Grant stumbled into two excellent choices when he placed William Strong and Joseph P. Bradley on the Court in 1870, the subsequent reversal in the *Legal Tender Cases* left an unpleasant suspicion of court packing.[9] No less damaging was the unseemly political maneuvering of Chief Justice Chase and his colleague, David Davis, both of whom wore their judicial robes uneasily as they partook of the great game of presidential politics.

With its reputation already damaged, the Court could ill afford the tragicomic events that attended Grant's efforts to find a Chief Justice. Certainly they were not inevitable, for there was no dearth of potentially fine appointees. Thomas M. Cooley, John F. Dillon, and Horace Gray among lower court judges; Samuel F. Miller and Joseph P. Bradley on the Supreme Court; former Justice Benjamin R. Curtis, Ebenezer R. Hoar, William M. Evarts, or George F. Edmunds in the national arena were all well-known Republicans of proven ability and integrity. The appointment of any one of these men would have been generally hailed as a fitting choice for Chief Justice. Such, however, was not to be the case.

As the summer of 1873 faded into autumn, speculation centered on Judge Ebenezer Rockwood Hoar, Grant's former Attorney General; Supreme Court Justice Samuel Miller; Edwards Pierrepont, a strong supporter of the President and a United States attorney; Attorney General George H. Williams, a former Oregon Senator; and two Administration leaders in the Senate, Oliver P. Morton of Indiana and Timothy O. Howe of Wisconsin. Finally, on November

[7] *Ex parte Merryman*, 17 Fed. Cas. 144 (1861). The story is told in Carl B. Swisher, *Roger B. Taney* (New York: The Macmillan Company, 1935), pp. 547–560.

[8] 14 Statutes at Large 44, ending the Court's jurisdiction in *Ex parte McCardle*, 7 Wallace 506 (1869).

[9] *Hepburn* v. *Griswold*, 8 Wallace 603 (1870), reversed in *Knox* v. *Lee*, 12 Wallace 457 (1871). The notion that the appointees were parties to a plot to reverse the *Legal Tender* decision is, however, false. Charles Fairman, "Mr. Justice Bradley's Appointment to the Supreme Court and the Legal Tender Cases," *Harvard Law Review*, LIV (1941), 977, 1128.

8, Grant offered the chief justiceship to one of his closest political allies, Senator Roscoe Conkling of New York. The delay, Grant wrote, was due to his conviction that the appointment should wait until Congress convened because "a Chief Justice should never be subjected to the mortification of a rejection. . . ." "The possibility of your rejection," he hastened to add, "was not dreamed of." [10]

Brilliant and incredibly arrogant, the lordly Sir Roscoe cut a broad swath on the national scene for two decades—first as a Radical, later as a Stalwart, but always as a spoilsman. With the patronage of the New York Customhouse as his base, Conkling dominated the state's Republican politics until 1881, when President Garfield and James G. Blaine combined to destroy his influence. Advocates of civil service and a purification of political life regarded Conkling, with good cause, as their archfoe. He returned the compliment, reminding them that "parties are not built up by deportment, or by ladies' magazines, or gush." As for the reformers, he had only scorn: "Their stock in trade is rancid, canting self-righteousness. They are wolves in sheep's clothing. Their real object is office and plunder. When Dr. Johnson defined patriotism as the last refuge of a scoundrel, he was unconscious of the undeveloped capabilities of the word 'Reform.' " [11]

Well-educated, shrewd, and forceful, the forty-four-year-old Conkling would certainly have brought excitement, though hardly dignity, to the Court. He was, however, quite uninterested in a judicial career and declined Grant's unsolicited proffer, writing him that transfer from the Senate to the Bench involved considerations "beyond my own interest and wishes." [12] "I could not take the place," he confided to friends, "for I would be forever gnawing my chains." [13] Representative James A. Garfield, who conceded Conkling's ability but felt that he was "not of the judicial mind," was taken aback by the rejection. "It is very rare that a man forty-four years of age puts aside so tempting a prize. It reminds me of the

[10] Alfred R. Conkling, *The Life and Letters of Roscoe Conkling* (New York: C. L. Webster and Company, 1889), pp. 460–461, cited hereafter as *Conkling*.
[11] *Conkling*, pp. 540–541.
[12] Conkling to Grant, Nov. 20, 1873, in *Conkling*, pp. 460–461; Conkling to Benjamin F. Butler, May 21, 1873. Benjamin F. Butler Papers, L.C.
[13] *Conkling*, p. 461.

refusal of the Younger Pitt in his early youth to accept a place in the Cabinet, saying that he declined any but the first place! Perhaps this is Conkling's reason." [14] Ohio's rising Congressman had probably put his finger on one of the main reasons behind Conkling's refusal. A man of intense political ambition, Conkling had only to recall the unhappy experience of Chief Justice Chase to whom the office, with "no favors to grant, no patronage to wield, seemed like retirement from public life." [15]

Meanwhile, other aspirants and their supporters were bidding for the position. The Supreme Court itself supplied two very active candidates, Justice Samuel F. Miller, a man of strong intellect who was one of the Court's dominant personalities, and Justice Noah H. Swayne, a man whose ambitions far outstripped his abilities. Miller had the support of War Secretary W. W. Belknap, and was widely endorsed by the legal profession. Additional backing came from the Washington *Chronicle*, a newspaper controlled by his son-in-law, Colonel Robert B. Corkhill. [16] Swayne's principal advocates were two fellow Ohioans, Interior Secretary Columbus Delano and Representative Garfield. Justice Swayne had cast longing eyes on the vacant seat left by Chief Justice Taney's death in 1864; [17] he now claimed that Grant had promised him the post should a vacancy again occur. Almost pathetic in his eagerness, Swayne repeatedly called on Garfield, who he hoped could prod the President's memory.[18] Far abler than Swayne was a third judicial candidate, Justice Joseph P. Bradley. A man of real stature, Bradley had an advocate in the Secretary of the Navy, George Robeson, and, though willing to accept the position, did little to encourage his nomination.

Sometime in late November Grant firmly decided against appointing from the Court. As early as mid-August the Associated

[14] Garfield's *Journal*, Nov. 13, 24, 1873. James A. Garfield Papers, L.C.

[15] Hugh McCulloch, *Men and Measures of Half a Century* (New York: C. Scribner's Sons, 1888), pp. 186–187.

[16] Charles Fairman, *Mr. Justice Miller and the Supreme Court* (Cambridge: Harvard University Press, 1939), pp. 250–257, cited hereafter as Fairman, *Miller*. In ch. xi Fairman gives a useful account of the struggle over the chief justiceship.

[17] David M. Silver, *Lincoln's Supreme Court* (Urbana: University of Illinois Press, 1956), pp. 189–191.

[18] Garfield's *Journal*, Nov. 13, 15, 17, 18, 24, 1873.

Press had reported that Grant would not elevate any of the judges.[19] Yet, when Garfield called on the President on November 18 to urge Swayne's appointment, he merely found him "in doubt what to do." [20] There was no indication that Grant (who by then probably suspected that Conkling would decline) had decided against the Court's candidates. But by the end of the month it became clear that none of the Justices would be promoted. Grant's coterie had other plans and Justices Miller, Swayne, and Bradley did not figure in them. Miller subsequently blamed Attorney General Williams, himself interested in the position, for the failure of his candidacy. Williams, he charged, convinced Grant that precedent was against giving the post to judges sitting on the Court.[21] To do so supposedly encouraged intra-Court rivalries and broke down the tribunal's detachment from politics—hardly an impressive argument at a time when Swayne and Miller were already deeply involved in lobbying for the chief justiceship. Lincoln gave a similar reason in also refusing to appoint the luckless Swayne.[22] In 1888, when yet another President bypassed a Court candidate, Justice Bradley was moved to protest the "popular prejudice" against elevating associate justices who, he argued, had the benefit of prior experience. Only the selection of a man possessing "eminence already acquired in statesmanship and knowledge of public law and public affairs" justified going outside the Court for a Chief Justice.[23] With President Taft's appointment in 1910 of Associate Justice Edward D. White as Chief Justice, the tradition that Bradley denounced as "senseless and absurd" came to an end.

At some point, although the dates are not clear, Grant reportedly offered the chief justiceship to two Senators who figured prominently in the early speculation, Timothy O. Howe and Oliver P. Morton.[24]

[19] N.Y. *Times*, Aug. 18, 1873.

[20] Garfield's *Journal*, Nov. 18, 1873.

[21] Fairman, *Miller*, pp. 264–265.

[22] Willard L. King, *Lincoln's Manager, David Davis* (Cambridge: Harvard University Press, 1960), p. 222.

[23] Joseph P. Bradley to Stephen J. Field, draft dated April 30, 1888. Joseph P. Bradley Papers, New Jersey Historical Society. Field had been an unsuccessful candidate for the chief justiceship.

[24] William D. Foulke, *Life of Oliver P. Morton* (Indianapolis-Kansas City: The Bowen-Merrill Company, 1899), II, 339–340; Duane Mowry, "Timothy Otis Howe," *Green Bag*, XV (1903), 514; N.Y. *Times*, Dec. 1, 1873.

Both, however, declined and on November 30 Grant turned to his Secretary of State, Hamilton Fish. He too refused the position, declaring with undue modesty that twenty years away from the bar had made him incompetent for the place.[25] That same day Grant suggested to Fish that a "temporary" appointment be offered to Caleb Cushing, with the understanding that Cushing resign before the presidential term ended. This particular scheme was the brainstorm of the irrepressible Benjamin F. Butler, one of the more colorful rascals on the post-Civil War scene and one of Grant's close advisers.[26] As for Caleb Cushing, a checkered national career marked him as a man whose only principle was to be on the winning side. A Whig congressman in the 1830's, he eventually joined the Democrats and served as Franklin Pierce's Attorney General, supported the *Dred Scott* decision, and presided over the secessionist Democratic convention that nominated Breckinridge in 1860. Finally, as a loyal Unionist, he became an adviser to the Lincoln Administration and a supporter of Grant's presidential bids. His ability and immense learning were widely admired, but many shared Garfield's estimate that he was "the highest type of political prostitute known to me in this country." [27]

More recently Cushing, assisted by William M. Evarts and Morrison R. Waite, had served as chief United States counsel before the Geneva Tribunal which arbitrated the *Alabama* claims dispute between the United States and Great Britain. This service obviously weighed heavily in Grant's mind and, on December 1, he presented to the Cabinet Butler's plan for temporarily appointing Cushing. According to Fish,

> The President referred to the fact that Sir Roundell Palmer, [British] Counsel at Geneva, had been made Lord Chancellor, and thought it would be a fitting return to advance our leading Counsel in return. . . . I expressed a very high estimate of Cushing's ability and fitness and the appropriateness of some recognition of those who

[25] Nevins, *Fish*, p. 661.

[26] Butler's original choice was Conkling. Conkling to Butler, May 21, 1873. Butler Papers.

[27] Garfield to L. L. Pinkerton, Jan. 14, 1874, Letterbooks. Garfield Papers. But see the sympathetic evaluation of Cushing in Claude M. Fuess, *Caleb Cushing* (New York: Harcourt, Brace and Company, 1923), II.

> represented us at Geneva, but felt the force of the objection to Cushing's age [seventy-four], and the question of the propriety of dispensing an office of that character on a conditional tenure.[28]

The Cabinet supported Fish, and Grant dropped the plan. It is perhaps no idle coincidence that the next President to consider seriously such a shabby move was Warren Gamaliel Harding. In 1921 Harding, whose administration paralleled Grant's in mediocrity and corruption, toyed with the idea of making aged and decrepit Justice William Rufus Day Chief Justice on the understanding that he resign in six months.[29]

Grant's next step proved equally inept. He nominated his Attorney General, George H. Williams, who had been skillfully furthering his own interests by persuading the President that it would be unwise to appoint from the Court. As Attorney General, he had displayed little competence as a lawyer and, although that was only a relatively minor matter in the Grant era, it soon became evident that Williams was open to damaging charges of corruption. While the New York Bar Association, the legal journals, and most of the press were branding Williams as unfit, the Senate Judiciary Committee, headed by the incorruptible George F. Edmunds, was uncovering information that ended Williams' dream for the chief justiceship. Allowing for the fact that some of the charges directed against the Attorney General were false, much remained that he could not explain. There were such matters as the purchase of an elegant landaulet (a convertible carriage) and servants liveries for his personal use from the Justice Department's contingent fund, the mingling of his personal accounts with those of the Department, and the activities of an ambitious wife who, for financial considerations, dispensed immunity from prosecution. "Landaulet" Williams, as the press quickly nicknamed him, was finished. When the President's staunchest senatorial supporters made it clear that they would vote against confirmation, Grant had Williams withdraw his name (he was re-

[28] Diary, Dec. 1, 1873. Fish Papers.

[29] Henry F. Pringle, *The Life and Times of William Howard Taft* (New York: Farrar and Rinehart, 1939), II, 958–959.

tained as Attorney General).[30] Corruption had its limitations, even in the Grant era.

Williams did not officially withdraw until January 7, 1874. Autumn had passed into winter and by then the Administration's friends were becoming restless. The New York *Times*, which in the optimism of mid-September had forecast that Grant's choice would be a wise and acceptable one, now described the contest for the position as "humiliating" and "scandalous." "Surely," the paper implored, "it cannot be difficult for the President to make a choice which will at least command the general respect of the country and the Bar, if it does not satisfy all classes of politicians." [31] But Grant, acting impulsively, now sent the name of Caleb Cushing to the Senate—a sure guarantee of another uproar. To many of the party faithful, who vividly recalled his long identification with the Southern fire-eaters, Cushing's latter-day conversion to Republicanism remained highly suspect. Charles Francis Adams judged him to be "a better man now than he ever was before," who would make "a safer judge" than any other likely Grant nominee.[32] The pro-Administration Washington *National Republican*, while it praised Cushing as "the foremost lawyer of the country," acknowledged that the nomination had taken the Cabinet "somewhat by surprise." [33] Most Republican newspapers and politicians, however, let out a roar. A "shocking error" said the New York *Times* and declared that "Jeff. Davis" himself could not have picked a man more pleasing to the Democrats.[34] Garfield noted the opposition of such congressmen as Judge Hoar and House Speaker Blaine and added that Cushing "has been a bitter opponent of republican ideas and is doubtless appointed as a mere 'locum tenens.' " [35] Edward L. Godkin's *Nation* spoke for liberal Republican

[30] Useful accounts of the Williams' fiasco occur in Fairman, *Miller*, pp. 259–261; Nevins, *Fish*, pp. 662–664; John P. Frank, "The Appointment of Supreme Court Justices: Prestige, Principles and Politics," *Wisconsin Law Review*, Volume 1941, 191–202.

[31] Sept. 15, 16, 1873; Jan. 9, 1874.

[32] Charles Francis Adams Diary, Jan. 14, 1874. The Adams Manuscript Trust (Microfilm, Massachusetts Historical Society).

[33] Jan. 10, 1874.

[34] Jan. 10, 11, 12, 1874.

[35] Garfield's *Journal*, Jan. 9, 1874.

opinion: "In the nomination of Mr. Cushing for Chief-Justice, it may be said that the President has at last entered the small circle of eminent lawyers and then with great care has chosen the worst man in it." [36]

The most effective attack came from the paper of Justice Miller's son-in-law, Corkhill's Washington *Chronicle*. Between January 10 and 14 the *Chronicle* featured a series of articles that, combined with the efforts of California Senator A. A. Sargent, who hated Cushing for personal reasons, defeated the appointment. Already under suspicion as a "copperhead," Cushing's hopes for confirmation ended with the uncovering of a letter he wrote to Confederate President Jefferson Davis on March 20, 1861, introducing a government clerk whom he described as a "practical man" and a "ripe and accomplished scholar with predominating literary tastes and habits." Quite harmless in itself, the letter, in the poisonous atmosphere of postwar Washington, left an implication of treasonous contact between Cushing and the political leader of the secessionist states. W. W. Belknap, the War Secretary and one of Justice Miller's backers, read the supposedly incriminating letter at a Cabinet meeting. Senator Sargent presented it to the Republican caucus. Meanwhile, the *Chronicle* also publicized it by printing a fraudulent version that depicted the government clerk as an experienced worker "in the Ordnance Department at Washington" who may be "of special service to you." [37]

In fact, the original version in itself was enough to destroy Cushing, and Justice Miller's biographer strongly contends that neither Miller nor Colonel Corkhill was guilty of deliberate forgery. It is nonetheless clear that Miller, motivated by his strong ambitions and a sincere conviction that the appointment was not in the public interest, played an important part in defeating Cushing. On January 18 he wrote a close friend that, while Attorney General Williams lacked ability and he was glad to see the rejection of the man "who had set the President against any appointment from the Bench," he could have adjusted himself to Williams' confirmation. They were once friends and the Attorney General would have been "more likely

[36] Jan. 15, 1874.

[37] Fairman, *Miller*, pp. 263–275; Nevins, *Fish*, pp. 664–665; Fuess, *Caleb Cushing*, II, 363–376.

to make my place on the bench influential and pleasant, than any other man the President will appoint." "I did not however lay a straw in his path," he continued, "and the 'Washington Chronicle' now under Corkhill's control preserved an absolute silence. But when Cushing was nominated we both broke ground openly and vigorously, and in three days we had him beaten." [38] Cushing indeed realized that he was "beaten" and on January 14 asked the President to withdraw the nomination. Grant, no closer to filling the vacancy than in June, had already decided to give up on Cushing.

Hamilton Fish now renewed earlier suggestions that the President appoint Judge Hoar, whose distinguished public career included service on the Massachusetts Supreme Judicial Court. Grant, however, was not particularly fond of Hoar and had dismissed him as Attorney General in 1870 in a cheap play to gain votes for his ill-fated Santo Domingo Treaty.[39] At a Cabinet meeting on January 14, the same meeting which sealed Cushing's fate, Fish suggested Hoar. "The President," he records, "mentioned that Hoar had yesterday told him that he was preparing a speech to be delivered soon, denying the power of Congress to emit legal tenders." Since the Supreme Court had earlier upheld such power and no legal tender questions were then pending, Grant merely seized upon Hoar's legal tender views as a convenient excuse. After some further discussion three names "eventually seemed to be the most acceptable": Lewis B. Woodruff, United States circuit judge for the second circuit; Morrison R. Waite, one of the American counsel at Geneva; and John F. Dillon, United States circuit judge for the eighth circuit. Two days later the Cabinet also considered circuit Judge Thomas J. Drummond, but Fish now placed Waite at the head of the list.[40]

A successful Ohio lawyer with a political career limited to a few comparatively minor forays into his state's Republican politics, Morrison Remick Waite first appeared on the national scene in 1872 when he participated in the Geneva Arbitration. As one of the three American counsel, the other two being Caleb Cushing and William M. Evarts, he helped prepare and argue the case that won the United

[38] Fairman, *Miller*, p. 264.
[39] Nevins, *Fish*, pp. 364–371.
[40] Diary, Jan. 14, 16, 1874. Fish Papers.

States fifteen million dollars while soothing nationalistic feelings aroused by England's friendly neutrality toward the Confederacy. Returning to his thriving Toledo law practice in the fall of 1872, Waite added to his growing prominence by winning election to the Ohio constitutional convention, which chose him as its president. And yet, throughout his life a man of modesty and moderate ambition, Waite gave little thought to succeeding Chase. Perhaps it occurred to him for a brief instant on May 14, 1873, when, as a member of a committee of the Ohio bar, he helped draft resolutions marking the death of Chief Justice Chase.[41] If so, it did not trouble him long. Certainly few of the politically conscious regarded Morrison Waite as a formidable candidate. His name was not among those believed to be under favored consideration and it is doubtful if one congressman in five could have supplied much information about the Toledo lawyer.

Waite's name, to be sure, appeared as a possibility in the press, particularly in Ohio and also in Connecticut, his family home. From Connecticut a cousin inquired of his chances, while Evarts, a longtime friend and recent colleague at Geneva, wrote to "congratulate you, also, in being a candidate for Ch. J. of U. S. If it costs you no more time, thought, or desire than it does me you will have the clear gain of honor without drawback of loss or burden." [42] Evarts was wise not to get excited over the chief justiceship, because Grant had no intention of appointing him. A Republican of markedly independent habits, he incurred the wrath of party regulars for successfully defending Andrew Johnson in the impeachment trial and later serving in that hated President's Cabinet. Conkling strongly opposed him, and Grant himself was personally cool.[43] As for Waite, he followed Evarts' advice, displaying a casual unconcern and rating his chances as poor.[44] In letters to Bancroft Davis, the American agent at Geneva and Assistant Secretary of State, one of his leading backers

[41] Charles Goddard to Waite, May 10, 1873. Morrison R. Waite Papers, L.C. All correspondence to and from Waite, unless otherwise indicated, is in the Waite Papers.
[42] John T. Wait to Waite, June 14, 1873; Evarts to Waite, June 16, 1873.
[43] Chester L. Barrows, *William M. Evarts, Lawyer, Diplomat, Statesman* (Chapel Hill: University of North Carolina Press, 1941), p. 198, 215, pp. 225–226, cited hereafter as Barrows, *Evarts;* Chester S. Lyman to Waite, Jan. 22, 1874.
[44] Henry B. Curtis to Waite, January 27, 1874.

for the post, Waite completely ignored the subject.[45] When Cushing received the nomination, Waite hoped for his confirmation. An influential supporter later chided him—"you never wrote a letter"—for failing to canvass for the position.[46]

His friends were less reserved. Samuel L. M. Barlow, a prominent New York lawyer, began a "campaign" on Waite's behalf during the summer of 1873. In Washington, Bancroft Davis and Elihu B. Washburne, who became his friends during the Geneva Arbitration, urged Grant to appoint Waite.[47] The bizarre sequence of events that began with Conkling's disdainful refusal, was followed by the malodorous nomination of "Landaulet" Williams and then the *opéra bouffe* surrounding Cushing's appointment, conspired heavily to favor a man like Waite. His honesty was unquestioned and, since he had few enemies, he could expect quick confirmation. For, with Grant, the problem was how to fill the vacancy at a minimum of further embarrassment. The President's fumbling efforts invited ridicule: when a congressman tauntingly suggested a bill abolishing the chief justiceship so as to spare him the mortification of further appointments, another wit retorted that this was quite unnecessary: Grant had long since destroyed the position.

Even before the unhappy Williams-Cushing nominations, Waite's name began to draw attention. After Williams withdrew in disgrace, press reports mentioned Waite as one of the more likely nominees.[48] When Grant decided not to appoint from the Court, he gained important backing within the Cabinet as Interior Secretary Columbus Delano shifted from Justice Swayne to Waite. Delano's relationship to Waite remains unclear. Both were Ohioans and both participated in the state's Republican politics during the war, but there is little evidence that they were close associates.

Despite reports that Waite was virtually unknown to the President and Cabinet,[49] Grant, from the beginning, kept him in mind as

[45] Waite to Bancroft Davis, Oct. 31, Nov. 7, 1873, J. C. Bancroft Davis Papers, L.C.
[46] Charles C. Beaman to Waite, Jan. 23, 1874; Samuel Barlow to Waite, Jan. 20, 1874.
[47] Barlow to Waite, Jan. 20, 1874; Waite to Bancroft Davis, June 16, 1877, Letterbooks; Waite to Washburne, n.d., 1873, Feb. 26, 1874. Elihu B. Washburne Papers, L.C.
[48] Chicago *Inter Ocean*, Nov. 28, 1873, Jan. 9, 1874; Washington *National Republican*, Jan. 8, 1874; N.Y. *Tribune*, Jan. 15, 1874.
[49] For instance, N.Y. *Tribune*, Jan. 19, 1874.

a possible nominee.[50] Early in 1873 when Waite came to Washington to be admitted to the Supreme Court bar—sponsored by Caleb Cushing in one of those little ironies so intriguing to historians—Grant invited him to dinner. The President's courtesies prompted Waite to tell a friend, "Nothing can exceed the kindness with which he has received me here." [51] By January 16, as the Fish Diary shows, he had become the probable nominee, and the Washington *National Republican* hastened to contact Waite's friends in order to get background information.[52] Although his candidacy, as a minor federal official reported, was in part "the work of the Ohio men here," [53] Ohio's best known politician was not among them. For Senator John Sherman knew so little about Waite that when his nomination became likely, he contacted Ohio's Representative from the Toledo district to get information. "M. R. Waites age 57—Born at Lyme, Conn't. Graduated at Yale 1837. Commenced practice law Toledo 1839," he was told.[54]

With Waite's nomination imminent, Roscoe Conkling's Senate friends sought to block the appointment by persuading the New York politico to change his mind. On January 18 Senators Timothy Howe and Hannibal Hamlin telegraphed Alonzo Cornell, a close ally of Conkling, that they had "the best of evidence that the President would like to renew the offer to Mr. Conkling." Waite, they argued, "has every requisite except repute . . . [and] it may be objected to Mr. Waite that he is the third or fourth choice and that he is unknown." [55] Conkling again demurred and the next day Grant nominated Morrison R. Waite of Toledo to be Chief Justice.

From the nation's press came a collective sigh of relief. The general response, though lukewarm and reserved, was one of thankfulness for having been spared from a Conkling, a Williams, or a Cushing. The influential New York *Tribune* suggested that at least the nomination was respectable and predicted that the Senate "will not venture to consider whether Mr. Waite is precisely the man for

[50] Chester S. Lyman to Waite, Jan. 22, 1874, reporting a conversation with Grant during the summer of 1873; George P. Este to Waite, Jan. 21, 1874.
[51] Waite to Bancroft Davis, Jan. 25, 1873. Davis Papers.
[52] R. B. Warden to Waite, Jan. 16, 1874.
[53] S. G. Arnold to "Dear Sir," Jan. 18, 1874. Waite Papers.
[54] Isaac R. Sherwood to Sherman, Jan. 16, 1874. John Sherman Papers, L.C.
[55] *Conkling*, pp. 463–464.

Chief Justice, but will look only to his respectable standing as a lawyer, as a citizen, and as a Republican, and gladly vote him into a seat where we had hoped never to see any one of less heroic stature than Marshall and Chase."[56] "The President," declared another liberal Republican journal,

> has, with remarkable skill, avoided choosing any first-rate man. Mr. Waite stands in the front rank of second-rate lawyers. . . . But he undoubtedly is a man of the highest character, and has the best possible standing at the bar of his own State. . . . On the whole, considering what the President might have done, and tried to do, we ought to be very thankful, and give Mr. Waite a cordial welcome.[57]

Predictably, the Washington *National Republican* hailed the nomination as "all that could be desired by Republicans,"[58] while the Ohio press found it "admirable" and "one that will be widely indorsed by the bar." Less cordial were the Germantown (Pa.) *Chronicle*, which described Waite as "a good representative of that respectable mediocrity which seems to be most esteemed just now," and the Chicago *Times*, which remonstrated: "Verily, the shades of Jay, and Marshall, and Taney, and Chase may arise to protest against a profanation of this venerated seat by a man so utterly incapable of filling it acceptably." A majority of the nation's editors, however, joined Samuel Bowles' Springfield *Republican* in "contrasting what is with what might have been . . . [and] congratulat[ing] the President upon his good choice, and the country upon its good fortune."[59]

Recalling the Washington *Chronicle's* bitter attack on Cushing, as well as its editor's relationship to Justice Miller, it is instructive to follow Colonel Corkhill's reaction. Not surprisingly, the first response was unenthusiastic. Waite lacked a national reputation, though, Corkhill acknowledged, "with a few years' experience he will fill the office creditably." The difficulty in making a really acceptable appointment from off the Court, the paper continued, "consists in

[56] Jan. 20, 1874.
[57] *Nation*, Jan. 22, 1874.
[58] Jan. 20, 1874.
[59] Press opinion as quoted in N.Y. *Tribune*, Jan. 21, 1874.

the transcendent ability of several of these old justices. Finding a new man to preside over them in the sense of being their superior would be exceedingly difficult." And, quoting the Boston *Evening Transcript* as its source, the *Chronicle* noted an allegation that in 1864 Waite had compromised his Republicanism by supporting General McClellan for the Presidency.

> We are not informed as to the correctness of the above charge. The nomination of Mr. Waite is before the United States Senate. It is presumed that there will be no unnecessary haste or action in the case. If it is true . . . that during the war he voted against the administration of Mr. Lincoln . . . he should not be confirmed by the Senate. It is of pre-eminent importance that the man who shall enter upon the duties of that high office shall have a clear and unsullied record in connection with the political history of the country for the past dozen years at least, and too much care can not be exercised in the examination of the record made by any man during that period who seeks this place.[60]

Although this was a canard, Cushing's experience emphasized the danger of uncontradicted rumors. Isaac Sherwood, the Representative from Ohio's Toledo district, telegraphed home to get an immediate denial. "I was able to contradict it of course," he told Waite, "but owing to the fact that it was being used against you in the Senate and by a portion of the press—after consulting with Senator Sherman, I decided to telegraph you." [61] Senators, eager to reassure themselves of the prospective Chief Justice's political soundness, sought out people who knew him. "When I got here," one Ohio friend wrote Waite, "I found myself in demand as an Ohio lawyer to be interviewed. Were you in favor of the Amendments? Did you vote for McClellan? Were you a radical? Were you a conservative? And many other things." [62]

The only basis for doubting Waite's orthodoxy was his unsuccessful run for Congress in 1862 as a conservative supporter of Lincoln against James Ashley, a Radical Republican and close asso-

[60] Jan. 20, 1874.
[61] Sherwood to Waite, Jan. 21, 1874.
[62] Aaron F. Perry to Waite, n.d., probably late Jan., 1874; also, George P. Este to Waite, Feb. 8, 1874.

ciate of Charles Sumner. This, however, hardly sufficed to impugn a man who had otherwise remained a loyal Republican and the charges of his political unreliability were easily disproven. "An Incorrect Rumor," said the *Chronicle* and upgraded its estimate of Waite: "There seems to be no doubt on the subject of Mr. Waite's soundness as a Republican, of his purity of character and culture as a gentleman, and of his high attainments as a lawyer. We do not question his ability, with experience, to fill the office well, and think he ought to be confirmed." [63]

Opposition collapsed quickly as the Senate even dispensed with hearings. After the delays of the Williams and Cushing nominations, this was indeed speedy action and suggests an eagerness on the Senate's part to be done with the political turmoil of the past eight months. Charles Sumner provided the only discordant note. He spoke against confirmation, arguing that an office of such importance ought not be filled by a comparative unknown. While he addressed himself to the greatness of the office and expressed interest in Waite's literary habits and the quality of his speeches, Sumner undoubtedly remembered Waite's effort to unseat his radical ally, Ashley.[64] Anxious for judicial vindication of the war amendments, he questioned Waite's commitment to the radical cause because, as he wrote a friend, "who will vouch for some accepted Republicans with whom technicality is a peril to principle?" [65] Sumner's opposition, however, went no further than abstention, and on January 21 a vote of sixty-three to nothing confirmed Morrison Waite as the nation's seventh Chief Justice.

Ulysses Grant had at last found a Chief Justice in a search superficially reminiscent of Lincoln's quest for a General. But Lincoln's search, which began with McClellan and then continued with Pope, Burnside, Hooker, and Meade—all of whom were tried and found wanting—was made by a strong-willed President determined to save the Union and who knew what he was looking for: a tough-minded

[63] Jan. 21, 1874.

[64] Aaron F. Perry to Waite, n.d., probably late Jan., 1874; Richard Waite to Rutherford B. Hayes, Aug. 13, 1888. Rutherford B. Hayes Papers, Hayes Memorial Library. On Sumner's relationship to Ashley see Nevins, *Fish*.

[65] Edward L. Pierce, *Memoir and Letters of Charles Sumner* (Boston: Roberts Brothers, 1894), IV, 588–589.

military leader who could combine military ability with the tenacity needed to crush the Confederate forces. General Grant was that military leader, but later, as a tragically miscast President, his attempt to fill an important post differed radically from Lincoln's. Without any fixed purpose, he regarded appointments as essentially personal gifts to be bestowed on those who won his gratitude. And this, along with his desire to nominate someone who could win easy confirmation, is the key to Waite's appointment. Recall Hamilton Fish's diary notation that Grant "thought it would be a fitting return to advance our leading Counsel [at Geneva]." Recall, too, that the Geneva Arbitration towers above the barren plain that is Grant's Presidency as one of its few substantial accomplishments. By ending America's dangerous feud with England in the late summer of 1872, it added to Grant's prestige just prior to a presidential election and at a moment when the Liberal Republican movement seemed most threatening.

Characteristically, Grant sought to reward those who had participated at Geneva—except Evarts whom he disliked and had appointed a counsel with great reluctance. To Cushing he gave the post of Minister to Spain; to Bancroft Davis, the hard-working agent, went the ambassadorship to Germany; and after Conkling's refusal he turned to Fish, who deserved much of the credit for the Geneva success, as his second choice for Chief Justice. Writing of Waite's nomination the day it went to the Senate, Fish strongly implied that it was a reward for services rendered. "It will prove a disappointment to some expectants," he wrote, "but some who felt themselves entitled to the nomination really had no right to expect it—some, who may have been professionally qualified, had no claims to consideration by a Republican Administration, and more had put it out of the power of the present Administration to give any further recognition." [66]

In appointing Justices Bradley and Strong, it is true, Grant chose men known to believe, as did the Senate majority which confirmed them, in the legality of the legal tender acts. Normally, however, his judicial and political appointments lacked a fixed purpose. No Presi-

[66] Fish to Robert C. Schenck, Jan. 19, 1874, Letterbooks. Fish Papers.

dent, of course, appoints judges obviously hostile to his views, but careful appointments, in the sense that they are thoughtfully weighed in terms of impact on future Court decisions, are characteristic of strong Presidents anxious for judicial sanction of their programs. Lincoln wanted judges that would uphold his administration's war policies, Theodore Roosevelt feared for the outcome of anti-trust prosecutions, Franklin Roosevelt sought to reverse a series of decisions that endangered his New Deal. But Grant, without a program, and regarding offices as gifts, could offer the chief justiceship to such unlike men as Roscoe Conkling, Hamilton Fish, George Williams, Caleb Cushing, and Morrison Waite.

Contributing to the success of Waite's candidacy was the support he enjoyed, especially after Swayne's elimination, among such Ohio politicians as Columbus Delano and Representatives Isaac Sherwood and Charles Foster. In an age when regional and state loyalties were far stronger than they are today, politicians and their constituents felt a sense of inner satisfaction when their state won an important appointment. Garfield, who judged Waite as "solid and good" but not brilliant, welcomed the appointment because "Ohio has secured the Chief Justiceship." [67] Within Grant's Cabinet it was more than coincidence that had New Jerseyite Robeson supporting Justice Bradley of New Jersey, Iowan Belknap supporting Justice Miller of Iowa, and Ohioan Delano supporting first Justice Swayne and then Morrison Waite, both of whom hailed from Ohio. Too much recognition for one state led to resentment. Referring to the undue influence of "Ohio men," a legal journal opposed the confirmation of Justice Matthews of Ohio in 1881, among other reasons, because "There is a spice of indelicacy in putting an Ohio man on that bench where the chief justice is an Ohio man, which is perceptible by everybody but Ohio people." [68] Following Waite's confirmation, Ohioans proudly responded by christening a new Lake Erie steamer the "Chief Justice Waite." In contrast, it is difficult to picture modern Californians gratefully reacting to President Eisenhower's elevation of their governor by naming a jet airliner the "Chief Justice Warren."

[67] Garfield to Major D. G. Swaim, Jan. 20, 1874, Letterbooks. Garfield Papers.
[68] *Albany Law Journal*, Feb. 5, 1881.

Thanks to the influence of local pride, the need of finding a man capable of winning confirmation, and Grant's desire to reward those who had given useful service to his Administration, Morrison Waite became Chief Justice of the United States. He was an obscure figure. The bare facts of his life—date of birth, schools attended, occupation, and political affiliation—had been duly printed in the newspapers announcing the appointment. Still, the *Albany Law Journal* wondered "who and what Mr. Waite is." [69] Who was this man suddenly called from obscurity to the seats of the mighty? What were the experiences which made up his life? What ideas and attitudes came with him as he began the journey from Toledo to Washington?

[69] Jan. 24, 1874.

2

CONNECTICUT: THE EARLY YEARS

Old Lyme on the Connecticut. Family Traditions.
Rod and Rule. The Pitfalls of Chewing Tobacco. Yale College.
Brothers-in-Unity. Yale Men and Conservatism.
Waite Reads Law. Rules for Life. A Young Man Looks West.

I WAS BORN IN A COUNTRY VILLAGE AND LIVED THERE ALL MY LIFE until I went to Ohio. . . . My father was a country lawyer until he was elected judge when I was about 18 years old. His habits of life were simple, and those of his family necessarily the same." [1] Thus did Morrison Waite describe his early years in Lyme, Connecticut, where he was born on November 27, 1816. A pleasant village at the mouth of the Connecticut River, Old Lyme, as it is now called, was already rich in historical memories during Waite's childhood. Names like Mather, Buckingham, and Griswold, all prominent in New England history, were associated with Lyme, and the little farming village proudly boasted of having played its part in the stirring events of the Revolution.[2]

Morrison himself could point to such ancestors as Judge Marvin Waite, one of General Washington's electors in the first presidential election, and Colonel Samuel Selden, a Revolutionary officer of some renown and the grandfather of his mother, Marie Selden Waite. His father, Henry Matson Waite, was a modest but capable lawyer who eventually became Chief Justice of Connecticut's Supreme Court of Errors. Lawyers' fees in the early eighteen hundreds were low and Henry Waite later told his children "that he never charged but one one hundred dollar fee in his life, and felt ashamed of it for years, but it was for saving a man's neck from the gallows." [3] His practice

[1] Waite to Clark Waggoner, Jan. 2, 1881, Letterbooks.
[2] Martha Lamb, "Lyme," *Harper's Magazine*, LII (1876), 313–328.
[3] Amelia C. Waite, "Memories" (uncompleted manuscript). Waite Papers.

was successful and a small inheritance provided enough to build a comfortable farmhouse. A man of culture and education, he impressed people as unpretentious and mild in temper—so much so, in fact, that when he won election to the Supreme Court of Errors, many wondered if his calm disposition would be a hindrance. Such doubts proved unjustified, and by the time he retired as State Chief Justice in 1854 Henry Matson Waite had established a reputation for "integrity, fair-mindedness, and firmness." [4]

In the Waite household, Morrison and four brothers and sisters grew up with Episcopalianism and Whiggery as dominant values. Family legend recalls a sternly religious great-grandmother who forbade cooking or sweeping on the Sabbath and "always entered church at the precise and proper moment." [5] Young Waite, however, was brought up in the less severe atmosphere of the "low" Episcopal Church. Always a devout Episcopalian, he never gave vent in later life to the sort of religious moralizing that characterized his contemporary, Stephen J. Field, also a son of New England. Like many of his property-holding colleagues in the legal and commercial professions, Henry Waite made the migration from Federalism and National Republicanism to Whiggery. Active in state politics, he served numerous terms in the state legislature, and Morrison became acquainted with "the distinguished men of the state" who often called at his home.[6] Whiggery came naturally to one brought up in such an environment. At the age of twenty-two he wrote his father of visiting Niagara Falls and having "the *honor* of looking over them with a son of Henry Clay." [7] The "Great Compromiser" and his mighty Whig associate, Daniel Webster, were, in fact, lifelong heroes and their portraits always occupied a prominent spot in Morrison Waite's study.

As a boy, he later recalled, most of his day was spent in school with little time (and probably not much need) for him to do chores on the farm. He spent, however, two summers "with my grandfathers

[4] Franklin B. Dexter, *Biographical Sketches of the Graduates of Yale College* (New Haven: Yale University Press, 1912), VI, 284.

[5] Lamb, "Lyme," 317.

[6] Waite to Waggoner, Jan. 2, 1881.

[7] Waite to Henry M. Waite, Oct. 22, 1838. Courtesy of Professor and Mrs. John B. Waite of Ann Arbor, Michigan.

who were both farmers, and there worked in farm work as boys did. My father's object in sending me there was to give me the benefit of outdoor life and exercise." [8] In company with others of his generation he began his education in a village schoolhouse. There he learned the joys of Webster's spelling book "with its four, and only four illustrations," of readers without narratives, and of Murray's Grammar, "ever associated in our memories with sundry visitations of the rod and rule, because some of his incomprehensible illustrations would escape us, as we were daily called upon to recite 'word for word' his dreamy platitudes." A boyhood friend described the Lyme schoolhouse as "the meanest looking building in the village, and almost hoary with age."

> It had never seen a coat of paint. Its windows and doors stood at all sorts of angles, but the right. Not an outdoor convenience of any kind for either sex. The larger scholars had an inclined plane for a desk on which to write, before which they sat upon benches made of the hardest kind of oak, and so polished by the use of years that our jack-knives could scarcely make an impression upon them. When facing about, that desk presented the sharp edge of an inch board as the only support to our bodies. Still, those seats were such a luxury compared with those on which the small children did penance for six long hours every day, that the little shavers envied us and looked forward to the day when they 'could sit upon the large bench' as a little Heaven of hope.[9]

Long winter hours in school were followed by carefree summer days, and the recollection of one of them has been preserved. Admiring grownups for their use of chewing tobacco, young Waite and his friends experimented with the likes of licorice root and Indian Posy. Despite strenuous chewing, they could not get their spittle to look quite like the real thing and so, one day, they retired to a pasture to try "the unadulterated black plug, ugly enough and strong enough to make a horse sick at the sight." The future Chief Justice and his companions became violently ill. "The joys of tobacco-chewing manhood lost much of their charms, and a more disgusted

[8] Waite to Waggoner, Jan. 2, 1881.

[9] Reminiscences of William Hill, undated newspaper clipping. Waite Papers. Hill, a friend of Waite, grew up with him in Lyme.

palefaced set of boys never wended their way home fearful of some parental or maternal interviewing." [10]

Finishing with the Lyme schoolhouse, Morrison Waite began preparing to follow his father to Yale. He spent a year studying Greek and Latin at one of the best of private schools, Bacon Academy in nearby Colchester, and then, at the age of seventeen, applied for admission to Yale College. Undoubtedly the year at Bacon Academy served him in good stead, for the "Terms of Admission" announced in the Yale Catalogue were decidedly stiff: "Candidates for admission to the Freshman Class, are examined in Cicero's Select Orations, Virgil, Sallust, the Greek Testament, Dalzel's Collectanea Graeca Minora, Adam's Latin Grammar, Goodrich's Greek Grammar, Latin Prosody, Writing Latin, Barnard's or Adam's Arithmetic, Murray's English Grammar, and Morse's, Worcester's, or Woodbridge's Geography." A note cautioned students that the exams in Latin, Greek, Geography and theoretical Arithmetic would be particularly "strict and comprehensive." [11] Waite passed the exams and, joining one hundred and twenty-five other young men, became a member of the class of 1837. Arriving at New Haven on October 1, 1833, he set out to furnish a room. This he did by spending $8.27 for "1 Tab," "1 Washbowl & Pitcher," "1 Lamp," "1 Lamp Filler," "1 Bedstead," "1 Desk," and "2 Chairs." [12]

Under its firm and austere President, Jeremiah Day, the Yale College that Morrison Waite knew was a model of regularity. President Day believed "mental discipline" to be one of the great objects of instruction and, as if to emphasize the importance of discipline in human affairs, his college exemplified order and routine. "His idea was to secure good order by reducing all the operations of the institution to the perfection of regularity. . . . Good order was to be maintained by requiring obedience to wisely established rules." [13] Compulsory chapel services began the day at five in the morning during summer, at six in the winter—"a rigid and often frigid rule," one

[10] Reminiscences of William Hill, unidentified newspaper clipping dated Jan. 31, 1874. Waite Papers.

[11] *Yale College Catalogue*, 1833–1834, p. 23.

[12] Expense Book, 1833–1839. Courtesy of Mr. M. R. Waite of Cincinnati, Ohio.

[13] William L. Kingsley, *Yale College* (New York: H. Holt and Company, 1879), I, 126.

of Waite's contemporaries called it.[14] After morning prayers in the chapel, "uniformly cold in winter and hot in summer," the students hurried to dreary recitation rooms for the day's first lesson.[15] Here they translated Folsom's Livy and Homer's Odyssey and were quizzed on their mastery of Day's Algebra and Playfair's Euclid. An hour for breakfast followed and then came two more recitations.

Timothy Dwight, who succeeded Waite by a few years, found such work unattractive and uninspiring. Limited almost exclusively to "the memorizing of rules and the solving of problems," [16] the one end in view was mental discipline: "to form," as the Catalogue gravely declared, "a proper *symmetry* and *balance* of character" that would give the mind "furniture, and discipline, and elevation." [17] And yet, Dwight admitted, "It was no weak, second-rate, half-useless education." [18] In addition to the Odyssey and Folsom's Livy, Waite and his young colleagues plowed through such classics as Adam's Roman Antiquities, Horace, Juvenal, Cicero's Orations, Tacitus' History of the Germans, and the tragedies of Aeschylus, Sophocles, and Euripides. Nor were the sciences—mathematics, astronomy, and natural philosophy—neglected. In men like Professors Benjamin Silliman and Denison Olmsted, Yale possessed two of the most distinguished American scientists of the first half of the century.

It would be entertaining to record that Morrison Waite, like Stephen Field, then a student at Williams, who was put on probation for "blowing a horn in the halls," [19] had a part in some colorful incident of undergraduate life. Such, however, was not the case. Waite was a serious young man. He studied hard, occasionally went visiting in New Haven, where, he wrote, "I always had the entree to the best society," [20] and kept a meticulous record of his expenses. He made Phi Beta Kappa, was a member of one of the oldest of the Senior societies, and gave much time to the debating activites that

[14] I. N. Tarbox, "The Chapel," in Kingsley, *Yale College*, I, 277.

[15] Timothy Dwight, *Memories of Yale Life and Men* (New York: Dodd, Mead and Company, 1903), pp. 12–13, cited hereafter as *Memories*.

[16] Dwight, *Memories*, p. 22.

[17] *Yale College Catalogue*, pp. 26–27.

[18] Dwight, *Memories*, p. 23.

[19] Charles Fairman, "The Education of a Justice," *Stanford Law Review*, I (1949), 241.

[20] Waite to Waggoner, Jan. 2, 1881.

were a staple of undergraduate life and, according to him, "an essential element in a complete collegial education." [21] The times were exciting, and issues such as the government's tariff policy, the nature of the Union, the question of internal improvements, and the proper federal policy toward the controversial National Bank were all grist for the mill of eager debaters.

Waite joined the Brothers-in-Unity debating society, and his college expense book records his involvement in its affairs with such entries as "Society Tax 2.50," "Constitutions of the U.S. .12½," and "Websters Speech .12½." [22] By the time graduation came, he had served on its finance committee and as its secretary, vice president, and president. At the Junior Exhibition he won an appointment to speak on "the character of Oliver Cromwell" and at commencement "on the science of government." [23] The picture that emerges of Waite as a student suggests the accuracy of a description by William Evarts, his friend and classmate: "Never rhetorical and never ostentatious, he was from the beginning until his graduation a most intelligent, a most faithful, and a most successful student, having always the respect of all in these qualities, and not less in the sobriety of his conduct and dignity of his character." [24]

Anson Phelps Stokes once claimed that Yale men shared four great characteristics: democracy, faith ("in God, in his country, in his University, in his fellow men"), constructive activity, and conservatism.[25] Morrison Waite, it can be safely assumed, believed with his hero Webster in "people's government, made for the people, made by the people, and answerable to the people." Certainly he had faith, including faith in the university which he loved throughout his life, and his work in the Brothers-in-Unity suggests at least the beginnings of what Stokes called "constructive activity." As for conservatism, the tale will unfold and this is not the place to define that slippery word. Assuming for the moment that the protection

[21] Waite to William Kingsley, June 16, 1877, Letterbooks.
[22] Expense Book, 1833–1839.
[23] Both speeches, unfortunately, are lost.
[24] "Supreme Court Proceedings in Memoriam of Morrison R. Waite," 126 U.S. 585, 605 (1888).
[25] Anson Phelps Stokes, *Memorials of Eminent Yale Men* (New Haven: Yale University Press, 1914), II, 375.

of property rights is among its essential elements, young Waite had been exposed to one important element in the conservative creed. From Adam Smith's popularizer, Jean-Baptiste Say, he learned that the property right was "the most powerful of all encouragements to the multiplication of wealth" and that it ought to be limited only when essential to national security or when it interfered with the right of third parties. "It is to be observed," Say lectured from the pages of his book, prescribed reading for Yale men during their Senior year, "that the right of property is equally invaded, by obstructing the free employment of the means of production, as by violently depriving the proprietor of the product of his land, capital, or industry; for the right of property, as defined by jurists, is the right of use, or even abuse." [26]

Say believed it "mere usurpation" for government to assert a right over the property of individuals. He denounced all forms of government price-fixing and glorified the free market where "the avarice of one part of mankind operates as a salutary check upon the improvidence of the rest." Recalling mercantilist practices of the recent past, and with the English corn laws still in hot dispute, he continued:

> The prevalence of erroneous views of the production and commerce of articles of human subsistence have led to a world of mischievous and contradictory laws, regulations, and ordinances, in all countries, suggested by the exigency of the moment, and often extorted by popular importunity. . . . Whenever a maximum of price has been affixed to grain, it has immediately been withdrawn or concealed. The next step was, to compel the farmers to bring their grain to market, and prohibit the private sales. . . . [But] in polity as well as morality, the grand secret is, not to constrain the actions, but to awaken the inclinations of mankind. Markets are not to be supplied by the terror of the bayonet or the sabre.[27]

Never at issue in America and eventually to be repealed in England, the specific laws which prompted this outburst regulated the price of grain. And yet, Say's warning against limiting the rights of

[26] Jean-Baptiste Say, *A Treatise on Political Economy* (Philadelphia: John Grigg, 1827), p. 72.

[27] Say, *Treatise on Political Economy,* pp. 138–139, 376, note.

property, his description of price-fixing as "usurpation," and his song of praise for the free market were rooted in a set of assumptions about the "laws" of economics and their relation to government that could apply to far more than English corn laws. Laws regulating the price of storing and transporting grain, passed in response to the demands of American midwestern farmers, Waite would one day be told, were as odious and destructive of property rights as the legislation which incurred Say's wrath.

Kent's famous *Commentaries on American Law* taught Yale seniors a similar lesson in the inviolability of private property. However, as befitted a great jurist, the Chancellor reserved to the courts a major share of the responsibility for their preservation. "Personal security, and private property," he solemnly intoned, "rest entirely upon the wisdom, the stability, and the integrity of the courts of justice." As an illustration Kent pointed to the Supreme Court's decision in the *Dartmouth College Case*, which "did more than any other single act . . . to throw an impregnable barrier around all rights and franchises derived from the grant of government."[28] We do not, of course, know how diligently young Morrison Waite studied these particular passages. But we do know that at Williams College, not so far from New Haven, another young man was learning a similar lesson. Remote as this then was, both were destined to clash on the Supreme Court, and Justice Field, who obviously learned well the lesson that private property was sacred, would use language implying that Chief Justice Waite neglected, or perhaps had forgotten, this part of his studies.

Graduating in the summer of 1837, Waite returned to Lyme to read law for a year with his father. Henry Matson Waite wanted all his sons to enter the legal profession, and there seems to have been no doubt that Morrison would be anything but a lawyer. Even before leaving Yale he prepared a list of "Law Books Wanted"—"Chitty's Pleadings," "Chitty On Bills," "Kents Commentaries," "New York Reps," "Blackstone," "Laws U.S.," "Coke on Littleton," and Story's "Commen. on Constitution" and "Conflict of Laws."[29]

[28] James Kent, *Commentaries on American Law* (New York: O. Halsted, 1826), I, 273, 392.
[29] Expense Book, 1833–1839.

The year of study completed, Morrison Waite, now twenty-two, prepared to strike out on his own.

Scant as is information about these early years, an image nonetheless begins to form. Coming from a respected and well-to-do Connecticut family, he had enjoyed the benefits common to children of his class: a comfortable home life, a thorough education at the best Eastern schools, and a training in one of the leading professions. He seems to have been a serious student, eager for success in the vocation that brought his father a measure of prominence. A hint as to the sort of influence exercised upon him by his education and family comes with a set of "rules for life" penned by George Waite, a younger brother who followed him to Yale and then practiced law until an early death.

> I must practice in economy in every profitable way. . . . I must make every honorable effort to get business. I must do in private as I would in public. I must improve every opportunity to speak in public. I must rise early in the morning. I must endeavor to make myself sociable and popular among my associates. I must improve every opportunity to cultivate the art of conversation. . . . And lastly, though by no means the least, I must do nothing of which I would be ashamed, if the whole world should find it out, keeping also in mind that passage of Scripture which says: "Know ye that for all these things, God shall one day bring thee to judgment." To be strictly temperate in eating and drinking, this I shall adopt. Write a plan for each succeeding day, at each evening, this I shall adopt. To beware of being too much influenced by the opinion of others, and in all cases act independently when I am in the right. Avoid confectionary shops.[30]

David Riesman's and William H. Whyte's complementary concepts of "inner direction" and the "Protestant ethic" were never illustrated more clearly than in this ambitious declaration. Moreover, the "rules" likely reflect values and attitudes common to all the Waite children. Morrison, to be sure, occasionally indulged himself with purchases of candy and ice cream while a student at Yale.[31] This

[30] Quoted in Mrs. John B. Waite, "The American Ancestry and some of the Descendents of Henry Matson and Marie Selden Waite" (unpublished manuscript). Courtesy of Professor and Mrs. John B. Waite.

[31] Expense Book, 1833–1839.

minor concession to earthly pleasure aside, his early years indicate a devotion to traditional Puritan standards. And when success finally came, he would insist with complete sincerity that "real and true success comes only through constant and untiring labor." To one young friend he gave this counsel: "Fix your mind upon what you will make your life employment—take hold of it at once and work until you achieve success. As a rule success can never be attained in any other way." [32]

As a young man Waite decided to "take hold" in northwest Ohio, then a frontier area. During the first half of the nineteenth century Connecticut held little appeal for the ambitious and the adventurous. Manufacturing was barely evident, farm and rural life followed crude patterns; and, attracted by the opportunities of the Western Reserve, many sons of Connecticut went West, reducing its population and further contributing to the stagnancy of life in the state.[33] An uncle, Horace Waite, worked as a merchant in Maumee, Ohio, a growing town in the northwest corner of the state, making it natural that his nephew should explore its possibilities. At the age of twenty-two Morrison Waite set out for Ohio.

[32] Waite to Nannie Hart, June 6, 1875, Letterbooks; to John Bemis, Feb. 12, 1876, Letterbooks.

[33] Jarvis M. Morse, *A Neglected Period of Connecticut's History 1818–1850* (New Haven: Yale University Press, 1933), pp. 7–21.

3

OHIO ATTORNEY

Waite's "Voyage of Discovery." Northwest Ohio.
Some Unpleasant Moments. The Junior Partner.
Affairs of the Heart. Beef at 6¼¢ a Pound.
Circuit Lawyer. Early Cases. M. R. & R. Waite, Toledo.
Growing Fame and Fortune. Business Ventures.
Railroads and Railroad Attorneys. A Community Law Firm.

LEAVING HOME IN THE FALL OF 1838, MORRISON WAITE MADE HIS WAY to Maumee, going first to Buffalo and then by water to Cleveland. The journey was pleasant and prompted a long letter to his father. "I stopped for a short time," he wrote, "at all the principal places on my way and looked up friends to show me the curiosities of their *cities*. At Cleveland I could almost imagine myself in Lyme. The Lyme folks at any rate seemed thicker than they did at home." He stayed in a hotel, politely refusing a distant relative's invitation to visit his home because "I had rather be independent." In this letter appears, also, probably the first professional advice of Waite's career given, appropriately enough, to his father:

> I saw Learned [?] at Locksport [N. Y.] and spoke to him concerning the lot of land. He said that it would be impossible to sell it at any price: but would himself give 60 dollars for it. It is more than you will have offered for it again for some time I think. It is out of the village some distance and in a part of the town which is not growing as rapidly as some others. I should advise you to send a deed to him as soon as convenient, for he offers more than it is worth.[1]

From Cleveland Waite pushed on to what, with an exaggeration born of optimism, was called "Maumee City." On the southwestern tip of Lake Erie and with a population of less than a thousand, Maumee was in the part of the state to be settled last. The "Black

[1] Waite to Henry M. Waite, Oct. 22, 1838. Courtesy of Professor and Mrs. John B. Waite.

Swamp," a wet, marshy tract between the Sandusky and Maumee Rivers, made farming difficult. A great drought during the summer of 1838 caused further hardship, making Maumee and nearby Toledo appear as harsh and unhealthy communities.[2] Not surprisingly, Waite found Maumee unattractive. Anxious to locate in a promising area, he discussed with his father the various possibilities open to him:

> At Buffalo I saw David M. Jewett.[3] He is on his way to Michigan and gave me an invitation to come out into that portion of the country. All others with whom I have conversed represent that state as presenting the best opening for lawyers. The practice is after the same plan with that of New York and of course the pay the same. It is probable that I should be compelled to study only one year and I have made up my mind to take a trip into the interior of that state before I settle myself down for the winter. I think my prospects would be better there than in Ohio. The practice in this state is about half way between the simplicity of that of Connecticut and the intricacy of that of New York. The fees are not as high as in New York and very difficult to collect. I think however that I should be content with a location in this place if it were not for the extreme unhealthiness of the climate. There are no good lawyers here and some considerable business with a prospect of more—but although Uncle Horace says it is not unhealthy—yet the pale & their [sic] faces of the inhabitants tell a different story. I do not think however that it is a[s] sickly here as at Toledo. The Western & Central parts of Michigan are said to be comparitively [sic] healthy and the country the most fertile of any part of this region. I was introduced to some lawyers at Cleveland—who of course advised me to settle in their place—and next go to Michigan. Kallamasoo—Marshall—Jacksonburg & several other towns along the central part of the state are recommended by all. At any rate I thought as I had come out on a voyage of discovery it would perhaps be well to take a turn out there. I have made arrangements to board with Mr. Chapman and read in the Allens office[4] probably if I should go back to Cleveland. I cannot get boarded there short of $3.50 or $4. a week. The clerk in the office of Payne & Wilson[5] as I was told by one of the partners

[2] Francis P. Weisenburger, *History of the State of Ohio, The Passing of the Frontier* (Columbus: Ohio State Archeological and Historical Society, 1941), III, 6–7, cited hereafter as Weisenburger, *Ohio*, III.

[3] The Jewetts were a Connecticut family known to the Waites.

[4] Perhaps the firm of William Allen, a well-known Ohio politician.

[5] A reference to the firm of Henry B. Payne and Hiram V. Wilson. Payne was also a prominent Ohio politician.

> probably made more than five hundred dollars over and above his expenses from pettifogging the last year. I was offered that situation in their office. I think if I do not conclude to stop in Michigan I think I shall go to Cleveland. There are no lawyers with whom I could study to advantage in this place. I shall start I think in about a week from here—after that I shall make up my mind what to do and shall settle down.[6]

Here, then, in this earliest of surviving letters is a glimpse of Morrison Waite as a young man: ambitious and alert, willing to weigh advice but making his own observations and decisions.

He did not, however, continue his "voyage of discovery" to Michigan and instead, on November 1, 1838, invested $31.43 in furniture to outfit a room in Maumee.[7] Waite had decided to take a chance on northwest Ohio. Despite its apparent unattractiveness, the Maumee-Toledo area was one of great possibilities. Even as Waite made his decision, two canals, the Wabash & Erie and the Miami & Erie, were under construction, which would turn the region into a center of commercial activity. Maumee's, and particularly, Toledo's port on Lake Erie became natural outlets for southern and western agricultural goods moving East and eastern manufactured goods destined for the river valley below Cincinnati.[8] Later, the coming of the railroad further enhanced the area's natural commercial advantages.

Without wasting time, he obtained a job with Samuel M. Young, a lawyer who had arrived in Maumee a few years before. Competent as a lawyer, Young had interests which attracted him to business and banking ventures and eventually he gave up law in favor of a career as Toledo's leading entrepreneur. One who knew Young well described him as "eminently a self-made man" who worked methodically and persistently while following "an economical course of living."[9] Although ten years older, he took an immediate and personal interest in Waite and, through a long life, became his closest

[6] Waite to Henry M. Waite, Oct. 22, 1838.
[7] Expense Book, 1833–1839.
[8] Henry Howe, *Historical Collections of Ohio* (Cincinnati: C. J. Krehbiel, 1900), II, 149.
[9] Clark Waggoner, *History of Toledo and Lucas County* (New York and Toledo: Munsell and Company, 1888), p. 500, cited hereafter as Waggoner, *Toledo History*.

and dearest friend. Their office was on the second story of a clapboarded frame building, "the next remove above a log cabin," and "had a thin coat of dingy white paint which gave it a neglected look." [10] Here Waite settled down to study for admission to the Ohio bar, but even before he gained formal admission in 1839, he was able to try petty cases before justices of the peace.[11]

On December 20, 1838, he took part in an action of "assumpsit for use & occupation," which was settled when the "Dft. paid 16 dollars & costs." A few weeks later Morrison Waite handled a case which he entered in his account book as "assumpsit—price & value of Horse damages $16." Other such actions, usually for breach of contract or right of property and involving small amounts of money, quickly followed.[12] What was perhaps Waite's first courtroom argument came during the spring of 1839 in the Woods and Bunting case. The dispute was a simple one: Woods sold to Bunting for $2,200 an old horse ferry crossing the Maumee River. Not long after, a bridge was built that destroyed the ferry's value. Waite represented Bunting, who claimed that Woods knew the bridge was to be built and had intentionally deceived him. Unfortunately, Waite became frightened, stammered, and almost broke down completely. With the presiding judge and opposing counsel encouraging him, he finally got through the argument, but lost the case. Discouraging as this early setback was, the experience was not an uncommon one for new lawyers. Waite recovered, won his next case, and from then on seems to have had little difficulty.[13] Indeed, Samuel Young thought well enough of him to offer the youthful attorney a junior partnership within five months of his arrival in Maumee. Morrison Waite proudly recorded the event by writing with a large scrawl in his expense book:

[10] Thomas Dunlap, "Chief Justice Waite," in *Addresses, Memorials and Sketches* of the Maumee Valley Pioneer Association (Toledo, 1897), pp. 30–31.

[11] It was unnecessary to be licensed for such cases. Conversation with Mr. Morison R. Waite of Cincinnati, May 12, 1961.

[12] Expense Book, 1833–1839.

[13] Scrapbook of newspaper clippings cited in Bruce R. Trimble, "The Life and Constitutional Doctrines of Chief Justice Waite" (Ph.D. dissertation, Cornell University, 1934), pp. 70–73. Trimble is the author of a book, *Chief Justice Waite, Defender of the Public Interest* (Princeton: Princeton University Press, 1938). The dissertation, however, contains original (and no longer obtainable) material that is not included in the book; subsequent citations of Trimble, *Waite,* refer to the dissertation.

S. M. Young &
M. R. Waite

Partnership Commenced April 20*th*
AD 1839 [14]

Because of the panic of 1837, economic conditions in Ohio were unsettled through the early 1840's. Overexpansion of credit and the turmoil caused by the Jacksonian war on the Bank of the United States led to a financial and business collapse that sharply increased the volume of litigation. Whatever its consequences for others, the panic kept the fledgling law firm of Young & Waite busy disentangling business complications, foreclosing mortgages, straightening out disputed property titles, collecting debts, and making settlements in the courts of bankruptcy. One of Waite's first assignments, for instance, was to help liquidate a Maumee insurance company that failed because of the poor state of its finances.[15] Since Young preferred to operate outside the courtroom, Waite took on the brunt of oral argument. He also did most of the detailed work such as bookkeeping, for which he always had a natural flair. Fees were low—a ride of many miles on horseback to try a small case before a justice of the peace for $5 was not unusual—but the firm attracted a large clientele and shrewdly encouraged litigation only when prospects for success were good.

Waite became a skillful pleader and a learned chancery lawyer, expert in real estate law and the history and status of legal titles. "I had no training in business," he once said, but "from my boyhood I was quick to learn and I always went about with my eyes and ears open." [16] William Baker, a lawyer and good friend during Waite's first years in Maumee, described him as an excellent business lawyer. "A strong common sense and practical knowledge of business methods and habits of thought," Baker recalled, "enabled him to not only give intelligent advice upon a business question, but to unravel and disclose to a court or a jury a fraud even if it lay concealed in the occult

[14] Expense Book, 1833–1839.
[15] Waggoner, *Toledo History*, p. 927.
[16] Waite to Waggoner, Jan. 2, 1881, Letterbooks.

mysteries of book-keeping." [17] A measure of the firm's rapid success is a report of the Lucas County Commissioners showing that by 1843, of nineteen attorneys in the Maumee-Toledo area, Samuel Young and Morrison Waite were among the top in earnings.[18]

With his career well under way Morrison Waite could turn to more intimate matters. While still a student at Yale he indicated his interest in a certain young lady: "Paid for basket for Amelia Warner .75," he dutifully put down in his account book.[19] Amelia Champlin Warner of Lyme was a second cousin, both being descended from Colonel Samuel Seldon who died a prisoner of war in New York during the Revolution. Engaged in 1838, they expected a long wait, but, as "Molly" Waite told the story, Samuel Young sent his partner home in 1840 to get married, "thus shortening our term of probation at least two years, telling him that there ought to be a wife in the firm and he was not ready to get married himself." Her surviving letters, written largely after her husband assumed the responsibilities of high public office, reveal her to be a thoroughly devoted wife and a woman of culture and education to whom he could confide his problems, fears, and aspirations. In these reminiscences Amelia Waite tells something of their early married life:

> We had little of this world's goods, but were just as happy as we were about as well off as our neighbors, at least we lived as well. When we were married my uncle (Henry L. Champlin) gave me one hundred dollars, with that we furnished our room and boarded with . . . Uncle Horace Waite for about eight months. Then we took a small house and my uncle sent me two hundred dollars with which we furnished the house comfortably. We then, as ever afterward, kept open house, indeed I do not know how to live otherwise even yet. For the first two years our annual expenses did not exceed six hundred dollars. . . .

To today's inflation-conscious housewife, who keeps a wary eye on the consumer price index, she paints a picture of living costs as remote as the semi-frontier society in which she lived:

[17] William Baker, "Memorial of Hon. Morrison Remick Waite," Ohio State Bar Association Reports, IX (1888), 177–178, and generally, 173–188. See also, Toledo *Commercial*, March 24, 1888.

[18] Waggoner, *Toledo History*, pp. 314–315.

[19] Expense Book, 1833–1839.

> The best cuts of beef were six and a quarter cents a pound, veal about the same, but pork and mutton not more than three or four cents. The hind quarters and saddle of venison were sold all through the winter at from fifty to seventy-five cents, for the whole half of the animal. . . . Turkey from twenty-five to thirty cents, and all the fat tender chickens you chose, dressed at six cents apiece. Quails and wild ducks in the same proportions. . . .[20]

To accommodate what soon was a growing family of four healthy children, three sons and a daughter, Waite built a good-sized colonial house with comfortable rooms.[21]

Such moderate prosperity as Morrison Waite now enjoyed he had earned. With most other western lawyers he spent much of his time riding circuit, usually on horseback, sometimes in wagons. Frequently the entire court, two or three lawyers and the judge, traveled in a body, going to the county seats scattered through the wilderness that was then northwestern Ohio. Saddlebags had but a limited capacity: Blackstone, Chitty, and perhaps a work on pleading and precedents made up the circuit lawyer's library. Beyond that, he was on his own, and as Waite's grandson wrote, "he most often triumphed who could clearly remember and state the rule of law applicable to the case at hand."[22] Together on a case one day, the next day the circuit lawyers might be in opposition, all the while sharing rooms in taverns and depending on each other for stimulation and companionship. Under such circumstances they came to know each other well; sham and deceit were readily apparent. One of Morrison Waite's circuit companions, Emery D. Potter, who served as a judge in the northwestern counties, later recalled their travels over a dozen counties "without roads, without bridges, and with log cabins at long intervals." At times they shared a hickory bedstead, sleeping under the same quilt, but no matter what the conditions, Waite always remained cheerful.

> He was remarkable for his adaptation to his surroundings. He was the genial gentleman in the log cabin and the palace, and the old men

[20] "Memories." Waite Papers.

[21] Toledo Biography Scrapbook. Toledo Public Library.

[22] Morison R. Waite, "Morrison R. Waite," *Western Reserve Law Journal*, I (1895), 95.

> and the children were delighted to call Mott Waite a friend. . . . He was never deemed a genius, but he was gifted with a large share of good common sense, and upon this by untiring industry he built . . . [his] fame. . . .[23]

Waite looked back on his circuit days with nostalgia. "The experiences of the time were rough," he wrote in 1881, "but they had heaps of enjoyment covered up in them." And, with the pride of a man who has proved himself, he wondered if "those of the present day" could have met the tests faced by him and his "old pioneer" friends.[24] "Didn't we laugh as heartily over our practical jokes," he wrote to an old circuit comrade, "as we ever did at any play—I am absolutely certain if I had grown up under different professional or social surroundings, I should not have been the same man I am. In fact, I think my success has been largely owing to that training."[25]

Alfred P. Edgerton, the recipient of this letter and a lifelong friend,[26] is the source of an anecdote that, from among a number of stories involving Waite, deserves to be preserved. On one occasion, while traveling together, a severe storm developed and prevented them from reaching their destination, the town of Hicksville. They were forced to stop overnight in a small cabin.

> It was a little affair of one room and an attic. The pioneer's wife hung up a blanket before the fireplace and behind this the future Chief Justice and myself stripped and dried our clothes. We slept in the attic, and the next morning upon pulling on my stockings I found a hole through which my big toe thrust itself. I pulled off the stocking and turned it wrong side out and put it on the same foot. Again the toe came through the hole, and Waite, who was watching my agony, said: "Why don't you put the stocking on the other foot, and the little toe will be in the hole?" I tried this plan and found it a success, and with this began my admiration for Judge Waite, which steadily increased as I knew him better.[27]

[23] Clipping, Toledo *Bee*, March 24, 1888. Waite Papers.

[24] Waite to Thomas Dunlap, Aug. 4, 1881. Toledo Public Library.

[25] Waite to Alfred P. Edgerton, Oct. 21, 1878, Letterbooks.

[26] Also a prominent Indiana Democrat and one of President Cleveland's Civil Service Commissioners.

[27] Clipping, Toledo *Commercial*, April 1, 1888. Waite Papers.

Circuit life, as Waite himself said, was one of the significant experiences in his professional background. On one level, the days on circuit provided a fund of stories which probably improved as they grew more distant. In later life, when things went hard, he found an outlet in recalling them. But, beyond this, the experiences on circuit brought out and sharpened some of his best qualities. Naturally amiable, he learned the art of being close friends in spite of disagreements. Men like Potter, Edgerton, and Rufus P. Ranney were all active and locally prominent Democrats, while Waite, first a Whig and afterwards a Republican, always opposed the Democracy. Yet Mott Waite, as friends called him, never allowed political differences —and in his day, with issues such as slavery, the Civil War, and Reconstruction, they could be hot and bitter—to interfere with friendships. "Isn't it strange," he once remarked, "that the democrats are so universally my friends." [28]

Getting along with people is perhaps just good common sense. In the northwestern Ohio of the 1840's the rewards went to those circuit lawyers who had precisely that quality. Judges who knew Waite during this period agreed that, while not a brilliant debater, he was a strong speaker and, more important, that "few lawyers could marshal the facts as succinctly as he." [29] With much of Ohio still close to frontier conditions, lawyers had to adapt pragmatically the old rules of the English common law in a new territory where the needs, desires, and customs were often novel. Blackstone or Chitty took a lawyer only so far as he argued in the rude taverns that served as courthouses. Then he was on his own mental resources and Waite, sensitive to facts, displayed ability and learning that revealed him to be "at once practical and philosophic." [30] A knack for human relations, adaptability, and common sense, along with a storehouse of pleasant memories, were the legacies of Morrison Waite's circuit days.

In a region where eager capitalists were busy building, trading, and investing, Young & Waite specialized in property cases. On oc-

[28] Waite to Amelia Waite, Feb. 18, 1874.
[29] Judge Lucien B. Otis in *Chicago Legal News,* March 31, 1888.
[30] R. B. Warden to E. Brooks, Jan., 1874. Waite Papers. Warden, one of Salmon P. Chase's biographers, had been a judge on the Ohio Supreme Court. See also, Toledo *Commercial,* March 24, 1888.

casion Waite accepted criminal cases involving murder or counterfeiting,[31] but the firm's main source of revenue came from disputes over land titles, tax assessments, mortgage foreclosures, breaches of contract, and claims against railroads. In 1844 he took and won his first case before the Ohio Supreme Court, an action of assumpsit in which a township recovered money from a man who had deserted his wife, making her a town pauper.[32] His name appears regularly thereafter in the Ohio Reports. Typical of the sort of case he handled was one in 1855 where he defended a settlement by which certain Maumee citizens, who had paid the cost of erecting buildings for the county government on the understanding that the county seat would remain in Maumee, were reimbursed when the seat was moved to Toledo. A board of County Commissioners subsequently challenged the settlement, but Waite successfully defended it.[33] While frequently a winner in cases such as *Butler* v. *Brown*, where he won a suit over title to land worth $22,000, or *Smith* v. *Toledo*, a suit to enjoin collection of a street assessment,[34] Waite was less fortunate in cases with public law implications.

In *Toledo Bank* v. *Bond*, for instance, he represented the Bank of Toledo, which sought to overturn a state tax on the capital stock of banks. Under an act of 1845 the legislature provided for the incorporation of banks on condition that they give the state 6 per cent of profits every six months "in lieu of all taxes." When in 1852 the legislature, acting under a new constitution, changed this system by passing an act taxing banks according to their capital stock, Waite & Young, representing the Bank of Toledo, challenged the new law. Relying chiefly on the *Dartmouth College* doctrine, they attacked the new tax as a violation of the federal Constitution's contract clause. The Ohio Supreme Court, however, ruled against the bank. It insisted that corporate franchises were subservient to the public welfare and that the legislature could amend private charters,

[31] A letter of Henry M. Waite dated Jan. 31, 1858, discusses Waite's participation in a murder prosecution. Trimble, *Waite*, p. 90, note; *Reed* v. *State*, 15 Ohio Rep. 217 (1846), where Waite unsuccessfully defended a counterfeiter; Waite to Ebenezer Lane, Oct. 26, 1854, in which he mentions his participation in divorce and slander suits. Ebenezer Lane Papers, Yale University Library.

[32] *Trustees of Springfield Township* v. *Demott*, 13 Ohio Rep. 105 (1844).

[33] *County Commissioners* v. *Hunt*, 5 Ohio 488 (1856).

[34] 5 Ohio 211 (1855); 24 Ohio 127 (1872).

which, the Court said, did not possess the essentials of a contract. And, in language that would one day be familiar to Chief Justice Waite, it rejected as "grossly absurd" the notion that legislative power can be bargained away.[35] Afterwards, Young & Waite won a measure of vindication when the federal Supreme Court, in another case involving the same act, struck it down as an unconstitutional violation of the contract clause.[36]

Again, in *Butler* v. *Toledo*, Waite & Young relied vainly on the contract clause.[37] Toledo had levied an assessment on lots bordering certain city streets that were to be improved. Because the assessment proved insufficient, the state legislature amended the city's charter so as to allow a reassessment to meet the higher costs. Waite, representing a party who purchased some of the lots after the original assessment, attacked the reassessment law for infringing on the contract clause and also the Ohio Constitution's ex post facto clause. It was, he claimed, "retro-active and operated to impair vested rights." The court turned aside both contentions and followed *Calder* v. *Bull*[38] in limiting the ex post facto clause to criminal proceedings.

Equally unsuccessful, though in this instance constitutional questions were not at issue, was his argument in a tax case, *Carrier* v. *Gordon*. Carrier, a merchant, tried to enjoin a county tax collector from collecting a tax on some lumber that he owned. Waite contended that, since Carrier was a nonresident of the state and intended to move the lumber as soon as navigation opened on Lake Erie, the property was only temporarily in the county and ought not be taxed. He continued:

> As a general rule, personal property has no *situs*, but follows the person of the owner. The law which governs it is the law of the owner's domicil. The legal presumption is, therefore, that all personal property is considered as being located (*situated*) at the place of the owner's domicil, and is under the law of that domicil. This presumption continues until a contrary intention of the owner appears.[39]

[35] 1 Ohio 622 (1853).
[36] *Dodge* v. *Woolsey*, 18 Howard 331 (1856).
[37] 5 Ohio 225 (1855).
[38] 3 Dallas 386 (1798).
[39] 21 Ohio 605, 606–607 (1871).

This argument, as well as its corollary that, under Ohio law, personal property could be taxed only if it belonged to a resident or a nonresident who had no intention to remove it, the state Supreme Court found invalid. It ruled that Ohio's laws made all tangible personal property subject to taxation, irrespective of the owner's residence, if it had *situs* in the state. Simple purchase of property with an intention to remove could not end tax liability, for this would make taxes "depend upon the mere intention of the owner, and subject to change as often as the owner changed his intention." "The safer and better rule," the Court concluded, is "to consider property actually in transit as belonging to the place of its destination, and property not in transit as property in the place of its *situs*." [40]

Despite such reverses, Waite & Young were often successful.[41] The firm prospered and in 1850 Waite moved to Toledo, which had become the county seat, to set up a branch office. Six years later Samuel Young gave up law in order to attend to his business interests and with Waite's younger brother, Richard, the firm was reorganized as M. R. & R. Waite. These were busy years for Morrison Waite as he pushed his income up to around $7,000 annually and built one of the Midwest's leading law offices. In 1854 we find him writing to Ebenezer Lane, a former Ohio Supreme Court judge with whom he frequently collaborated and who had asked him to help in an important case in another part of the state. Unless a replacement could be found, Waite replied, he would have to refuse and go instead to Napoleon, Ohio, where "I have several cases . . . which I am under some obligation to attend to. They have been continued several times because I could not go and attend to them." [42] A year later he was again pressed for time due to "some business in N.Y. which I cannot omit." [43] During this period his father, then Connecticut's Chief Justice, boasted to friends that "Morrison has as great a proportion of cases as usual, more than any other lawyer," and that his was

[40] At 609.

[41] Among many cases see, for example, *Horton* v. *Horner*, 14 Ohio Rep. 369 (1846), *Frost* v. *Lowry*, 15 Ohio Rep. 200 (1846) and *Morris* v. *Way*, 16 Ohio Rep. 470 (1847).

[42] Waite to Lane, Oct. 26, 1854. Lane Papers, Yale.

[43] Waite to Lane, Aug. 21, 1855. Lane Papers, Yale.

"the largest library in northern Ohio (unless it may be in Cleveland) of any practicing lawyer." [44]

Among fellow attorneys Waite won respect for his ability to pierce quickly through the real merits of a dispute. He preferred, in fact, to arrange out-of-court settlements with opposing counsel.[45] Charles W. Hill related how, as a green young lawyer, he had his first encounter with Waite. Since Waite had an established reputation, Hill approached the case with considerable fear. The two opposing attorneys took testimony in private, and before it was submitted to the judge, Waite invited Hill to lunch. Recalled Hill:

> During our lunch he told me that he thought we could settle that case just as well as Judge Latty, and asked me if I would be willing for him to fix the terms of settlement. I replied that that was rather a strange method of procedure and I would like to know how he would settle it first. He then made a plain statement of the justice of the case, and proposed a settlement in accordance with this. His ideas as to how the case should be settled was exactly the same as mine, and I could not have asked for better treatment.[46]

The story is told that on another occasion Waite was defending a party in an action in the Common Pleas Court of Lucas County. Pressed by business, he neglected to file an answer in the specified time. Technically this meant that the defendant's case lost by default, but the custom among local attorneys was to give the defense a reasonable time after default to answer. Moreover, the presiding judge pointed out that the case could not be tried for some time anyway, and that no harm would result by following the custom. But Waite's opposing attorney, a new lawyer in Toledo with a reputation for sharp practices, brashly insisted on a judgment by default. Meanwhile, Waite hastily looked over the lawyer's petition and called the court's attention to a fatal defect which, according to a strict construction of the law, entitled him to have the case dismissed with costs thrown on the plaintiff. Waite, however, permitted the at-

[44] Letter to Henry M. Waite, March 27, 1854, and Henry M. Waite to Samuel Lawrence, July 23, 1856, quoted in Trimble, *Waite*, p. 66, p. 97, note.

[45] Baker, "Memorial of Morrison R. Waite," 177.

[46] Undated clipping of the American Press Association. Waite Papers.

torney to amend his pleadings, dryly remarking that, "If I give him time to amend his petition, he may be willing to grant me a few minutes to prepare my answer." He subsequently won the case.[47]

This reputation for integrity and legal ability, as well as one for charging low fees, grew with the firm and, in turn, also contributed to its success. "He was not indebted," Judge Warden noted, "for his heavy docket to a heavy conscience." [48] Hill, who fought many cases with and against him, agreed: "I don't believe that Waite ever advocated the cause of a dishonest client." [49] The reputation appears well deserved. After he and Ebenezer Lane had jointly settled a claims case involving $18,000, Waite told Lane to "let the Company send me whatever you think is right and I will be satisfied." [50] George Bancroft, the great nineteenth century historian, wrote M. R. & R. Waite to ask if they would sell some land he owned in Michigan. His inquiry, coming as it did in 1859 from distant Massachusetts, is an indication of Waite's increasing reputation. Waite's reply, distinguishing him from what Judge Warden called "mere lawyers of the money-getting, pushing, bustling order," [51] explains one of the reasons for his growing reputation:

> We should very cheerfully undertake the sale and management of your lands if we thought we could do as well as some parties residing in the same County where they are situated. Cooley & Croswell [Waite's correspondents at Adrian, Michigan] [52] are prompt and efficient. . . . We think your interests will be better cared for by them and we therefore beg leave to refer you to them.[53]

Accompanying Waite's legal success was a growing involvement in business affairs. To a large extent he was simply participating in the expansion and prosperity enjoyed by Ohio in the decades following 1850. Particularly was this evident in manufacturing and transporta-

[47] John M. Killits, *Toledo and Lucas County, Ohio* (Chicago and Toledo: S. J. Clarke, 1923), I, 644.

[48] R. B. Warden to E. Brooks, Jan., 1874. Waite Papers.

[49] Undated clipping of the American Press Association. Waite Papers.

[50] Waite to Lane, Oct. 29, 1855. Lane Papers, Yale.

[51] R. B. Warden to E. Brooks, Jan., 1874. Waite Papers.

[52] The firm of the famed Thomas M. Cooley.

[53] Waite to Bancroft, May 16, 1859. George Bancroft Papers, Massachusetts Historical Society.

tion: in thirty years, from 1850 to 1880, the value of manufactured goods increased five and one-half times to almost $350 million annually; in transportation the 1850's rank as Ohio's great era of railroad building with track mileage multiplying tenfold to three thousand miles by 1860.[54] Toledo more than shared in this growth. A village of 2,000 in 1840, without sidewalks, which regarded a privately subscribed main street walk of wooden planks as a "grand improvement," [55] Toledo grew to 12,000 by 1860 and 50,000 by 1880. The "Black Swamp" was drained and northwestern Ohio became prosperous farming country. Where the Miami & Erie and the Wabash & Erie canals had served earlier to channel trade through the region, the coming of the railroad contributed even further to Toledo's economic well-being. By 1880 thirteen railroads passed through the city carrying scores of products east and west, and Toledo had become Ohio's third city. The metropolis of the northwest, it was the home of hundreds of industries, ranked as one of the nation's major grain markets, and its miles of docks made it the finest harbor on the Great Lakes.[56]

To Morrison Waite this was far more than statistics. It was part of his own experience. Samuel Young, his former law partner, made a small fortune in banking, railroad investments, and municipal enterprises. A few miles away, another close friend and the uncle of Rutherford Hayes, Sardis Birchard, beginning with next to nothing, had become a wealthy banker and merchant.[57] Waite never became rich, but his business activities and legal practice gave him a very comfortable income. During the summer of 1852 he served as one of Toledo's representatives at a meeting held in Logansport, Indiana, to spur the construction of the Wabash & Western Railway, a project

[54] Eugene H. Roseboom and Francis P. Weisenburger, *A History of Ohio* (New York: Prentice-Hall, Inc., 1934), pp. 314–328.

[55] H. S. Knapp, *History of the Maumee Valley* (Toledo: Blade Publishing House, 1872), p. 551.

[56] Howe, *Historical Collections of Ohio*, II, 150–152; Roseboom and Weisenburger, *Ohio*, p. 309; Eugene H. Roseboom, *History of the State of Ohio, The Civil War Era* (Columbus: Ohio State Archeological and Historical Society, 1944), IV, 26–27, cited hereafter as Roseboom, *Ohio*, IV.

[57] On Birchard and his friendship with Waite see, Harry Barnard, *Rutherford B. Hayes and His America* (New York: Bobbs-Merrill, 1954), cited hereafter as Barnard, *Hayes;* Waite to Hayes, April 8, 1873. Rutherford B. Hayes Papers, Hayes Memorial Library.

much desired by the city's business interests.[58] A few months later Morrison Waite presided over the birth of the city's first utility, the Toledo Gas-Light and Coke Company. Stock subscription books were opened in his office; $100,000 was raised and he became a director of a company whose direct descendant today supplies one hundred thousand inhabitants and two hundred industries in metropolitan Toledo.[59] Other business ventures followed. With Samuel Young he served as a director of the Toledo National Bank. He held a similar position in the North Western Savings Depository and in 1860 helped organize the Toledo Street Railroad Company, acting as one of its directors for a few years.[60]

At the same time M. R. & R. Waite obtained an increasing number of cases involving railroads, which after the mid-1850's were the dominant factor in the state's economic life. Professionally, the firm specialized in tax assessments and claims, and Waite at one time or another represented such local roads as the Northern Indiana, the Southern Michigan, the Cleveland & Toledo, and the important Lake Shore & Michigan Southern.[61] During the early 1870's he earned his largest fee—$25,000—for representing the interests of the Atlantic & Great Western Railroad's English bondholders. That railroad, a crucial cog in handling the mighty Erie Railroad's western traffic, had an unhappy history in the years after the Civil War. Continuing financial difficulties forced the Atlantic & Great Western through a succession of receiverships and reorganizations until it finally came under the Erie's control. It became a pawn in James McHenry's and General McClellan's ultimately successful effort to rid the Erie system of the unscrupulous Jay Gould.[62] When the McHenry-McClellan

[58] Waggoner, *Toledo History*, p. 413.

[59] Waggoner, *Toledo History*, p. 781; Toledo *Blade*, Sept. 20, 1953.

[60] Knapp, *History of the Maumee Valley*, pp. 631–633; Waggoner, *Toledo History*, p. 422.

[61] *Northern Indiana R. Co.* v. *Connelly*, 10 Ohio 160 (1859); *Muhl's Administrator* v. *Southern Michigan R. Co.*, 10 Ohio 272 (1859); *Wagner* v. *Cleveland & Toledo R. Co.*, 22 Ohio 563 (1872); *Lake Shore & Michigan Southern R. Co.* v. *Perkins*, 25 Mich. 329 (1872); Waite to Lane, May 20, 1856, discussing Waite's defense of the Michigan Southern & Northern Indiana (later the Lake Shore & Michigan Southern) against a suit by an injured brakeman. Ebenezer Lane Papers, Chicago Historical Society.

[62] Stuart Daggett, *Railroad Reorganization* (Cambridge: Harvard University Press, 1908), p. 51; Julius Grodinsky, *Jay Gould* (Philadelphia: University of Pennsylvania Press, 1957), Chaps. II–VI; *Financial and Commercial Chronicle*, XVII, Oct. 18, 1873, 511.

group wrested the Erie from Gould's hands, the New York firm of Barlow, Larocque & Macfarland retained Waite to look after the legal affairs of the Cleveland and Mahoning, a subsidiary of the Atlantic & Great Western.[63]

Close friends such as Samuel Young, who was a director of the Cleveland and Toledo, a road that Waite represented on occasion and part of the Vanderbilt empire; Rufus P. Ranney, an attorney for the Cleveland and Pittsburg, which was operated by the Pennsylvania Railroad; and Hugh J. Jewett, for many years president of the Erie, were deeply interested in railroad affairs. One of his sons, Christopher Waite, served as superintendent of the Cincinnati and Muskingum Valley Railway and later as vice-president of the Cincinnati, Hamilton and Dayton. Waite himself owned fifty shares in the latter road and was from 1871 to 1874 a director and vice-president of the Dayton and Michigan, a road leased in perpetuity to the Cincinnati, Hamilton and Dayton.[64]

By the time he went on the Supreme Court, Morrison Waite was known in business and railroad circles, and as if in confirmation of this, his appointment brought a flood of congratulatory messages from old clients. Levi P. Morton of Morton & Bliss, one of the dominant financiers of the age, sent warm greetings. Amasa Stone, then managing the Lake Shore & Michigan Southern for Commodore Vanderbilt, wrote, "I regret to part with you as an associate in the service of this Co." Similar sentiments came from the Home Insurance Company of New York, the Missouri Valley Life Insurance Company of Kansas, the Bank of Attica in Buffalo, the Columbus and Hocking Valley Railroad, and the Chesapeake and Ohio Railroad [65]—a measure of the success attained by the young man who, thirty-six years earlier, overcoming his doubts about "the extreme unhealthiness of the climate," had concluded that "there are no good lawyers here and some considerable business with a prospect of more."

[63] W. W. Macfarland to Waite, May 9, 1873; S. L. M. Barlow to Waite, June 7, 1873; numerous letters in the papers of Samuel L. M. Barlow. Henry E. Huntington Library, California.

[64] C. B. Marsh to Waite, July 13, 1874; Henry V. Poor, *Manual of the Railroads of the United States* (New York: H. V. & H. W. Poor, 1869–1873), 1869–70 and 1873–74 editions, pp. 25–26 and p. 50.

[65] Morton to Waite, Jan. 20, 1874; Stone to Waite, Jan. 20, 1874; letters received, Jan., 1874. Waite Papers.

Surveying a small part of this evidence from a socialist orientation, Gustavus Myers hastily concluded that Waite was "a railroad attorney" and, while on the Court, a tool of powerful corporations.[66] Waite's judicial behavior belies the label. Even so, the general image of Morrison Waite is that of a railroad attorney who redeemed himself on the bench. As a consequence, Waite becomes something of a paradox: the corporate hireling who, once on the Court, miraculously proclaimed his independence and showed a striking unconcern for the railroads he formerly served. The paradox, however, is only apparent. Waite was not a "railroad attorney" in the sense in which the term is normally used—and this despite the fact that he sometimes defended railroads, sympathized with capitalist enterprises, and participated in business. To begin with, after the 1850's no business lawyer worth his salt could avoid involvement in railroad cases. Railroads became an integral part of the nation's business life and lawyers inevitably were caught up in their affairs, either defending or prosecuting them in the multitude of cases that they spawned.

But more important, Morrison Waite's practice, though impressive, was of a different scope than that of lawyers such as Evarts, Choate, Goudy, and Jewett. These men, accurately described as railroad attorneys, worked in the great cities of New York and Chicago, devoting themselves almost exclusively to serving large corporate interests. William Evarts' law firm drew its clientele from New York's prominent merchants, bankers, and men of immense wealth. His partner, Joseph H. Choate, earned fees of $80,000 annually, refused to enter a court for less than $500, sat on the boards of numerous powerful corporations, and generally moved in the top social and business circles. William C. Goudy gave all his attention to being general counsel for the Chicago & North Western Railway, as did John N. Jewett for the Illinois Central.[67]

By contrast, Waite worked in a city of fifty thousand that was provincial in comparison to New York or Chicago. The firm of M. R. & R. Waite certainly represented powerful interests such as the Lake

[66] Gustavus Myers, *History of the Supreme Court of the United States* (Chicago: C. H. Kerr and Company, 1912), p. 537.

[67] For a general picture of railroad attorneys see Benjamin R. Twiss, *Lawyers and the Constitution* (Princeton: Princeton University Press, 1942).

Shore & Michigan Southern or the Atlantic & Great Western—most commonly when their affairs at Toledo were involved—but it was essentially a community firm whose doors were open to the local townsfolk. Typically, not long before Waite's accession to the bench, the firm carried three such minor cases to the Ohio Supreme Court: it represented parties who variously sued to recover the value of a barge lost on Lake Erie, to reclaim $500 misappropriated by a justice of the peace, and to enjoin the collection of a Toledo street assessment.[68] Once, Waite journeyed all the way to Chicago solely to look after the interests of a minor heir and widow.[69] In representing railroads the firm did not find it necessary to tie itself to one or two companies, and, quite naturally, in some instances represented parties suing railroads.[70] In fact, the records of the state Supreme Court show M. R. & R. Waite handling relatively minor property cases far more often than cases involving railroads. At the time of Waite's appointment the *Nation* unintentionally put its finger on this fact when it complained that "the most competent lawyers for judicial functions . . . will be found in the great seaports and centres of finance and industry." Waite, Godkin's journal insisted, was "probably less fitted to preside over the Supreme Court than one who has long practiced in a great emporium of foreign commerce like New York or Boston." [71]

Had Morrison Waite not gone on the Court, he might well have become, like his friend Evarts, more exclusively involved with railroad affairs. By 1874 he was at the peak of his professional career, known by businessmen with national interests, and, as his work for the Atlantic & Great Western implies, increasingly sought after by large corporations. M. R. & R. Waite, with a reputation for skill and integrity, ranked as one of Ohio's leading law firms.

[68] *Daniels* v. *Ballantine,* 23 Ohio 533 (1872); *Aucker* v. *Adams & Ford,* 23 Ohio 543 (1873); *Smith* v. *Toledo,* 24 Ohio 127 (1873).

[69] *Chicago Legal News,* March 31, 1888.

[70] Waite to Lane, July 21, 1857. Lane Papers, Yale; *Toledo & Wabash R. Co.* v. *Daniels,* 16 Ohio 390 (1865).

[71] Jan. 22, 1874.

4

LAWYER-POLITICIAN

Waite Joins the Whigs. Cider and Cheers for "Old Tip."

Democracy in Frontier Ohio. Party Worker.

Term in the State Legislature. The Irrepressible Conflict.

"Honest Mott Waite" for Congress. "Union for the Sake of Union."

Campaigning Against the Copperheads.

Legacy from the Frontier. Government by the People.

"THERE HAS BEEN SO LITTLE OF MY PUBLIC LIFE," CHIEF JUSTICE Waite told an inquirer, "that it is very easy to find dates." [1] This was no modest denial of previous fame. With the exception of his immediate successor, Melville W. Fuller, Morris Waite went on the Court having less public recognition than any who preceded or followed him as Chief Justice. But, though nationally insignificant, Waite's public activities prior to 1874 were meaningful and significant to him. Certainly they occupied much of his time. Almost from the moment of his arrival in Maumee he was active as a local Whig politician. Today, the lawyer in a middle-sized community may, if he chooses, participate in politics; he is, however, expected to be active in civic affairs, heading a fund drive or giving time to a community improvement program.[2] In the mid-nineteenth century "civic" was defined more broadly to include politics—partisan politics—and nearly all lawyers gave freely of their time to party affairs. Accordingly, Morrison Waite did his share in what, inevitably, was the party of his choice, first the Whig and later the Republican Party.

He moved effortlessly into the Whig Party. His father had served the Whigs as a representative in the Connecticut legislature, and as a young man Morrison Waite warmly admired the party's giants, Daniel Webster and Henry Clay. As a lawyer concerned with property rights, as a businessman anxious for the development of a

[1] Waite to Charles Lamman, April 30, 1875, Letterbooks.

[2] On the modern middle-class phenomenon of "civic virtue" see Andrew Hacker's discussion in his "Politics and the Corporation," Fund for the Republic Occasional Paper, 1958.

national canal and rail system, and as the son of Federalist ancestors whose faith lay in the Union, it would have been surprising had Morrison Waite not joined the Whigs. The Ohio Democracy of the 1840's, possessed of a powerful Locofoco wing favoring radical control of the state's banks and burdened with the necessity of supporting the Southern slavocracy,[3] was singularly unappealing to this Yankee lawyer, who sympathized with merchants and bankers.

For his debut into partisan politics Morrison Waite chose an exciting event: the 1840 log cabin presidential campaign, which pitted William Henry Harrison, "Old Tippecanoe," against Andrew Jackson's protegé, Martin Van Buren. Taking a cue from Jackson's successful bids in 1824 and 1828, the Whigs resurrected the somewhat aged General Harrison. In a campaign whose utter vacuity should comfort modern critics who mourn the image-making and shallowness of today's electioneering, Harrison, a gentleman farmer and man of wealth, was put across as the hero of the Battle of Fallen Timbers and a rugged pioneer who dwelled in a log cabin. Van Buren, whose political views were actually closer to those of the low-income groups, was handicapped by the lack of a war record and by his aristocratic tastes, leaving him open to Whig taunts that he strutted about in a ruffled silk shirt and drank champagne from silver goblets. Handicapped though they were, the Ohio Democrats fought back as best they could, accusing Harrison of such mild character defects as being immoral, failing to pay his debts, and selling white men into slavery.[4]

One of the highlights of the early part of the campaign, the drive to nominate Harrison, occurred at Columbus on February 22, 1840, and it marks Morrison Waite's entry into state politics. A few days earlier the Lucas County Whig organization had named him a delegate to the state convention. Now he witnessed some captivating sights. Despite a combination of rain and the spring thaw, which turned Columbus into a mud hole, twenty thousand partisans assembled to cheer for Old Tippecanoe. After the convention endorsed his candidacy the Whigs put on a mammoth parade of gigantic floats and demonstrations. Ross County sent a double log cabin with "Old Tip" drawing cider from a barrel; the Maumee Valley Whigs con-

[3] Weisenburger, *Ohio*, III, 406–440.
[4] Weisenburger, *Ohio*, III, 394.

tributed a replica of Fort Meigs, which Harrison had defended against the British in 1813; Columbus supplied eight white horses to draw a mounted canoe whose stern contained a Buckeye tree in full leaf ("the handiwork of Whig ladies in Columbus"). Jackson County Whigs marched smartly by, wearing ribbons with the couplet:

With Tip and Tyler,
We'll bust Van's biler.

Harrison, of course, won the nomination and the election. Waite no doubt congratulated himself on the small part he played in the victory that had Ohio giving its native son a handsome majority of over 23,000 votes. As secretary of the Lucas County party organization, a post to which he was elected after the Columbus convention, he had actively campaigned for the Whig ticket.[5]

It was fitting that Morrison Waite's first political activity should be the democratic and vulgar log cabin campaign. Though he called himself a Whig and in the next decade and a half marched under the banner of a party committed to privilege and vested property rights, in a very important sense he was a Jacksonian. Waite may have regarded Old Hickory as a crude and arrogant demagogue, quite likely he disliked the spoils system, and most certainly he opposed Jackson's bank policy. Jacksonianism was, however, something more than the sum of the testy General's personality and politics. It was rule by the people and particularly the faith that the people should and *could* rule. As the propertied classes learned in 1800, in 1828, and again in 1932, the triumph of a party opposed to government-sponsored privilege did not mean the destruction of all property rights or the coming of the commune. It did mean the triumph of men opposed to entrenched privilege and who appealed to, and claimed to speak for, the great mass of people. Whatever the interpretation of the impulses and motives that moved the Jacksonian Democrats might be,[6] Jacksonian Democracy popularized, put into the climate of opinion, at least three major ideas: all the people (white

[5] Waggoner, *Toledo History*, pp. 332–334; Waggoner to Waite, April 4, 1882.

[6] Arthur M. Schlesinger, Jr., *The Age of Jackson* (Boston: Little, Brown and Company, 1945); cf., Marvin Meyers, *The Jacksonian Persuasion* (Stanford: Stanford University Press, 1957).

males) should rule without suffrage restrictions; government should serve all the people; and the average person had sufficient ability to fill positions of responsibility in self-government.

Morrison Waite, who grew up when the Jacksonian movement was at its peak, and lived in a frontier community, unquestioningly accepted these propositions. While it enjoyed support in urban areas, the Jacksonian movement had a strong agrarian flavor and its roots were deepest in the frontier. When Waite departed from sedate and cultivated Connecticut in 1838, he stepped into a typically Jacksonian community. Northwest Ohio was primitive, and Maumee, a village of eight hundred, was on the frontier. Frontier life, romantics to the contrary, does not make men virtuous. But life in the frontier community of Maumee and later in Toledo did provide for him a unique opportunity and environment. Men such as Waite participated in making the region a prosperous center of commerce, all the while governing themselves. When, at the height of the dangerous Hayes-Tilden disputed election, Waite comforted himself with the thought that "the great good sense of the people" would exert a beneficial influence,[7] he spoke with the faith of a man to whom the notion of "the people" and their relation to government was not rhetoric but experience: the Commissioners of Lucas County voting to build a road from the Maumee River to Lower Sandusky, the Toledo City Council, of which he was a member, deciding to ban liquor sales on Sundays, the leading citizens of Toledo successfully agitating to acquire railroad service for their city. Government, as Waite knew it, was close to the people. Its officials were known and responsive to the local citizenry, and (the crucial element) the decisions made by the political bodies familiar to Waite—County Commissions, City Councils, local party organizations, and state legislature—seemed and *were* important. They hit, as the expression goes, "close to home," and it was home that counted, not distant Washington.

When, during the log cabin campaign, Morrison Waite joined ardent Whigs in shouting their candidate's praises in such boisterous songs as "General Harrison's Quick Step" and "The Hurrah Song" ("poverty he thinks no crime, But welcomes it at dinner time"), he

[7] Waite to Edward Browne, Jan. 15, 1877, Letterbooks.

was doing something more than adding to the cries of partisans. The shouts for "Old Tip" and "the humble farmer from North Bend" were also shouts heralding the victory of the democratic idea in American thought and practice. Waite's hero, Webster, had suggested the possibilities of casting conservative appeals in a popular idiom. His Second Reply to Hayne—the government of the United States "is, Sir, the people's Constitution, the people's government, made for the people, made by the people, and answerable to the people"—was a masterful step in this direction. At Yale Waite had purchased speeches by the "Godlike Daniel"; later, as a youthful lawyer on the northwest Ohio frontier, his first political activity was in the first thoroughly popular presidential campaign. So it was only natural that, as a loyal Unionist during the Civil War, Morrison Waite was still quoting the Reply to Hayne and using Jacksonian language about people's government.

Not all political activity, however, was as exciting, or successful, as the log cabin campaign. Throughout the 1840's and 1850's Waite served the Lucas County Whigs in routine capacities—secretary at meetings, president of conventions, and stump speaker for party candidates. A typical instance came in the 1842 state and congressional election. Under the 1840 census the state's Democrats, who controlled both branches of the legislature, reapportioned (the Whigs claimed "gerrymandered") Ohio's congressional districts. Sensing an issue and, of course, seeing their interests threatened, Ohio Whigs denounced the reapportionment. In Lucas, the Whig Central Committee issued a declaration, signed by Waite and four other committeemen, calling for a mass meeting. "RALLY, WHIGS, AND KILL THE MONSTER!" proclaimed the leaflet which denounced the gerrymander as "a rare animal of the genus Locofoco . . . so trained that he could destroy annually, for ten years to come, from twenty-five to thirty thousand Whig votes." Labeling the Democrats "Hypocrites" who "prate about 'Equal Rights' and 'Democracy,'" the committee asked "Farmers, Mechanics, Merchants and Professional Men" to rally "and make one more struggle for the election of honest men, the ascendancy of correct principles," and, in a somewhat more prosaic vein, "the payment of the Contractors and Laborers on the Public Works!" However, the Ohio Democrats won and increased their majority in the legislature.[8]

Again, in 1844, Waite campaigned for the unsuccessful presidential ticket headed by Henry Clay. Two years later he made his first run for elective office when a convention of Whigs asked him to oppose William Sawyer, a conservative Democrat, then holding the seat in the fifth congressional district. Following national party policy, the convention nominating Waite adopted resolutions defending their lukewarm support of the Mexican War, demanding an aggressive policy toward Great Britain in the Oregon Boundary Dispute, and, still true to Clay's "American System," favoring high duties on imports. Finally, they pledged "to Morrison R. Waite, this day nominated for Congress, our hearty and unanimous support—we will elect him if we can."[9] The qualification, "if we can," reflected Whig uncertainties in northern Ohio and their poor prospects for success. Caught by the growing antislavery movement on one side and by the need for conservative Southern support on the other, the irreconcilable pressures soon to destroy the Whig Party were already being felt in 1846. Particularly was this so in northern Ohio where influential politicians such as Edward Wade and Joshua R. Giddings, increasingly dissatisfied with Whig equivocations, were defecting to the abolitionist Liberty Party.[10]

Barely thirty years old and eager to build a reputation as a responsible attorney, Waite accepted a worthless nomination from a sense of duty. A lawyer who rode circuit with him during these years recalled the campaign:

> [O]nce upon a time you was around making some speeches as a candidate . . . for the good old *Whig party* and we met and "bedded" together after you had an evening speech . . . at the little town of Montpelier quite in the woods of N Western Williams Co.
>
> You told me, I remember, how your canvass had disgusted you with the ways, tricks & machinations of party politicians, and how much nobler and more honorable was adherence to professional

[8] Waggoner, *Toledo History,* pp. 334–348.
[9] Toledo *Blade,* July 22, 1846.
[10] Roseboom and Weisenburger, *History of Ohio,* pp. 218–224; Weisenburger, *Ohio,* III, 432–440.

practice. I knew & felt you was making the canvass as a sheer matter of duty, and without the most forlorn hope of success.[11]

Toledo's *Blade* commended "M. R. Waite, Esq." as "a young gentleman of distinguished talents, and excellent character,"[12] but the campaign was listless, and as expected, he lost by a wide margin. Morrison Waite, who thirty-five years from then would still be doing unpleasant tasks because "I have not yet got over the notion that whatever it is my duty to do must be done,"[13] had at least served his party in the manner expected of a small-town lawyer.

The "momentous question" that, "like a fire bell in the night," awakened and terrified Jefferson as the old sage spent his last days at Monticello, figured more prominently in Waite's next campaign. As abolitionist pressure which now spoke through the Free Soil Party grew, northern Ohio Whigs were forced into a stronger stand. In the late summer of 1849, with Waite presiding as convention president, Lucas County Whigs declared that "slavery is opposed to natural law, the spirit of a Republican Government and the tendency of the age." And, resolved the convention,

while we recognize the right of our sister States to regulate their internal policy, we regard Slavery as a grievous moral, social and political evil, and that the efforts of our Government, both State and National, should be so directed as to effect the entire eradication of the same and its consequent evils from our favored land.[14]

These resolutions, hoped the Toledo *Blade*, ought to be "*anti-slavery* enough to satisfy the most ultra *Free Soiler*."[15] A few weeks later district Whigs chose Waite to be their candidate for the state legislature, repeating their condemnation of slavery "as an infraction of human right." But, as the Whig resolutions showed, their disapproval of slavery owed more to economic than to human implications. After briefly condemning the peculiar institution on moral grounds, the Lucas Whigs denounced its practical effects: the destruction "of

[11] Charles Case to Waite, March 26, 1874.
[12] July 22, 1846.
[13] Waite to Thomas Dunlap, Aug. 4, 1881. Toledo Public Library.
[14] Waggoner, *Toledo History*, p. 343.
[15] Aug. 11, 1849.

equality of power in the general government" by enlarging the representation of those "against northern and western policy," the promotion of "a system of laws destructive of domestic industry," and the limitation of free labor by "retarding the natural growth of population and improvement" through "the appropriation of large tracts of land for the benefit of the few." On this platform Morrison Waite ran against a Democrat and a Free Soiler, winning by a mere fifty-eight votes his only important elective office, a term in the 1849–1850 Ohio House.[16]

A dispute over a bitterly contested Senate seat, a lengthy struggle over apportionment, and difficulty in organizing the House—compounded by the fact that six Free Soilers held the balance of power between the other two parties—made the session a political free-for-all.[17] Henry Matson Waite, experienced in the ways and wiles of state politics, warned his son that "the question with politicians is not always what is right, but what will most avail the party." "I fear," he went on, "that you will have a long session and that you will become heartily sick of legislation before it is ended—But as the Californians say you will have an opportunity of seeing the elephant—of seeing how demagogues manage." [18] His prediction of a long and acrimonious session was correct. Morrison Waite left Columbus feeling thoroughly dissatisfied. "If the State does not hereafter suffer from what we have done this winter I am no prophet. More wholesale reckless Legislation I never dreamed of." [19]

During his brief legislative career Waite served on the Judiciary Committee; he busied himself primarily with judicial matters, as, for instance, the times of meetings for county courts and the various details related to a constitutional convention scheduled for 1851. One such detail was the date to be set for the election of convention delegates. It became the occasion for a debate which provides a good insight into the political attitudes of the thirty-three year old Waite. Democrats wanted the election postponed as long as possible to allow voters time to familiarize themselves with the issues. They further

[16] Toledo *Blade,* Sept. 3, 1849; Waggoner, *Toledo History,* p. 343.

[17] Weisenburger, *Ohio,* III, 477–478.

[18] Henry M. Waite to Waite, Jan. 10, 1850. Courtesy of Professor and Mrs. John B. Waite.

[19] Waite to Lane, March 22, 1850. Lane Papers, Yale.

claimed that the existing constitution required that the choosing of delegates coincide with the date set for the regular state elections, which would have meant deferring the election until October, 1850. The Whigs favored a much earlier date, in April, and eventually succeeded in getting it adopted. Speaking in support of an early election, Waite easily demonstrated that Ohio's "constitutional law" did not require the selection of delegates at any specific time; the Democrats later dropped this argument. But was it "expedient" to separate the two elections? Waite answered that it was essential to divorce the convention election from the extreme partisanship characteristic of the regular elections; separating the two elections, he contended, diminished the likelihood that the choice of convention delegates would be influenced by purely political considerations. On the other hand, mixing the two elections would mean the selection of "ultraist" delegates from each party and the consequent inability of the convention to frame a constitution neutral enough to win ratification. Next, he turned to the objection that since it was already early February an April election would attract too few voters. Waite's reply illustrates one of the most persistent elements in his political philosophy, faith in popular democracy.

> I ask gentlemen here to revert to their own experience in this matter, and tell me if the people are not always out when there is an important political or even local election. Can they not cast their minds back to an election of a Justice of the Peace, where every vote was polled for that election? There never was a time in the history of the politics of Ohio . . . when an important election of any kind did not bring the people out to the polls. Have we time to inform the people of the passage of this bill, in time for an April election? Suppose this bill does not become a law until the last of next week. Cannot you and I and all directly inform the people of its passage? Would we not do the people a greater service by franking home copies of the bill, than by sending the political speeches which we are accustomed to frank at all times? . . . Depend upon it, when the first Monday in April comes the people will be at the polls and vote for their man.[20]

[20] *Ohio State Journal* (Columbus), Feb. 11, 1850; and also, the issues of Feb. 19 and 22, 1850.

Waite's legislative actions and votes showed him to be a typical member of Ohio's Whig Party, the party of "friends of the business classes and defenders of banks." [21] Faced with a choice between two bank-tax bills, one increasing rates beyond those fixed by their original charter, the other providing for increases only with the consent of the affected banks, he denounced the former as a bill to "suppress" banks. The "bank haters," as the Whig *Ohio State Journal* (Columbus) labeled the Democrats, failed in their efforts, and a Whig-Free Soil coalition passed the more moderate measure. Two years later, when the legislature adopted the harsher bank-tax law giving rise to the case of *Toledo Bank* v. *Bond*, Waite represented the bank and renewed his opposition, arguing that the tax unconstitutionally impaired the obligation of contracts.[22] On another economic issue he opposed a bill "to regulate labor, prevent oppression and establish ten hours as a legal day's work," voting instead for an amendment designed to kill the proposal by providing "that if such person shall not work ten hours in a day he shall forfeit and pay ten dollars to his employer." And when, he wrote Ebenezer Lane, a bill providing for the service of mesne process (intermediary legal writs which precede final court orders) on railroads passed the Senate, "I tried to tack on an amendment in the House requiring demand to be made of the Company before suit [could be] brought but it was no go." [23]

Proposals for bond issues found him less sympathetic to railroads. He signed a Judiciary Committee report opposing legislation which would permit municipal corporations and counties to authorize taxes for railroad construction.[24] Bond authorizations were not a party issue and Waite's votes suggest skepticism toward many of the schemes then so popular. Thus, on February 11, 1850, he voted against authorizing the Commissioners of Shelby County to subscribe additional funds to the Bellefontaine & Indiana Railroad. He opposed similar plans for financing a number of the other railroads and would-

[21] Roseboom, *Ohio*, III, 125.

[22] *Ohio State Journal*, March 20, 25, 1850; Toledo *Blade*, Oct. 6, 1862; 1 Ohio 622 (1853). In 1856 the federal Supreme Court agreed with Waite by declaring the tax unconstitutional. *Dodge* v. *Woolsey*, 18 Howard 331.

[23] *Journal*, Ohio House of Representatives, Volume 1849–50, 305–306. Ohio Historical Society, Columbus; Waite to Lane, March 22, 1850. Lane Papers, Yale.

[24] Clipping of Toledo *Commercial*, March 30, 1888. Waite Papers.

be railroads which proliferated during the 1850's—the Central Ohio Railroad, the West Liberty Central Railroad, and the Scioto & Hocking Valley Railroad. A bill incorporating a turnpike company also met with his disapproval. He supported instead an unsuccessful amendment providing that "nothing in this act shall be so construed as to compel them who do not vote for a tax under this act to pay any portion of the tax so assessed." [25]

On the slavery question then fragmenting the parties, as it would soon the nation, Waite took the line followed by northern Ohio Whigs. General Zachary Taylor had already felt the power of the abolitionist movement, which was especially strong among the New Englanders in the Western Reserve. In 1848 Taylor had lost Ohio's presidential electors because of his inability to hold antislavery Whigs, who bolted to support the Free Soil ticket. As the state's 1849 legislative session opened, the Whigs aimed at regaining the support of the antislavery movement. The antislavery platform on which Waite had been so narrowly elected mirrored these hopes, as did too his votes in the House. Among them were votes permitting a convention of Negroes to use the House chamber for an evening meeting, opposing a motion condemning abolitionist agitation, and supporting a bill "for the protection of personal liberty," which would have prohibited Ohio citizens and state officers from taking any steps to assist in the recapture of fugitive slaves.[26]

One debate elicited Waite's comments on the status of the Negro. A bill before the House proposed amending an 1831 law denying Negroes admission to poorhouses. The Judiciary Committee recommended against passage (it was rejected by a vote of fifty-three to nine) and Waite explained the committee's reasons. These hinged on the fact that recent decisions of the Ohio courts made it possible for destitute Negroes to receive support; they were still, however, excluded from the poorhouses. According to Waite, the state was obliged to support any suffering person, whether Negro or white. But he doubted that the mere admission of Negroes to poorhouses served their best interests. On the contrary, it would become "a

[25] Ohio House *Journal*, Volume 1849–50, 480–481, 499, 526, 548, 605–606; Volume 1850, 78–79, 267–268.

[26] Ohio House *Journal*, Volume 1849–50, 133–134; Volume 1850, 337, 341.

fruitful source of oppression" by putting them into contact "with persons who would despise them, and strive to render their situation as unhappy as possible." Since Negro paupers were now receiving aid, he deemed it unnecessary to amend the law even though he wanted all relics of the state's black laws repealed. "So soon as public sentiment will admit," Waite concluded, "every friend of humanity will desire to see every invidious distinction abolished, and a perfect admission of equality to every class of the human race." Although equivocal, this position differed markedly from that of the Democratic legislators. These described the Negro as a subhuman species, not entitled to any rights, and condemned the proposed poor-law revision as "infernal fanaticism." [27]

Despite its efforts, which, as in the case of the poor-law amendment, were often rather temporizing, the Whig Party failed to recoup the losses suffered in 1848. To be sure, President Zachary Taylor had learned his political lesson and he opposed Henry Clay's compromise, thereby winning antislavery support and enhancing Whig prospects. But Taylor's untimely death placed Millard Fillmore in the presidential chair. The new President approved the Compromise of 1850—highly favorable to the slavery interests—and the Ohio Whig Party soon disintegrated.[28]

Morrison Waite's brief career as a state legislator ended with the session. He did not seek reelection, most likely because of disgust with state politics and a desire to build up his law office. In the spring of 1850 he unsuccessfully contested a seat in the state's constitutional convention and the next year he served one term on the Toledo City Council. Alderman M. R. Waite introduced "an ordinance requiring all places in which liquors were sold, to be closed on Sunday." Personally fond of wines and not averse to an occasional taste of the stronger stuff, Waite was a mild supporter of the temperance movement which swept Ohio prior to the Civil War. Joining other leading Toledo citizens, he signed a manifesto backing "a strict and uncompromising execution" of state prohibition laws because it "will enhance the best interests of all the people, promote private happiness,

[27] *Ohio State Journal*, Feb. 13 and 14, 1850.
[28] Roseboom and Weisenburger, *Ohio*, pp. 223–224, 235–240.

secure public good order, and save the wretched from increased wretchedness." [29]

Apart from this one term on the City Council, Waite's political activity fell to a minimum as he concentrated on his growing legal practice. After Congress passed the proslavery Kansas-Nebraska Act in 1854, repealing the Missouri Compromise, he and other Whigs joined antislavery Democrats and Free Soilers in forming a temporary party known as "Anti-Nebraska" which was soon absorbed into the Republican Party.[30] His political participation, however, remained confined to purely local matters. Thus, shortly after the beginning of the Civil War he wrote Salmon Chase, Lincoln's Treasury Secretary, discussing in great detail patronage matters affecting Toledo Republicans. Concluding the letter, he added an afterthought about the rebellion. "How refreshing it is to see the union of feeling here at the North in the present troubles. We are *all* enthusiastic administration men. Party is entirely forgotten." [31]

The harmony that so pleased Waite was, unfortunately, only temporary, fed by the patriotic war fever which gripped the North following the firing on Fort Sumter. As the Union armies suffered severe reverses and casualty lists mounted, it became painfully clear that not all Ohioans were "administration men." On the contrary, the state was riven with political fissures. At one extreme a powerful movement of "Peace Democrats" led by Clement L. Vallandigham, the fiery copperhead, came close to treason, clamoring for a negotiated peace and resisting Lincoln's repressive war measures. At the other, radical Republicans, dissatisfied with Lincoln's conduct of the war and angered by his refusal to support immediate emancipation, kept up an incessant pressure aimed at forcing the President to accept their position. In the middle, loyal Republicans, old Whig conservatives, and "War Democrats" formed a Union Party to back the beleaguered President.

For Morrison Waite, who never wavered in defending Lincoln's conservative and moderate policies, this political dissension had im-

[29] Waggoner, *Toledo History*, p. 721.
[30] Waggoner, *Toledo History*, p. 344, 525.
[31] Waite to Chase, May 6, 1861. Salmon P. Chase Papers, L.C.

mediate consequences. Not especially keen to enter Congress, he was led by the political situation in the Toledo district to accept a congressional nomination.[32] Like the party at the state and national level, Toledo Republicans were badly divided over the war as they met in the summer of 1862 to nominate a candidate for Congress. James M. Ashley, who held the seat, was a radical Republican of the deepest hue. A close friend of Charles Sumner and later prominent in the drive to impeach President Johnson, Ashley demanded that the administration make abolition its primary goal. At the same time he sharply attacked Lincoln for failing to prosecute the war vigorously. Unable to unite on a candidate, the convention split into two factions. Radicals renominated Ashley; conservatives, with some Democratic support, drafted Morrison Waite to contest the seat as a pro-Lincoln Union candidate. The third aspirant for Ashley's seat was a Peace Democrat, Edward L. Phelps, who ran as "the white man's candidate," the foe of Sumner's "vile gang," and an "avowed enemy of Negro freedom." [33]

In the style of the day and spurred by the passions unleashed by a bitter war, the campaign was rough and hard-fought. Ashley denounced Waite as "the Vallandigham candidate," and Waite's supporters responded by accusing Ashley of defrauding the government "of many dollars" and sundry "violations of pledges." Phelps' backers impartially blasted both rivals for sustaining the President "in his high-handed usurpation of power." [34] Waite's slogan was "Union for the Sake of Union" and his basic position simple: preservation of the Union as the main object of the war; immediate emancipation only as a war measure if deemed necessary by the President as Commander in Chief; and amendment of the Constitution as an essential step in attaining the desirable goal of Negro freedom. Clark Waggoner, editor of the Toledo *Blade*, veteran of many Toledo political wars and a close associate of Waite, spoke authoritatively for the conservative candidate:

[32] Waggoner, *Toledo History*, p. 526; Benjamin R. Cowen, "Morrison Remick Waite," in William D. Lewis (Ed.), *Great American Lawyers* (Philadelphia: The John C. Winston Company, 1909), VII, 97.

[33] Napoleon *Northwest*, a Democratic paper, quoted in the Toledo *Blade*, Oct. 6, 1862.

[34] Toledo *Blade*, Oct. 6, 1862.

Mr. Waite

He believes that the rebellion ought to be put down.
He believes that the Government should use all means necessary thereto.
He believes that black men are no better than white men and should be employed by the Government, in any way that may be found practicable, for the suppression of the rebellion.
He believes that fanatics, who are for the Union if Slavery can be destroyed, and don't care a snap for it, if Slavery is not destroyed, are too fanatical to be safe counsellors, or reliable supporters of the Government in Congress.[35]

Waite stumped northwest Ohio emphasizing his support for Lincoln's policy of "patient waiting" as illustrated by the President's preliminary proclamation that on January 1, 1863, slaves in states still in rebellion would be declared free. The Fulton *County Union* reported a typical Union Party rally at the town of Ottokee where Waite spoke in early October. It was, said the paper, "a grand success."

The recent heavy rain and bad condition of the roads did not dampen the ardor of the friends of honest Mott Waite, or the Union cause. They came from every nook and corner of the country, and brought their women folk and boys, babies and bannners. The Court House was crowded to suffocation, and the address of Mr. Waite, which was quite lengthy, was listened to with the deepest interest. . . . He sought not to conceal anything and gave his views with a freedom and honesty that was most convincing. Union men of all political antecedents were more than satisfied with his views. . . .

The Wauseon Brass Band favored the meeting with some excellent music.[36]

Returning to Lucas County, Waite delivered his major campaign speech at Toledo on October 6. At the outset he declared his opposition to slavery. It was his desire that the United States be "the first" nation of the earth and this could be attained only with free institutions and free labor. Slavery, he urged, retarded the development of large areas of American territory. The slave state of Ken-

[35] Toledo *Blade*, Aug. 22, 1862.
[36] Oct. 3, 1862, quoted in Toledo *Blade*, Oct. 6, 1862.

tucky, said Waite, despite its better climate and soil, was less productive than free states such as Ohio or Illinois. However, a legislator

> could have no power to interfere with Slavery in the States. Congress could pass laws to punish crime and declare the forfeiture of property, as had been done; but in this case there must be a trial of the individual charged, and no forfeiture could result until such trial and conviction.

And so, while he favored abolition,

> Congress has no right to interfere with the institution in the States, except in the punishment of crime. —This is the rule for Congress in peace and war. No new power is given that body by the war. To get this the Constitution must be peaceably amended in pursuance of its own terms.

But though denying congressional radicals the right to abolish slavery, he gave it to the President under his power as Commander in Chief. "Slavery was beyond question," Waite insisted, "the chief strength of the Rebels." By freeing Southern whites to fight in the rebel armies, it gave the Confederacy an element of power that the President could destroy. For, he concluded, the rebellion brought with it war and the laws of war. Lincoln could "do anything warranted by the laws of war to strengthen his own army." Indeed, as a Commander it was his duty "to weaken the enemy—take his property of every kind and nature; and his life itself, if necessary, to this end." [37]

Waite's position was popular in Lucas County, which he carried by a margin of two to one, but Ashley took the district with 7,013 votes to 5,850 votes for Waite and 5,234 for Phelps—a good illustration of how sharply the war divided Ohioans. In spite of the defeat, Waite remained active in state politics. From the war's beginning he had been prominent in furthering the Union cause. Much of his time between 1861 and 1865 was spent making speeches and signing declarations supporting the administration, promoting enlistments, and raising funds for the relief of soldiers' families.[38] Such efforts were

[37] Toledo *Blade*, Oct. 6, 7, 1862; Waggoner, *Toledo History*, p. 351.
[38] Waggoner, *Toledo History*, pp. 84–124.

necessary, for, as his own defeat showed, the administration's popularity in Ohio was dangerously low. The excessively harsh measures employed against Peace Democrats by overzealous Union commanders, and particularly, the continuing and costly setbacks suffered by the federal armies, hurt the administration on two sides. Both radicals and pro-Southerners found cause for severe disaffection. When the outspoken rebel sympathizer, Clement Vallandigham, safely ensconced across the border in Canada, opened his campaign for Governor in 1863, the administration faced real trouble. Vallandigham, who had reacted to General Burnside's order decreeing arrest for enemy sympathizers by screaming that "He despised it, spit upon it, he trampled it under his feet," may have been a demagogue. He was also courageous and sincere in his beliefs. Most important, his peace platform had appeal to a war-weary people.[39]

Confronted with this challenge, the Union Party threw its full support behind John Brough, a War Democrat, as its candidate for Governor. Waite campaigned extensively for Brough in the northwest, stressing that the war was "a War for the Republic; and he who is not for it is against it." Always his emphasis was on "the integrity of the Union," and he quoted his old hero, Webster, exhorting his listeners to maintain the Union "now and forever—one and inseparable." When a heckler interrupted his speech at a Union meeting in Toledo, Waite reminded the man that "this Government is better than any other you could find" because "it has made you and me all we are, and we should defend it." [40] Vallandigham showed strength in polling one hundred and eighty-seven thousand votes, but the great Union victories at Vicksburg and Gettysburg in the summer of 1863 were powerful campaign arguments. Brough received one hundred thousand votes more than his rival, vindicating the national administration and easing the threat posed by the copperheads. Governor Brough sought to reward the Toledo lawyer-politician with a seat on the State Supreme Court. Waite declined, preferring to keep his law practice. He stayed active, however, as an adviser to Brough and an advocate of the Union cause.

[39] Roseboom and Weisenburger, *History of Ohio,* pp. 279–285; Roseboom, *Ohio,* IV, 404–423.

[40] Waggoner, *Toledo History,* pp. 95–96, 111, 352.

Morrison Waite spoke accurately when he declared that there had been "little of my public life." Even when Waite's service at the Geneva Tribunal and his brief presidency over the Ohio Constitutional Convention of 1871 are added to the rest of his public career —three unsuccessful runs for state office, a term in the state legislature, and a year as a Toledo alderman—the record remains unimpressive. Waite's state of Ohio had hundreds of men with similar records, most of whom were forgotten within a few years of their death. Had Morrison Waite not gone on the Supreme Court, he, unlike William Evarts or Caleb Cushing, would soon have been consigned to oblivion. In Toledo, where most people knew each other personally, it was hard to avoid such civic-political service. Certainly there is no evidence that Waite hungered for public office; there is much to suggest the exact opposite, that, feeling a loyalty to certain interests, his political activity was merely a response to "duty."

Yet, if his public record is thin, it has nonetheless a meaning and a significance. Raised in the Jacksonian Era by a Whig father, he naturally joined the party of Webster and Clay, both of whom spoke the language of popular democracy. Moving to a frontier community, soon involved in the almost populistic log cabin campaign, he witnessed real self-government. To Waite "the people" was no abstraction. It was a visible power which governed Toledo and made its influence felt at Columbus. Moreover, this government, which in the proper hands could provide order and promote the banking systems, roads, and canals essential to commerce, was not an evil, but an instrument of good. In politics, Whiggery and later Republicanism were the obvious outlets through which he expressed his concern for the well-being of financial and commercial interests. As a prospering business lawyer he shunned the radical—be it of the ultra-abolitionist or the Southern sympathizer. His approach to the slavery crisis was, from his point of view, hardheaded: slavery was a moral wrong, a violation of the natural law; it was also a practical wrong because inefficient and harmful to the interests of free white labor. Above all, the Union, which created the conditions for prosperity, had to be preserved. All the while, however, as he had since the log cabin campaign, Waite held a simple—but deep—faith in popular government and the people's ultimate wisdom.

With the war over and the Union preserved, Waite shied away from further political involvement. The Civil War meant, in Louis Hacker's phrase, "the triumph of American capitalism"; the nation's economy was booming and the firm of M. R. & R. Waite shared in the prosperity. But wars have political as well as economic after-effects. One such after-effect was the *Alabama* claims dispute.

5

GENEVA:

"Peace hath her victories"

Confederate Steamship Alabama. *American Claims.*

The Geneva Tribunal. "A Mr. Waite of Toledo" Named Counsel.

Paris and Geneva. Arbitration Endangered.

The Toledo Attorney Files a Brief. Victory in Peace.

Travels and Pleasures in Europe.

Ohio's Constitutional Convention. Presiding Officer.

The Chief Justiceship. The Challenge Ahead.

IN THE SPRING OF 1862 A WARSHIP TEMPORARILY CHRISTENED THE "Enrica" steamed out of the port of Liverpool. Two years later this ship, better known as the *Alabama*, was sunk by a Union vessel, the *Kearsarge*, in the waters outside Cherbourg harbor. Between these two events the *Alabama* and its fellow Confederate cruisers captured hundreds of Union merchant ships and destroyed millions of dollars worth of Northern property. The saga of these cruisers did not, however, end with their sinking or the close of the war. Built in English shipyards, outfitted with British armaments, and often seeking haven in the ports of the Empire, the cruisers caused a severe crisis in Anglo-American relations.

Annoying to the North, Britain's early recognition of Confederate belligerency had justification in international practice and would not in itself have strained relations. But Britain's neutrality, especially in the crucial early stages of the war, is best described as a friendly neutrality toward the South. Despite the repeated protests of the United States Minister, Charles Francis Adams, the British Government, some of whose officials were anxious to see America divided into two or more states, blinked at numerous violations of Britain's neutrality laws. The result was the construction and escape of the Confederate cruisers, which drove Union merchant ships from the sea and seriously damaged the North's war effort.

From the war's outset, Lincoln's Secretary of State, William Seward, and Minister Adams sought not only to prevent the Confederacy from acquiring additional cruisers—this object was eventually attained—but also pressed claims against Great Britain. These were of two kinds. The first were for property losses suffered by American interests. Far more troublesome were the second, the national or indirect claims based on the increased insurance costs for American shipping and the transfer of cargoes from United States to neutral ships. In addition, some Americans charged that the early recognition of Southern belligerency and the activities of the cruisers prolonged the war, thereby adding to Britain's indirect liability.[1] Emerging victorious from the war and feeling its newly developed military power, the North demanded that Britain pay some form of acceptable compensation. Under President Johnson an attempt was made to settle the issue. Lord Clarendon, the British Foreign Minister, negotiated a treaty with Reverdy Johnson, the American envoy. Ignoring the really contentious matters of the allegedly "premature" recognition of Southern belligerency and the damages caused by the rebel ships, the treaty merely provided that the citizens of either country could reciprocally submit claims.

Agreed to in the closing days of President Johnson's hapless Administration, the Johnson-Clarendon Convention of 1869 went to the Senate shortly after Grant's accession, only to be repudiated by a vote of fifty-four to one. Prior to the Senate's defiant rejection, Charles Sumner, Chairman of the Foreign Relations Committee, and never a man to weigh words carefully, delivered a bitter, almost warlike, attack on Great Britain. With some justification he denounced the treaty for avoiding the real issues. Then, in threatening language, he advanced the indirect claims in their most extreme form. According to Sumner, had it not been for the British-built cruisers, the war would have ended with Gettysburg. Great Britain, therefore, was liable for all American war costs incurred after the summer of 1863, a sum estimated at $2,125,000,000 which, he helpfully suggested, could be satisfied by the annexation of Canada.

Sumner's preposterous claims and the cries of other jingoes such as Benjamin "Glorious Ben" Butler produced in turn a predictable reaction of defiance across the Atlantic. By 1870 the two countries

[1] Nevins, *Fish*, ch. viii is excellent on the *Alabama* claims dispute; see also James Ford Rhodes, *History of the United States* (New York: The Macmillan Company, 1906), VI, ch. xxxviii.

were close to a diplomatic break. Thanks, however, to the patient and brilliant efforts of Grant's Secretary of State, Hamilton Fish, relations gradually improved. Finally, in 1871, the Treaty of Washington was negotiated and subsequently approved by the Senate. Besides settling other matters in dispute, it provided for an international board of arbitration to pass on the American claims and affirmed the principle that during wartime a neutral nation ought to use "due dilligence" in preventing either belligerent from acquiring warships within its jurisdiction or using its ports as a naval base. To assist the five arbitrators, who were to meet in Geneva, the British Government agreed that they should assume that during the war Britain sought to act upon the principle of "due dilligence." Both sides avoided the ticklish indirect claims controversy. The British negotiators, fearful of home opinion and the Tory opposition, were loath to admit their validity. They supposed that the question had been disposed of by Great Britain's expression of regret embodied in the treaty. The American negotiators led by Fish, conscious of jingoist sentiment in the North, felt they could not drop the indirect claims and assumed that, along with those for actual property damage, they would go before the arbitrators. Unfortunately, subsequent developments illustrated the dangers of such "good natured vagueness" in diplomatic negotiation, and the Geneva Tribunal almost died stillborn.[2] But, for the moment, the indirect claims were brushed under the rug. Each nation agreed to appoint an agent to submit its basic case to the tribunal in December of 1871; legal counsel would then prepare further arguments to be submitted later the next year.

As American agent, President Grant chose J. C. Bancroft Davis, his Assistant Secretary of State and a nephew of George Bancroft. He then turned to the problem of finding three counsel, making as his first choices William M. Meredith, a leader of the Philadelphia bar and a Secretary of the Treasury in Zachary Taylor's Cabinet, Caleb Cushing, and former Supreme Court Justice Benjamin R. Curtis. When Meredith and Curtis declined because of ill health, Grant relented from an earlier determination that "under no circumstances" would he appoint William M. Evarts, and succumbing to Secretary

[2] Nevins, *Fish*, pp. 528–529.

Fish's insistence, selected the highly regarded New York lawyer.[3] A Cabinet meeting on November 10, 1871, took up the subject of a third counsel. Various prominent names were mentioned: Richard Henry Dana, Lyman Trumbull, Matt Carpenter, Charles O'Conor, Edwards Pierrepont, Jeremiah Black, and Ebenezer Rockwood Hoar. And "Mr. Delano," Fish recorded in his diary, "names a Mr. Waite of Toledo, who, he says is the equal of any man in the Country as a Lawyer." Four days later President Grant decided to follow his Interior Secretary's suggestion and directed Fish to offer Waite the appointment. So unknown was Waite that Columbus Delano had to write the Secretary of State to tell him that " 'Morrison R. Waite Toledo Ohio' gives you name and address." [4]

To Morrison Waite the appointment came as a complete surprise. He was in New York attending to legal business when two telegrams, one from Fish, the other from Delano, reached him after being forwarded from Toledo. His first reaction—and it tells something of Waite's ambitions and modesty—was that the telegrams were part of a practical joke.[5] Friends persuaded him differently and on November 24, 1871, Fish was able to announce Waite's acceptance of the position.[6] Pleased to be working with his old Yale classmate in what he called "this honorable employment," Waite wrote to Evarts that "the appointment came upon me very unexpectedly, but it is none the less acceptable on that account." [7]

Back in Toledo, Waite prepared to leave for Washington and then Paris where the American counsel planned to prepare their arguments. Before his departure "the substantial men of Toledo" tendered him a complimentary dinner, featuring a fancy bill of fare that began with mock turtle soup and ended with Madeira jelly and Malaga grapes. In brief remarks thanking his hosts, Waite discussed the significance of the Geneva Arbitration. It was, he said, symbolic of the progress of civilization. Already the barbarous modes of set-

[3] Barrows, *Evarts*, p. 198; Frank W. Hackett, *Reminiscences of the Geneva Tribunal of Arbitration* (Boston: Houghton Mifflin Company, 1911), pp. 73–83, cited hereafter as Hackett, *Reminiscences*.

[4] Diary, Nov. 10, 14, 1871; Delano to Fish, Nov. 14, 1871. Fish Papers.

[5] Clipping, Toledo *Commercial*, March 31, 1888. Waite Papers.

[6] Diary, Nov. 24, 1871. Fish Papers.

[7] Waite to Evarts, Dec. 1, 1871, quoted in Barrows, *Evarts*, p. 199.

tling disputes between individuals were being superseded by more peaceful and Christian methods. He continued,

> Why may not nations as well as individuals settle disputes without resort to arms, and cases between two nations be tried before tribunals of their own selection? When that time shall come, then will commence that new era when wars shall end and nations the shedding of blood for the settlement of disputes which can best be adjusted before properly constituted peaceful tribunals. May God speed that day.[8]

With these thoughts Morrison Waite, accompanied by his wife, his unmarried daughter Mary, and a son to give him secretarial aid, departed for the Geneva Arbitration. Arriving at Paris in the winter of 1872, he settled down for some months of exacting labor: preparing that part of the American brief that showed where the Confederate cruisers had been built and how they obtained every piece of armament and ton of coal they had used.[9] One of Waite's greatest legal skills was an ability to mass relevant facts, and this he now did, shrewdly building his argument by citing material culled from Britain's case to show precisely how the cruisers received aid in violation of Britain's own neutrality laws.[10] Though uninteresting, this detailed work was essential to proving the American charge that Britain's policy, or at best her negligence, resulted in the giving of substantial assistance to the Confederacy.

Even as Waite compiled his brief, it seemed that it might never go before the arbitrators. The indirect claims controversy, so conveniently ignored by the treaty's negotiators, flared up again and nearly wrecked the arbitration. Bancroft Davis, in preparing the basic American statement, to the complete surprise of the British, reasserted these claims in their extremest form. Accusing the wartime British Government of a "conscious unfriendly purpose toward the United States," Davis placed on Great Britain all war costs incurred after Gettysburg—adding, for good measure, an interest of seven

[8] Toledo *Commercial*, Dec. 19, 1871.

[9] Kenneth B. Umbreit, *Our Eleven Chief Justices* (New York: Harper & Brothers, 1938), p. 306.

[10] *The Argument at Geneva* (New York: D. Appleton and Company, 1873), chs. vi–x, cited hereafter as *Argument*.

per cent! Faced with the prospect of paying over four and a half billion dollars, the British Government, its opposition, and the popular press reacted with understandable fury, threatening to end the arbitration unless the indirect claims were withdrawn. Ironically, neither Secretary of State Hamilton Fish nor the American counsel took these claims seriously. They were included to appease the Sumners and Butlers just prior to a national election in an era when pulling the British lion's tail was almost as fashionable as waving the bloody shirt. Beyond this, they were intended to bolster American claims for direct damages caused by the cruisers. In fact, Fish, knowing well that America might be neutral in future European wars, hoped to have the Tribunal pass on the indirect claims and establish that a neutral was not liable for indirect and remote injuries resulting from her negligence.[11]

Under gloomy circumstances, the Tribunal convened in Geneva on June 15, 1872. Britain sought an eight-month adjournment to permit the two nations to negotiate a supplementary convention. Hamilton Fish, however, still hoped to avert the collapse of the treaty he had so painstakingly engineered. Cooperating with British diplomats similarly interested in continuing the arbitration and using the American arbitrator, Charles Francis Adams, as an intermediary, a face-saving compromise was arranged. While not formally passing on the indirect claims, the five arbitrators issued an advisory opinion holding such claims invalid.[12] All parties were now reasonably satisfied—Fish because the national claims, a possible skeleton in the American closet, had been buried; American jingoists because they had the pleasure of reading Bancroft Davis' lecture to Great Britain; Britain's Government because the arbitrators would not consider the extravagant demands made in the American case.

Finally, in mid-July the Tribunal began hearing arguments on the question of direct damages. Waite was able to report to Elihu B. Washburne, the American Minister to France, that "everything is going on smoothly" and "gives evidence of a reasonably favorable

[11] Nevins, *Fish*, pp. 519–534; Rhodes, *History of the United States*, VI, 365–369; Waite to Fish, draft dated, Feb. 2, 1872.

[12] Rhodes, *History of the United States*, VI, 370–372; Hackett, *Reminiscences*, ch. vii.

result."[13] Cushing, the senior counsel, and Evarts carried the brunt of the argument. Waite had not expected to argue before the Tribunal, but when a hot dispute developed over the meaning of "base of naval operations" and whether Britain incurred liability by allowing Confederate cruisers to coal in the Empire's ports, Bancroft Davis persuaded a reluctant Waite to present the American side.[14] At issue was an important point, for under the Treaty of Washington both powers prohibited the use of neutral ports or waters as "the base of naval operations" by one belligerent against the other. Roundell Palmer, Britain's counsel and later Lord Chancellor, interpreted "base of naval operations" narrowly, insisting that it meant the use of neutral territory to carry on hostile operations or to shelter preparations for attack. Belligerent vessels, he argued, could lawfully enter a neutral port to receive supplies and make repairs and then continue on to assault an enemy. "The connection between the act done within the neutral territory and the hostile operation which is actually performed out of it, must (to be within the prohibition) be 'proximate'; that is, they must be connected directly and immediately with one another."[15]

Filing a written argument on August 8, Waite squarely challenged Palmer's definition. A "base of naval operations," he countered, is not merely a place from which naval operations are carried into effect or from which a belligerent strikes against an enemy. Rather:

> It is any place at which the necessary preparations for the warfare are made; any place from which ships, arms, ammunition, stores, equipment or men are furnished, and to which the ships of the navy look for warlike supplies, and for the means of effecting the necessary repairs. It is, in short, what its name implies—the support, the foundation, which upholds and sustains the operations of a naval war.

Using this broader definition as a springboard, Waite went on to argue that, given the Federal blockade of Southern harbors, the British ports became essential to Confederate naval operations. This, beyond doubt, was the case: so "notorious" was Confederate reliance

[13] Waite to Washburne, July 18, 1872. Washburne Papers.
[14] Hackett, *Reminiscences*, p. 306.
[15] *Argument*, pp. 434–535.

on British ports that it even became a subject of comment in the House of Commons. Especially objectionable was the fact that much of it occurred after the insurgents, in procuring the *Florida* and the *Alabama*, had admittedly violated Britain's own neutrality laws. The argument was a good one. It temporarily waived the other controversy as to whether the British Government failed to exercise "due dilligence" in preventing the acknowledged violation of her laws that occurred in the construction and escape of the rebel cruisers.

Waite hammered away, pointing out that the United States repeatedly asked Britain to deny the cruisers the use of her territory and that Lord Russell, the Foreign Minister, later admitted that the insurgent activities were "totally unjustifiable and manifestly offensive to the British Crown." Surely, he contended, Britain "owed no comity to a nation that had abused her hospitality. She was under no obligation to open her ports to a belligerent that violated her neutrality. . . . It was a privilege she could grant or not as she pleased." But, instead, Britain took no action. He cited statistics showing how the *Alabama* and the *Florida* regularly refueled at Britain's Caribbean ports. And, thus, Waite concluded:

> The nation, whose authority and dignity had been so grossly offended in the construction and outfit of these vessels, was the first to grant them neutral hospitalities. From that time her ports were never closed to any insurgent vessel of war; and permission to coal, provision, and repair was never refused. . . . The number of visits made by these cruisers to all ports of all other neutral nations during the war did not exceed twenty. . . . [But] the hospitalities extended by Great Britain in this form to the insurgents [twenty-five visits] were greater than those of all the world beside, and yet more serious offenses had been committed against her than any other neutral nation.[16]

Today, the arguments and statistics cited in Waite's reply to Roundell Palmer may seem dry as bones. For the industrious Toledo attorney, however, these few pages of argument, written in Geneva during the summer of 1872, represented the greatest achievement of his professional career. Along with his other contribution to the

[16] *Argument*, pp. 513–519.

United States argument, it played a part in the arbitrators' decision: a finding of British liability for the raids of the *Alabama*, *Florida*, and *Shenandoah* and an award to the United States of fifteen and a half million dollars. The successful outcome of the Geneva Arbitration had other meanings as well for Morrison Waite. It confirmed his hope that "nations as well as individuals" could settle disputes peacefully and so commence a "new era" when wars would end and nations no longer shed blood. He had, after all, participated in one of the first instances where two major powers arbitrated a serious and aggravating dispute. Well might he respond at a dinner in Toledo after his return to a toast to "The Geneva Arbitration" by quoting Milton's affirmation: "Peace hath her victories no less renowned than those of war."

In other ways, too, the Geneva Arbitration was a broadening experience. For one thing, it gave him and his wife their first opportunity to travel in Europe. More important, it placed Waite in intimate contact with prominent figures in American public life—Caleb Cushing, Bancroft Davis, Robert C. Schenck, and Elihu Washburne. Especially did he delight in spending time with William Evarts. Unlike his Yale classmate, Waite lacked brilliance as an after-dinner speaker or as a master of the *bon mot*, but he keenly appreciated these qualities and spent many hours with Evarts.[17] Other rewards included the beginning of a warm and lasting friendship with Montague Bernard, one of the two British counsel, and the enjoyment of a high popularity among the younger men in the American party such as Charles C. Beaman and Frank W. Hackett, both of whom went on to attain eminence as lawyers. Hackett's first impression of Waite was that of a tolerant and broad-minded "man of good sense and sound judgment." He later described "the real man" as "frank" and a "most lovable of companions" who was "ever consulting the comforts of others." [18]

Along with the social amenities, politics were not forgotten during the months in Europe. Waite had barely reached Paris when Richard Waite wrote to tell him that some of the Republican leaders

[17] Barrows, *Evarts*, p. 205.
[18] Hackett, *Reminiscences*, pp. 83, 284.

in the Toledo district wanted him to make another try for Congress. Knowing his brother's desires, Richard Waite passed the word around that his interests were "in quite a different channel from that of politics." [19] If, however, Morrison Waite personally had, as his brother put it, "no special love for the science" of politics and "no axe to grind," [20] he felt quite concerned about national events in the summer of 1872. Conservative Republicans, seeking reconciliation with the South, and reformers, concerned about Civil Service and the low standard of government morality, joined hands to form that curious hybrid: the Liberal Republican Movement. Four years of growing disillusionment with Grant finally crystallized in a bolting movement that placed some leading Republicans—Carl Schurz, Horace Greeley, Charles Sumner, Jacob D. Cox, David Davis, Lyman Trumbull, and Charles Francis Adams—in opposition to the Grant Administration. Their improbable alliance with the Democratic Party appeared quite dangerous to Republican regulars, though, as subsequent events showed, the even more improbable nomination of Horace Greeley assured Grant's re-election.[21]

Not a bitter partisan, certainly no spoilsman, Morrison Waite nonetheless had little admiration for these early mugwumps. He always valued party regularity; of Lyman Trumbull, who made the transition from Radical Republican to Independent Democrat, he once said that "when a man gets to 'lying around loose' as he has done, it wont do to bet on him." Even his good friend Evarts came in for some sharp words when he hesitated to support Rutherford Hayes in 1876: "I hope he will learn by & by that he must be either the one thing or the other in politics." [22] Moreover, Waite's image of Ulysses S. Grant as one of the saviors of the Union never faded. On occasion he criticized his conduct, but his final judgment was that "He will go down to history as a really great man—and he deserves to do

[19] Richard Waite to Waite, Feb. 11, 1872, Sept. 13, 1872; J. M. Gloyd to Waite, Aug. 5, 1872.

[20] Richard Waite to Waite, May 5, 1872.

[21] Earle D. Ross, *The Liberal Republican Movement* (New York: H. Holt and Company, 1919).

[22] Waite to Amelia C. Waite, Nov. 16, 1876; Waite to Edwards Pierrepont, Oct. 29, 1876, Letterbooks.

so."[23] Since President Grant had given Waite a measure of distinction by appointing him one of the Geneva counsel, it is not surprising to find him "afraid" of Greeley's election. Likely he agreed with a friend who denounced "the Greeley treachery" which led "an old Rep. to merge himself in the Dem. Party and to help defeat his own."[24] As judicious and moderate a man as Hamilton Fish called the Liberal Republicans "snakes" and "rebels" in a "barefaced, profligate, unprincipled coalition" that was part of "a wicked effort to obtain spoils."[25]

One of the many criticisms made by the Liberal Republican-Democratic press during the summer of 1872 against Grant concerned his handling of the Geneva Arbitration. Papers such as the *World* and the *Tribune* of New York and the *Commercial* of Cincinnati rebuked the President and his Secretary of State for having pressed the explosive indirect claims.[26] Fearful of a possible Greeley victory, Waite penned a lengthy defense of the Administration's course and sent it to Samuel R. Reed, a well-known Ohio journalist with the Cincinnati *Gazette*. Reed immediately replied, saying he had incorporated Waite's letter, adding "only a little of my own," into an editorial that would be received "by the Rep. press as a model" for the "complete vindication of the Administration and the counsel in the case."[27]

Morrison Waite's defense began by noting that, as early as 1862 and repeatedly thereafter, Minister Adams, under instructions from Secretary of State Seward, demanded redress from the British Government for national and private claims. Originally, such requests were quite reasonable, requesting compensation only for indirect losses due to the transfer of commerce from American shipping and the increased cost of maritime insurance. Then Waite shrewdly took a slap at Charles Sumner, who now supported the Liberal Republican ticket. With the Senate's rejection of the Johnson-Clarendon Con-

[23] Waite to Amelia C. Waite, Nov. 16, 1876.

[24] Waite to Washburne, July 18, 1872. Washburne Papers; Samuel Reed to Waite, Aug. 11, 1872.

[25] Nevins, *Fish*, p. 608.

[26] Nevins, *Fish*, p. 605.

[27] Reed to Waite, Aug. 11, 1872. Waite's original letter, dated July 21, 1872, is lost, but its text appears in the Cincinnati *Gazette*, Aug. 13, 1872. Reed wrote the editorial's introduction, but the remainder clearly follows Waite's style.

vention, he wrote, Sumner "added to the claims which had been before made, the one for the cost of the prolongation of the war." He "magnified greatly the offense of Great Britain in prematurely issuing her proclamation of neutrality." As a consequence, Sumner inflamed "the popular mind," and when General Grant's Administration came to power, it not only inherited the indirect claims as presented by former administrations but also in the extreme form advanced by Sumner.

"In a spirit of frankness, and with a desire to remove the danger of a constantly rasping grievance," Waite continued, Secretary Fish offered to accept payment of the direct losses in full satisfaction of all claims. Britain refused, admitting no liability, and proposed instead "to try the case from the bottom up." Accordingly, the United States agreed to arbitration "to decide first by principles of public law whether Great Britain was liable at all." And so:

> The effort that followed was one made in good faith on our part to establish a mode of settling international disputes by means of international courts. These courts would not make public law, but would declare what the law is. There may not be a marked distinction between making law by the courts and declaring what the law is; but the proceeding is familiar to all who have business in the courts of this and other nations, where every day the Judges declare what the law is, not by showing that it has before been enacted or promulgated by any competent tribunal, but by showing what reason and sound judgment require it should be.

Because the United States was often neutral and knew that the indirect claims could be turned against it in later conflicts, it sought a judgment on the question. The Tribunal's opinion rejecting such claims, though not technically a judgment in the award, achieved this aim. Thus, Grant's Administration, the inheritor, not the creator, of the indirect claims, did its duty in presenting them. At the same time it gained an opinion from an international body that was likely to favor future United States interests.

Interesting as the statement is in giving Morrison Waite's views on the *Alabama* claims and his conception of the public law function of courts, it also reveals his strong commitment to the Grant Administration. His defense was clever and, it might be added, tenable. Presented with a nasty international dispute and the impossible indirect claims, the Administration handled itself well, neatly disposing of the indirect claims by insisting that it was in the national interest to have them decided against the United States. In turn, Waite's fervor in defending Grant owed something to the fact that he was associated with one of the very few achievements of Grant's eight years in office. Because of these efforts, it seems clear, Grant rewarded Waite with the chief justiceship. Whether or not Grant knew of Waite's statement, he clearly linked him with the Geneva Tribunal's decision, which on September 14, 1872, awarded the United States fifteen and a half million dollars and "redounded enormously to the credit of the Administration" just prior to the election.[28]

Upon his return home, the sequence of events that began when Columbus Delano suggested to Grant "a Mr. Waite of Toledo" as one of the Geneva counsel continued their course. Morrison Waite now found himself something of a hero. A parade and turnout of the local citizenry welcomed his arrival at Toledo. Yale honored him with a Doctor of Laws. And, when the state legislature decided to sponsor a new constitutional convention, both parties endorsed Waite as the Toledo district's candidate and he won an uncontested election.

Taking his seat at Columbus on May 13, 1873, he was immediately nominated for the convention's presidency and won the post on the sixth ballot. This, to be sure, was an honor and an indication of Waite's growing stature. But state constitutional conventions can be boring and its members intoxicated with the sound of their own words. As the convention's members droned on through the summer months, Waite described it as "a drag" and complained, "I am satisfied no one can find in the 'good book' any authority for calling together one hundred & five talking men to make a constitution." [29]

On his part, he did little to contribute to the verbiage—most of which lost its meaning after the state's voters rejected the convention's draft constitution. Since he normally sat in the presiding officer's

[28] Nevins, *Fish*, p. 605; Ross, *The Liberal Republican Movement*, pp. 41–42.
[29] Waite to Washburne, n.d., 1873. Washburne Papers.

chair, he had few opportunities for debate. One problem, however, that of judicial reform, engaged Waite's full attention. Like the United States Supreme Court, as Chief Justice Waite would soon learn, Ohio's Supreme Court labored with a badly overcrowded docket, which seriously delayed the dispensation of justice. To unclog the congestion, some of the delegates proposed the creation of a circuit court to hear appeals from the district courts. This circuit plan, which the convention adopted, also changed the existing procedure by making the new circuit court the final arbiter for all questions of fact.

Waite strongly favored these limitations of Supreme Court jurisdiction and presented the convention with an array of facts showing the steady growth in the Court's docket and the long delays, usually four years, in reaching final judgments. In combatting the charge that denying the Supreme Court jurisdiction on fact questions would not relieve its docket, he made a quick trip to the clerk's office. There he gathered statistics comparing the flow of Court business prior to 1845 and from 1853 to 1858, when it could not review fact questions, with periods during which it had such power, and easily proved that it was a major cause of the unmanageable docket.[30] The problem, as Waite saw it, was simple: to "relieve the court from a portion of its duties without doing injustice to the people of the State." Replying to an argument that the legislature, not the convention, ought to set the Court's jurisdiction, he also had a ready answer:

> When we make a Constitution and establish a court, we have the right to say what shall be the jurisdiction of that court, and we are not infringing upon the province of legislation when we do so. . . . We are creating a court and defining its duties. It is for the people to determine when the question comes before them, whether we have provided such a one as they want.

Since the proposed circuit court was to be popularly elected, another delegate wondered if the fact that the people were to choose judges having the responsibility of making final judgments in certain cases would make for a court of superior talent. Without any hesitation, Waite replied:

[30] J. G. Adel, *Official Report of the Proceedings and Debates of the Third Constitutional Convention* (Cleveland: W. S. Robison & Co., 1873–1874), I, 724, 727, 737, cited hereafter as *Convention Proceedings.*

> Certainly. If you make a court worth something the people will put a man that is worth something into it, but if it is worth nothing, you will have a man there that is worth nothing. The people are careful in the selection of those to whom they entrust their important interests.[31]

Although upon his election as convention president Waite claimed, perhaps overmodestly, unfamiliarity with the duties of a presiding officer, he earned wide praise for his "ability, courtesy, and impartiality." [32] George Hoadly, later a Democratic Governor of Ohio, described Waite as wisely guiding over one hundred occasionally "inharmonious" men with a "sunny" temper and a common sense that "was large and broad, and he had no antagonisms with any man. No appeal was ever taken from any decision he made." [33] Private opinions confirm the public statements. John W. Herron, delegate from Rutherford Hayes' district, told the former governor, "I have got to know Waite very well and like him very much. He makes a very good presiding officer though I think we have lost a good deal in not having him on the floor." After his "surprise" appointment to the Court, Herron again gave an estimate of Waite:

> I have had fine opportunities of knowing him since I have been in the Convention—and can sincerely say that he will make himself a good reputation in the position. His clear mind—good judgment—great industry and strong constitution will enable him to do a good work on the Supreme Bench. . . . I shall be very sorry to part with him. We have no other man in the Convention that can begin to equal him as presiding officer.[34]

Indeed, the presiding officer was so congenial that one of Hayes' political supporters, who found the convention "a good place to electioneer," suspected "that our President, Mr. M. R. Waite," had designs on the governorship— "judging from his agreeable manner, & constant mingling with the members." [35]

[31] *Convention Proceedings*, I, 724–725.
[32] *Convention Proceedings*, II, pt. 1, 965.
[33] "Memorial Before the Association of the Bar of the City of New York," (specially printed in 1890). Waite Papers.
[34] Herron to Hayes, Jan. 17, 1873 [*sic*—1874]; Jan. 26, 1874. Hayes Papers.
[35] Dudley W. Rhodes to Hayes, June 11, 1873. Hayes Papers.

Whatever political ambitions Morrison Waite had, and probably he had none, they came to an end January 19, 1874, when President Grant made him Chief Justice of the Supreme Court. A nice touch was added to the convention's good humor at the announcement of Waite's appointment. One of the delegates moved the creation of a committee to felicitate the new Chief Justice, and Waite, still in the presiding chair and with the members laughing, ruled the motion "entirely out of order." [36] He stayed a few days in Cincinnati, where the delegates now met, to wind up his convention duties. Manning Force, Hayes' commander during the Civil War, reported "a good deal of gayety in the city. Mr. Waite and his family are in full round of lunches, dinners, receptions and parties and having a good time." "I like them," he added, "the new Chief Justice is a sterling man." [37]

From Cincinnati he went back to Toledo to settle his business affairs and pack for the journey to Washington. As at the convention, more dinners and receptions celebrated what Waite called "my unexpected honors," and he told Hayes that since the appointment "sixty seconds have made short minutes with me." [38] To others he spoke of going on the Court with "fear and trembling" and thanked them for their words of encouragement. Such words "bear me up," he wrote. "I shall try and not disappoint the expectation of my friends." [39] In saying this he was not expressing a merely conventional modesty. Morrison Waite, deeply apprehensive about taking his seat on the Court, meant every bit of it. He read the national newspapers, and all the flattering praises in the Ohio press or from the convention's delegates could not drown out the voices that dubbed him "mediocre." Some papers carried reports that the Court's members regretted his nomination because he lacked sufficient reputation.[40] His own friends in Washington told him not to expect a warm reception from the judges, some of whom felt strongly entitled to sit in the seat he was about to occupy. "They will for some time regard you with very critical eyes," one of them warned. Another

[36] *Convention Proceedings,* II, pt. 1, 769.
[37] Force to Hayes, Jan. 26, 1874. Hayes Papers.
[38] Waite to Hayes, Feb. 11, 1874.
[39] Quoted in Baker, "Memorial of Hon. Morrison Remick Waite," 183; George P. Este to Waite, Feb. 8, 1874.
[40] N.Y. *Times,* Jan. 21, 1874.

friend reported that if any of the justices "are eating roots of bitterness, the fact will not be visible." [41] Visible or not, it hardly was reassuring to know that he soon would be presiding over a group of men who regarded him with jealousy and doubted his abilites—particularly so when the group included such names as David Davis, Stephen J. Field, Samuel F. Miller, Joseph P. Bradley, and William Strong.

For this task, however, Morrison Waite was not entirely unprepared. He came from a family with a judicial tradition. His father, a chief justice of a state court, had hoped to see his eldest son on the bench. "Defeated for election as member of Congress," noted Henry Matson Waite in 1862. "Not sorry. Would rather see him judge of a higher court." [42] Lacking a national reputation, Waite by 1874 had nonetheless become one of Ohio's most respected attorneys, judged by those who knew him as a man of common sense and integrity. Furthermore, as Justice Bradley later observed, "his efficient service on the Geneva Commission had secured to him the confidence of those who were familiar with the details of that great arbitration." [43]

To Washington, then, he brought, if not brilliance, solid legal competence. As a man who had lived in a Jacksonian frontier community, he also brought a sturdy faith in popular government, a faith he had reaffirmed only a few months earlier in reminding his fellow convention delegates that the people are careful in taking care of their interests. But most important in the immediate months ahead, Morrison Waite brought to the Court a way with men. "For the first year," a good friend wisely counseled, "you will have to give quite as much to your tact—your amiable bearing—fine natural generousness of nature—your knowledge of men, and a careful watch not to offend their sensibilities—as to your real ability as a lawyer and probably more." [44]

[41] George P. Este to Waite, Feb. 8, 1874; Aaron F. Perry to Waite, n.d., 1874 (probably late Jan.).

[42] Letter dated Jan. 29, 1862, quoted in Trimble, *Waite*, p. 269, note.

[43] Bradley to Stephen J. Field, draft dated April 30, 1888. Bradley Papers.

[44] George P. Este to Waite, Feb. 8, 1874. Este, a General during the Civil War and subsequently a Washington lawyer, had worked in the firm of M. R. & R. Waite.

6

THE NEW CHIEF JUSTICE

Arrival in Washington. Social Trepidations and Experiments.
"Getting the Hang of the Barn." First Day in Court.
Brethren of the Bench. Letters to Home.
Nathan Clifford, Custodian of Court Ceremonies.
Unjudicial Jealousies. First Opinion and Final "Test."

ON THE EVENING OF FEBRUARY 16, 1874, A TRAIN FROM NEW YORK pulled into the Washington railroad station. From the train stepped a middle-aged man of medium height and stocky build. He carried himself well, his large head, covered with thick iron-gray hair, erectly poised on his shoulders. His eyes were dark and piercing, though kindly. Well-trimmed whiskers and a clean-shaven upper lip revealed a large mouth, a large nose, and a heavy chin. Morrison Remick Waite, the new Chief Justice, had arrived in the nation's capital. Despite, as he told his wife, "a hard ride" on "the most uncomfortable" seat in the palace car, "I came through alive and found all the bell boys" in the Arlington House "to meet the 'Chief Justice.' " "As I went into the [hotel] office it was whispered from all 'there he is.' " The next morning, he continued, "a servant was assigned me in the house, and altogether I was 'the man.' Went quietly to breakfast and took a seat by the side of Gov. Fenton, who at once made me known to the headwaiter. . . . All eyes were on me of course and I read my paper." [1]

Amelia, his wife, whose health was not good at the time, and his daughter Mary Frances, known as "Nany" to her parents and friends, stayed in Toledo, planning to follow later. In a sense their separation was fortunate, as it led to a number of revealing letters that provide an excellent window through which to observe Waite in one of the most trying periods of his life. "All eyes," as he well knew,

[1] Waite to Amelia Waite, Feb. 22, 1874. The reference is to Reuben E. Fenton, a former New York governor serving in the Senate.

were upon him. Not only was Waite personally an unknown quantity, but the background against which he took his seat was tense. Two of the Court's senior members, Justices Miller and Swayne, felt the chief justiceship rightfully belonged to them; their jealousy, lingering from what Justice Bradley called "a scramble for place," complicated the always delicate relationships which exist between the judges, and made Waite's task doubly difficult.[2]

On February 18 Waite wrote his wife, apologizing for not writing sooner and explaining that "it has been jump, jump, jump all the time." The fast pace had begun five days before in New York. First came visits to many of the city's prominent lawyers and bankers—Samuel L. M. Barlow, Charles O'Conor, George Bliss, Levi P. Morton, and, of course, William Evarts. Between visits he found time to order his judicial robes at a tailor shop where, "as I went into the store in rushed the people to see the new Chief Justice." After dining with two old Ohio friends, Alfred P. Edgerton and Judge Rufus P. Ranney, he went to the home of Edwards Pierrepont, who had arranged an elaborate party in the hope of attracting Waite later in the evening. There he met more of the great names in New York's legal and financial aristocracy: Samuel Tilden, Marshall O. Roberts, Edwin W. Stoughton, William Allen Butler, William H. Vanderbilt, and the editor of the *Nation*, E. L. Godkin. "I was quite at my ease," he wrote, "and the whole thing was a success." With evident satisfaction, he added:

> I may be mistaken, but unless I misjudge, the N.Y. bar and certainly a large part of the commercial men are well satisfied with my appointment than they would have been with Evarts or Pierrepont. Mr. O'Conner [sic], who is the acknowledged leader of the bar, and has been for many years paid me the compliment of saying in so many words.[3]

The day, however, was not far distant when "the commercial men" would have been happier had Evarts been sitting in the Chief Justice's chair.

[2] Bradley quoted in Charles Fairman, "What Makes a Great Justice? Mr. Justice Bradley and the Supreme Court 1870–1892," *Boston University Law Review,* XXX (1950), 62–63, note.

[3] Waite to Amelia Waite, Feb. 18, 1874.

In Washington the round of visits and dinners continued as Morrison Waite made himself known to the nation's political leaders and, most importantly, to the Justices of the Supreme Court. On February 17 came a call on the President:

> I was most cordially received [by General Orville Babcock] until the President sent for me in the room and he gave me the warmest greeting. It was all any one could ask from any one. He kept me until it was time for the Cabinet to get together, and I was formally presented *to* them as they came in. I am not yet inducted into the office, and I am therefore [not] availing of my privilege of having other[s] presented to me. But it was pleasant, and all seemed to be glad it was me.

This formality completed, Waite set out to establish cordial relations with the men over whom he would soon preside.

> From the President, I took a carriage and went immediately to Judge Swayne's. I found him ready to receive me and on my invitation he took the carriage with me to see the other judges. Judge Clifford was out of town, but we saw his wife, a good motherly old lady and I am inclined to think I left a good impression there. Then went to Judge Field's and found that all had gone out—then to Judge Bradley's and saw him and his wife. I liked them very much and I am inclined to think they were not inclined to dislike me. He at once made arrangements to give me a dinner and I am to go there on Friday. It was arranged on the call. Judge Hunt was out of town & Mrs. Hunt was making visits so I did not see any one there. Judge Davis & Judge Miller were also out of town. Then went to Judge Strong and he said he knew more about you than me as he had been posted by his brother. This call upon the Judges proved to be a strike.
>
> It seems to have been watched for & Belknap (Sec. of War) said the other evening to me that "a little common sense well applied was an excellent thing"—that my call was just the brightest thing that could have been done and disarmed all criticism—that I had been watched and this thing was more spoken of than anything else could have been in my favor. I left all the Judges feeling that all were disposed to be kind.
>
> [That evening] I went to call on Senators Sherman & Thurman, and saw them both with their wives.[4] Nothing could be more cordial

[4] John Sherman (1823–1900) of Ohio, Republican Senator and Secretary of the Treasury under Hayes and Secretary of State in the McKinley Cabinet; Allen G.

than my reception. Thurman told me something about the nomination which I was glad to know, but which I can't put on paper. From there I went to the President's . . . reception which was a terrific jam. The President saw at least two thousand people pass in front of him during the evening. I was immediately taken behind him in the blue room and there had a reception of my own. Of course next to the President I was a great object of curiosity . . . [and] when all was over went up stairs with the President and took a glass of wine. . . .

Wednesday I went to call on the Sec. of State and Mr. Delano. I made long calls on each and they seemed very glad to see me. In the evening took my dinner at Bancroft Davis' and stayed fairly late with Davis up stairs in his library. He and his wife are apparently as much tickled with the appointment as any one could be. He told me a great many things it was important for me to know & Mrs. Davis instructed me in some of the requirements of etiquette.[5] Before we separated a dinner was arranged for me Wednesday at which I am to meet Sir Edward Thornton and some of the Foreign ministers. . . .

Thursday I called on the Cabinet, that I did not see on Wednesday and on General Sherman. At the office of the Sec. of the Navy, I met Mr. Parke Godwin, one of the editors of the [New York] Evening Post, who told me among other things of his writing of an article on Provincialism about the time of my nomination which did a great deal of good. . . .

After this I went to call on Judge Miller who was one of the prominent candidates for Ch. J. and from whom I was told I might expect some harsh criticism. But I got along nicely with him, and left him with a feeling that if he was not already he might be made a good friend.

In the evening was Mr. Delano's dinner. . . . All the Judges who were in town were present [and also the] President, members of the Cabinet, Senator Sherman, Sherwood & [unclear]. I was seated at the left of Mr. Delano and between him & Judge Strong. Everything was just as pleasant as anything could be and when I came away Judge Miller, who had been watching me closely all the evening put out his left hand & grasped mine, in a manner that satisfied me if I was able to do my share of the work I need not fear him. The President after dinner took especial pains to sit beside me and staid quite a long time after we came out.[6]

Thurman (1813–1895) of Ohio, lawyer, Civil War "Peace Democrat," and ranking Democratic Senator on the Judiciary Committee.

[5] Mrs. Davis was an expert in the social graces. Hackett, *Reminiscences,* pp. 96–97.

[6] Waite to Amelia Waite, Feb. 22, 1874.

At the dinner, "before the liquid refreshments had qualified the crudities," Attorney General Williams looked at the Justices and remarked *sotto voce*, "Did you ever see so many corpses at one funeral?" Benjamin Rush Cowen, Delano's assistant, and the source of this story, might have added that Williams himself was one of the corpses. Judge Rockwood Hoar, also a disappointed aspirant, provided his own *bon mot*. Alluding to the Cushing and Williams nominations, he referred to Waite as "that luckiest of all individuals known to the law, an innocent third party without notice." [7]

Besides being initiated into Washington social life at Columbus Delano's dinner, Waite had also, that same day, gone to the Senate.

> I went into the office of the Marshal of the Court and had him introduce to me all the inferior officers and the servants. . . . It seemed an entirely new thing & they were all apparently delighted. Judge Chase kept himself on the dignity of this office and permitted no one to interfere with him.
>
> Friday I went to see Judge Cartter on the bench of the Supreme Court of the District.[8] For this I hear I have been somewhat criticized. It was thought to be letting down the dignity of my office. However, I don't think it is much disliked. From there I went to the House. The members came rushing up to me and all at once Judge Hoar, who had been a prominent candidate for the office, moved that the House take a recess of ten minutes in order that the members might be introduced. Then I was taken to the open space in front of the Speakers Chair and was formally introduced to all.[9]

A first impression may not be lasting, but it does count. Waite was determined to make a good one. He took the extra trouble of personally calling on the judges, and seeing that the visits were well received, proudly described them as a hit. Feeling insecure, he was highly sensitive to signs of approbation or disapprobation and acted so as to avoid needless criticism. When personal friends planned elaborate private dinners in his honor, he gracefully declined. Such displays, he said, give an impression of "undue glorification" ill-suited to one so recently and unexpectedly honored. He acted similarly in

[7] Cowen in Lewis, *Great American Lawyers*, VII, 109–110.

[8] D. K. Cartter of Ohio, Chief Justice of the Supreme Court of the District of Columbia.

[9] Waite to Amelia Waite, Feb. 22, 1874.

another small matter. John W. Wallace, the Court Reporter, sought to learn Waite's preference as to how he should be titled. Until 1864 it had been "Mr. Chief Justice Taney," but Chase had this changed to "The Chief Justice"—"by analogy," Wallace suggested, "to the head of the Executive department, 'The President.'" Waite replied that he had "no preference whatever," would not have advised the change made by Chase, but that, "I am not myself inclined to open the door for criticism upon what has been done by going back to the old way."[10]

Waite's insecurity and caution—strong and real as they were—should not be overdrawn. As in most men, feelings of confidence struggled in his breast with doubts of adequacy. New York's legal and commercial leaders, after all, had indicated their satisfaction. And, significantly, he opened the long letter describing his first week in Washington with a characteristically simple and direct remark: "I am getting the hang of the barn a little and soon I hope to be quite at home." More dinners followed while he marked time, waiting to be sworn in as soon as the Court finished delivering opinions already decided. On the twenty-eighth he again wrote home:

> Wednesday I met the Judges at the consultation room and heard them read opinions. Today they are at the same work, but I don't go. I shall take my seat on Wednesday [March 4]. There is to be a grand rush of ladies to see the performance which I am to make as simple as possible. However, there is something due to the position I suppose.[11]

Among those witnessing the ceremony was Congressman James A. Garfield, and General Garfield, as he was commonly addressed, set down this description of the installation of the nation's seventh Chief Justice:

> At twelve o'clock went to the Supreme Court and saw Mr. Waite sworn in as Chief Justice. The associate justices in new gowns took their seats leaving the central seat vacant. Mr. Waite sat down in the Clerk's chair. After court was opened Mr. Middleton the clerk

[10] George P. Este to Waite, Feb. 8, 1874; Waite to Amelia Waite, Feb. 18, 1874; Wallace to Waite, Aug. 31, 1874; Waite to Wallace, Sept. 10, 1874.

[11] Waite to Amelia Waite, Feb. 28, 1874.

> read the commission of Mr. Waite and administered the oath. The other judges in the meanwhile sitting when the new Chief Justice approached the vacant chair. The others arose and bowed to him and were seated. And Judge Field next read an opinion. The simplicity of this performance impressed me very much. The Court room was crowded. There were present two college classmates of the Chief Justice Messrs Evarts and Pierrepont.[12]

What thoughts, one wonders, crossed the judges' minds as they politely rose and bowed while Waite settled himself into the Chief Justice's chair? Seated on comfortable leather armchairs placed on a low dais in the semicircular chamber, the old Senate hall where Clay, Hayne, Webster, and Calhoun once vied for mastery, was one of the strongest benches in the nation's judicial history. Some of Morrison Waite's associates in "the heaven of legal ambition," as an enthusiastic writer described the Court,[13] rank among the handful of truly great justices. Surely in this category were two of Lincoln's appointees, Samuel Freeman Miller and Stephen J. Field, both of whom, like their new Chief, were born in 1816. Beginning as a poor Kentucky farm boy, Miller had two careers, one as a rural doctor and, after studying law on his own, one as a country lawyer. Moving to Iowa, participating actively in Republican politics, he fast became a leader in the western bar. Appointed by Lincoln in 1862, Miller in his judicial position stressed the importance of personal liberties and reflected a hostility to corporate and financial wealth. Blunt, self-confident, and, prone to vanity, Miller was a dominant figure on the postwar Court, though his lack of legal training sometimes limited his effectiveness.

No less forceful was Stephen Field, a "War Democrat," also appointed by Lincoln in 1862, but his social and economic sympathies were enlisted in a cause different from Miller's. Through a long judicial career of nearly thirty-five years—in typical stubbornness, Field hung on to his seat despite infirmity so as to surpass Marshall's record of service—he unashamedly sought to make the Court an instrument for the defense of vested property rights. A transplanted

[12] Garfield's *Journal,* March 4, 1874. Garfield Papers.

[13] Mrs. John A. Logan, *Thirty Years in Washington* (Hartford: A. D. Worthington, 1901), p. 408, pp. 410–411.

New Englander, who prided himself on being a rugged Californian, Field, as Waite was about to learn, was tactless, querulous, and given to annoying fits of self-righteous moralizing. Yet, for all his faults, Stephen Field remains one of the Court's most colorful judges. Dusty pages of the U.S. Reports still crackle with the fire of Judge Field's burning convictions, and the bearded, passionate judge, whose feuding sparked the celebrated *Neagle* case,[14] is a constant reminder that raw human drama is often the stuff of constitutional litigation.

If a forcefully held judicial position, intellectual curiosity, and depth of legal knowledge are the hallmarks of judicial greatness, then Joseph P. Bradley stands at the top in a charmed circle with Joseph Story, Oliver Wendell Holmes, and Benjamin N. Cardozo. A self-made man of complete integrity, Bradley enjoyed a successful career representing some of New Jersey's most powerful railroads until put on the Court in 1870 by President Grant. Once on the bench, he showed marked independence toward the corporate interests he formerly defended, frequently upholding economic regulation and assuming a nationalistic position in constitutional interpretation. Whatever his personal opinions, Bradley, unlike Miller, displayed no resentment toward his new Chief. Instead, the two men struck up a close relationship, and Waite, particularly in his early years on the Court, often wisely relied on Justice Bradley. Appointed at the same time as Bradley was William Strong who had served with distinction on Pennsylvania's Supreme Court. Although a capable judge, Strong's memory has been obscured by a comparatively short tenure and the fact that many of his opinions dealt with Civil War confiscation problems and common-law cases, subjects of little current interest. Sympathetic to the claims of corporations, he normally voted with Field on economic issues, but he was a devout leader in the Presbyterian Church and a gentleman, and there was nothing of the other's cantankerousness about him.

Of the other four judges who bowed to Morrison Waite as he sat down, less need be said. In the roll call of Supreme Court Justices

[14] The almost incredible story behind *In re Neagle*, 135 U. S. 1 (1890), and Field's part in it, is the subject of ch. xiii in Carl B. Swisher's *Stephen J. Field, Craftsman of the Law* (Washington: The Brookings Institution, 1930), cited hereafter as Swisher, *Field*.

they march by in the ranks, at best competent and generally undistinguished, though their votes inevitably played a part in constitutional history. Two of them, Nathan Clifford of Maine and David Davis of Illinois, had impressive public records. A states'-rights Democrat of the old school and the senior associate, Clifford's commission dated back to 1858 when he was appointed by President Buchanan following a career as a congressman, an Attorney General, and a minister to Mexico. His opinions, most of which involved commercial and admiralty law, were, like his size, ponderous. By the time Waite came on the Court, old age had made him an obstinate and rather trying man. David Davis, also a massive man, can hardly be dismissed as a nonentity. "Lincoln's Manager" at the 1860 Republican Convention, and after 1877 an independent in an almost evenly divided Senate, David Davis is a commanding figure. His nomination as a presidential candidate by the National Labor Reform Party in 1872 suggests the direction of his judicial votes—opposition to corporate and financial interests—and also the reason why, despite the fact that he sat on the Court from 1862 to 1877, his judicial career is not noteworthy. Personally honest, Davis was always first the politician and only second the judge. As Miller once observed, he governed "every act of his life by his hope of the Presidency." [15]

Noah H. Swayne, the weakest of Lincoln's appointments, could boast of a successful career as an Ohio lawyer and little else. Unduly impressed by his own mediocre talents, Swayne took himself very seriously, and hoping for the chief justiceship when Chase died, used his influence against Miller. For this, and because of his unwavering support of bondholders in the municipal bond cases that pitted railroad against agrarian interests, he won Miller's undying enmity. Finally, there was Ward Hunt of New York, appointed by President Grant in 1872 at Roscoe Conkling's behest.[16] Decent and kindly as a person, he is chiefly remembered for holding on to his seat for three years after becoming totally incapacitated, waiting for Congress to vote him a retirement pension.[17]

[15] Quoted in Fairman, *Miller*, p. 373.

[16] Fish Diary, Dec. 3, 1872. Fish Papers.

[17] This brief survey draws on Charles Fairman's *Miller* and his articles, "The Education of a Justice" and "What Makes a Great Justice?"; Swisher, *Field;* Williard L. King, *Lincoln's Manager, David Davis* (Cambridge: Harvard University Press, 1960).

This was the Waite Court in 1874. Whatever might be the judges' conflicting emotions, Chief Justice Waite felt on his part that he had gone through the ceremony "with reasonable success" and "did not belittle the place or myself." A dinner for the judges and their wives "was pleasant and the Chief Justice does not seem to have made many enemies. They all appear willing to give me a fair trial, and so far have not found any reason to snub me to say the least." Beginning to miss his wife, he asked her to join him as soon as possible. "You will be kindly received," he wrote, and "need not be afraid of yourself. All you need do is to be yourself." He gave the same advice to his daughter Mary, who, he was sure, would have a "splendid time": "She will [be to] Washington society just what seems to have made me extra popular—natural." [18]

During the next few weeks Waite wrote frequently, describing his first experiences as Chief Justice. On March 8 he assured his wife that he was bearing up under the strain "most nobly." "I don't hear all," he wrote, but such criticisms as came his way were "all kind." Since "my friends appear so much satisfied I feel that I have not been very severely handled." After giving accounts of various dinners, he continued:

> Tuesday night I dine with the Clerks of the Court and that so far as I know ends my weeks engagements, except that Judge Hunt wanted me to dine with him one day during the week. . . . Saturday I went through my severest ordeal. It was to meet the Judges in consultation for the first time and when as a matter of course severe criticism would be in order. I got through with it very successfully I think. At any rate there was nothing to cause any uneasiness or discomfort on my part. It was a pretty easy time and my nerves were as cool as it is possible to be for a wonder, and so it has been all the time since I have been here. I have been perfectly self-possessed and have made very few mistakes. . . .
>
> Won't it be good to see you, and how many there are who want to get a first look at you. You will have to be prepared for a long look, a strong look, and a look altogether. All I have got to say—keep cool—take it & it will not be found very hard to take.
>
> I cant write about my sensations as to the gown or otherwise. I

[18] Waite to Amelia Waite, March 5, 1874.

will tell you all at some time. They were strange sometimes, but yet I seem to take to them naturally.[19]

Five days later he wrote again:

So far I have got through nicely and the pleasantest thing of all is that my last dinner invitation has been complied with and I am this P.M. without a single invitation ahead. Had a most delightful dinner at Judge Hunt's last evening. There were only ten and were happy. If I can judge from the look on their faces, the Ch. J. did not lose any of his friends.

Today was the funeral of Mr. Sumner. We all attended officially and in our robes. I suppose one of these days I shall get to feel that I am entitled to my place. But it is not an easy job. The "boy" of the Court must be made of different material from me, if he can, in his gown, pass through the crowd and hear the crowd say "there is the new Ch. J." and "that must be Judge Waite," without saying to himself, what does all this mean. I suppose I shall realize it all bye & bye, but it seems strange now. Judge Clifford is the martinetest of all martinetts [*sic*]. It was a question of what ought to be done. Should we go in single or double file. Judge C. said "double file until we come to the chamber and then single." So we double, but just as luck would have it, when he & I came to take the double, I put myself on the wrong side of him. He said, "take the other side, if you please, Mr. Chief Justice." So I did and therefore I was in place. And coming out of the Senate Chamber, ahead as I was, because I had found out that was my place, I dropped back at the outside door to make the double front (there I put myself on the proper side). When the time to move came he said "look out for these steps Mr. Ch. J." & so I did, but I am inclined to the opinion that if he had not been slightly paralysed in his underpinning he might not have been quite as thoughtful of where & how I put my feet.

We live to learn, darlings, & if we keep our eyes & ears open we do learn. Come here with that feeling. You are the best of any of them. Feel that you are so, and everybody will acknowledge it to be true. I have learned a heap since I have been here. The result is, take the place that belongs to you, not offensively, but let every body feel that it is yours.[20]

Many years afterwards, Attorney General Williams described Justice Clifford as "proud of his official position" and "the impersona-

[19] Waite to Amelia Waite, March 8, 1874.
[20] Waite to Amelia Waite, March 13, 1874.

tion of the highest style of judicial decorum and propriety." He recalled accompanying the judges on their annual call on the President at the opening of the 1873 term when Clifford was acting Chief Justice and that "the extreme punctiliousness with which he conducted that ceremony was interesting to behold." [21] According to one report, Clifford called the new Chief's attention to his unfamiliarity with the Court's formalities and suggested that it would be best if he continued presiding until Waite learned them. After reportedly seeking advice, Waite rejected Clifford's suggestion, telling his friends, "I am going to drive and those gentlemen know it." [22] As he wrote his wife, he was fast learning not to let feelings of humility stop him from taking his rightful place. Being Chief Justice and wearing a gown felt "strange," but "yet I seem to take to them naturally."

On March 14 he wrote again, saying he was glad to be "out of the dinner business" and that his reception remained "cordial." The judges, he went on,

> apparently are well satisfied with me, and from my experience with them twice in the consultation room I feel sure that when I get the hang of the work I shall be able to keep up my end of the whiffle tree. I went to get Judge Strong to come and play a game of whist last night and showed him your pictures. He says he has most enthusiastic accounts of you from his brother. They are all waiting to see you, but you need not be afraid to meet any of them.[23]

"Every second is so full," he said in his next letter, "and I am so anxious to do all the work that is put upon me, and to do it well." Apparently he was back in "the dinner business" for he wrote of one given by Sir Edward Thornton, the British Ambassador—and Waite still felt the strangeness of his new position:

> It was a little funny. I took out Lady Thornton. Judge Swayne was at the right of Sir Edward. Senator Sherman at Lady Thornton's

[21] George H. Williams, "Reminiscences of the United States Supreme Court," *Yale Law Journal*, VIII (1899), 298.

[22] Cowen in Lewis, *Great American Lawyers*, VII, 110–111. That Clifford made the suggestion seems likely, but Benjamin Rush Cowen's version of the event must be treated with some doubt. Cowen claimed that Waite came to him for advice. Perhaps, but Cowen was not a particularly close friend, making it doubtful that Waite would solicit his advice. Waite's own common sense was just as likely to tell him that he could not afford, even temporarily, to take a back seat.

[23] Waite to Amelia Waite, March 14, 1874.

left. Sec. Delano at Sir Edward's left. Gen. Schenck at my right, Evarts at Judge Swayne's right & Gen. Sherman at Sec. Delanos left. It seems a little strange to be put naturally so much above all these dignitaries and our dignitaries. But I suppose in time I shall become used to it. However, your *green* husband has made but few mistakes so far—I don't know how much they may laugh behind my back.[24]

A week later he told of his work on the Court:

This has been my busiest week. Every day in Court hard at work and harder at work outside of the Court room. It is all new and I have adopted the plan of going to the bottom of all new questions so that when I once understand it fully, I shall not have to look it up again. I had a hard Habeas Corpus case given me last Saturday week. The Judges were equally divided and I had the casting vote. I took the week to examine it and yesterday when, in consultation, I gave my opinion two, out of the four Judges of a different mind originally, agreed with me. So I had the satisfaction of believing that work was well done.

Then we had a great many cases submitted to us last week. I had to examine all of them and prepare myself to state intelligently the questions to be decided. That was a labor and thus I have been compelled to . . . [unclear—work evenings?]. On Friday night I sat up until one and was up again at seven. I went to Court with nearly all the cases prepared for presentation and Judge Miller and Judge Davis on our way down from the Capitol both complimented me on my dispatch of business. I have as yet read no opinions, in Court, and have prepared none. When I pass that test successfully I shall put myself where I have nothing more to fear, if I keep up to my standards. It has been in some respect an anxious five weeks since I left you, and yet not so much so as when I left you I supposed it would be. Some how I have found myself equal to taking everything as it comes and not being overcome. If I had put on any airs, I think I know enough of human nature to know that there would have been many obstructions put in the way of my march. But I did not, and every body seems to have stood aside to see what I can do. Therefore if I fail, the disgrace is all the more terrible. I hope I may not. Everything is 'rose color' now, and while I cannot ask that shall continue always, I do hope I may be able to keep it about me until I feel at home where I am.

[24] Waite to Amelia Waite, March 19, 1874. Robert C. Schenck was American Minister to Great Britain; General William Tecumseh Sherman was the ranking officer in the federal army.

Still doubtful, he now began to reveal a feeling of healthy satisfaction, of pleasure, in being Chief Justice of the United States. In the retrospect of "an anxious five weeks" he gave free rein to his inner sentiments:

> The only drawback upon my enjoyments of the past month has been that you could not be here to see how heartily I have been welcomed. As we have struggled up the hill together, it would have been no more than right that we should have stood side by side to take the first look at the prospect which was to be seen from the top. But one of these days we will get settled at the top and then we will enjoy it all. You do not know how pleasant it is to sit down and *look* at it. If I was quite sure I was looking at the *real* picture, I should be satisfied with my outlook. When you come, if it looks the same to you, I shall be satisfied that *our* place is a good place. An ill natured man would have had some rebuff in my place while he was . . . [unclear—taking this position?]. I have had nothing of the kind. Q.E.D. I am not an ill natured man on general principles. Am I on special? You my darlings, (I mean all of you) can only tell. I am troubled, and therefore almost as a necessary consequence am sometimes brought near to ill nature. . . .
>
> When I come to home & all it has of mine I get sentimental. It is almost 34 years since you & I Molly first promised each other that our two lives thereafter should be one life. When a promise is made it don't always keep—Ours has kept, and the time has at last come when we are sure the promise was made to bind us into one. Don't say this [is] 'twaddle.' It may be, but it is pleasant twaddle to me.[25]

Morrison Waite's reception had been mixed. To his wife he repeatedly insisted—probably to relieve her from worry—that everyone was treating him most cordially. This, however, was not the case. Secretary Delano's assistant declared that some Court members received him "with a coolness bordering on discourtesy"; Attorney General Williams' comment at the Delano dinner suggests the same thing; and Hugh McCulloch, a well-known Washington figure, who subsequently changed his estimate radically, spoke for many in regarding Waite's appointment as "unmerited and injudicious."[26]

[25] Waite to Amelia Waite, March 22, 1874.

[26] Cowen in Lewis, *Great American Lawyers*, VII, 109–110; McCulloch, *Men and Measures of Half a Century*, pp. 352–353. McCulloch served as Secretary of the Treasury in three administrations, those of Lincoln, Johnson, and Arthur.

Shortly after the appointment Justice Swayne had written to Waite that "we shall all be glad to see you here," but seven years later, on the occasion of Swayne's retirement, Waite noted that "unfortunately . . . our relations have not always been as cordial as I wished them to be." [27] Ward Hunt sent the new Chief Justice a warm letter and gave him, as did Justice Bradley, a dinner. Justice Strong greeted Waite amicably and David Davis told his wife that he liked his new Chief. To a friend he wrote, "He is not a great man, but then he dont pretend to be one. He is a fair lawyer, with pleasant manners; is of undoubted integrity & has good abilities." [28]

Clifford, however, treated the new Chief as an interloper, and two of the Court's leading members were uncomplimentary in their private remarks. Said Miller: "We have had our new Chief Justice with us now three weeks, twice in conference. He is pleasant, a good presiding officer, *mediocre*, with fair amount of professional learning." [29] Field commented with characteristic pungency:

> That matter—the Chief Justiceship is at last settled. We have a Chief Justice. He is a new man that would never have been thought of for the position by any person except President Grant. He is a short thick set person, with very plain—indeed rough features. He is gentlemanly in his manners and possesses some considerable culture. But how much of a lawyer he is remains to be seen. He may turn out to be a Marshall or a Taney, though such a result is hardly to be expected. My objection to the appointment is that it is an experiment whether a man of fair but not great abilities may make a fit Chief Justice of the United States—an experiment which no President has a right to make with our Court.[30]

[27] Swayne to Waite, Jan. 26, 1874; Waite to Swayne, draft dated, Jan. 24, 1881. In the same letter, however, Waite also said, "In my heart of hearts I shall always thank every member of the court for my cordial reception"—a statement hard to reconcile with other facts and probably made as a courtesy to an old man.

[28] Hunt to Waite, Feb. 8, 1874; Waite to Amelia Waite, Feb. 22, 1874; Waite to Amelia Waite, March 13, 1874; Mrs. Davis to Davis, March 11, 22, 1874; Davis to Julius Rockwell, Aug. 18, 1875, quoted in King, *David Davis*, p. 287.

[29] Miller to William P. Ballinger, March 21, 1874, quoted in Fairman, *Miller*, p. 349.

[30] Field to Matthew P. Deady, March 16, 1874. Deady Papers, Oregon Historical Society. Much of the fascinating correspondence between Field and Deady, an Oregon federal district judge, appears in one of Howard Jay Graham's many fine articles, "Justice Field and the Fourteenth Amendment," *Yale Law Journal*, LII (1943), 851.

Joseph P. Bradley made much the same argument in 1888 when he criticized Melville W. Fuller's appointment. Though "a very estimable man, and a successful practitioner," this "hardly fills the public expectation for the place of Chief Justice of the United States." Granted, he may "by happy accident turn out to be an admirable appointment. But an appointment to this place ought not to depend for its success on accident & good fortune." [31] Besides underscoring the possessive feeling of institutional reverence which the justices come to have for "our Court," these comments make it clear why Morrison Waite felt so apprehensive. Unlike Marshall, Taney, or Chase at the time of their appointments, his public stature was negligible. He would have understood well the feeling of his successor, a man whose plight was much the same. Referring to such famous judges as Miller, Field, Bradley, and Harlan, Chief Justice Fuller found "no rising sun for me with these old luminaries blazing away with all their ancient fires." [32] But, at least, Fuller's appointment had not been preceded by a farcial public spectacle and he was President Cleveland's first choice, not a fifth or seventh choice—if, as some claimed, Grant also offered the chief justiceship to Senators Howe and Morton.

Because of this background of hostility from some of the judges, and because of his own self-doubt, Waite occasionally still expressed fears. "Nothing but constant watchfulness will keep me from falling in. That I constantly have before me and it is sometimes oppressive," he wrote in 1875.[33] Generally, however, such sentiments become rare after the first few weeks. Although Waite often made clear his determination to work hard and be remembered as a successful Chief Justice, he also felt increasingly confident. "I have got a splendid messenger," he said to his wife near the end of his first month. "You would be amused to see how naturally I take to being waited upon." [34] And, some months later, after referring to various maneuverings in Toledo politics: "Aren't I glad I am out of the ring. I tell you it is not a bad thing to feel that you are in a good place for life, even

[31] Bradley to Field, draft dated April 30, 1888. Bradley Papers.
[32] Willard L. King, *Melville Weston Fuller* (New York: The Macmillan Company, 1950), p. 127.
[33] Waite to John T. Wait, Oct. 24, 1875, Letterbooks.
[34] Waite to Amelia Waite, March 25, 1874.

though you have to pinch a little to keep within a salary." [35] What he had called his final "test," giving an opinion, came on April 13. Opinion writing was hard because "it is new—that kind of work. I have one prepared but shall not read it until one week from today. I must confess I hate to begin." [36] The opinion Waite referred to was *Tappan* v. *Merchant's National Bank*, a suit challenging the legality of a county tax on the shares of a national bank incorporated under federal law.[37] Melville Fuller, who, as fate would have it, also appeared in Waite's last case, argued unsuccessfully for the bank. Speaking for a unanimous Court, Waite upheld the tax with an opinion that was well received; [38] no doubt, he felt relieved at having passed another hurdle.

The spring of 1874 had been difficult for the new Chief Justice. A humble but very conscientious man, Morrison Waite wanted desperately to do well. "A judge," he well knew, "is not made by his commission," and his ambition was to "be considered not unworthy the place." [39] But while the personal adjustment had its unpleasant moments, particularly so under the circumstances in which he took his seat, the really hard work lay ahead. In addition to fairly routine common-law, admiralty, and patent cases which ate up valuable time —the nineteenth century Court had little control over its docket— new and pressing problems confronted Chief Justice Waite and his colleagues.

There was, for one thing, the whole question of economic regulation. By 1874 the outline of modern American society had clearly emerged: urban and industrial, it revealed great disparities of wealth and poverty, while small groups of men, accountable to no one, controlled the banks, railroads, and industries which were the economic sinews of the new nation. As those at the bottom of the economic scale felt the burdens of irresponsible economic power, there came demands for public regulation. First to protest were the western farmers who believed themselves oppressed by the giant railroad corporations. Those to be regulated naturally fought back, attacking

[35] Waite to Amelia Waite, July 15, 1874.
[36] Waite to Amelia Waite, April 6, 1874.
[37] 19 Wallace 445 (1874).
[38] Waite to Amelia Waite, May 21, 1874.
[39] Waite to Rufus King, May 4, 1875, Letterbooks.

the regulatory legislation on many fronts, but especially in the courts. From this conflict came some of the Waite Court's most significant and difficult decisions.

Of equal urgency and significance was the Reconstruction period's greatest social and human problem: that of the newly freed slaves. The problem of the Negro, a "freedman" by virtue of the North's victory, a citizen in name, thanks to the war amendments, ("the southern question," as it was popularly called) presented the Waite court with perhaps its major challenge in constitutional statesmanship. Only nine days after being sworn in, Chief Justice Waite marched in Charles Sumner's funeral. One of the staunchest radicals and one of the Negro's truest friends was gone. But the new amendments and the recent civil rights legislation—in a sense, Sumner's real memorial—were still largely uninterpreted. How would they fare in the cases that, even as the judges of the Supreme Court paid their last respects to the great Massachusetts Senator, sat on the docket waiting for decision?

7

CONCILIATION: THE COURT FACES THE SOUTHERN QUESTION

Demise of the Radicals. Pressures for Reconciliation.

The Case of the New Orleans Butchers. War Amendments Amended.

Racial Conflicts. Judge Bradley on the Enforcement Acts.

Appeals Before the Supreme Court. The Chief Prepares an Opinion.

Dissenting Views. Public Reaction.

Political Impact of United States *v.* Cruikshank *and* United States *v.* Reese.

A Court of Conciliation.

IF THE CIVIL WAR WAS, IN CHARLES A. BEARD'S PHRASE, "THE SECOND American Revolution," the war amendments were, in a sense, "the second American Constitution." [1] To the Waite Court fell the task of giving it meaning by passing on the controversial civil rights legislation that rested on the Fourteenth and Fifteenth Amendments. A wise remark once made by Hamilton Fish serves as an appropriate preface to this discussion. His friend, Bancroft Davis, then the Court Reporter, sent him a volume of the reports he had prepared. Fish replied:

> Thanks for Part II Vol 109—U.S.R. Well—you begin with a lesson not yet learnt by the Honorable Members who *think* that they make laws for the Country. Dear innocent fools—[Senators] Anthony, Edmunds & the rest of them—do they yet know that they only formulate a map of stuff printed as the Statutes of the U.S. but that nine fellows, sitting in black gowns make the "*Laws*" of the U.S. I am not quite sure whether to think this tending in a good or in an evil direction. Was it not John Randolph? who said that the Book of *Kings* follows close after the Book of *Judges*—and some one said, Well! what if it does? [2]

The judges, as many have pointed out, do not, Mr. Dooley to the contrary, follow the election returns by keeping an eye cocked on

[1] John P. Frank and Robert F. Munro, "The Original Understanding of 'Equal Protection of the Laws,'" *Columbia Law Review*, L (1950), 134.
[2] Fish to Davis, Jan. 24, 1884. Bancroft Davis Papers.

the biennial voting results. Insofar as the Court reflects national trends, it is because its members are themselves part of American society, and normally the relationship is quite complex, with Court decisions both reflecting and contributing to national policy. Such was the case when the Waite Court took up the vexing question of civil rights. By 1874 the idealism that had sparked the efforts to assist the Negro in his climb up from slavery was no longer evident. All the "old" Republican radicals, to follow Louis Hacker's distinction, were either dead or politically impotent, replaced by "new" radicals. In place of men like Thaddeus Stevens, Charles Sumner, and George W. Julian, original abolitionists sincerely committed to political, social, and economic equality for the Negro, a different breed of radicals occupied the positions of power. Roscoe Conkling, John "Black Jack" Logan, and James G. Blaine, these were the men who now claimed to speak for the freedman. But their support of him was purely opportunistic, rooted in the Republican Party's precarious majority status. For, pending the creation of an alliance with Western interests sympathetic to industrial capitalism, the votes of the easily manipulated Southern Negroes were essential to the party's managers.[3] It followed, of course, that once the Negro ceased to serve Republican interests, agitation on his behalf would be quietly dropped.

Through the early 1870's pressures for a reconciliation of North and South gained strength. Southern whites, to begin with, remained thoroughly unreconstructed and by 1875 had "redeemed" eight of the old rebel states. Writing to the Attorney General, a federal district attorney described one of the techniques—in addition to threats, murder, and ballot stuffing—used to oust the "Black Republicans" in Mississippi:

> [C]annon were purchased and used [prior to an election] as the *loudest argument*. In Loundes, Colfax and Monroe, particularly, these cannon were frequently fired by day and night, were carried to different places in the country where there was to be public speakings, or gatherings, and often fired on the route. . . . The effect of this kind of *argument* on the colored voters, who, as you

[3] Louis M. Hacker, *The Triumph of American Capitalism* (New York: Columbia University Press, 1947), pp. 339–345.

> may know, are naturally peaceable, timid and cowardly, as the results of slavery, can be more readily imagined and understood than described.[4]

Within the North and West the Democracy applauded and championed the cause of reconciliation. Meanwhile, the Republican Party itself moved closer to an abandonment of the Negro and a policy of reunion. Upon taking office in 1869 President Grant announced a policy of leniency, saying, "Let us have peace"—which prompted Henry Adams' acid comment that "the Executive asked only to be let alone. This was his meaning when he said: 'Let us have peace.' "[5] Republican leaders such as Blaine, Logan, and Conkling, however, still felt the need for Southern Negro votes, and they persuaded Grant to use federal troops and vigorous legal prosecutions to sustain the remaining Republican state governments. By the end of his second term Grant, supported by many prominent Republicans, again shifted, favoring conciliation and the complete elimination of carpetbag rule.[6]

Behind this shift lay a number of factors, none more influential than economic ones. The implacable hostility of the whites resulting from attempts to give the Negro real political power had caused serious turmoil and violence in the South. Unsettled conditions hindered recovery, and many Northern businessmen demanded a policy of moderation to foster the area's economic expansion. "When theories of Negro equality," a student of the period has perceptively written, "resulted in race conflict, and conflict in higher prices of raw cotton, manufacturers were inclined to accept the view of the Southern planter rather than that of the New England zealot."[7] *Hunt's Merchant's Magazine* and the *Commercial and Financial Chronicle*, the two leading business journals of the postwar era, made

[4] Henry B. Whitfield to Edwards Pierrepont, Nov. 6, 1875. Source Chronological File (Mississippi) of the Department of Justice, National Archives, R.G. 60, cited hereafter as Source Chronological File, NA. See also the account of William A. Dunning, a writer sympathetic to the white South, in his, "The Undoing of Reconstruction," *Atlantic Monthly*, LXXXVIII (1901), 440–441.

[5] *The Education of Henry Adams*, p. 267.

[6] Nevins, *Fish*, pp. 289–294, ch. xxxv.

[7] Paul H. Buck, *The Road to Reunion* (Boston: Little, Brown and Company, 1937), p. 154.

Morrison Waite's boyhood home in Lyme, Connecticut

.yme as it appeared in the mid-1870's

The American Party to the Geneva Arbitration

A likeness of Chief Justice Waite probably drawn in 1874

The Supreme Court in 1876

Justice Stephen J. Field

Cartoon criticism of Justice Field in a California journal

The Supreme Court in 1882

"Our Overworked Supreme Court," cartoon by Keppler in Puck, *December 9, 188*

Left to right: Woods, Blatchford, Harlan, Gray
Miller, Waite, Matthews, Bradley, Field

e I Street Home in Washington

Morrison Remick Waite, 1888

it clear that so long as Negro majorities controlled state legislatures, so long would capital avoid the South.[8]

Adding a powerful voice was the ex-radical, Horace Greeley. In 1862 he was attacking Lincoln's policy of moderation; by 1868 he was suggesting an alliance between the commercial men of North and South. Indeed, the Liberal Republican Movement of 1872, whose ticket he headed, showed how deeply many Republicans yearned for a new Southern policy. Like Greeley, Edward L. Godkin also did an about-face, summarizing the new attitude when his *Nation* opposed what eventually became the Civil Rights Act of 1875: "The Reconstruction period is ended, and the negro in future will occupy such a position as his industry and sobriety entitle him to. Such bills as the one we have been considering do nothing for him but turn his friends into enemies." [9]

Editors of other influential Northern journals, *Harper's*, *Scribner's*, and the *Atlantic*, responded in similar fashion. Earlier the Negro had been a hero and the Southern white a rebellious villain; the roles were now reversed and Northern readers avidly consumed literature emphasizing the virtues of the white South.[10] In truth, of course, the average Northerner never regarded the Negro as his equal. At best he had been pitied, and during the early 1870's the cause of the usually poor, ignorant, and illiterate Negro seemed more and more like a poor substitute for the national reconciliation which most Americans sincerely desired. When it became clear that the price to be paid for Negro equality included continuing military rule and a certain amount of violence—at the cost of business profits—there could be but one outcome. Capitalism was on the march and surely the Republican Party, its political prophet, would not stand in the way.

[8] Vincent P. DeSantis, *Republicans Face the Southern Question 1877–1897* (Baltimore: Johns Hopkins Press, 1959); William B. Hesseltine, "Economic Factors in the Abandonment of Reconstruction," *Mississippi Valley Historical Review*, XXII (1935), 191–210.

[9] Sept. 14, 1874, quoted in Charles Warren, *The Supreme Court in United States History* (Boston: Little, Brown and Company, 1926), II, 601–602, cited hereafter as Warren, *Supreme Court*. The shift in the *Nation's* editorial policy is traced in Hampton M. Jarrell, *Wade Hampton and the Negro* (Columbia: University of South Carolina Press, 1949), pp. 36–37, note.

[10] Buck, *Road to Reunion*, pp. 130–134.

Against this background the Supreme Court began passing on Congress' civil rights legislation. In brief, this legislation wiped out discriminatory state laws, safeguarded voting, granted the President broad powers to protect federal rights, and guaranteed the Negro equal accommodations in public places.[11] None of this legislation was interpreted prior to 1876, though the Court bypassed two earlier opportunities to speak on civil rights.[12] The pre-Waite Court, however, did render one landmark opinion having profound implications for the fate of the war amendments and the civil rights legislation. That opinion came in the *Slaughter-House Cases* (1873), which challenged the power of the carpetbag Louisiana legislature to grant an exclusive monopoly in New Orleans to a single firm of butchers thereby driving all competitors out of business.[13] Former Supreme Court Justice John A. Campbell, the brilliant attorney for the disfranchised butchers, attacked the state law with an armory of weapons drawn from the new amendments. He especially pressed the argument that it abridged the "privileges and immunities" guaranteed to "citizens of the United States" by the Fourteenth Amendment. Among these privileges Campbell listed the right to engage in a business of one's choosing.

By the closest of votes, five to four, the Court disagreed with Campbell. Justice Miller, who gave the majority opinion, rejected Campbell's expansive reading of the privileges and immunities clause. Conceding that the war amendments gave some added powers to the federal government in guaranteeing Negroes freedom from state discrimination, Miller insisted that the states retained most of their prewar authority. Seizing upon a distinction between United States and state citizenship, he claimed that the Fourteenth Amendment left fundamental rights to the protection of the states. The privileges and immunities clause, in his view, merely protected such rights as the right to pass freely from state to state, to have diplomatic protection,

[11] It is summarized in Robert K. Carr, *Federal Protection of Civil Rights* (Ithaca, N.Y.: Cornell University Press, 1947), pp. 37–39.

[12] *Blyew* v. *United States,* 13 Wallace 581 (1872); *United States* v. *Avery,* 13 Wallace 251 (1872). Note should be taken of *Railroad Co.* v. *Brown,* 17 Wallace 445 (1873), which held that a railroad operating under a federal charter in the District of Columbia might not segregate passengers.

[13] 16 Wallace 36.

to use the navigable waters of the United States, and to obtain the writ of habeas corpus (none of which, in fact, really depended on the Fourteenth Amendment). In short, the war amendments had not radically changed the federal nature of the Union.

No Negroes appeared as litigants, nor were any federal laws in dispute. Instead, the disputants were a Reconstruction state government and a handful of dispossessed white butchers. The result of their dispute was a double irony. In attacking the Louisiana law on behalf of the butchers, Campbell—a states'-righter who resigned from the Supreme Court in 1861 to secede with his native Alabama—had relied on a far-reaching interpretation of the Fourteenth Amendment. He lost. But so too did the Negro. Miller's analysis of the amendment strongly implied that the recent civil rights laws, which were intended to fulfill the amendment's high purposes by aiding the freedman, were unconstitutional. His opinion included two overriding assumptions, both seemingly fatal to the civil rights legislation: that the states retained most of their original powers and that the privileges and immunities clause (potentially of the greatest importance in giving the freedman tangible rights) protected only a very small category of rights. Campbell, then, had won, not as the butchers' attorney, but as a Southerner and a Democrat hostile to broad national powers.

Democratic politicians immediately perceived the decision's significance. It augured well for the future and provided a bright new symbol to use in their fight to end Black Republican rule. Unable to block the passage of the war amendments during the late 1860's (the Democrats had then asserted that their enactment would produce a centralizing national government totally destructive of the states), they suavely reversed course once the amendments were ratified. The new argument was that they were minimal in scope: they forbade slavery and barred *state* legislation overtly discriminating against Negroes. Apart from this, Democrats and Southerners insisted that state powers remained undiminished, and, most assuredly, the suddenly unradical amendments failed to confer any general civil rights power on Congress. These arguments, already well-developed as early as the 1870 and 1871 debates over the Enforcement Acts,[14]

[14] For example, *Congressional Globe,* 41st Cong., 2nd Sess. 3841, 3661–3666 (1869–1870); 41st Cong., 3rd Sess. 1270–1285, 1633–1655 (1870–1871).

again did service in the mid-seventies debates over the Sumner Civil Rights Act. Now, however, they had the benefit of judicial confirmation. Democratic orators studded their anti-civil-rights speeches with eloquent tributes to the "incorruptible judiciary" and copious quotations from Justice Miller's *Slaughter-House* opinion. "It amounts to this," declaimed Alexander H. Stephens, once the Confederacy's Vice President, "that these amendments do not change the nature and character of the Government. Soul-inspiring words are these!" [15] "Soul-inspiring words" indeed—to white Southern souls, if not to Negro ones.

This decision, so unfortunate to Negro interests, was in part a consequence of the form in which the first major case raising questions about the war amendments came to the Court. As Charles Fairman has pointed out, Campbell's argument was essentially a plea for laissez faire—that any abridgement of a citizen's economic rights "raised a federal question, and that if the Court considered the state action unreasonable it should thereupon declare it unconstitutional." [16] Predictably, Justice Field, staunch believer in Adam Smith's economic theory, enthusiastically endorsed Campbell's argument. His dissenting opinion, contending that the privileges and immunities clause aimed at all "hostile and discriminating" state legislation, invited the Court to become a censor of all laws threatening property rights.[17] To Justice Miller, whose basic attitude was one of judicial self-restraint and wide scope to the states' police power, the Campbell-Field position seemed a dangerous perversion of the Fourteenth Amendment. Thoroughly disagreeing with the economic assumptions underlying their arguments, he met the challenge head on by writing an opinion that interpreted the amendments narrowly and left state legislative power unimpaired.

In consequence of this sharp clash of judicial attitudes triggered by the *Slaughter-House Cases*, the Fourteenth Amendment was something less than a *tabula rasa* when Chief Justice Waite first con-

[15] *Congressional Record*, 43rd Cong., 1st Sess. 380 (1873–1874). Democratic reliance on the *Slaughter-House* decision was extensive. The speeches reported on pages 405–406, 419–421, 428–429, and 4083–4090 are representative.

[16] Fairman, *Miller*, p. 181, and generally, pp. 179–186.

[17] 16 Wallace 36, 83, 100–101.

fronted it in 1875. The case was *Minor* v. *Happersett*, and again, though Negroes were not involved, their interests were. Mrs. Virginia Minor, a resident of Missouri, sought to vote. Claiming that as a United States citizen she was entitled to all the "privileges and immunities" guaranteed by the Fourteenth Amendment, among which she included the right to vote, Mrs. Minor asked the Court to void Missouri's laws granting the elective franchise only to men. Reassured by an earlier ruling that states could refuse to license women lawyers,[18] Missouri did not even bother to contest the case. In denying the plea for a unanimous Court, Waite declared that prior to the adoption of the amendment, suffrage was not a right of citizenship. Since "the amendment did not add to the privileges and immunities of a citizen" but "simply furnished an additional guaranty for the protection of such as he already had," Mrs. Minor was without a remedy.[19]

Despite this decision, Waite sympathized with the women's rights movement. He believed that "if a woman does a man's work and does it as well as he can, she ought to have a man's pay"; he had a woman as family physician during the later years of his life and, with Justices Davis and Miller, unsuccessfully favored admitting women as members of the Supreme Court bar. [20] Yet here, as in all other areas, Waite construed the war amendments narrowly, almost always allowing a wide scope to state authority. To a Toledo suffragette with whom he was friendly he wrote, "I hear Miss Anthony" and "the ladies criticised my work somewhat sharply—of course it was a pleasure to be assured that you ladies at home gave me the credit of deciding according to our [*sic*] honest convictions." [21]

Walker v. *Sauvinet* continued the narrow interpretation. In that case Waite prepared an opinion holding that the privileges and immunities clause did not guarantee a jury trial in common-law suits.[22] The really significant definition of the war amendments' effect on

[18] *Bradwell* v. *Illinois*, 16 Wallace 130 (1873).
[19] 21 Wallace 162, 171 (1875).
[20] Waite to P. H. Dowling, Nov. 21, 1875, Letterbooks; Docket Book, Oct. Term 1876. Waite Papers. In 1879 Congress passed a law admitting qualified women lawyers to the Supreme Court bar.
[21] Waite to Mrs. Sarah Williams, June 6, 1875, Letterbooks.
[22] 92 U.S. 90 (1875).

Negro rights came in two cases decided during the 1875 term, *United States* v. *Cruikshank* and *United States* v. *Reese*.[23] Both featured the sort of racial conflict that became common when white Southerners tried to regain power. *Cruikshank* had its origins in a political meeting attended by over three hundred Louisiana Negroes early in 1873 in the town of Colfax in Grant Parish. Tension ran high because Republican and Democratic rivals claimed the offices of sheriff and judge. When a Negro posse, led by a sheriff commissioned by the state's carpetbag governor, occupied the Colfax courthouse, a white band attacked, killing from sixty to one hundred Negroes. Almost one hundred whites were indicted by the Justice Department for violating the Enforcement Act of 1870, yet it was possible to arrest only nine. A subsequent jury trial resulted in guilty verdicts but Circuit Judge William B. Woods and Justice Bradley, who had jointly presided, could not agree whether the indictments were valid. Bradley believed them to be faulty and the case was taken to the Supreme Court.[24]

At issue in *Cruikshank* was a part of the Enforcement Act making it a crime for two or more persons to act or conspire to act in such a way as to prevent citizens from enjoying any rights secured by the laws and Constitution of the United States. The defendants allegedly violated this law by interfering with the Negroes' right to hold a peaceful assembly, to bear arms, to vote, and to equal protection of laws safeguarding persons and property. During the summer of 1874 Bradley prepared a circuit opinion declaring that under the Constitution the affirmative protection of the fundamental rights of citizenship "does not devolve upon . . . [the federal government], but belongs to the state government as a part of its residual sovereignty."[25] Turning to the amendments, he found that the Fifteenth conferred a right, the right "to be exempt from the disability of race . . . as respects the right to vote." This, he thought, gave Congress power to furnish redress against hostile state laws and, also, "outrage, violence, and combination on the part of individuals." But

[23] 92 U.S. 214; 92 U.S. 542 (1876).

[24] Homer Cummings and Carl McFarland, *Federal Justice* (New York: The Macmillan Company, 1937), pp. 241–246.

[25] 25 Fed. Cas. 707, 710 (1874).

the Fourteenth gave Congress no affirmative power: "the only con- constitutional guaranty of such privileges and immunities is that no state shall pass any law to abridge them." [26] As for the indictments, they were all defective, failing to aver improper state action and containing no allegation that the acts complained of were designed to deprive the injured parties of any rights on account of their race.

But in 1871 when a racial conflict in Alabama raised questions almost identical to those presented by *Cruikshank*, Bradley had advised Circuit Judge Woods that the Fourteenth Amendment's privileges and immunities clause secured—by *direct* federal intervention within the states—all the "fundamental" rights guaranteed in the Constitution "either as against the action of the Federal government, or the State governments." [27] This suggestion had been adopted by Woods in the neglected case of *United States* v. *Hall* (1871) upholding a series of indictments based on the Enforcement Act.[28] Since Bradley also had read the amendments generously when dissenting in the *Slaughter-House Cases*, his opinion in *Cruikshank* represented a striking change in position. To a friend who disagreed with his new interpretation he wrote, "My own mind is rather in the condition of *seeking the truth*, than that of dogmatically laying down opinions; and I am very glad that the Louisiana case is now in a position in which it can be brought before the Supreme Court, and receive the deliberate and well considered judgment of the whole Court." [29] Diary notations confirm the great importance Bradley attached to the case; he took two weeks to write the opinion and then immediately sent it to prominent Cabinet members and Senators as well as to all the justices.[30]

At the same time, *United States* v. *Reese* also came before the Court, presenting related questions. Two white inspectors of a municipal election in Kentucky refused to receive and count the vote of one William Garner, "a citizen of African descent." They were then

[26] 25 Fed. Cas. 707, 712–714 (1874).

[27] Bradley to Woods, draft dated Jan. 3, 1871, and draft dated March 12, 1871. Bradley Papers. See also Bradley's dissents in *Blyew* v. *United States*, 13 Wallace 581, 595, and the *Slaughter-House Cases*, 16 Wallace 36, 111.

[28] 26 Fed. Cas. 79.

[29] Bradley to Frederick T. Frelinghuysen, draft dated July 19, 1874. Bradley Papers.

[30] Diary, June 12–July 1, 1874. Bradley Papers.

indicted in United States Circuit Court for violating sections three and four of the Enforcement Act. These sections substituted federal election procedures for those of the state when local officials prevented qualified citizens from voting and made offenders subject to criminal penalties.

Both were argued during the 1874 term and, in effect, asked the Court to explain what the war amendments meant for the Negro. In *Reese* B. F. Buckner, the counsel for the white defendants, launched a three-pronged assault, attacking the indictments as faulty for failing to allege that the inspectors' denial was based on racial considerations, arguing the unconstitutionality of the Enforcement Act, and skillfully developing a very limited interpretation of the amendments. Sections three and four were denounced for attempting to reach "any" wrongful act on the part of election officers instead of being limited to actions which wrongfully discriminated because of race. Hiram Reese's attorney further denied that the Fifteenth Amendment, which "amounts merely to an inhibition to the States against any discrimination on account of race, color, or previous condition of servitude," gave Congress substantive power to regulate state elections.[31]

On behalf of the United States, Attorney General Williams and Solicitor General S. F. Phillips concentrated on broad constitutional questions. They argued that the Fifteenth Amendment gave Congress affirmative power to prevent and punish any racially discriminating actions interfering with voting in either state or national elections. While admitting that sections three and four had a wider application than necessary, they nonetheless insisted that it covered Reese's behavior.[32] Their argument in *Cruikshank* was along the same line. Here the challenge was to section six, prohibiting actions intended to deny any citizen the enjoyment of his federal rights. As in *Reese*, the indictments were attacked as too vague. In a brief argument Williams and S. F. Phillips declared that the Fourteenth Amendment gave Congress responsibility for directly enforcing all rights

[31] Brief for Defendants in Error, pp. 6–35, *United States* v. *Reese*, 92 U.S. 214 (1876). Buckner made the same argument about the Fourteenth Amendment: that it merely inhibited discriminatory state legislation.

[32] Brief for the United States, pp. 21–29, *United States* v. *Reese*.

and privileges growing out of United States citizenship. Without being very clear as to what these rights were, they asserted that the indictment was "properly set forth according to technical rules" and that

> the counts in question are not to be read as referring to other rights than those which the courts of the United States can thus protect. If there be any "right to vote," or if there be any "rights and privileges" whatever which may be thus protected, these counts refer to them and to them only. . . . If the learned counsel for the defendants can show that the counts taken in some large sense, include rights . . . [of the victims] because of their connection with another political society [i.e., the states], that are not in this particular way to be protected by the courts of the United States, we reply that such a conclusion is not material, without a demonstration that there are no rights (to vote &c.,) enjoyed because of connection with the United States. So that there be some such we are not interested in this connection to say whether certain rights are upon this or that side of the boundary.[33]

In other words, not bothering to clearly indicate whether the states or the federal government were responsible for the protection of a citizen's fundamental rights, they simply asserted that "if" there were any basic rights intrusted to the federal government, then the indictment covered them.

Recalling that Justice Bradley's circuit opinion showed great concern over the question of whether the states or the federal government was now responsible for protecting fundamental rights,[34] the government's brief was, to say the least, uninspired. In contrast, the defense submitted a brief twice as long. Its well-constructed presentation, duplicating arguments frequently heard on the floors of Congress, hammered hard at crucial points which the government had treated casually: that the amendments applied only to state legislation, that the amendments were not intended to revolutionize federal-state relations, and that the victims' rights depended on state protection.[35] Nor did the United States match the impressive legal talent

[33] Brief for the United States, pp. 26–27, *United States* v. *Cruikshank*, 92 U.S. 542 (1876).
[34] 25 Fed. Cas. 707, 710 (1874).
[35] Brief for Defendants, *United States* v. *Cruikshank*.

assembled to defend the perpetuators of the Grant Parish Riot—eight attorneys including such first-rate lawyers as John A. Campbell, Philip Phillips, and Reverdy Johnson.

Of especial interest is the oral argument made by one of the defense lawyers, David Dudley Field, Justice Field's brother. Attacking the Enforcement Act, he maintained that the war amendments did not grant Congress affirmative power to legislate in areas where possible state discrimination might occur. "That protection of the Federal Government which the whites could not have claimed before the blacks cannot claim now." The amendments merely proscribed discriminatory legislation, and "the only constitutional mode of [congressional] enforcement is by judicial remedies to establish and enforce the nullity." For instance, a state law depriving a person of property without due process of law by declaring that A. shall have a farm belonging to B. could be judicially voided. By suggesting that courts, not legislatures were to enforce the amendments, Field—a noted corporation lawyer—allowed the judiciary ample scope to protect property interests even as he denied that the amendments could do much for the Negro.

If the government failed to compete with the defense in talent and breadth of argument, neither did it match its eloquence. David Dudley Field concluded with a burst of oratory, finding it "difficult to speak of the pretensions upon which this legislation rests" and summoning the Court, "the Constitution of the country," to preserve "the Republic of our fathers":

> The first two words of the national motto [*e pluribus unum*] are as much a part of it as the last. They have never been changed since its use began. They have been borne in every battle, and on every march, by land or sea, in defeat or in victory. They are still blazed on our escutcheon, and copied on every seal of office. May the motto never be mutiliated or disowned. I would have it written on the walls of the Capitol and of every Statehouse. I would wish it written on the ceiling of this chamber, that upon every turning of the face upward, the eye might behold it. In its three words is written a faithful history; may they abide for ages, witnesses of the past and pledges of the future.[36]

[36] Argument of David Dudley Field for Defendants, pp. 24–26, 33–35, *United States* v. *Cruikshank.*

As the Court deliberated, federal attorneys and judges working in the Southern states waited for the result with intense interest.[37] Many of them already felt pessimistic about enforcing the Negro's voting rights. After a Mississippi election in 1875, which saw four Negroes murdered and Republican voting strength in Columbus drop —from twelve hundred to seventeen—the district's federal attorney reported that prosecutions would be "utterly futile":

> Notorious violations of the election laws have been absolutely ignored by grand jurors who had direct and personal knowledge of the violation. It is impossible to get the witnesses, *who have personal knowledge of the facts*, to tell the truth, or what they know, even, in presence of the grand jury, for fear of their lives, or for considerations of policy, protection of personal friends, accomplishment of political and party purposes &c. The same reasons apply to petit juries. . . .
>
> The only hope now is through the officers and Court of the United States. If these fail, then a large mass of the people here are without remedy, or protection, *by reason of the practical nullification of the Constitution and laws of the Country*.[38]

But those challenging the Enforcement laws were supremely confident. Even before the oral argument in *Cruikshank* Philip Phillips had "but little doubt that Judge Bradley's decision will be sustained." [39]

Accurate though the prediction was, it took the Waite Court a while to reach its decision. Both cases were argued early in 1875; re-arguments were heard in October, and on November 6 the Justices agreed to throw out the indictments. That evening Chief Justice Waite sent Justice Clifford a note asking him to write the opinions. "When I supposed that the enforcement cases would be decided on constitutional grounds," Waite wrote, "I felt it to be my duty to try and write the opinions myself." But, since the judges "decided not to have any intimation in the opinion upon constitutional ques-

[37] Cummings and McFarland, *Federal Justice*, pp. 241–246; William W. Davis, "The Federal Enforcement Acts," in *Studies in Southern History and Politics* (New York: Columbia University Press, 1914), pp. 225–226; Woods to Bradley, Dec. 28, 1874. Bradley Papers; Hugh L. Bond to Waite, Nov. 15, 1875.

[38] Henry B. Whitfield to Edwards Pierrepont, Nov. 6, 1875. Source Chronological File (Mississippi), NA.

[39] Phillips to P. Hamilton March 13, 1875, Letterbooks. Philip Phillips Papers, L.C.

tions," he preferred not to take the cases. "You are perfectly familiar with criminal law and I am not," he told Clifford, who readily agreed to write the opinions. What happened next is not entirely clear. On November 20 the judges, sitting in consultation, heard Clifford read his draft opinions and rejected them. Thereupon Waite took back the cases and began preparing opinions deciding *Reese* and *Cruikshank* essentially on constitutional grounds. Justice Clifford's drafts, finding for the defendants because of technical flaws in the indictments, became concurring opinions. Perhaps the aging Clifford was confused. A letter he wrote the Chief Justice on November 21 analyzing the indictments in *Reese* disagrees substantially with the opinion he filed.[40] Or perhaps the judges concluded, after all, that the constitutional questions had to be faced. At any rate, it seems clear that, beginning with Justice Bradley on circuit, the Court handled the cases gingerly, keenly aware of their political implications.

Three months later the Court approved Chief Justice Waite's opinion. On March 26, the day before the decisions were announced, he wrote Justice Miller:

> I thank you very much for calling my attention to my omission [in *Cruikshank*] to refer to the Slaughter House cases. I am so little accustomed to citing cases as authority, except when I quote, that I too often omit it when I should not. It will give me great pleasure to make the notation, which is certainly due. . . . I am glad the opinion meets your approbation. It is not easy for a new beginner in such matters to come before such old heads for criticism.[41]

A reference to Justice Miller's opinion was "certainly due." Waite's opinion in *United States* v. *Cruikshank* drew heavily on the assumptions of the *Slaughter-House Cases.*

In upholding Justice Bradley's opinion, Chief Justice Waite did not accept David Dudley Field's bid to void the Enforcement Act. He nonetheless severely narrowed its scope, arguing that the American system embraces federalism, limited government, and dual citizenship[42]. As a consequence, the indictments were defective, for, follow-

[40] Waite to Clifford, Nov. 6, 1875, Letterbooks; Clifford to Waite, Nov. 7, 1875, Nov. 21, 1875; 92 U.S. 214, 231.

[41] Waite to Miller, March 26, 1876, Letterbooks.

[42] 92 U.S. 542, 550 (1876).

ing *Barron* v. *Baltimore*,[43] Waite declared that the rights allegedly denied by the defendants—to assemble, to bear arms, to life and liberty, to vote—preceded the federal Constitution and depended on the states for their protection. The Fifteenth Amendment gave citizens a new constitutional right, exemption from discrimination on racial grounds, but the indictments failed to aver race as the element motivating the defendants, and the United States was not responsible for local breaches of the peace. Other counts were similarly defective for being too vague and not specifying the exact federal right allegedly denied. Neither could the Fourteenth Amendment cover the indictments:

> [It] prohibits a State from denying to any person within its jurisdiction the equal protection of the laws; but this provision does not . . . add anything to the rights which one citizen has under the Constitution against another. The equality of the rights of citizens is a principle of republicanism. . . . [But] that duty was originally assumed by the States; and it still remains there. The only obligation resting upon the United States is to see that the States do not deny the right. This the amendment guarantees, but no more. The power of the national government is limited to the enforcement of this guaranty.[44]

Both in spirit and language this clearly foreshadows the *Civil Rights Cases* where the Waite Court struck down the Civil Rights Act of 1875 with the explanation that the Fourteenth Amendment only authorized Congress to prevent discriminatory "state action"; the behavior of private individuals, it held, fell beyond this limited sphere.[45] In one respect, however, Chief Justice Waite took a generous view of federal power, suggesting that when a petition or assembly had a direct relationship to federal affairs, rights were involved which the Constitution protected against private as well as governmental threats.[46] This dictum later took on meaning in certain voting cases and—in the hands of willing judges—offers an op-

[43] 7 Peters 243 (1833).
[44] 92 U.S. 542, 554–555.
[45] 109 U.S. 3 (1883).
[46] 92 U.S. 542, 552–553.

portunity for expanding the scope of protected "federal" rights.[47]

Eight justices accepted Waite's language and Justice Clifford concurred separately. All agreed in dismissing the indictments. Similar unity prevailed in the companion case of *United States* v. *Reese.* With the exception of Justice Hunt who dissented and Clifford who again concurred on technical grounds, six of the judges joined Chief Justice Waite in voiding sections three and four of the act. Where in *Cruikshank* the Court found the indictments defective in failing to allege a specific intent of racial discrimination, here parts of the act itself were struck down for the same reason. Although, wrote Waite, the Fifteenth Amendment secured citizens the right to be free from discrimination in exercising the elective franchise, sections three and four did not expressly limit the punishable offenses of election inspectors to acts based on racial grounds, but, rather, were aimed at "all persons, who, by force, bribery, &c., hinder, delay, &c., any person from qualifying or voting."

Penal statutes such as these, the Chief Justice admitted, ought to be construed strictly, but here was a law which "radically" changed state election procedures. And if, taking the statute as a whole, it was apparent that "it was not the intention of Congress thus to limit the operation of the act [to instances of racial discrimination], we cannot give it that effect."[48] Congress had failed to provide "appropriate legislation" to punish the offenses charged in the indictment:

> It would certainly be dangerous if the legislature could set a net large enough to catch all possible offenders, and leave it to the courts to step inside and say who could be rightfully detained, and who should be set at large. This would . . . substitute the judicial for the legislative department of the government. . . . Within its legitimate sphere, Congress is supreme, and beyond the control of the courts; but if it steps outside of its constitutional limitations, and attempts that which is beyond its reach, the courts are authorized to . . . annul its encroachments upon the reserved powers of the

[47] *Ex parte Yarbrough,* 110 U.S. 651 (1884); *United States* v. *Powe,* 109 F. (2d) 147 (1940); Carr, *Federal Protection of Civil Rights,* pp. 49–50, 105, 204, carefully develops this point.

[48] 92 U.S. 214, 219–220 (1876).

> States and the people. . . . To limit this statute . . . would be to make a new law, not to enforce an old one.[49]

Justice Ward Hunt, one of the Supreme Court's anonymous toilers, probably had the best of it in his dissenting opinion. To him —but to him alone—"the intention of Congress on this subject is too plain to be discussed"; the Fifteenth Amendment protected Negroes against violations of their right to vote, and, as its title distinctly indicated, the Enforcement Act was intended to do just that. As Hunt correctly observed, sections one and two, giving a general statement of the act's purposes and requiring equal voting opportunities, made specific references to the Fifteenth Amendment's prohibition of racial discrimination in voting as the evil to be prevented. While the following two sections did not include the word "race" in providing penalties and alternate voting procedures, both sections contain such references as "the wrongful act or omission *aforesaid* of the person or officer." Hunt insisted that "aforesaid" obviously referred to the specific prohibitions against discrimination in the preceding sections and that, given the act's title and manifest purpose, the Court could easily have construed the sections so as to uphold their constitutionality.[50] Despite the force of this contention, the majority decided instead to notify Congress that unless it crossed every "t" and dotted every "i" the Court would not sustain its civil rights legislation.

For his part, the Chief Justice was well pleased. When Circuit Judge Hugh Bond, who worked with him in the fourth circuit, teased him about "that 'Dred' decision of the enforcement case," Waite replied, "Sorry for the 'Dred,' but to my mind there was no escape."[51] He told his brother that the opinions "meet with the most unexpected encomiums. The papers in N.Y. both Rep. & Dem. are to a certain extent enthusiastic." To his cousin he wrote:

> I am getting tired. The past few weeks have borne upon me. The two opinions I read last Monday, and which have been some-

[49] 92 U.S. 214, 221.
[50] 92 U.S. 214, 239–256.
[51] Bond to Waite, April 4, 1876; Waite to Bond, April 4, 1876, Letterbooks.

> what commented upon during the week cost me a heap of hard work, to say nothing of the anxiety. Of course, it is gratifying to see that they have as a rule been kindly commented upon. Some of the Senators have found it hard work to swallow them, but still thus far they have given me no severe criticism.[52]

Waite's fear of a possible hostile reaction was groundless. The Republican New York *Times*, which three years earlier had blasted the Grant Parish Riot as a "fiendish deed," endorsed the decisions and spoke of "the admirable clearness and emphasis of the opinions." Whitelaw Reid's New York *Tribune* told its readers that the Enforcement Act was the "odious" product of a "greedy and malignant partisanship." The influential Springfield *Republican* also nodded approvingly, and, though somewhat fearful that the decision might encourage abuses against the Negro, the Chicago *Tribune* felt no hesitation in praising the opinions for a "clearness of thought and trimness of expression" which "will commend the new Chief-Justice to the confidence of his countrymen." So favorable was Northern reaction that the Richmond *Enquirer* ran an editorial lauding "the improved temper of the North" as a "return to reason." [53]

Congressional reaction also spoke volumes. A scant decade before, the Supreme Court had been an object of suspicion, censured and threatened by the then ascendant Radicals. At one point, to prevent the reputedly pro-Southern justices from passing on the Reconstruction acts, Congress abruptly curtailed the Court's jurisdiction and blocked it from giving an opinion in a case already argued and awaiting decision.[54] *Cruikshank* and *Reese* would have provoked outraged howls in the 1860's; in 1876 Congress accepted them with the mildest of taps on the Court's wrist.

While the *Cruikshank* case drastically narrowed the scope of permissible civil rights legislation, the decisions seemingly left intact

[52] Waite to Richard Waite and to John T. Wait, March 28, April 2, 1876, Letterbooks.

[53] N.Y. *Times*, April 16, 1873, March 28, 29, 1876; N.Y. *Tribune*, March 29, 1876; Springfield *Republican*, March 29, 1876; Chicago *Tribune*, March 29, 1876; Richmond *Enquirer*, March 30, 1876.

[54] *Ex parte McCardle*, 6 Wallace 318 (1868); Warren, *Supreme Court*, II, chs. xxix–xxx.

congressional power to prevent voting discrimination. Early in the summer of 1876 Senate Republicans forced passage of a bill reenacting the provisions voided in *Reese*, explicitly confining their operation to denials based on race. But a resurgent Democracy firmly controlled the House and there was no chance of the bill becoming law; it was not even introduced in the lower chamber. With national elections due in the fall, the Senate vote served merely as a gesture to those Negroes not yet disenfranchised that the party of Lincoln still kept the faith. The really striking feature of the Senate's behavior was its gentlemanly deference to the Court, its willingness to accept the idea that it, rather than the judges, was to blame for the flaws in the Enforcement Act. One Republican, Indiana's Oliver P. Morton, described the decisions as regrettable and vague, but even his remarks lacked sting.[55] 1876 was an era—not a decade—removed from 1866. In 1876 there was no acrimonious denunciation of the Bench, no Thad Stevens to rail against judicial infamy, though perhaps his ghost stirred uneasily.

Where Congress acquiesced and Republican editors described the decisions as wise, Democratic and Southern newspapers reacted with undisguised glee. The New York *World*, which once called Waite mediocre, suddenly discovered his merits. "An exquisite piece of legal acumen, a sound utterance of political wisdom," it said of his *Cruikshank* opinion and concluded: "Chief-Justice Waite in this decision and in the terms of its utterance, has vindicated his disposition and his capacity to emulate the fame of JAY, MARSHALL AND TANEY." "This has the ring of the true metal," declared the Richmond *Enquirer*, echoing other Southern papers, "and we congratulate the learned Chief Justice on the utterance of doctrines worthy of the fathers." [56] Some, as did the New Orleans *Time*, took time to explain what the decisions meant for the Negro: "The colored

[55] *Congressional Record*, 44th Cong., 1st Sess. 4068 and generally, 4057–4075 (1876). Needless to say, Democrats praised the rulings. Original Senate reaction came late in March, 1876, when Republicans called for an investigation of election frauds in Mississippi. Criticism of the Court was muffled. *Congressional Record*, 44th Cong., 1st Sess. 2064–2076, 2105–2120 (1876).

[56] N.Y. *World*, March 28, 1876; Richmond *Enquirer*, March 28, 29, 1876; Louisville *Courier-Journal*, March 28, 31, 1876; Atlanta *Constitution*, March 30, 1876.

suffragan, if not already conscious of the fact, must soon know that his prerogatives, under the constitution as amended, are no greater than those of any other citizen." [57]

Just what prerogatives Negroes enjoyed in the eyes of white Southerners became evident in the years after 1876. Negro voting dwindled steadily as the whites regained total political domination in the states of the Old South. Obviously the Supreme Court's decisions in *United States* v. *Cruikshank* and *United States* v. *Reese* were not the sole causes, being but one of the elements in a much larger picture which included the North's felt need for reconciliation—a need which found political expression in the famous Compromise of 1877. Within this context *Cruikshank* and *Reese* assume significance in arranging one of the essential conditions for North-South reconciliation: the ending of meaningful political participation by the Negro.

It had been difficult enough before 1876 to enforce the voting rights of Negroes, convictions occurring in only twenty per cent of the cases; following the decisions the task became impossible. *Reese* and *Cruikshank* themselves were test cases upon which depended the fate of numerous prosecutions.[58] In 1875 over two hundred prosecutions were started in the South, in 1878 only twenty-five.[59] Fear of reprisal kept many Negroes from the polls, and those who went usually failed to get their votes counted. State officials naturally encouraged violations, and *Reese* and *Cruikshank* hampered the efforts of the United States attorneys. They stand for "the classical theory of an imperium of imperio," one of them complained in 1879. "The contest is unequal, until Congress reconstructs its reconstruction acts." This same attorney, the federal attorney in Charleston, South Carolina, gave a vivid description of his plight:

> I have been forced by the unfortunate condition here, to give to Reese et al and Cruikshank et al my severest study. I made last spring a careful abstract with notes, of these and all kindred cases and came

[57] March 29, 1876.

[58] R. H. Marr and John A. Campbell, Motion to advance *United States* v. *Cruikshank*, Nov. 5, 1874; B. F. Buckner to D. W. Middleton, March 30, 1877, concerning *United States* v. *Reese*. Supreme Court Appellate Case File, National Archives.

[59] Davis, "The Federal Enforcement Acts," p. 224.

to the conclusion then, which is much stronger now, that with the single exception of a few sections, relating to the elections of federal officers, the federal election laws are a delusion and farce. . . . If red shirts [a term for white bands] break up meetings by violence, there is no remedy, unless it can be proved to have been done on account of race &c, which cant be proved; because the people can only peaceably assemble under the Constitutional guarantees, to petition Congress &c. It is hard to sit quietly and see such things, with the powerful arm of the Government, bound in conscience to protect its citizens, tied behind its back by these decisions. With colored men crowding my office, it is hard to make them understand my utter helplessness. . . .

Of course under all sorts of pretexts, and arbitrarily where there is no pretext, the Managers of Elections, three at each precinct, appointed by three Commissioners of election, in turn appointed by . . . [the governor] reject and refuse to permit colored men to register. . . . The object is clear to break down the republican strength. I examine the statutes but Reese et al says the legislation is not "appropriate," because the section has not the mystic words "on account of race &c.," nor has Congress yet provided "appropriate legislation". . . .

I have not registered yet, and although I always do, feel like it would be wasting that much time. Suppose I vote, will it be counted and if I cant protect myself, how can I protect my friend of African descent. . . .[60]

Thus did the Supreme Court's decisions have their impact. In practical terms they show that the Court, in facing the Southern question, marched in step with the national mood. "It is pretty clear to my mind," a federal district judge in Mississippi observed shortly before the decisions were announced, "that the judgment of our wisest Republican Jurists and Statesmen is now against Federal interference in such [voting] cases but, to leave it to the State authorities and the good sense of the people." [61] And so it was. The Court that emasculated the Enforcement Acts and the war amendments was a Republican Court; its principal architects in these cases—Judges Waite, Miller, and Bradley—were Northerners and Republicans

[60] L. C. Northrop to Charles Devens, Jan. 14, 1879, Nov. 11, 1879. Source Chronological File (South Carolina), NA.

[61] Judge R. A. Hill to W. W. Dedrick, Sept. 9, 1875. Source Chronological File (Mississippi), NA.

whose credentials were unimpeachable. To suggest that they consciously fashioned a policy of conciliation would be impossible to prove and unjust to their motives: to Miller it was a matter of resisting Judge Field's attempt to turn the Fourteenth Amendment into a roving license for judicial supervision of the economy; to Bradley, the legal scholar and craftsman, it was a question of undogmatically "seeking the truth"; to Waite, a judge consistently devoted to the idea of broad state powers in all areas, there was "no escape" from the Court's conclusions.

More often than not, however, the national environment gradually finds expression in the Supreme Court's decisions. Judges live and breathe in the atmosphere of their day, and in 1876 reconciliation was in the air. "The day of our complete deliverance," the Richmond *Enquirer* hopefully proclaimed, "may be still longer postponed, but it will come at last, and we shall not be disposed to complain so long as our present rate of speed is maintained." [62] *United States* v. *Cruikshank* and *United States* v. *Reese* were the opening phases of the Compromise of 1877—heralding the day of "complete deliverance," which, for the white South, was just around the corner.

[62] March 30, 1876.

8

GUARDIAN OF THE COMPROMISE OF 1877

Cordiality in the Centennial Spirit.

Hayes-Tilden Election Crisis. North and South Strike a Bargain.

Judicial Validation. Commerce and Civil Rights.

Nullification of the Civil Rights Laws.

An Ex-Slaveholder's Dissent. The Lost Cause of the Negro.

"MEN OF THE SOUTH, WE WANT YOU. MEN OF THE SOUTH WE LONG for the restoration of your peace and your prosperity. We should see your cities thriving, your homes happy, your plantations teeming with plenteous harvests, your schools overflowing, your wisest statesmen leading you, and all causes and all memories of discord wiped out forever." [1] So spoke the editors of *Scribner's Monthly* as they extended the olive branch across the Mason-Dixon line, bidding the South to join the North in celebrating the one-hundredth anniversary of the Republic's birth. An invitation so cordial could hardly be refused. To the Philadelphia Centennial Celebration of 1876 the South sent exhibits and representatives. Its exhibits were intended to lure Northern capital southward; its representatives, such as the poet Sidney Lanier, who contributed a cantata, and the Mississippi political leader, Lucius Quintus Cincinnatus Lamar, who gave an oration, to develop still further the North's good will. Both efforts succeeded, and for many Americans the Centennial became an exercise in reconciliation as well as a commemoration of national independence.

It was in this spirit that Morrison Waite responded to a die-hard radical who asked him to block the invitation given a member of the Lee family to read the Declaration of Independence at the Centennial's opening ceremonies on July 4:

[1] Quoted in E. Merton Coulter, *The South During Reconstruction 1865–1877* (Baton Rouge: Louisiana State University Press, 1947); also, Buck, *Road to Reunion*, pp. 134–142.

> The nation has been preserved in its entirety and I preside over a court which is common to all its parts. In fact, I must not permit myself to know that it has parts. Neither can I, in my position, know the antecedents of any one—All are equal before me. It is my duty, in my place, to cultivate that feeling so that I may at all times and in all places be prepared to act without prejudice.[2]

Even while Northerners and Southerners visited Philadelphia to mingle as Americans and gaze at the fruits of the new industrial order—fruits more likely to be widely distributed if Americans could live together harmoniously—the nation faced and resolved its most serious crisis since 1861. The crisis was the Disputed Election of 1876; its resolution, the Compromise of 1877. Only the bare bones of these events need be noted. As their candidate to succeed Grant the two parties nominated men who shared much in common: Samuel J. Tilden and Rutherford B. Hayes were political moderates and men of integrity; both could wear the mantle of "reform," and both were equally acceptable to the men of Wall Street. National politics remained nonetheless largely sectional, and Republicans, including Hayes, who favored a mild Southern policy, still waved the bloody shirt furiously. For his part, Tilden had a good record as New York's Democratic governor, making the outcome doubtful and the campaign an absorbing one. The Fourteenth Amendment did not, the Supreme Court had held, confer upon women the right to vote, but even the Chief Justice's wife wished she had the right: "I am so excited over election I . . . look out of the window at the Engine House [in Toledo] and wish I could have a hand in. Later Mary says she never wanted to vote before but she does now. I told her I felt as if I could not be satisfied with one vote. I should want to vote all day." [3]

On November 8 the American people learned that Samuel Tilden had carried enough Northern states and most of the South to gain a tiny majority of the popular vote. South Carolina, Louisiana, and Florida, however, were nominally controlled by the Republicans and here conflict arose. Without electoral votes from at least one of these states Tilden lacked a majority; with the votes from all three

[2] Waite to Alice Sandford, Feb. 14, 1876, Letterbooks.
[3] Amelia Waite to Waite, Nov. 7, 1876.

Hayes had the necessary majority—185 to 184. In all but form the white Democracy controlled these states and claimed to be legitimately in power; the upshot was competing state governments which filed conflicting election returns. Adding to the confusion, which included charges of Democratic intimidation of Negro voters and countercharges of unlawful interferences by federal troops on behalf of the Republicans, was the fact of divided government in Washington. Because Republicans controlled the Senate and Democrats the House, a count of the electoral vote became impossible. Finally, in late January, 1877, a Democrat-sponsored bill to create a special Electoral Commission to pass on the disputed returns picked up enough Republican support to get through Congress. After wading through the legal morass spawned by the fight for the Presidency, the Commission, composed of ten congressmen and five Supreme Court justices—Clifford, Field, Miller, Strong, and Bradley—divided along straight party lines and recommended that Congress certify the Republican electors. This Congress did, though not until an effort by Northern Democrats to filibuster completion of the count was defeated by a Republican-Southern Democrat coalition a mere two days before the end of Grant's term. On March 4, 1877, Chief Justice Waite administered the oath of office to his friend from northwest Ohio, Rutherford B. Hayes.

Southern Democratic cooperation was essential to the peaceful installation of Hayes, and to obtain it North and South struck a bargain. Most superficially, the bargain involved the sort of horse trading common to American politics: in return for their cooperation in seating Hayes and their promise not to mistreat the Negro, Southerners were to be rewarded with the withdrawal of federal troops and the recognition of the Democratic governments in South Carolina and Louisiana. Actually, as C. Vann Woodward's research shows, the Compromise of 1877 was considerably more than a simple political deal.[4] What was attempted was nothing less than a rebuilding of the Republican Party. By a policy of active cooperation with the old Southern Whigs, who before the war had taken their

[4] *Reunion and Reaction* (New York: Doubleday Anchor Edition, 1956); *Origins of the New South 1877–1913* (Baton Rouge: Louisiana State University Press, 1951); *The Strange Career of Jim Crow* (New York: Galaxy Book Edition, 1957).

cues from Eastern financial and commercial interests, many of Hayes' close advisers hoped to bring the South's nascent capitalists permanently into the Republican camp. Federally-sponsored railroad construction and a remission of the Negro to the control of the states were among the inducements offered the South. In turn, Republicans would benefit by becoming a truly national party, acquiring a stability which would make it better able to defend capitalism against the disturbing influences of the various Western heresies propounded by agrarians, Greenbackers, and silverites.

Despite its appeal to such ex-Whigs and conservative Democrats as Lamar of Mississippi, Joseph E. Brown of Georgia, and Wade Hampton of South Carolina, men whose moderate racial policies made them acceptable in the North, the effort to reconstruct the Republican Party failed. But in a more subtle sense, as Woodward cogently points out, the alliance worked. Southern Whigs aligned themselves with the Conservative Eastern wing of the Democratic Party, which "was as devoted to the defense of the new economic order as the Republicans. A way was therefore found for Conservatives to cooperate across sectional barriers as they had in Federalist and Whig days." [5]

As these events and adjustments took place the Supreme Court was no idle spectator. At one level the justices gave Hayes the Presidency. Five of them served on the Electoral Commission and from their ranks came the odd vote, Judge Bradley's, which made an eight to seven majority for the Republican candidate.[6] Were this all, the commission's vote would mark only an isolated incident in Court history (important, to be sure, in the seating of Hayes and in showing that on occasion the justices have been dragooned into temporarily doffing their judicial robes in favor of more obviously political duties), but the Waite Court's involvement in the social and political adjustments of the late nineteenth century went much deeper.

Even before the Disputed Election its decisions in *United States* v. *Cruikshank* and *United States* v. *Reese* had encouraged the elimination of Negro voting, making clear that the Supreme Court re-

[5] Woodward, *Reunion and Reaction*, p. 265, and in general, chs. xi–xii.
[6] The Waite Court's relationship to the commission is discussed in ch. xiv.

garded the Reconstruction era as over. Subsequently it put the official stamp of constitutional approval on the Compromise of 1877. For in one crucial matter—that of the historical Negro question—this compromise, unlike earlier ones, proved more lasting. "There were," as Woodward has written, "no serious infringements of the basic agreements of 1877—those regarding intervention by force, respect for state rights, and the renunciation of Federal responsibility for the protection of the Negro." [7] With the exception of one or two decisions which, though they ultimately grew into significant precedents, had little impact beyond the immediate cases, the Negro became the forgotten man of American constitutional law. No less than the Confederacy was his the Lost Cause.

Within a year of the Compromise of 1877 the Negro again lost in the Supreme Court. Louisiana's Reconstruction legislature had passed a civil rights statute requiring public carriers operating in the state to give all passengers equal facilities without regard to race. A Negro woman, Mrs. Josephine DeCuir, boarded a Mississippi River boat at New Orleans, intending to travel to Vicksburg, and was refused accommodation in a cabin reserved for whites. On appeal of her suit to the Supreme Court, the carrier challenged the law as an unconstitutional violation of congressional power over commerce. Three Justices—Miller, Strong, and Hunt—supported the law in conference, yet withheld dissenting from what Chief Justice Waite was able to announce as a unanimous decision against the validity of the civil rights act.[8] Despite Congress' exclusive power over interstate commerce, Waite admitted that states might regulate instruments of commerce wholly within their jurisdictions. Indeed, except when interstate commerce was involved, their control was exclusive.[9] But the problem was a difficult one:

> The line which separates the powers of the States from this exclusive power of Congress is not always distinctly marked. . . . Judges not infrequently differ in their reasons for a decision in which

[7] Woodward, *Reunion and Reaction*, pp. 265–266.

[8] *Hall* v. *DeCuir*, 95 U.S. 485 (1878); Docket Books, Oct. Term 1877. Waite Papers. John Marshall Harlan, appointed to succeed David Davis, did not participate. Clifford concurred specially.

[9] Citing *Willson* v. *Blackbird Creek Marsh Co.*, 2 Peters 245 (1829); *Munn* v. *Illinois*, 94 U.S. 113 (1877); *C., B. & Q. R. Co.* v. *Iowa*, 94 U.S. 155 (1877).

> they concur. Under such circumstances it would be a useless task to undertake to fix an arbitrary rule by which the line must in all cases be located. It is far better to leave a matter of such delicacy to be settled in each case upon a view of the particular rights involved.

Here, however, Louisiana's law was "a direct burden upon interstate commerce": "While it purports only to control the carrier when engaged within the State, it must necessarily influence his conduct to some extent in the management of his business throughout his entire voyage." [10]

As the more recent invalidation of a Virginia statute requiring segregation on interstate busses demonstrates,[11] *Hall* v. *DeCuir* is something of a two-edged sword—applicable as well against state segregation laws affecting interstate commerce. This, however, was not the immediate consequence of Mrs. DeCuir's loss in the Supreme Court, which gave yet another indication of the federal judiciary's willingness to leave the Negro problem to the states. Between 1881 and 1891 nine Southern states hastened to pass Jim Crow laws segregating transportation. Lower federal courts cooperated, ignoring *DeCuir*'s dual implications and advancing instead the doctrine of separate but equal: transportation might be segregated if the facilities were substantially equal. In the 1890's the Supreme Court itself ratified separate but equal, and overlooking *DeCuir*, gave its approval to state segregation laws impinging on interstate commerce.[12]

Disappointing as these decisions were to proponents of Negro rights, they had considerably less significance than the Court's rulings limiting assertions of federal power. With the Southern states firmly in white hands, the federal government remained the Negro's last hope for civil rights protection. To be sure, the realities of the Compromise of 1877 made prospects for positive federal action on his behalf as dim as the rapidly fading memory of Charles Sumner.

[10] 95 U.S. 485, 488–489.

[11] *Morgan* v. *Virginia*, 328 U.S. 373 (1946); cf., *Bob-Lo Excursion Co.* v. *Michigan*, 333 U.S. 28 (1948).

[12] *Louisville, N. O. & T. R. Co.* v. *Mississippi*, 133 U.S. 587 (1890); *Plessy* v. *Ferguson*, 163 U.S. 537 (1896); *C. & O. R. Co.* v. *Kentucky*, 179 U.S. 388 (1900); Sarah M. Lemmon, "Transportation Segregation in the Federal Courts Since 1865," *Journal of Negro History*, XXXVIII (1953), 174–193.

Still, the Negro and such loyal supporters as Robert Ingersoll and Wendell Phillips might at least hope that the principle of federal intervention would survive, to be reasserted again in some future, more hospitable period.

Any such hopes came to an end in 1883. In *United States* v. *Harris* the justices voided section two of the Enforcement Act of 1871, a provision which aimed at Ku-Klux activities by making it a crime for two or more persons to conspire or go in disguise upon a highway or another person's premises for the purpose of depriving them of the equal protection of the law or their privileges and immunities. This, said the Court, exceeded the authority conferred by the war amendments; Congress lacked power to legislate directly as to the acts of private persons.[13] Nor could the section be used in a case where a federal right, that of a Chinese alien to do business in a California town on equal terms with Americans, was guaranteed by treaty between the United States and China. Speaking for the Court four years after the *Harris* ruling, Chief Justice Waite stood by his declaration in *Reese* that this was the sort of statute which the Court could not divide into constitutional and unconstitutional parts.[14] Simultaneously with *Harris* the Court upheld an Alabama law making adultery or fornication between Negro and white a more serious crime than the identical offenses committed by two members of the same race. This, it declared, did not violate the Fourteenth Amendment's equal protection clause because the law applied equally to both races.[15]

It was, however, the *Civil Rights Cases* (1883) nullifying the Civil Rights Acts of 1875, which guaranteed equal accommodations in inns, public conveyances, and places of public amusement, that pleased the South most and best signifies the Supreme Court's role as constitutional guardian of the Compromise of 1877. While in both North and South the act was often violated, there was no firm pattern of anti-Negro discrimination during the seventies and eighties. They were scarcely accepted as social equals, yet it was not uncommon to see Southern Negroes, particularly in the cities, mingling with

[13] 106 U.S. 629 (1883).
[14] *Baldwin* v. *Franks*, 120 U.S. 678 (1887).
[15] *Pace* v. *Alabama*, 106 U.S. 583 (1883).

whites in streetcars, restaurants, saloons, and theaters.[16] The Civil Rights Act encouraged such nondiscrimination and, perhaps most important, stood as a symbol: to the Negro for his aspirations, to the white Southerner for the rigors of Reconstruction.

In voiding the act Justice Bradley, speaking for seven of his brethren, made explicit what in *Cruikshank* had been implicit. The Fourteenth Amendment "does not authorize Congress to create a code of municipal law for the regulation of private rights; but to provide modes of redress against the operation of State laws, and the action of State officers, executive or judicial, when these are subversive of the fundamental rights specified in the amendment." The Thirteenth Amendment was also irrelevant. Applying its prohibition against involuntary servitude "to every act of discrimination which a person may see fit to make as to the guests he will entertain, or as to the people he will take into his coach or cab or car, or admit to his concert or theatre," he declared, "would be running the slavery argument into the ground." [17] One of these cases involved discrimination on an interstate railroad, and Waite's language in *DeCuir* implied that Congress might regulate in this area.[18] But Bradley dismissed the contention as a question "not now before us." And finally he expressed a concluding thought on the subject of civil rights legislation:

> When a man has emerged from slavery, and by the aid of beneficent legislation has shaken off the inseparable concomitants of that State, there must be some stage in the progress of his elevation when he takes the rank of a mere citizen, and ceases to be the special favorite of the laws, and when his rights as a citizen, or a man, are to be protected in the ordinary modes by which other men's rights are protected.[19]

Clearly, the welcome mat was not out for Negroes on their way to the Supreme Court.

Only one judge dissented, ex-slaveholder John Marshall Harlan, appointed to the Court by President Hayes in 1877 as a representa-

[16] Woodward, *Strange Career of Jim Crow,* ch. i.
[17] *Civil Rights Cases,* 109 U.S. 3, 11, 24–25 (1883).
[18] 95 U.S. 485, 490.
[19] 109 U.S. 3, 19, 25.

tive of the South. His thirty-four page opinion, attacking the majority for its "narrow and artificial" reading of the amendments which destroyed their "substance and spirit" by "a subtle and ingenious verbal criticism," ranks among the powerful dissents of Court history. To accept the majority's narrow concept of "state action," Harlan argued, reduced the amendments to delusive, "splendid baubles." He rejected Bradley's implied distinction between "social" and "civil" rights, insisting that the act aimed solely to protect legal rights. A colored citizen's right, he wrote, "to use the accommodations of a public highway, upon the same terms as are permitted to white citizens, is no more a social right than his right, under the law, to use the public streets of a city or town." [20]

The Court's refusal to decide whether the commerce clause gave Congress power to legislative civil rights provoked an especially strong rebuttal:

> I beg to suggest that that precise question was substantially presented here in [*Hall* v. *DeCuir*]. . . . Might not the act of 1875 be maintained in that case, as applicable at least to commerce between the States, notwithstanding it does not, upon its face, profess to have been passed in pursuance of the power of Congress to regulate commerce? Has it ever been held that the judiciary should overturn a statute, because the legislative department did not accurately recite therein the particular of the Constitution authorizing its enactment?

Harlan closed by calling Bradley's description of the Negro as a special favorite of the laws "scarcely just":

> The statute of 1875, now adjudged to be unconstitutional, is for the benefit of every race and color. What the nation, through Congress, has sought to accomplish in reference to that race, is—what had already been done in every State of the Union for the white race—to secure and protect rights belonging to them as freemen and citizens.[21]

[20] 109 U.S. 3, 26, 48, 59.

[21] 109 U.S. 3, 26, 60–61. For an excellent discussion of Harlan's civil rights views see, Alan F. Westin, "John Marshall Harlan and the Constitutional Rights of Negroes: The Transformation of a Southerner," *Yale Law Journal*, LXVI (1957), 637–710.

However much the dissent may appeal today, in 1883 Justice Harlan was but a minority of one. Beyond the bench a few voices protested. Colonel Ingersoll denounced the decision for allowing "a contemptible white man to trample upon a good colored man," saying the country needed "another constitutional amendment or a new Court." At scattered places in the North Negro ministers presided over protest meetings. Washington's *National Republican* was mildly critical, but let the Court off easily: "it has simply decided that a faulty method for securing equal rights to all citizens was selected. It is now necessary to do that work over again." Much stronger language came from Frederick Douglass, the early Negro leader and orator, who attacked the decision as "a concession to prejudice" and contrary to Christianity, the Declaration of Independence, and the spirit of the age.[22]

Douglass was vainly invoking an age that had passed with Thad Stevens and Charles Sumner. The North's most influential papers rushed to embrace the decision, emphasizing the principle later popularized in William Graham Sumner's dictum, "Stateways cannot change folkways." [23] Noting that the Civil Rights Act had failed to revolutionize the Negro's status, the Chicago *Tribune* blandly concluded that "the denial of its validity will not entail any more social discrimination against them in the future than has preceded in the past." The New York *Times* was glad to see the Negro problem remanded to the states, where "it rightly belongs," and denounced the law as "mischievous":

> It has kept alive a prejudice against the negroes and against the Republican Party in the South, which without it would have generally died out. It has furnished demagogues like [Benjamin F.] Butler with the means of misleading the colored race, arousing hostility among Southern whites, and rendering the Republican Party ridiculous. . . . The judgment of the court is but a final chapter in a history full of wretched blunders, made possible by the sincerest and noblest sentiment of humanity, but in which the cunning and

[22] Oct. 16–20, 1883; N.Y. *Times,* Oct. 26, Nov. 9, 1883.

[23] Rayford W. Logan, *The Negro in American Life and Thought* (New York: Dial Press, 1954), pp. 170–175, cited hereafter as Logan, *Negro Life.* Harlan's dissent did, however, gain the approval of many smaller newspapers. Westin, "John Marshall Harlan," 683–684.

conscienceless scheme of the Butler school have played the larger part.[24]

To no one's surprise, the South showered the Court with bouquets of praise. Its Senators issued complimentary statements; its press, such as South Carolina's Charleston *News and Courier*, congratulated the justices for nullifying "the most objectionable provisions of the Republican political legislation" and defining the Fourteenth Amendment "as the Democratic Party, from the beginning defined it." [25] In Atlanta the decision was literally applauded:

> There was a wild scene in the opera-house last night when the announcement of the civil-rights decision was made. White men stood on their feet and cheered and ladies gave approving smiles, the quietude of the colored gallery was noticeable. Not a note of applause came from those solemn benches; their occupants were dumfounded. The feeling of the colored people today is deep, and in their ignorance they imagine the effect may be much more than reality. The white people are jubilant.[26]

The South's elation was justified. Had the line of decisions which began with the *Slaughter-House Cases* and culminated in the Court's invalidation of the Civil Rights Act gone the other way, the federal system would have been permanently altered. "Taken together," as Benjamin F. Wright has said, "they constitute one of the two or three greatest setbacks to the extension of national power in our history." [27] True, the Waite Court recorded some notable nationalizing decisions,[28] but on the key issues it faced—civil rights and economic regulation—the judges cast their votes for states' rights.[29]

Despite their reverses, Negroes won a few minor victories. *Strauder* v. *West Virginia* voided a state law explicitly limiting jury service to whites as contrary to the Fourteenth Amendment's equal

[24] Chicago *Tribune,* Oct. 17, 1883; N.Y. *Times,* Oct. 16, 18, 1883.
[25] Oct. 19, 1883.
[26] N.Y. *Times,* Oct. 18, 24, 1883.
[27] Benjamin F. Wright, *The Growth of American Constitutional Law* (Boston: Houghton Mifflin Company, 1942), p. 95.
[28] E.g., *Pensacola Tel. Co.* v. *W. U. Tel. Co.,* 96 U.S. 1 (1878); *Pacific Railroad Removal Cases,* 115 U.S. 1 (1885); *Wabash, St. L. & P. Ry.* v. *Illinois,* 118 U.S. 557 (1886).
[29] But cf., Warren, *Supreme Court,* II, ch. xxxv.

protection clause; *Ex parte Virginia* extended the principle to prohibit similar discrimination on the part of state officers charged with selecting juries.[30] Even these quite moderate affirmations of the freedman's rights were too much for Southern sympathizers. Judges Clifford and Field, the Court's two Democratic members, protested that the decisions would destroy the independence of the states. The *Nation* called them "an unexpected stride in the direction of centralization." A noted constitutional historian, George Ticknor Curtis, thanked Field for his struggle "against the consolidating and destructive tendencies of the present majority," wondering "how it is that men can be so illogical and so blind to the first principles of our constitutional system." So also did the Democratic leader, Senator Thomas F. Bayard, who felt utterly dismayed "that the spirit of revolution could have so invaded" the Court thereby prostrating "all the barriers against complete centralization." [31]

Virginia v. *Rives*, decided at the same time, showed how exaggerated, almost comic, such fears were. Two Negroes on trial for murder challenged the constitutionality of their indictment and trial by exclusively white juries in a county where no Negro jurors had ever been chosen. It ought to be presumed, said the Court, that, even if a state officer had consciously discriminated in selecting jurors, the state court "will redress the wrong." Assertions that Negroes had never served as jurors "fall short of showing that any civil right was denied, or that there had been any discrimination against the defendants because of their color or race. The facts may have been as stated, and yet the jury which indicted them, and the panel summoned to try them, may have been impartially selected." Moreover, Negroes were not entitled to have representation, as such, on juries.[32] As a consequence, the Negro's right to freedom from discrimination in the selection of juries became meaningless. All that was necessary to keep Negroes off juries was the avoidance of open, public discrimination. Not until the 1930's did the Court begin going behind

[30] 100 U.S. 303, 100 U.S. 339 (1880); also *Neal* v. *Delaware*, 103 U.S. 370 (1881); *Bush* v. *Kentucky*, 107 U.S. 110 (1883).

[31] *Nation*, quoted in Warren, *Supreme Court,* II, 611; George Ticknor Curtis to Field, March 9, 1880, Bayard to Field, March 15, 1880. Stephen J. Field Papers, Berkeley Library, University of California.

[32] 100 U.S. 313, 322–323 (1880).

surface appearances to prove the more covert means of keeping Negroes off juries.[33]

A series of congressional election cases also contributed to a mild expansion of federal power. In *Ex parte Siebold* the Court upheld a conviction of state election officers accused of ballot stuffing in violation of the Enforcement Acts. Under the "times, places, and manner" clause of the Constitution Congress could, it ruled, enact laws making it a penal offense for any election officer to violate any state or federal duty in the conduct of congressional election.[34] Equally significant was the Court's decision in *Ex parte Yarbrough.* "The right of the people peaceably to assemble," Chief Justice Waite had declared in *Cruikshank,* for anything "connected with the powers or duties of the national government, is an attribute of national citizenship, and, as such, under the protection of, and guaranteed by, the United States." [35] Justice Miller's opinion in *Ex parte Yarbrough,* sustaining the conviction of nine men for beating a Negro who voted in a congressional election, gave real content to Waite's dictum. It meant, in effect, that the Court recognized voting in national elections as a federal right which Congress might protect against both public and private abuse.[36]

Although it eventually grew into a leading civil rights precedent,[37] the case did little for the late nineteenth century Negro. If anything, Negro voting continued to decline. Efforts made in the late 1880's to get Congress to pass a "Force Bill" making the Fifteenth Amendment more effective ended in complete failure. By 1900 Congress had repealed most of the surviving civil rights statutes and the post-Waite Court continued the process of attrition.[38] Meanwhile, Southern states perfected "legal" techniques which, in one form or another, disenfranchised the Negro for another fifty years.[39]

[33] Beginning with *Norris* v. *Alabama,* 294 U.S. 587 (1935).
[34] 100 U.S. 371 (1880); *Ex parte Clarke,* 100 U.S. 339 (1880).
[35] 92 U.S. 542, 552–553.
[36] 110 U.S. 651 (1884); *United States* v. *Waddell,* 112 U.S. 76 (1884); Carr, *Federal Protection of Civil Rights,* pp. 50–51.
[37] *United States* v. *Classic,* 313 U.S. 299 (1941); *Smith* v. *Allwright,* 321 U.S. 649 (1944); *Screws* v. *United States,* 325 U.S. 91 (1945).
[38] *James* v. *Bowman,* 190 U.S. 127 (1903); *Hodges* v. *United States,* 203 U.S. 1 (1906).
[39] Until the decision in *Smith* v. *Allwright,* 321 U.S. 649 (1944), ended the white primary. On the decline in Negro voting see Logan, *Negro Life,* pp. 110–116; Warren, *Supreme Court,* II, 617–618.

As the century drew to a close, whites, North and South, considered the Negro question settled. Looking upon him as inferior in ability and unfit for self-government—in a word, as the American peasantry—Northerners came to believe that white supremacy was in the best interest of both races. Certainly it was in the best interest of Northern capital which flowed steadily into the South.[40]

While a glance at the daily newspaper is sufficient reminder that the Negro question is anything but settled, the Compromise of 1877 proved enduring enough to restore Southern stability and so open the South to the capitalism that was the order of the day. However unfortunate, the nineteenth century Negro's low social and economic status made inevitable his dominance by the better trained and organized whites. Only the determined use of federal force could have given him an element of political security, and after 1877 any willingness to sustain such force totally disappeared in the North. Instead it wanted reunion; the Hayes-Tilden election crisis provided the excuse for the desired accommodation—an accommodation which had as one of its essential elements the remission of the Negro's destiny to the states. The Supreme Court saw to it that the bargain was not violated.

[40] DeSantis, *Republicans Face the Southern Question*, pp. 49–50, p. 221.

9

THE CHIEF JUSTICE AND THE NEGRO

Moderate Politician, Moderate Judge.
The Southern Circuit Welcomes Waite. Bleeding South Carolina.
Charleston's Great Political Trial. The Chief Justice Presides.
Dismay at the Unreconstructed South. A Mistrial.
Wade Hampton. Revived Hopes for the "New Departure."
Negro Schooling Promoted. Salvation Through Education.

SUPREME COURT HISTORY HAS BEEN ENLIVENED BY STRONGMINDED judges who valiantly, though often vainly, resisted the judicial attitudes of their day. One thinks of Justice Story dissenting from what he regarded as the Jacksonian judges' profanation of the true faith, of Holmes and Brandeis protesting the course of a majority bent on reading their economic views into the Constitution. During the late nineteenth century the dissenter's mantle was shared by two judges. Stephen J. Field normally slipped it on when the Court confronted questions of economic regulation; for use in civil rights cases he handed it to John Marshall Harlan, whose frequent challenges to the majority led his colleagues to joshingly suggest that he suffered from "dis-sent-ery." [1] Morrison Waite, on the other hand, rarely parted company with the majority on either issue.

Especially in the civil rights cases his position was that of the Court. He spoke for it in the first two major cases, *United States* v. *Cruikshank* and *United States* v. *Reese*, denying claims pressed by Negroes. In *Hall* v. *DeCuir* Waite departed from his otherwise consistent support of state laws allegedly interfering with interstate commerce in order to strike down a Louisiana antisegregation statute. Even in the few instances where the majority took a charitable view of Negro claims, he favored a strict construction of the Court's power over state proceedings. Thus, he dissented from the majority's conclusion in *Neal* v. *Delaware* that a Negro being tried for murder was denied equal protection of the law in a case where the trial court re-

[1] Harlan to Waite, n.d., probably late fall, 1883.

fused to consider his uncontroverted allegation that state officers purposely excluded Negroes from juries. To Chief Justice Waite "the mere fact that no person of color had been allowed to serve on juries where colored men were interested" did not prove discrimination and was insufficient to justify reversing the state court.[2] He dissented on similar grounds in another jury case, *Bush* v. *Kentucky*,[3] and stood with the majority in the *Civil Rights Cases*, assigning the case to Justice Bradley and obviously approving of his opinion. Among Waite's papers are various newspaper clippings defending the Court's decision. One of them, written by Ralph P. Lowe, a former Chief Justice of Iowa, he labeled "Judge Lowe's Vindication of the Civil rights decision," marking off this passage:

> If the plaintiffs had a right to the use of the theatre, the hotel or the railway car, which was violated, it was a simple trespass, for which the laws of the state would give a redress, but for which the constitution of the United States has provided none, and for this defect in the constitution the court is not responsible, and there exists no power in congress, as before stated, to make laws which are not authorized by the constitution, and if congress enacts such laws, the judges of the supreme court would violate their solemn oaths if they enforced them. Now the feeling against the court because of this decision is extremely unjust, since it did not make the constitution nor act of congress in question, and it is still more unjust when it is remembered that this same court has enforced the rights of the colored man to vote, his right to sit on juries, to become a witness, his right to personal freedom, to make contracts, and to enforce them. . . .[4]

There is naturally no single "key" to Chief Justice Waite's civil rights decisions. It is indeed a risky—and rather presumptuous—undertaking to spin out an intricate web supposedly explaining a judge's motivations for, as likely as not, such a web will owe more to the weaver's imagination than to the thoughts and motives of the victim thus "explained." What can be profitably done, however, is

[2] 103 U.S. 370, 398 (1881).
[3] 107 U.S. 110, 123 (1883).
[4] Citing such cases as *Strauder* v. *West Virginia* and *United States* v. *Cruikshank*. The article appeared in the St. Louis *Republican*, Nov. 16, 1883, and was intended to answer Frederick Douglass and Robert Ingersoll who had criticized the decision.

to explore the dominant influences encountered by the judge in his environment, take note of his relevant observations, and examine his judicial opinions and votes—in short, to present a picture which speaks for itself.

In the case of Chief Justice Waite's reaction to civil rights problems several elements converged to help shape his response. Although Ohio had been a hotbed of abolitionist sentiment, Waite's political career stamped him as a moderate. Not until the Whig Party foundered on the shoals of the Kansas-Nebraska Act in the mid-1850's did he leave the party of his father. And then he immediately identified himself with the conservative wing of the Republican Party, defending Lincoln against radical criticisms by emphasizing that salvation of the Union was the war's first object. As Chief Justice it was but an easy jump to translate this concern for the Union, this feeling that the well-being of the American people depended on national unity, into judicial decisions which aided the cause of reconciliation. To Waite, as well as to colleagues such as Bradley and Miller, this love for the Union was a powerful influence. Where the Union represented a positive value of the first rank, the Negro's interests in these cases seemed far less compelling. The blunt fact is that acceptance of the Negro as a man in all respects equal to the whites was alien to the preponderance of late nineteenth century opinion. But to judge Waite according to modern standards of what constitutes social justice for the Negro is essentially irrelevant. His conception of the Negro was shaped by differing social attitudes, widely held by many other good men whose understanding of the Negro was limited by the imperfect knowledge of their day. By contrast, that value, love of the Union, which weighed so heavily in the civil rights cases, was a workaday concern for a majority of men in his time, men who, after all, had experienced a corrosive Civil War and knew full well the great cost of disunion.

Waite also knew that Grant, who more than any man could claim distinction as the South's conqueror, favored an end to carpetbag rule.[5] When Rutherford Hayes, a friend with whom Waite shared many attitudes, assumed the Presidency committed to a policy of con-

[5] Waite to Pierrepont, June 16, 1877, Letterbooks; Nevins, *Fish*, pp. 853–856.

ciliation, it became almost inevitable that the Chief Justice would pursue a similar course. Moreover, remission of the Negro problem to the states was thoroughly consistent with Waite's conviction that the federal system reserved large spheres of power to state authorities. While by no means hostile to federal power in areas other than civil rights,[6] in his basic judicial posture Waite was a disciple of Taney, not Marshall. Before he came on the Court, nearly all of his public career had been with state and local units of government; it was only natural for Morrison Waite to believe that the difficult Negro problem could be handled best at the state level.

Finally, while he reflected the prejudices of his day in regarding the Negro as somewhat inferior, Waite felt deep concern over the freedman's plight. Even as he denied his claims in the Supreme Court he spent long hours in efforts aimed at bettering the Negro's lot through education. The diffusion of knowledge and the construction of schools, not legislation, seemed to him the best means of elevating the Negro. Among men of Waite's class participation in such philanthropic endeavors was a commonplace, a form of *noblesse oblige*. In Waite's case it went further, for his commitment was a real one.

These attitudes, a desire for national reconciliation, a faith in state government, and a feeling that the Negro's hopes lay in education, were never consciously articulated by Waite as explanations for his civil rights decisions. Rather, they lie in the background, implicit in his words and actions, and are best revealed by examining his circuit experiences during the trial of the *Ellenton Cases*, which occurred shortly after Hayes' inauguration, and by glancing briefly at his efforts to educate the freedman.

Until 1891 the justices were burdened with the necessity of holding court in their respective circuits. Waite's was the fourth, a Southern circuit which included the states of Maryland, Virginia, West Virginia, and North and South Carolina. Deference to state authorities made him immediately popular among the Southerners. On Waite's first circuit trip a Richmond newspaper joyously discovered that one of his opinions read like those "of the olden time." "Instead

[6] *Pensacola Tel. Co.* v. *W. U. Tel. Co.*, 96 U.S. 1 (1878); *Sinking Fund Cases*, 99 U.S. 727 (1879); *United States* v. *Lee*, 106 U.S. 196, 223 (1882) (dissenting).

of trying to override the state courts," the *Dispatch* continued, "the Chief Justice quotes them as authority." Everywhere he received a good reception from lawyers and press. Immensely pleased, Waite sent his wife numerous clippings from what he called "the rebelest of rebel papers." [7] But when he came to hold circuit in Charleston, South Carolina, in the spring of 1877, relations between the rebels and the national judiciary were strained.

Hayes had withdrawn the federal troops from South Carolina a month after taking office, and the redeemer, Wade Hampton, securely held the reins of government. The new President, however, decided not to drop a series of Justice Department prosecutions which stemmed from a racial riot during the bitterly contested election of the previous fall—and these prosecutions the white South Carolinians regarded as rank political harassment. To regain control of the state in 1876 the whites had embarked on a massive pre-election campaign aimed at either frightening Negroes from voting or coercing them into voting Democratic. Techniques varied from subtle forms of intimidation, tacitly approved by Hampton, to open violence patterned on the so-called "Mississippi Plan." In the upcountry county of Edgefield, for instance, a Negro milita company parading in Hamburg refused to permit the passage of a buggy carrying two white men. A white-instigated riot quickly followed in which six Negroes were killed. One of the participants, Benjamin "Pitchfork Ben" Tillman, later explained the object of the "Hamburg Massacre": "It had been the settled purpose of the leading white men of Edgefield to seize the first opportunity that the Negroes might offer to provoke a riot and teach the Negroes a lesson; as it was generally believed that nothing but bloodshed and a good deal of it could answer the purpose of redeeming the state." [8]

A like opportunity to instruct Negroes in the desirability of white rule arose in neighboring Aiken County. Two Negroes attempted to

[7] Waite described his pleasant reception in letters to his wife dated June 7, 12, and 17, 1874. The Richmond *Dispatch* was dated June 6, 1874; it referred to Waite's circuit opinion *In re Deckert*, 7 Fed. Cas. 334 (1874), which supported the state's courts in holding part of a federal bankruptcy law to be unconstitutional because it changed existing rights between creditors and debtors in a nonuniform manner.

[8] Quoted in Francis B. Simkins and Robert H. Woody, *South Carolina During Reconstruction* (Chapel Hill: University of North Carolina Press, 1932), p. 487, note.

rob the house of a white woman, giving the whites a pretext for organizing a posse. They pursued the fugitives, capturing and executing one of them; the second found protection with a band of armed Negroes. Sporadic fighting then broke out around Ellenton, and before federal troops succeeded in restoring order, two whites and fifteen to one hundred Negroes lost their lives.[9] As a sequel to the riot, the federal government obtained grand jury indictments charging twelve Aiken County whites with violations of the Enforcement Acts. South Carolinians reacted in predictable fury by denouncing the indictments, which were returned just before the November election, as part of a politically inspired effort to keep the state in Republican hands.

Once it was evident that the cases would come to trial, Chief Justice Waite's presence became inevitable because Circuit Judge Hugh L. Bond was roundly distrusted by Southerners who looked upon him as an incorrigible radical. D. T. Corbin, the federal attorney in South Carolina, wanted a speedy trial and asked Waite to hold a special term of the Circuit Court in late November. South Carolina was then in the very center of the hysteria arising from the Disputed Election. Granting Corbin's request would have had the nation's highest judicial officer presiding at a trial charged with political implications under the most trying circumstances. Already Waite had turned aside an appeal from the Democratic National Chairman, Abram S. Hewitt, that he go to South Carolina to decide a habeas corpus case growing out of the dispute over who had won the state's electoral votes. Now he submitted Corbin's special-term motion to the full Supreme Court, which unanimously voted against it. Waite then wrote Corbin that "with our docket of 950 cases" it was "simply impossible" for him to leave Washington. To Judge Bond he wrote, "A trial of these cases in the midst of the present excitement could do no good as far as verdicts." [10]

Accordingly, the *Ellenton Cases*, as they were called, were postponed to the spring. But when Waite arrived in Charleston, accom-

[9] Interpretations vary: Simkins and Woody, *South Carolina During Reconstruction*, pp. 505–506; cf., Jarrell, *Wade Hampton and the Negro*, pp. 77–82.

[10] Waite to Hewitt, Nov. 27, 1876, Letterbooks; Washington *National Republican*, Nov. 28, 1876; Waite to Corbin, Nov. 16 and to Bond, Dec. 25, 1876, Letterbooks.

panied by Judge Bond, Southerners still resented the federal prosecution. The Charleston *News and Courier* gave daily front page billing to the cases under the headline, "THE GREAT POLITICAL TRIAL," charging that "the Radicals knowing that with negro witnesses at $1.50 per day, and a packed jury containing some of the worst and most degraded men in the State, there was a chance to obtain revenge from their inglorious defeat at the election . . . and the . . . cases were revived." [11] On May 15, 1877, the government opened the case of *United States* v. *Butler*, accusing Andrew Pickens Butler, an ex-Confederate Colonel, and eleven other defendants of violating two sections of the Enforcement Acts: section six of the Act of May 31, 1870, prohibiting conspiracies of two or more persons intended to deprive citizens of "any right" secured by the federal Constitution and laws, and section two of the Act of April 20, 1871, proscribing similar conspiracies intended to deprive citizens of their right to vote and to support candidates in federal elections.

An account of the trial's opening appeared in the *News and Courier:*

> The scene in the United States Court room yesterday . . . was one that will bear description. The room itself is an oblong quadrangular hall, built for the purposes of a club, admirably suited for billiard tables and a bar, but altered for a court room by having a stage and sort of pulpit erected at the end opposite the huge entrance, and a railing run across from side to side about midway between the entrance and the stage. Windows reaching from the ceiling to the floor on either side cast an abundance of light upon the scene. This hall is historically noted as the place of assembly of the famous Ringed, Streaked and Striped Convention, by which the present Constitution of the State was adopted, and the reign of the carpet-bagger, scalawag and negro inaugurated. It seems fit that the same hall that witnessed the first organization of the political rogues should also behold their last desperate effort to be avenged upon the people whom they cannot rule. Yesterday the stage, rostrum, pulpit, or whatever else the unsightly box which serves as the legal "bench" may be called, was occupied by Hon. Morrison R. Waite, Chief Justice of the United States, and Hon. Hugh L. Bond, Judge of the Fourth Circuit; below and in front of the Judges in the

[11] May 15, 1877.

> clerk's desk sat the clerk of the Court, and his assistants, while on either hand constables stood in waiting. The representatives of the press and the reporters for the government occupied a table at the right of the clerk's desk. The jury seats on either side next the wall were occupied mostly by negroes, only a few decent white men being visible among them. . . . The space outside the railing was occupied by a motley crew, mostly negroes, while the doorway was thronged with eager spectators, generally white people, who had not time to stay long, but whose places were filled as soon as they passed away.[12]

In its case the government relied on circumstantial evidence, the actions and declarations of the defendants, to prove a conspiracy. It introduced, for instance, the declaration of one defendant "that the leading rascals of the Republican party were going to be killed before the election. That the Democrats would wade to their saddle-skirts in blood to carry the election." Another defendant, it charged, went to the house of one of the Negro victims, "took out a list which he called a 'dead list,' and read from it the names of several prominent colored Republicans in that vicinity who were to be killed." According to the prosecution, Colonel Butler commanded over two hundred armed men who, joined by other white bands, terrorized Negroes in Aiken County:

> Two of the defendants, Paul and John Bowers, went into the house [of a colored woman] and found there one Wilkins Hamilton, a nephew of Joanna. He had been shot in the leg the night before at Union Bridges [the scene of a skirmish between whites and Negroes]. He was unarmed when these two entered the house, and offered them no resistance. Five pistol-balls were shot into him by these two men, in the presence of his aunt, killing him instantly. They rejoined the column, and proceeded with it to Ellenton. Near the station they killed another colored man, John Kelsey, who was trying to escape from them. Afterwards the column turned and went by the house of some colored people named Kelsey. Six young colored men had eaten dinner there. As they heard the advancing column of mounted men they ran from the house. David Bush and Sam Brown, a deaf and dumb boy, were killed by the whites in the field near the house. Warren Kelsey was killed in his yard, in the

[12] May 16, 1877.

presence of his wife and family, while begging for his life and promising to vote the Democratic ticket.[13]

Defense attorneys countered by claiming that the whites had gathered to execute a warrant for the arrest of the Negroes suspected of robbery and that the Negroes began a riot which forced Colonel Butler's men to act in self-defense. Outside the courtroom the *News and Courier* did its best to discredit the prosecution. On the twenty-third its feature story was "Horrible Tales of Murders Repeated Ad Nauseam"; on the twenty-fourth, "End of the Government's Bugaboo Stories." It attacked the federal attorneys as "unscrupulous," their charges as "flimsy," and their witnesses as "hired prevaricators and perjurers." Negro witnesses were uniformly described in an insulting manner:

> Paul Weston: This was a most comical-looking darkey, his eyes executing a rapid succession of winks for a minute at a time, and his mouth twisted up into the most quizzical expression imaginable. He might at first sight have been mistaken for a good-humored negro, but before the cross-examination was over he exhibited a most villainous temper.[14]

Such tactics distressed Waite. He had come to Charleston brimming with hope for the success of President Hayes' policy of reconciliation. In order to weaken the Democrats in the South he favored Administration appointments drawn from "the most respectable men of the Democratic party," and while in April he accurately forecast the failure of Republican efforts to organize the House with Southern Democratic support, his prognosis remained cheerful. "Hayes will in the end succeed," he asserted, "for he certainly is in accord with the sentiment of the people and they bring the politicians [into] line generally." [15] The Ellenton trial upset him. On May 20 he wrote his wife:

> We are having a hard time here. This trial is likely to last into next week . . . though we sit from 10 until two and from five until 9 or 10.

[13] *United States* v. *Butler,* 25 Fed. Cas. 213, 218–220 (1877).
[14] May 22–28, 1877.
[15] Bond to Waite, March 9, 1877; Waite to John T. Wait, April 11, 1877, Letterbooks.

The people of the city are very bitter about it. I am inclined to think they are not quite as cordial towards us as they were when we came. The newspapers are very bitter though thus far they have let me alone. Once or twice they have given Judge Bond a dig, but they misrepresent the testimony very badly and abuse the witnesses, who, it seems to me, are unusually intelligent for their condition. Some of their stories are almost beyond belief. It is so difficult for us who have lived amidst other circumstances to comprehend such a state of society. Negroes, so far as the case thus far shows, were shot down in cold blood without any cause or provocation. I am exceedingly anxious to hear what possible excuse can be given for the acts which seem to be admitted on all hands.

Did I write you about the dinner at Judge Magrath's? We had there Gen. Butler who is charged with being one of the Hamburgh victers [*sic*], and Mr. Youmans, one of the counsel of the defendants in this case and Mr. Trenholm, a son of the old secretary of the Confederate states.[16] He, however, is one of the most intelligent gentlemen I have met down here. Somehow, I feel that the two sections will never in our times come together cordially again. They praise Gov. Hayes and his policy, say he is popular, but I am afraid will never do a thing to help him along with the policy he has begun. They will take all the offices he will give, but will give him nothing in return. That looks to me like the present situation here. The truth is I am less hopeful of good results now than I used to be. Still I would not have the President change his policy. It is the only thing that can be done, and if it is not successful it wont be his fault.[17]

So bitter were Southern feelings that, as Waite implied, some Charlestonians were less than hospitable to the Chief Justice. Northern papers later reported, "Socially he was ostracized—unceremoniously 'cut' by the influential whites of the place." This was exaggeration and Waite denied it, insisting that he had been well received, though he added, "it was sometimes hard for them to be as cordial as they might otherwise have been." [18]

Further testimony Waite found "horrid" and "sickening." He again wrote home on May 24:

[16] Andrew G. Magrath, a former governor and state judge; Matthew C. Butler, a political associate of Wade Hampton; Leroy F. Youmans, State Attorney General.

[17] Waite to Amelia Waite, May 20, 1877.

[18] N.Y. *Times*, June 22, 1877; Waite to William Aiken, June 18, 1877, to Samuel Young, June 20, 1877, Letterbooks.

The truth is that, in my opinion, the people here are really, at the moment, in heart further from reconstruction than they have been since the war. They have received the first fruits of success over what they assume to have been their enemies and they have gone back to their original idols. They are willing to receive from the President's policy all it will give, but I have not seen one that is willing to give anything in return, except to say that he, and some others he will name, "will take the office." Perhaps that is the only way there is to *real* reconstruction, and I am sometimes inclined to think it is. But that is all you can make out of the present condition of things, so far as I can discover. But today the bitterness of hate in the general Charlestonian is as deep and determined as it ever has been since the war. Republicanism here has "given up," and they all know it. That with them is triumph. The only hope from the administration now is the "loaves & fishes." If I were Hayes I would look over the whole field of the enemy and select out men of real merit and the greatest ability. Those that have the interest of South Carolina at heart and who know its people. They should have brains, energy and tact and I would offer to them the best offices. All I would ask for would be personal fitness for the place and ability to control public sentiment. Then things might take care of themselves. I don't know but I am wrong but that is the only road out of the present trouble that I can now see. The truth is I am thoroughly disgusted.[19]

A few days later Chief Justice Waite charged the jury of six Negroes and six whites. Following his reasoning in *United States* v. *Cruikshank* and *United States* v. *Reese*, he told them that to prove guilt they had to find an unlawful conspiracy to deprive Negroes of their federal voting rights on account of race or color:

[T]he defendants are not on trial for the killing of Bush, or of any other of the numerous homicides that were committed during the disturbances which followed the alleged attack by two negroes. . . . The shocking detail of these transactions, which have been given in evidence, are to be considered by you with reference to their bearing upon the existence of the alleged conspiracy to prevent by force, intimidation, or threats the support and advocacy by Bush of the election of Smalls, or to intimidate him on account of his race or color in the free exercise of his right to vote. However much you may deprecate the acts which have been described by the witnesses, the punish-

[19] Waite to Amelia Waite, May 22, 23, 24, 1877.

> ment of those guilty of them has been committed by the laws to other courts than this. Power for that purpose exists in the government of the state, and under our political system the courts of that government can alone be resorted to for the trial and conviction of such offenders.

Taking note of Southern criticism, he asked the jurors "to lift yourselves above the political arena" and disregard charges that *United States* v. *Butler* was a "political trial." It "is political only in the sense that it grows out of an alleged offence against the political rights of a citizen of the United States, secured to him by the national constitution." And he concluded:

> That a number of citizens of the United States have been killed, there can be no question. But that is not enough to enable the government of the United States to interfere for their protection. Under the constitution that duty belongs to the state alone. But when an unlawful combination is made to interfere with any of the rights of national citizenship secured to citizens of the United States by the national constitution, then an offence is committed against the laws of the United States, and it is not only the right, but the absolute duty of the national government to interfere and afford to its citizens that protection which every good government is bound to give.[20]

Although acknowledging the existence of federally enforceable rights, the charge leaned heavily in the direction of states' rights. This reflected the Chief Justice's conviction that in most matters, despite the amendments, local authorities retained control over personal relations. Privately he wrote, "The defence has made a strong case against their liability—under this indictment, but nothing to excuse the inhumane barbarity of the conduct of some of the persons implicated. More unprovoked murders were never proven than has been done in some of these cases, but unfortunately the guilty parties are not on trial for that." [21]

Because the charge was Waite's first, he was anxious, hoping it would not be criticized. The unpleasant trial had become a strain—"up at five or six every morning for that is the only time I have for work"—and he confessed, "I don't care to be called upon to do much

[20] 25 Fed. Cas. 213, 224–226.
[21] Waite to Amelia Waite, May 27, 1877.

more of that kind of work." [22] But lawyers on both sides complimented his labors, and the Southern press found Waite's sympathy for dual government statesmanlike. Recalling his opinion in the *Cruikshank* case as one of the first indications "to the Southern people that law and constitution existed for them," the Charleston *Journal of Commerce* commended the Ellenton charge "for its perspicuity, force and general impartiality." [23] "A Clear, Dignified and Impressive Address," headlined the *News and Courier*, which did not, however, ease its attacks on the trial. On June 4 it gave this picture of two Negro jurors as they came into court to give the verdict:

> M. K. Holloway (mulatto Radical) appeared with a look of indifference upon his face, not as though he was indifferent to remain for months longer, draw his three dollars per diem, and vote every time against innocent men.
> Cato T. Stewart (negro Radical) looked as though he had just returned from the cotton plantation, where he had had a hard day's work of it. Of the jurymen ever drawn in the United States Court, this small, filthy looking negro ignoramus certainly beats them all.[24]

As many expected, the jury deadlocked on racial lines, the Negroes voting for conviction, the whites for acquittal, and Waite declared a mistrial. Prior to the trial Governor Wade Hampton had pressured the President to drop the prosecution. Hampton, whom Hayes came to admire as a moderate and fair-minded Southern leader, now renewed his request, promising to drop state prosecutions against carpetbaggers accused of corruption and pleading the cause of "peace and quiet in the State." [25] One year after the trial Hayes' Attorney General wrote Waite a long letter asking his opinion of the *Ellenton Cases*, in effect, putting in the Chief Justice's hands the decision as to whether or not to resume prosecution. Waite took his time about replying—for him, an uncharacteristic gesture—and, after complimenting the federal attorney's handling of the case, quite properly refused to express an opinion, "as the cases are still pending and may

[22] Waite to Amelia Waite, June 1, 1877.
[23] June 2, 1877.
[24] June 2, 4, 1877.
[25] Jarrell, *Wade Hampton and the Negro*, pp. 135–137, 175–179; N.Y. *Times*, Aug. 3, Oct. 12, 1877.

come before me again for trial." [26] This ended matters until President Hayes wrote Waite in confidence late in 1878 asking for a copy of the Ellenton charge—obviously in order to study it before reaching a final decision. Prosecution was never resumed.[27]

Glad to be done with the trial, Chief Justice Waite began the trip northward, no doubt looking forward to the summer vacation which he and his family always spent at his old Connecticut home in Lyme. Morrison Waite was a natural-born optimist and soon he was cheerful again. From Richmond he wrote to Amelia Waite:

> We reached Columbia last evening at 5 o'c and left at 12 at night. Gov. Hampton called on me and staid a full half hour. I took occasion to give him a full account of the Ellenton trials and to express to him my ideas of his duty. He is a gentleman and I was glad to have an opportunity of seeing him. As you know the jury disagreed. All the papers are full of compliments for my charge. If possible the democratic papers are the most so. I found an article in the Richmond paper of Sunday when I got here this morning, which was perhaps as complete as any I have seen. The lawyers on the part of the defence said it was all they could wish and Corbin who was for the prosecution said it was the best he had ever heard or read. Of course, all this is pleasant. The Charleston papers, that have done every thing [they] possibly could to embarrass the trial and misrepresent, said they could not ask for a change of a single word. I notice it was telegraphed to N.Y. and the Herald of Sunday speaks of it in the highest terms.[28]

That Wade Hampton, a patrician of the prewar South Carolina aristocracy, should make a good impression on Waite, as he did also on Hayes, was to be expected. Though not an old Whig, as was the Chief Justice, his roots were in the conservative wing of his party. A moderate in racial matters, this Rebel military hero billed himself as the first man in the South to advocate Negro voting. Politically allied with the rising class of Southern capitalists, Hampton hoped the

[26] Charles Devens to Waite, March 11, 1878; Waite to Devens, March 25, 1877, Letterbooks.

[27] Hayes to Waite, Nov. 14, 1878. Apart from the report of *United States* v. *Butler* at 25 Fed. Cas. 213 there are no surviving records. Following "an intensive search" through old papers of the Fourth Circuit, officials of the Federal Records Center failed to locate any documents relating to the *Ellenton Cases*. Acting Chief, Federal Records Center to author, Oct. 24, 1960.

[28] Waite to Amelia Waite, June 5, 1877.

Negro would support the commercial and financial interests of the towns against the leveling demands of the upcountry radicals. If the President and the Chief Justice were somewhat naive in expecting that national reconciliation could be achieved without overly sacrificing the Negro, the moderation and sincerity of men like Hampton in South Carolina and Lamar in Mississippi gave a plausibility to their hopes. While Hampton's motives were mixed, he sought to fulfill his pledges of fair play for the Negro; ultimately, though, his conservative faction lost the state to Negro-hating populists led by Martin W. Gary and "Pitchfork Ben" Tillman.[29]

Waite's experience at Charleston made him more cautious but did not shake his faith in the Compromise of 1877. As he astutely observed to his son, "The President's Southern policy, as it is called, is no *policy* at all— He simply accepted what time and circumstances had already accomplished and he had the good sense to make a virtue of his necessity." [30] He doubted whether "the new departure" would improve party chances in the old Confederate states. Still, it would benefit Northern Republicans, for "it is perfectly certain that the people of the north were tired of keeping men in office by the help of the general government." And, always the optimist, he soon viewed the *Ellenton Cases* as a beneficial influence. "All *White* Charleston was arrayed against the trial," he told a Toledo friend, yet it "has done them good": "They see now just what has been done in some parts of the State and I don't think there will be a repetition of just such crimes. Perhaps this simple experience may have done all the work that is necessary." [31] Four years later he was still sanguine:

> Garfield's four years will break up a solid south— Always they say loud enough to be heard that the Republicans can do more for us than the democrats. A little encouragement will I am sure add to this sentiment, and when I see that our politics are no longer sectional, I shall feel that the war is at last over.[32]

[29] Jarrell, *Wade Hampton and the Negro;* Woodward, *Origins of the New South*, pp. 85–86, 209–210, 321, and *The Strange Career of Jim Crow*, pp. 36–37. Simkins and Woody, *South Carolina During Reconstruction*, p. 547, take a less charitable view of Hampton's Negro policy.

[30] Waite to E. T. Waite, Oct. 21, 1877; to Pierrepont, June 16, 1877, Letterbooks.

[31] Waite to Waggoner, June 20, 1877, Letterbooks.

[32] Waite to Park Matthewson, Nov. 21, 1880, Letterbooks.

In retrospect few would deny that the "new departure" so warmly supported by Waite and ratified by his Court's decisions enjoyed at least partial success. Only a fervent wish in the breasts of most Americans as the year 1877 began, by the close of Rutherford Hayes' term national reconciliation was fast becoming a reality: when an assassin's bullet struck his successor, the whole nation suffered and then mourned; when, a decade and a half later, Manifest Destiny took American soldiers to Cuba, North and South fought and died together as they had not done since the Battle of Chapultepec half a century earlier. But reconciliation had its cost; there was, to adapt Herbert Agar's phrase, a price of reunion. As Rayford Logan has well said in evaluating Hayes' Southern policy:

> However well-intentioned Hayes may have been, he had accomplished only one of the two tasks that he had set for himself. He had pacified the country in so far as a threat of a new civil war between the North and the South was concerned and he had allayed the bitterness between the two sections. But he had abandoned "the poor colored people of the South" to the "honorable and influential Southern whites." He had kept his part of the bargain but had been unable to hold the other parties to their agreement. White supremacy was more securely entrenched in the South when he left the White House than it had been when he entered it.[33]

Yet, almost paradoxically, the President who sacrificed the Negro for national reconciliation and the Chief Justice whose Court gave it a constitutional blessing spent the rest of their lives promoting Negro education in the South. It might be said that the inconsistency is more apparent than real, that the nineteenth century gentleman typically devoted himself to humanitarian causes. It might also be said that the Peabody and Slater Funds, both largely concerned with subsidizing Negro education in the South, and with which Waite and Hayes were prominently associated, were dedicated to freeing the Negro from the bonds of ignorance so that he would be less susceptible to the appeals of demagogues—and hence less likely to harm the economic interests of the upper class. Both assertions have some validity.

[33] Logan, *Negro Life*, p. 35.

People naturally expected the Chief Justice of the United States to lend his name to uplifting causes. Believing that man, particularly with a stiff dose of education, could improve his condition, Morrison Waite amply fulfilled social expectations: he was a member of the Association for the Reform and Codification of the Law of Nations; he was vice president of the Organization for the Better Endowment of Washington and Lee University; and he served as president of the American Institute of Civics, which aspired to "teach our youth the lessons which shall kindle the fires of patriotism" and "inspire them with a sense of the nobility of citizenship." [34] Hayes was of course similarly identified with the work of the righteous.

Second, there can be no doubt that many who gave their time and money to Negro education hoped thereby to keep America safe for capitalism. George Peabody, the Massachusetts money-broker who gave millions to Southern education, "loved," in the quaint words of an admirer, "to accumulate." [35] His fund, like that of the Connecticut industrialist, John F. Slater, was operated by men who dominated business, North and South: J. Pierpont Morgan, William Aiken, Morris K. Jessup, Alexander H. H. Stuart, Robert C. Winthrop, George W. Riggs, and Alfred H. Colquitt. The effect, if not the conscious intent, was to secure cooperation between Northern financiers and their counterparts in the South. These men argued that unless education insured order and trained a skilled and reliable working class, capital would not flow southward.[36] Or, as one Peabody trustee put it: "Five millions of untrained, uneducated citizens is a fearful factor in the problem of the future. We shall take care of them, or they will take care of us." [37]

Nonetheless, Waite and Hayes had a commitment to Negro education which far transcended *noblesse oblige* and class interest. Overburdened with administrative duties, the Chief Justice, who became

[34] From a leaflet in the Waite Papers.

[35] J. L. M. Curry, *Peabody Education Fund* (Cambridge: John Wilson and Son, 1898), p. 16.

[36] Merle Curti, *The Social Ideas of American Educators* (New York: C. Scribner's Sons, 1935), p. 263, generally, ch. vii.

[37] *Proceedings* of the Peabody Education Fund (Boston: John Wilson and Son, 1867–1899), II, 267.

a Peabody Fund trustee in 1874, nevertheless found time to faithfully attend biennial meetings and serve on its committees—though he twice declined honorary degrees from Harvard because he was too busy. When John Slater decided to endow a similar fund in 1881, Waite acted as a go-between to persuade Hayes to head the trustees, served as vice president of the board, and became absorbed in its affairs.[38] Most indicative of Waite's commitment, however, was the fact that he publicly identified himself with efforts to have Congress pass a bill for Negro education. In 1880 he helped revise a Peabody report, "Education for the Colored Population of the United States," which had been drafted by Alexander H. H. Stuart of Virginia. The report, a strong and eloquent appeal for federal funds to educate the Negro, took its main assumption straight from Thomas Jefferson: "If a nation expects to be ignorant and free, in a state of civilization, it expects what never will be." Waite signed the report, which also answered criticisms that federal aid to education was unconstitutional, and it went to Congress.[39] Despite the report and lobbying by the Peabody Fund's agent through the 1880's, New Hampshire Senator Henry W. Blair, Congress' leading supporter of federal aid to education, failed in numerous attempts to get a bill passed.[40] What is significant here is that Waite, normally a model of judicial propriety, should, in effect, lobby on behalf of a controversial bill and give an ex parte opinion of its constitutionality. Nothing else better illustrates his desire to see the freedman educated.

Much the same can be said of Rutherford Hayes. Following retirement from office he plunged zestfully into the work of the Peabody and Slater Funds. When the Slater Fund began operation he exulted:

> I will now try to make the most of this good charity. . . . To make the colored people respected and influential, they must be successful in accumulating property—in doing the work which our civili-

[38] *Proceedings* of the Peabody Education Fund, IV, 11–13; Charles R. Williams (Ed.), *Diary and Letters of Rutherford B. Hayes* (Columbus: Ohio State Archeological and Historical Society, 1924), IV, 42, 343, cited hereafter as *Hayes Diary;* Waite to Hayes, May 22, 1884. Hayes Papers; William A. Slater to Waite, Dec. 1, 1884, Oct. 3, 1887. Waite Papers.

[39] *Proceedings* of the Peabody Education Fund, II, 269–298.

[40] For the reasons see Curti, *Social Ideas of American Educators*, pp. 272–273; Logan, *Negro Life*, pp. 192–193; Woodward, *Origins of the New South*, p. 64.

zation prizes most highly. Let them be not merely bookish scholars, but good mechanics and good business men. Let them show architects, civil engineers, and the like.[41]

The bias was in favor of industrial education—it led the young W. E. B. Dubois to complain to the former President, "I find men willing to help me thro' cheap theological schools, I find men willing to help me use my hands before I have got my brains in working order, I have an abundance of good wishes on hand, but I never found a man willing to help me get a Harvard Ph.D." [42] But Hayes—who helped Dubois get his education—was sincere in believing industrial education, such as that of the famed Hampton Institute, the speediest road to the Negro's amelioration. Moreover, like his friend on the Supreme Court, Hayes was no lackey of the robber barons; indeed, had the business leaders known some of the thoughts troubling the former President during the 1880's they would have been shocked—perhaps even denounced him, in the vocabulary of the day, as a "communist." [43]

Hayes' latest and best biographer has speculated that some of his zeal for Negro education "was by way of penance for the failure of the South to do as much for education of Negroes as it had promised him, and as he, in turn, had in effect promised would be done." [44] This concern, one might further speculate, was a more general compensation for the neglect of the Negro which followed the Compromise of 1877. The same can be said, though tentatively and speculatively, of Morrison Waite. With Hayes he shared in making the policies that returned the freedman to the control of his old masters. Also like Hayes, he shared the hope that planter gentlemen of Wade Hampton's stripe could deliver on their promises of fair play for the Negro—a hope which all too soon proved illusory. Chief Justice Waite, as his comments during the Ellenton trial show, was not insensitive to the Negro's plight. He was sickened by the excesses of

[41] *Hayes Diary*, IV, 76.

[42] Dubois to Hayes, May 25, 1891, in Louis D. Rubin (Ed.), *Teach the Freeman, The Correspondence of Rutherford B. Hayes and the Slater Fund* (Baton Rouge: Louisiana State University Press, 1959), II, 205.

[43] His dedication to Negro education is discussed by Rubin, *Teach the Freeman,* I, xiii–lv. On Hayes' attitude toward corporations see ch. xi, *infra.*

[44] Barnard, *Hayes*, p. 506.

some Southern whites, yet he and his Court made it unlikely that much could be done to prevent such abuses. And so, in educating the freedman he found, in a sense, an avenue to make up to the Negro for what he had denied him from the bench.

The equation also has its reverse side: precisely because Morrison Waite held a deep faith in the ameliorative power of education he felt that it, rather than the sanctions of federal legislation, offered the best means of improving the Negro's condition. It is true that remitting the Negro problem to state control tied in with his customary deference to state powers while reflecting the desire he and most Northerners had for national reconciliation. It was made easier, however, by his faith in the efficacy of education, a faith which took him so far as to step off the Court and advocate congressional appropriations. So strong indeed was the faith, that even respect for states' rights did not deter him from seeking federal aid in the face of the reality which confronted the freedman: "Having for generations been held in slavery, they had no opportunity of obtaining education, of acquiring property, or of qualifying themselves for the intelligent discharge of the duties of citizenship. They are not responsible for their ignorance." [45]

Neither the Slater nor Peabody Funds radically changed the Negro's lot. If he began the second half of the century as a degraded slave, he ended with a status not much better: that of a second-class citizen. Still, the efforts to "teach the freeman," though comparatively small, were tangible evidence that the Negro was not completely forgotten. The institutions it supported brought forth individuals as unlike as Booker T. Washington and W. E. B. Dubois.[46] Both made important contributions toward lifting their race up from second-class citizenship. Nor—for all the hypocrisy, for all the self-serving ends which motivated some of the Northerners eager to educate the Negro—is it entirely clear that education was not for the Negro, as it has been for most Americans, in Lincoln's phrase, his "last, best hope." Not until he acquired property and was freed from ignorance—and

[45] "Education for the Colored Population," *Proceedings* of the Peabody Education Fund, II, 282.

[46] Rubin, *Teach the Freeman,* I, lii–liii.

thus better understood how much he suffered from discrimination—could he effectively challenge his white masters. In voting for national reconciliation as well as for Negro education, Morrison Waite showed that, in these respects at least, he was a true son of his age.

10

THE WAITE COURT, DUE PROCESS, AND *MUNN* v. *ILLINOIS*

Capitalism on Wheels. Farmers and Railroaders.
The Granger Movement. Regulation and Resistance.
Business Goes to Court. Issues and Arguments.
The Brethren Consult. A Landmark Decision. Waite's Opinion.
The Public Interest. Field, Justice, Dissenting.
Munn *v.* Illinois *at the Bar of History.*
Due Process and Subsequent Regulation Cases.
Concessions or Commonplaces?
The Power to Regulate: Defeat and Victory.

"TRIUMPHANT DEMOCRACY"—WITH THESE TWO WORDS A FORMER Bobbin boy from Dunfermline, Scotland, sought to describe his adopted country at the height of the Gilded Age.[1] Andrew Carnegie, who struck gold in the drab processes of manufacturing iron, would have spoken with greater accuracy had he chosen "Triumphant Capitalism" as his descriptive phrase. For the capitalism which Alexander Hamilton had dreamed of in the days when America belonged—heart and soul—to Thomas Jefferson was everywhere evident less than a century after his death. Urban, industrial, and capitalistic: this was the essence of the country after the Civil War. Between 1870 and 1890 the population doubled, rising to seventy-six million, and it increasingly found its home in the cities. Where one-fifth of the population was urban in 1870, the percentage climbed to one-third during the next three decades. No less spectacular was the growth of capital invested in manufactures which grew nineteenfold from 1850 to 1900 while the value of manufactured products jumped twelvefold. Were a date chosen to symbolize the final passing of Jefferson's dream of an agrarian nation, it would have to be 1890, the year which Frederick Jackson Turner saw as marking the end of Frontier America. That year, for the first time, the value of the country's manufactured goods surpassed that of the farm, the orchard, and the dairy.[2]

[1] Andrew Carnegie, *Triumphant Democracy* (New York: C. Scribner's Sons, 1886).

[2] Louis M. Hacker and Benjamin B. Kendrick, *The United States Since 1865* (New York: Appleton-Century-Crofts, Inc., 1946), p. 186.

Things, said Emerson, were in the saddle, and few things were more important than business. As a Tammany Hall leader put it, journalism, politics, medicine, "all professions, arts, sports—everything is business." [3] Nothing was more businesslike than railroading, the businessman's business. Appropriately, many of the period's most able men lent their talents to crisscrossing America with shiny rails. A burgeoning commerce required fast and dependable transportation, and the Vanderbilts, Harrimans, and Stanfords volunteered to fill the need—knowing, as very practical men, that the path of the railroad was often the path to immense personal fortune.

Essential as the railroads were to the country's economic development, their owners and operators won few popularity contests among Western farmers during the 1870's. At first they were greeted with open arms, the mere rumor that railroad surveyors were in a particular locality being "enough to fill the hearts of every settler with joy." [4] The honeymoon rarely lasted long. No one, least of all the farmers, denied the railroads' utility. Farmers, after all, depended on the roads to get their produce to market. Many mortgaged their farms to buy railroad shares and paid high local taxes to finance the bonds which lured the iron horse into their region.

For all their efforts the harvest was a bitter one. Once established, or so the small farmers charged, the railroads paid scant heed to their interests. Company officials were often overbearing, and worst of all, the rates were high and discriminated in favor of large shippers who received special rates. To further fan the fires of agrarian discontent, the economic balance of the post-Civil War period was heavily weighted against the American farmer. A high tariff protected manufacturers, forcing farmers to buy domestic necessities at exaggerated prices while selling their own products—which, because of the wartime boom, were being overproduced—in an unprotected market. Having borrowed inflated money to expand agricultural production during the war, many faced debt collectors who demanded payment in an appreciated currency. While the price of corn declined

[3] Richard Croker, quoted in Thomas C. Cochran and William Miller, *The Age of Enterprise* (New York: The Macmillan Company, 1956), p. 2.

[4] Dakota Railroad Commission, (1885) quoted in Robert E. Riegel, *The Story of the Western Railroads* (New York: The Macmillan Company, 1926), p. 144.

32 per cent and that of wheat 49 per cent, the money with which the farmer had to pay for debts contracted in the flush of inflationary optimism rose 20 per cent in value.[5]

What followed was almost inevitable. Acting in a time-honored tradition that went back at least as far as the Massachusetts Shayites of the preceding century, the farmers struck boldly to cure their ills. None, in their eyes, was worse than that caused by the Eastern-dominated railroads which oppressed them with high rates, and through bribery and the lubricant of free passes, sought to dominate their legislatures. Known to history as the Granger Movement,[6] the protesting farmers of the 1870's aimed to place railroad corporations under the control of public authorities. These, they hoped, would be responsive to the interests of those who tilled the earth. Although the rumblings of agrarian discontent were heard throughout the farming regions of the South and West, farmers scored their biggest victories in Illinois, Minnesota, Iowa, and Wisconsin. It was here that the Patrons of Husbandry and farmer-dominated Anti-Monopoly parties successfully pressured legislatures into passing laws regulating railroads. These naturally varied from state to state, but the main features were similar: establishment of maximum rates for railroad freight and passengers and for the storing of grain by direct legislative enactment or by regulatory commissions; prohibition of discriminatory rates between places by means of the so-called "shorthaul" clauses; and encouragement of competition by forbidding the consolidation of parallel lines.[7]

If the regulatory laws were a tribute to the political power of organized farmers, the victims of their wrath showed why the entrepreneurs of the Gilded Age were renowned for skill and resource-

[5] Solon J. Buck, *The Granger Movement* (Cambridge: Harvard University Press, 1933), pp. 1–34; cf., Theodore Saloutos, "The Agricultural Problem and Nineteenth-Century Industrialism," *Agricultural History*, XXII (1948), 166–167, for the view that ruinous competition, not the railroad rates, lay at the heart of the farmers' difficulties.

[6] As a matter of historical fact the Patrons of Husbandry or Grange, which gave the movement its name, reached its peak influence in 1873–1874, well after other farmer protest movements made themselves felt on Western legislatures. The term "Granger Movement" is used here to refer to all agrarian efforts to regulate railroads during the 1870's. See Buck, *Granger Movement*, p. 123.

[7] Buck, *Granger Movement*, chs. iv–v; Charles Fairman, "The So-called Granger Cases," *Stanford Law Review*, V (1953), 592–620, cited hereafter as "Granger Cases."

fulness. Having failed to prevent the laws from passing, the railroad leaders turned to a variety of weapons in their struggle to avoid regulation. In some instances the corporations strove to project an image of sweet reasonableness, cooperating with the regulatory commissions and willingly adjusting grievances by arbitration. Even the normally insensitive William H. Vanderbilt ("The public be damned") felt the breath of popular opinion; he counseled a policy of caution that would "keep the public with us." [8] But more often than not the policy was one of resistance. Railroad agents fought to repeal or weaken the laws and educate the public to their undesirability. They insisted that regulation was against the farmer's best interests and pointedly threatened that it would discourage further construction, an effective point, for even the bitterest foes of "the octopus" wanted increased railroad service—at a fair price.

Education took other forms as well. In some cases the roads aimed to make the laws unpopular by raising rates to their full maximum in those areas where they had been low. In others, they reduced service and threatened its complete abandonment.[9] Or, alternatively, the laws were disregarded with impunity. The president of the powerful Chicago, Burlington & Quincy decided to ignore Iowa's "mousing RR Commrs" who, he complained, went snooping about to find if shippers were paying excessive rates. "We have and shall pay no attention to the Iowa law," he told subordinates. "We shall increase our rates on certain kinds of freight so as to make any reduction we are compelled to make good, and probably something more." [10]

Above all the railroad corporations put their faith in the courts—not the elective state courts where decisions were likely to mirror popular desires, but the federal courts. These, the corporations felt supremely confident, would decide there was no power to regulate and declare the Granger laws void as an odious interference with vested rights. "Happily," one executive proclaimed, "we have the law on our side, having the right under our charter to make our own rates for freight and passengers and we intend to maintain our rights

[8] Thomas C. Cochran, *Railroad Leaders, 1845–1890* (Cambridge: Harvard University Press, 1953), p. 157.

[9] Fairman, "Granger Cases," 604; Buck, *Granger Movement*, pp. 159–166.

[10] James M. Walker to John N. Denison, May 26, July 10, 1874, in Cochran, *Railroad Leaders*, pp. 489–490.

in the courts."[11] Armed with advisory opinions from three distinguished lawyers, Ebenezer R. Hoar, Benjamin R. Curtis, and William M. Evarts, who pronounced the laws unconstitutional, the railroads licked their wounds and prepared "to fight it out."[12]

Despite careful preparations and the brilliance of their many attorneys, the railroads lost the first round in the state and lower federal courts. The Wisconsin, Iowa, Minnesota, and Illinois laws all survived constitutional tests; eight cases from the Midwest were then appealed to the Supreme Court.[13] The first to reach the Court was *Winona & St. Peter Railroad Co.* v. *Blake,* a Minnesota case docketed during the fall of 1873. Related cases from the other states followed, the Illinois case being somewhat unusual. Unlike the others which involved state-chartered corporations, it involved an unincorporated partnership unable to contend that the regulatory laws unconstitutionally impaired the obligation of contracts by limiting a charter-granted right to set rates. Ira Munn and George L. Scott, operators of a Chicago grain warehouse called the Northwestern Elevators, sought to reverse a conviction and a $100 fine for illegally operating without a license and for charging rates higher than those prescribed by the 1871 Illinois Warehouse Act.

All cases, however, raised a common question: the extent of the legislative power to regulate business. This was the crucial issue and it emerged repeatedly in the briefs and in the individual oral arguments heard by the Court during its 1875 term. Chief Justice Breese of the Illinois Supreme Court had upheld the state's right, under its "inherently unlimited legislative power," to prescribe maximum rates for warehousemen Munn and Scott. Moreover, his opinion insisted that regulation which might possibly impair the value of property

[11] John Denison to Jacob B. Jewett, Oct. 15, 1875; to N. W. Beckwith, April 7, 1873; James M. Walker to Denison, July 10, 1874, in Cochran, *Railroad Leaders,* p. 308, 390; James G. Randall (Ed.), *The Diary of Orville Hickman Browning* (Springfield: Illinois State Historical Society, 1933), II, 423, cited hereafter as *Browning Diary.*

[12] James M. Walker to Charles E. Perkins, May 16, 1874, in Cochran, *Railroad Leaders,* p. 489. Extracts from the Hoar-Curtis-Evarts opinions appear in "The Wisconsin Railroad Acts," *American Law Review,* IX (1874), 55–62.

[13] In 1873 the Illinois Supreme Court invalidated a regulatory law due to some minor deficiencies. *C. & Alton R. Co.* v. *Illinois,* 67 Ill. 11. The law, promptly repassed to meet the objections, was subsequently upheld. For the reason as to why Illinois' railroad legislation was not included among the *Granger Cases* see Fairman, "Granger Cases," 623.

was not confiscation in violation of the Fourteenth Amendment's due process clause. The opinion cited numerous instances where the Illinois legislature had regulated property and throughout emphasized legislative discretion in selecting means to further the public welfare.[14] Here, in sharp outline, was a challenge for the nation's business leaders to whom governmental interference was anathema—except, of course, when the interference favored them with generous charters, protective tariffs, and land grants. To fill the breach caused by Judge Breese's opinion and lower-court decisions in the other *Granger Cases*, the railroads rushed in a veritable battalion of talented lawyers. The roll call of their attorneys reads like a "Who's Who" of the post-Civil War American bar: Orville H. Browning, Edwin W. Stoughton, William C. Goudy, William M. Evarts, David Dudley Field, John W. Cary, Charles B. Lawrence, John N. Jewett, Silas W. Sanderson, Burton C. Cook, and Frederick T. Frelinghuysen.[15]

From this great reservoir of legal brilliance came a flood of arguments that had nonetheless a basic consistency. First, the attorneys flatly denied the right of state legislatures to regulate the prices charged by railroads and warehouse operators. As bars to such regulation they relied most heavily on the "genius and spirit" of American institutions and the Fourteenth Amendment's guarantee that states were not to deprive persons of liberty or property without due process of law. These, presumably, provided vested property rights with a preferred position against governmental meddling. Second, they urged a consideration of policy, forecasting dire results if the legislation was permitted to stand. The Granger laws, one attorney declared, were "the beginning of the operations of the commune in the legislation of this country." Not quite so, corrected another, who compared the laws with Communism: "the latter divides property ratably between the plundered and the plunderers, while the former takes all for the Grangers." [16] Third, as all good lawyers must, they bombarded the laws with subsidiary arguments; these were drawn

[14] Transcript of Record, pp. 3185–3187, *Munn* v. *Illinois*, 94 U.S. 113 (1877).

[15] Useful sketches appear in Fairman, "Granger Cases"; Twiss, *Lawyers and the Constitution*.

[16] John W. Cary, Brief and Argument for Appellants, p. 83; Edwin W. Stoughton, Statement and Points for Appellants, p. 17, *Peik* v. *C. & N. W. R. Co.*, 94 U.S. 164 (1877).

from the state constitutions and especially from the federal constitution's contract and commerce clauses.

Somewhat outclassed by the star cast of railroad attorneys, James K. Edsall, Luther S. Dixon, and Marsena E. Cutts served as able defenders of the states' interests. Backed by an impressive chain of lower-court victories they quietly urged that by regulating powerful monopolies the laws promoted the general welfare. Any person who pursued a public calling and enjoyed such a position "that the people must of necessity deal with him" on his terms, Illinois Attorney General Edsall contended, was liable to rate regulation in order to prevent extortion and abuse of position.[17] This the railroad attorneys vehemently denied, but their position was difficult. Railroads had frequently benefited from state and federal land grants, while during the 1860's and 70's the Supreme Court repeatedly upheld the issuance of tax-supported county and municipal bonds designed to aid railroads on the reasonable theory that they were constructing public highways.[18]

The railroads tried hard to minimize these recognitions of the public character of their business. Granted, they said, the roads were built for public use and subject to police regulations in the interests of safety but the "ownership is exclusively in the Company. It is their right to operate and control it in their own way." [19] Nor could a legislature declare that a private business was of such public concern as to warrant state control. "Who, until now, ever heard of making private property public by a constitutional or legislative declaration," exclaimed John N. Jewett in the Illinois warehouse case:

> [I]s it within the scope of legislative power to make a private business a public office, and private property the seat of its exercise, and then impose terms thereon? . . . The entire community are interested in the trades and employments of the cobbler and the tailor. Declare them by constitutional provision or legislative enactment, to be public officers, and we have then, public cobblers and public tailors,

[17] Edsall, Argument, p. 47, *Munn* v. *Illinois.*

[18] E.g., *Gelpcke* v. *Dubuque,* I Wallace 175 (1864); *Olcott* v. *The Supervisors,* 16 Wallace 678 (1873); Fairman, *Miller,* ch. ix. The general pattern of aid is described in Carter Goodrich, *Government Promotion of American Canals and Railroads* (New York: Columbia University Press, 1960).

[19] Cary, Brief, p. 32, *Peik* v. *C. & N. W. R. Co.;* C. B. Lawrence, Brief and Argument, pp. 18–28, *Winona & St. P. R. Co.* v. *Blake,* 94 U.S. 180.

> with compensation fixed by law. The ridiculousness of this result may be no argument against its possibility; but the bare statement of it is repugnent [sic] to a constitution which does not permit slavery. . . .[20]

An even more difficult task was to explain away the numerous past instances of state-regulated prices. At one time or another Illinois fixed compensation for the use of public ferries, public mills, hackmen, and draymen; regulated the weight and price of bread; and set interest rates for the loaning of money.[21] Price regulation was a commonplace in English law and equally familiar in American practice. During the Revolution eight of the rebelling states passed laws regulating the price of almost every commodity in the market, and while these acts were clearly war measures, positive state action in the economic field continued well into the nineteenth century.[22] There was more boldness than accuracy in William Goudy's opening statement in the *Munn* case:

> For the first time since the Union of these States, a legislature of a State has attempted to control the property, capital and labor of a private individual, by fixing the prices he may receive from other private persons, who choose to deal with him.[23]

Past instances of price regulation were distinguished as "exceptions to the principles upon which our government has been administered." Interest rate laws, said Goudy, grew out of the "peculiar relation" of money to government which made and issued it "and therefore is primarily subject exclusively to government control"; regulation of ferry and mill tolls had their origin in the prerogatives of the Crown which granted the franchises; as for the regulation of draymen and hackmen, this was an acknowledged part of the English common law

[20] Further Argument, p. 23, *Munn* v. *Illinois*.
[21] Opinion of C. J. Breese, Transcript, p. 3187, *Munn* v. *Illinois*.
[22] Franklin D. Jones, "Historical Development of the Law of Business Corporations," *Yale Law Journal*, XXXV (1926), 906–920; Note, "State Regulation of Prices under the Fourteenth Amendment," *Harvard Law Review*, XXXIII (1920), 838–839; Oscar and Mary F. Handlin, *Commonwealth Massachusetts 1774–1861* (New York: New York University Press, 1947); Louis Hartz, *Economic Policy and Democratic Thought: Pennsylvania 1776–1860* (Cambridge: Harvard University Press, 1948); James N. Primm, *Economic Policy in Missouri 1820–1860* (Cambridge: Harvard University Press, 1954).
[23] Brief and Argument, p. 1, *Munn* v. *Illinois*.

but "it has hitherto stood, solitary and alone, an exception to the theory and practice of our government."[24] In the famous *Income Tax Cases* of 1895 Joseph H. Choate called on the Court to correct "a century of error" by reversing its earlier rulings sustaining the constitutionality of federal income taxes.[25] In the *Granger Cases,* counsel asked the justices to reverse history itself.

This the Waite Court was not prepared to do. Contrary to the *American Law Review's* confident prediction that it would void the laws and "restore public confidence in the rights of private property, now severely shaken," [26] in March, 1877, Chief Justice Waite spoke for a seven man majority that upheld the states in every case. An undated memorandum he later prepared gives the sequence of events:

> Munn vs. Illinois
>
> argued Jan. 14, 18, 1876
>
> Railroad cases
>
> argued from Oct. 25 to Nov. 4, 1875—
>
> At the consultation on the 29th of April 1876 they were continued until the next term under advisement.
>
> ---
>
> At the consultation on the 14th of Oct, they were set down peremptorily for a final vote on the 18th of Nov.
>
> ---
>
> On the 18th of Nov. all the Judges except Field and Strong voted for the judgment in Munn vs. Illinois. The same vote was in all the other cases except in Winona & St Peter vs. Blake. Judge Clifford did not vote. My impression is his doubt rose on the question of contract in the charter.
>
> ---
>
> The opinions were prepared while the Electoral Commission was in session, and read in conference on the 26 of February. As Judge Davis was to leave the bench on the 4th of March the judgments were announced on Monday the 1st of March, and Judge Field was given leave to prepare a dissent at his leisure.

[24] Brief, pp. 37–47, *Munn* v. *Illinois.*
[25] 158 U.S. 601 (1895).
[26] "The Potter Act at Washington," *American Law Review,* IX (1874), 235.

> The opinion was printed in advance and considered carefully by all the Justices who concurred in the judgment, and also by Judge Strong [who dissented].[27]

In preparing his opinions Waite received valuable assistance from Justice Bradley. Shortly after the conference vote Bradley sent him a note:

> I have reduced my notes in the Granger cases into a sort of general *Outline of Views* on the questions involved. The authorities referred to, particularly, in the first portion may be of service to you. Make just such use of it as you please. I wrote it out to steady my mind and judgment, and to see how each proposition would appear on paper. I feel more than ever sure that our conclusion is right. And now I dismiss the cases from my mind except to hear your opinion, which I feel sure I shall approve, for I think we look at the subject much in the same point of view.[28]

The "Outline View" ran to twenty-three manuscript pages. It covered all the points at issue and entitles Bradley to recognition as co-author of the famous *Munn* opinion—a fact which Waite admitted when he returned it with the endorsement, "Had it not been for the within I could never have won your approbation of my own." [29]

Starting from the premise that the principal question was "whether the legislative authority extends to the regulation of the charges to be exacted for transportation on railroads, and for receiving and delivering grain in the Elevator Warehouses," Bradley—a former counsel and director of New Jersey's ruthless and monopolistic Camden and Amboy Railroad—stated the fundamental principle which decided the cases:

> Wherever a particular employment, or a business establishment becomes a matter of public consequence so as to affect the whole public and to become a '*common concern*' it is subject to legislative regulation and control. Whatever affects the community at large ought to

[27] In July–Dec. 1876 correspondence. Waite Papers.

[28] Bradley to Waite, Nov. 20, 1876.

[29] Discovered by Professor Fairman, the "Outline View" is published in the appendix (670–679) to his article on the "Granger Cases."

> be subject to such regulation, otherwise the very object of legislative power—the consulting of the general good—would be subverted. Unrestricted monopolies as to those things which the people must have and use, are a canker in any society, and have ever been the occasion of civil convulsions and revolutions. A people disposed for freedom will not tolerate this kind of oppression at the hands of private corporations or powerful citizens.[30]

To illustrate, he listed past instances of legislative rate regulation and showed that in England the common carriers had always been subject to regulation. He further pointed out that the English common law recognized the principle of rate regulation. Ever the legal antiquarian, Bradley dug up an obscure seventeenth century treatise, *De Portibus Maris,* and so introduced its author, Lord Chief Justice Hale, to American constitutional law. Concerned with the question of legal interests in seaports, Lord Hale reasoned that in a public port where "the king or subject have a publick wharf, unto which all persons that come to that port must come," the fees "for cranage, wharfage, pesage, &c." cannot be arbitrarily excessive:

> For now the wharf and crane and other conveniences are affected with a publick interest, and they cease to be *juris privati* only; as if a man set out a street in new building on his own land, it is now no longer bare private interest, but it is affected with a publick interest.[31]

Bradley quoted this language and, by way of historical analogy, noted that Lord Hale had applied it to public ferries and wharves. With the main problem—legislative power to regulate rates—resolved, he easily disposed of the railroads' remaining objections. Reasonableness of rates, he concluded, was a legislative, not a judicial, question; nor were the laws invalid because of the contract or commerce clauses. The corporations' charters in no way reserved for the railroads an exclusive right to set rates; finally, in the absence of congressional regulation, the states were free to regulate commerce within their borders.

[30] In Fairman, "Granger Cases," 670.

[31] In Fairman, "Granger Cases," 656. Lord Hale is discussed in Breck P. McAllister, "Lord Hale and Business Affected with a Public Interest," *Harvard Law Review,* XLIII (1930), 759.

Taking Bradley's exposition as a guide, Chief Justice Waite prepared his opinions while the country was worrying its way through the Hayes-Tilden disputed election crisis of 1876. He worked hard, anxious as usual to produce an acceptable opinion in what he knew was a case of major importance. Later he wrote, it "kept my mind and hands at work all the time." [32] As soon as completed, the opinion was circulated among his brethren, who gave it a thoughtful reading. Samuel Miller returned it after "a careful consideration" saying, "I approve unreservedly of all you have said and I think it well said and equal to the occasion which is a very great one." He added one exception, noting that in the railroad cases he might say a few words to indicate that he reserved opinion as to the effect of possible congressional regulation of interstate commerce on the state laws.

In reply, Waite thanked him. "I confess that I am weak enough to feel pleasure when my friends are satisfied with what I have tried to do well." To meet Miller's objection he proposed adding a sentence suggested by Justice Swayne. The Court, it said, did not hold that "under the form of regulating state affairs" the states might impinge on Congress' power over interstate commerce, but, rather, that such infringement had not occurred in the cases at bar.

From Bradley who, as much as anyone, had plumbed the issues presented by the cases, also came an encomium:

> I listened very attentively to your opinion when you read it to me, and if any thing had struck me to correct, I should have called your attention to it. I have read over the proof again hastily. I see nothing I would wish to alter. I think it, as I said before, an admirable opinion —terse, correct, & safe.[33]

When one turns to Chief Justice Waite's opinion in *Munn* v. *Illinois* there is however a sense of letdown. The decision upholding in broad terms the legislative power to regulate business for the public interest, is surely one of the Supreme Court's memorable rulings. Yet, as Professor Felix Frankfurter commented, "even in his most famous

[32] Waite to D. M. Bain, Feb. 25, 1877, Letterbooks. With the exception of one memorandum giving some examples of state price regulation, none of his working papers remain. See July–Dec. 1876 correspondence. Waite Papers.

[33] Miller to Waite, late Feb. 1877; Waite to Miller, Feb. 24, 1877, Letterbooks; Bradley to Waite, Feb. 22, 1877.

opinion Waite lacked art." Style is not substance; when it came to substance Waite proved himself a first-rate lawyer and an able judge. But style can further substantive purposes and the lack of it was Waite's greatest handicap, largely responsible for his underrated status today. "Humdrum, matter-of-fact, dry lawyer's English unrelieved by the flashing word or the overtone of meaning," Frankfurter has well said, "is not likely to carry a judge's reputation down the stream of history." [34]

In an age when many public men vastly overrated their abilities —Roscoe Conkling and Matt Carpenter vainly imagined they were Daniel Webster—the Chief Justice was refreshingly frank about his limitations. "The difficulty with me is that I cannot give the *reasons* as I wish I could," he told Justice Field—a judge, incidentally, never handicapped by an inability to employ rhetoric on behalf of his objectives. To Justice Horace Gray, a good craftsman, he once wrote, "Can't you tell me the secret of your *style*. I wish I had it— Simple words properly used express so much." [35]

There is a second reason for the opinion's matter-of-fact quality. Despite its political and economic significance, the majority regarded their decision as unexceptional. A decision upholding laws which, as Bradley wrote in his "Outline View," do "little more than carry out, and give practical effect to, the Common Law" was no bold, new departure. In its very nature the opinion lacked the fervor characteristic of a call for a new constitutional interpretation. That, spiced with the drama of dissent, was reserved for Stephen J. Field's opinion which rattles with clever imagery and striking phrases. Waite's opinion was merely, in his own eyes, a reaffirmation of traditional principles of constitutional adjudication.

Chief Justice Waite's major assumptions in the *Munn* case—and they characterize his basic judicial position—followed those of his famous predecessor, Roger Brooke Taney. These were a recognition that property rights are not absolute, a broad view of the states' police powers, and a conscious deference to legislative policy judgments.

[34] Frankfurter, *The Commerce Clause under Marshall, Taney and Waite* (Chapel Hill: University of North Carolina Press, 1937), p. 79, 85, cited hereafter as Frankfurter, *Commerce Clause.*

[35] Waite to Field, April 28, 1882. Field Papers; Waite to Gray, Feb. 21, 1884. Horace Gray Papers, Supreme Court Library.

Members of a society, Waite declared, necessarily part with some of their privileges; government may pass laws "requiring each citizen to so conduct himself, and so use his own property, as not necessarily to injure another." This was the origin of the states' police powers which he defined by quoting Taney's celebrated statement in the *License Cases:* they "are nothing more or less than the powers of government inherent in every sovereignty to the extent of its dominions," the "power to govern men and things." [36] The ensuing laws of course might be unwise, power might be abused, but, said Waite in one of his few well-known statements, "For protection against abuses by legislatures the people must resort to the polls, not to the courts." [37]

Applying these assumptions to the cases at hand led him to uphold the legislation without reservation. From "time immemorial," he wrote, England and later the United States, had known price regulation. Never before had it been attacked as an unconstitutional interference with private property. Congress, though limited by the Fifth Amendment which contained a due process clause similar to that of the Fourteenth Amendment, twice passed laws (in 1820 and 1848) regulating the prices charged in Washington by private wharfs, chimney sweepers, operators of hackney carriages, wagoners, and auctioneers. Then, Waite gave what he called "the principles upon which this power of regulation rests":

> Looking . . . to the common law, from whence came the right which the Constitution protects, we find that when private property is "affected with a public interest, it ceases to be *juris privati* only." This was said by Lord Chief Justice Hale more than two hundred years ago . . . and has been accepted without objection as an essential element in the law of property ever since. . . .[38]

Here, obviously, Waite was borrowing from his brother Bradley's "Outline View," too freely, in fact. Where Bradley used Lord Hale's treatise in its historical context—to illustrate "merely one instance" of how price regulation had been justified—Waite converted it into *the* universal proposition governing legislative price fixing. Unless the

[36] 5 Howard 504, 583 (1847).
[37] 94 U.S. 113, 124, 133–134.
[38] 94 U.S. 113, 125–126.

public interest principle was meaningless, applying, as Justice Field feared, to every enterprise "engaging the attention and labor of any considerable portion of the community" in which the public had an interest,[39] Waite's usage implied two categories of business: those affected with a public interest, where regulation was permissible, and those not affected where, presumably, regulation was forbidden. A private letter Waite wrote shortly thereafter gave just such an interpretation:

> The great difficulty in the future will be to establish the boundary between that which is private, and that in which the public has an interest. The Elevators furnished an extreme case and there was no difficulty in determining on which side of the line they properly belonged.[40]

According to modern critics, this apparently mechanical distinction between the public and private spheres fatally marred the *Munn* opinion. Professor Charles Fairman laments Waite's bungling of Bradley's more precise reference to Lord Hale; it turned, he claims, what should have been a decisive opinion into "an unsatisfactory exposition of a monumental holding." [41] If this is so, Justices Miller and Bradley share the responsibility with Waite. Both wholeheartedly approved it after, in their words, "careful" and "attentive" study. Since they were then busy with their service on the Electoral Commission, it seems especially hard to believe that Bradley, who took so great an interest in the decision, would have let a faulty opinion slip by—had he detected any weaknesses.

The fact remains that the public-interest doctrine theoretically lends itself to contradictory purposes. "If the court may affect," a critic has written, "it may refuse to affect; if it may throw about an industry the cloak of public interest, it may refuse the covering of that protective garment." [42] Precisely this happened in the 1920's. The

[39] 94 U.S. 113, 141.

[40] Waite to James Sheldon, March 30, 1877, Letterbooks.

[41] Fairman, "Granger Cases," 656–659. It should be noted that Professor Fairman, to whom all students of the post-Civil War Court are indebted, did not have access to the Waite-Bradley-Miller correspondence on the *Munn* case when he prepared his article.

[42] Walton H. Hamilton, "Affectation With Public Interest," *Yale Law Journal*, XXXIX (1930), 1110; see also, McAllister, "Lord Hale," 767–768.

public-interest doctrine became twisted into a limitation on regulation as laissez-faire judges gave birth to a series of decisions striking down state regulatory laws.[43] But were these rulings legitimate progeny of Morrison Waite's opinion? The answer, surely, is No, for the votes cast in those decisions were products of a conception of the judicial function vastly at odds with that dominant on the Waite Court. *Munn* v. *Illinois*, after all, implicitly accorded the legislative branch of government a leading role in deciding which enterprises had acquired a public character; viewed as a whole, the opinion—its mood, its dicta, and, most of all, its conclusion—is a brief in behalf of judicial deference to legislative decisions. Moreover, this attitude of self-restraint characterized the handling of economic cases throughout Waite's tenure on the Court. If the public-interest doctrine had reactionary undertones, they were peculiarly latent. For more than four decades they slumbered until awakened by the property-conscious Chief Justice William Howard Taft and his like-minded colleagues; but their decisions against business regulation owed much to their conception of the judge's role and little to Waite's formulation.

Waite, to be sure, misapplied Lord Hale's remarks; he could as well have sustained the laws under the general power of legislatures to regulate in the public welfare. Even so, the public-interest doctrine, taken together with the general attitude of deference to legislatures which provides its proper setting, has its own force. The Chief Justice's concept of "business affected with a public interest" was pragmatic and flexible; by adding modern grain elevators and railroads to Lord Hale's category, he demonstrated just how flexible the doctrine could be.[44]

[43] *Wolff Packing C.* v. *Court of Industrial Relations*, 262 U.S. 522 (1924); *Tyson* v. *Banton*, 272 U.S. 418 (1927); *Ribnik* v. *McBride*, 277 U.S. 350 (1928); *Williams* v. *Standard Oil Co.*, 278 U.S. 235 (1929); and *New State Ice Co.* v. *Liebmann*, 285 U.S. 262 (1932), inverted the public interest doctrine so as to justify the overturning of various state laws regulating economic relationships.

[44] The question may also be raised as to whether Bradley's (or, for that matter, any) approach was invulnerable. The "Outline View" proposed that business be adjudged subject to regulation when it "becomes a matter of public consequence." But when was a business "of public consequence"? In fact, the "Outline View" suggested that the permissibility of regulation depended on the existence of monopoly conditions. In the *Sinking Fund Cases* (1879) he and Waite clashed on this very point, Bradley insisting that the public interest doctrine was limited to "practical monopolies." Dissenting at 99 U.S. 700, 747; cf., Waite's statement at 719. And see Brewer, J., dissenting in *Brass* v. *Stoeser* (1894), a case upholding grain storage

In other ways Waite's opinion showed the pragmatic bent which characterized his judicial attitude. Chicago's fourteen grain elevators, controlled by a mere thirty persons, stand at "the very 'gateway of commerce,' " to the East "and take toll from all who pass." "Their business most certainly," he continued,

> "tends to a common charge, and is become a thing of public interest and use". . . . Certainly, if any business can be clothed "with a public interest, and cease to be *juris privati* only," this has been. It may not be made so by the operation of the Constitution of Illinois or this statute, but it is by the facts. . . .
>
> For our purposes we must assume that, if a state of facts could exist that would justify such legislation, it actually did exist when the statute now under consideration was passed. For us the question is one of power, not of expediency. If no state of circumstances could exist to justify such a statute, then we may declare this one void, because in excess of the legislative power of the State. But if it could we must presume it did. Of the propriety of legislative interference within the scope of legislative power, the legislature is the exclusive judge.[45]

With the Illinois Warehouse Act sustained, the Granger railroad cases fell easily into place.[46] Most likely the Court chose *Munn* as its main vehicle of expression because it presented the issue of regulation free from the commerce question of continuous transportation through the states and free from any claim of contract rights under incorporation laws.[47] These issues the Court dismissed summarily. It rejected counsel's objection that the grain elevators were part of interstate commerce and hence beyond state control. Waite admitted that the roads had an impact beyond state lines, but ruled that until Congress undertook to legislate for interstate commerce the states

regulation in a non-monopolistic situation by reliance on the *Munn* doctrine. Brewer invoked Bradley's "practical monopoly" test to attack the legislation. 153 U.S. 391, 405.

[45] 94 U.S. 113, 132–133.

[46] Disposed of along with *Munn* were: *Chicago B. R. Co.* v. *Iowa*, 94 U.S. 155; *Peik* v. *C. & N. W. R. Co.*, 94 U.S. 164; *C., M. & St. P. R. Co.* v. *Ackley*, 94 U.S. 179; *Winona & St. P. R. Co.* v. *Blake*, 94 U.S. 180; *Coleman* v. *McIlrath, Recr. of the Southern Minnesota R. Co.*,—unreported—see Fairman, "Granger Cases," 621; *S. Minn. R. Co.* v. *Coleman*, 94 U.S. 181; *Stone* v. *Wisconsin*, 94 U.S. 181 (all cases 1877). Illinois' railroad legislation was sustained in *Ruggles* v. *Illinois*, 108 U.S. 526 (1883).

[47] Miller, J., in *Wabash* v. *St. L. & Pac. R. Co.*, 118 U.S. 569 (1886).

might regulate within their borders.[48] The claims under the contract clause, strenuously urged by the railroad attorneys, were turned aside with equal ease. Only an explicit permanent grant of power to set rates, unlimited by reservations in the incorporation laws and constitutions of the states, could block the states' rightful authority to regulate in the public interest.[49]

Although rooted in the common law and in historical practice, there was nevertheless something truly remarkable in this decision by a Republican Court during the nation's most capitalistic phase. For the first time and in broad terms it sustained state power to regulate business. Waite, "because the interests involved were so important," anticipated adverse criticism. Of the correctness of his decision he had no doubt: "The position taken seemed to me to be the only safe one. Necessarily the power is a dangerous one, but that may be said of all and any other in the hands of dishonest legislators." [50] Still, to offset potential criticism, Waite wanted it known that a solid seven-man majority supported the ruling. He therefore arranged to have it announced before the retirement of David Davis, who had been elected to the Senate.[51]

Justice Field, to whom every case involving property rights was an Armageddon where the forces of order and decency contended with those of anarchy, dissented with his customary vehemence. Waite's opinion was "subversive of the rights of private property." "If the power can be exercised as to one article, it may as to all articles, and the prices of everything, from a calico gown to a city mansion, may be the subject of legislative direction." [52] He informed David A. Wells "that the doctrine announced by the majority of the Court practically destroys the guaranties of the Constitution intended for the protection of the rights of private property." [53] Newspapers were more restrained. Except for a few (the New York *Tribune*

[48] *Peik* v. *C. & N. W. R. Co.*, 94 U.S. 164, 178.

[49] And he rejected the strained argument that the regulation impaired contract rights between the companies and their bondholders. *C., B & Q. R. Co.* v. *Iowa*, 94 U.S. 155, 161–163; *Peik* v. *C. & N. W. R. Co.*, 94 U.S. 164, 175–176.

[50] Waite to S. J. Andrews, March 27, 1877; to James Sheldon, March 30, 1877, Letterbooks.

[51] Undated Waite memorandum in July–Dec. 1876 correspondence.

[52] 94 U.S. 113, 136, 152.

[53] Field to Wells, June 29, 1877. David A. Wells Papers, N.Y. Public Library.

called the decision "an advanced guard of a sort of enlightened socialism"), editorial comment was favorable. The *Herald* of New York noted with satisfaction that the Supreme Court has weakened the power of the rapacious handful dominating the railroads; the Chicago *Inter-Ocean* believed "that any other view would leave the people wholly at the mercy of the railway and warehouse companies"; and most of the midwestern press adopted similar expressions.[54]

Nevertheless, for a momentous holding *Munn* v. *Illinois* attracted little attention.[55] In part this was a consequence of its being announced on March 1, 1877, during the Disputed Election crisis. Northern Democrats were still filibustering the electoral count; not until Rutherford Hayes' inauguration three days later did the tense nation breathe a bit easier. Even then all eyes stayed on the new President as he chose a Cabinet, withdrew federal troops from the South, and engaged in an internecine power struggle with the Conkling faction of his party. There was a second reason. By 1877 agrarian discontent had temporarily subsided. Following the bad times caused by the Panic of 1873, relative prosperity returned to the farm belt in the late seventies. This, together with inept organization in the farmers' movement, led to a decline of their most powerful body, the Patrons of Husbandry. In turn, the railroads made a comeback, and by the time they were validated by the Court, many of the Granger laws had been weakened or repealed.

This, however, was not the case in Iowa. The Court's decision in *C., B. & Q.* v. *Iowa,* affirming the Railroad Tariff Law of 1874, distressed Robert Harris, the president of the Chicago, Burlington & Quincy:

> I do not see how I can recommend our people to invest more in Railroads [in Iowa]. . . . Why should those who invest their means in useful business of providing transportation for their fellow citizens be the only persons whose property should have no protection under

[54] Some of the press opinion is sampled in Warren, *Supreme Court,* II, 581–589; Chicago *Inter-Ocean,* March 2, May 3, 1877; *Iowa State Register* (Des Moines), March 3, 31, 1877.

[55] Thus, the Chicago *Inter-Ocean* of March 2, 1877, buried its account of the cases in a short column on page five. Such midwestern papers as the Detroit *Free Press,* the Topeka *Daily Blade,* and the Dubuque *Times-Journal* ignored the cases during March 1877.

> the law? No matter what rates the Legislature may prescribe—however, *unreasonable* in reason—they become *in law* reasonable charges. Would any farmer or manufacturer or professional man be willing to submit his property to such control? [56]

Within a year the Burlington's property regained the protection of the laws: Iowa's railroads joined forces and by a judicious combination of cajolery, threats, manipulation of newspapers, and bribery induced the legislature to repeal the regulation law.[57] Leaders of other railroads agreed with the president of the Burlington but remained generally subdued until 1879 when Court rulings began hurting their pecuniary interests. As practical men concerned with immediate realities, they were not the sort to scatter their fire on what had temporarily become a dead issue.

Despite the initially mild reaction, contemporary opinion during the 1870's and 1880's regarded *Munn* v. *Illinois* as giving blanket approval to public regulation of the nation's economy.[58] It is therefore paradoxical that many twentieth century legal historians have depreciated Waite's opinion, describing it as something quite different from a powerful assertion on behalf of the legislative power. One scholar has called it "another of the landmarks in the growth of the judicial power"; to Professor Robert G. McCloskey the case has a "Janus-like character" because "the basic premise that the property right is ultimate was now fuzzily accepted." [59] *Munn* v. *Illinois* becomes, not a major victory for public regulation, but, instead, the ideological forerunner to *Lochner* v. *New York* (1905), that *bête noire* of the Progressives which denied states the right to limit working hours.[60] Why? In part the reasons are situational, stimulated by the inversion of the public-interest doctrine which occurred in the ten-year span between

[56] Harris to Brown, Metelman and Company, March 27, 1877, in Cochran, *Railroad Leaders*, p. 350.

[57] Fairman, "Granger Cases," 615–616.

[58] See the writings of Thomas C. Cooley cited in Twiss, *Lawyers and the Constitution*, pp. 37–38; William M. Foster, "Doctrine of Property Affected by a Public Interest," *Yale Law Journal*, V (1895), 49; Charles C. Marshall, "A New Constitutional Amendment," *American Law Review*, XXIV (1890), 908; Christopher G. Tiedeman, *A Treatise on the Limitations of Police Power* (St. Louis: F. H. Thomas, 1886), pp. 235–236. Business reaction to the Waite Court is discussed in chs. xi–xii, *infra*.

[59] Benjamin F. Wright, *Growth of American Constitutional Law*, pp. 99–100; McCloskey, *American Conservatism in the Age of Enterprise*, pp. 79–80.

[60] 198 U.S. 45.

1924 and 1934.[61] But the primary source of the criticism is one sentence that Waite inserted in the opening part of his opinion. Counsel for the railroad and warehouse companies had insisted that the Granger laws violated the due process clause of the Fourteenth Amendment. Waite denied their claim but admitted that "under some circumstances" legislation might violate due process [62]—a boon, critics charge, to the proponents of laissez faire. It was, McCloskey writes, "a concession whose value was beyond emeralds and rubies," a back-handed recognition "that the due process clause of the Fourteenth Amendment imposed a substantive limit on economic legislation." [63]

This charge, which raises important questions about the Waite Court's relationship to business, merits exploration. Conventional accounts of Court history, for instance those of Edward S. Corwin and Benjamin F. Wright, portray due process as making a spectacular growth in the decisions of the seventies and eighties. They begin with the premise that the concept of due process has two distinct meanings. There is, first, procedural due process, which is limited to matters of procedure—notice, specific charges, fair hearings, and similar safeguards in judicial trials and administrative proceedings; second, there is substantive due process, which concerns itself with the essential wisdom and justice of governmental actions. It is then asserted that, while prior to the Civil War due process had largely a procedural content, during the postwar decades skilled corporation attorneys led a not unwilling Court to accept the Fourteenth Amendment's due process clause as a substantive limitation on public efforts to regulate business.[64] Although the crude "conspiracy theory" of the Fourteenth

[61] The cases are cited in note 43. The ruling in *Nebbia* v. *New York*, 291 U.S. 502 (1934), sustaining New York's program for regulating the milk industry buried the restrictive interpretation of the public-interest doctrine and marked a return to the permissive spirit of *Munn* v. *Illinois.*

[62] 94 U.S. 113, 125.

[63] McCloskey, *The American Supreme Court* (Chicago: University of Chicago Press, 1960), pp. 129–130.

[64] Among numerous works see, in addition to McCloskey, Edward S. Corwin, *Liberty Against Government* (Baton Rouge: Louisiana State University Press, 1948), ch. iv, which recapitulates his earlier articles on due process; Sidney Fine, *Laissez-Faire and the General Welfare State* (Ann Arbor: The University of Michigan Press, 1956), ch. v; Charles G. Haines, *The Revival of Natural Law Concepts* (Cambridge: Harvard University Press, 1930), ch. vi, and his, "The History of Due Process After the Civil War," in *Selected Essays on Constitutional Law* (Chicago:

Amendment—the Amendment as part of an evil capitalistic plot—has now been buried,[65] the conventional picture is that of a far more refined conspiracy: it opens with Thomas Cooley pointing the way to court-enforced censorship in his *Constitutional Limitations* (1868); continues with railroad attorneys, echoed by Justice Field, picking up the cry in the *Slaughter-House* (1873) and *Granger Cases* (1877) that the Fourteenth Amendment limits legislative regulation of property; and finally closes with Waite and his brethren—normally depicted as eager to give laissez faire an assist—gradually but stealthily adopting the doctrine until, in *Lochner* v. *New York* (1905), judicial reaction in the form of substantive due process is unfurled in all its glory.

On closer examination this version of the Waite Court's response to the due process clause becomes grossly unsatisfactory. Apart from numerous contradictions,[66] it fails to reckon with the fact that so-called substantive due process was widely accepted well before 1868, the year the Fourteenth Amendment was adopted. In its earliest days American constitutional interpretation recognized higher law limitations on governmental actions affecting property. Though not at first

The Foundation Press, Inc., 1938), I, 268; Twiss, *Lawyers and the Constitution;* Wright, *Growth of American Constitutional Law*, pp. 95–107.

[65] By the diligent research of Howard Jay Graham: "The 'Conspiracy Theory' of the Fourteenth Amendment," *Yale Law Journal*, XLVII–XLVIII (1938), 371 and 171; "Builded Better Than They Knew," *University of Pittsburgh Law Review*, XVII (1956), 537. Wallace Mendelson, "A Missing Link in the Evolution of Due Process," *Vanderbilt Law Review*, X (1956), 446, shows that the separation of powers concept, itself regarded by many judges as a natural limitation on legislative actions, was absorbed into state due process and law of the land clauses by many of the outstanding jurists of the ante-bellum period. Mendelson, however, 134–135, adopts the standard interpretation of the Waite Court's handling of due process.

[66] To cite only a few: why did Bradley repeatedly vote in favor of railroad regulation if, as charged (Wright, *Growth of American Constitutional Law*, p. 99; McCloskey, *American Supreme Court*, pp. 121–123), his *Slaughter-House* dissent made him an advocate of the Fieldian laissez-faire position? Do *Bartemeyer* v. *Iowa*, 18 Wallace 129 (1874) and *Loan Association* v. *Topeka*, 20 Wallace 665 (1875) really, as the writers in note 64, *supra*, indicate, represent striking reversals—in less than two years!—of Judge Miller's position in the *Slaughter-House Cases*, 16 Wallace 36 (1873)? Field was persuasive, but is it logical to assume he could so easily shift Miller, himself an exceptionally strong-minded judge? Why is it reasonable to emphasize (Twiss, *Lawyers and the Constitution*, p. 121, 136) Justice Harlan's majority opinion in *Mugler* v. *Kansas*, 123 U.S. 623 (1887), *upholding* an exercise of regulatory power as a verbal steppingstone to *Lochner* v. *New York*, 198 U.S. 45 (1905), a case in which Harlan registered a powerful dissent? Why not attach equal importance to his dissent in *Bowman* v. *Chicago*, 125 U.S. 465, 509 (1888), where he gave a broad statement of the police power?

included under the rubric of due process, these higher or natural law limitations, thanks to the craftsmanship of such judges as Ruffin, Kent, Marshall, and Story, soon found their way into state and federal reports.[67] Before long, however, due process notions (in addition to the federal, most state constitutions included "due process" and the related "law of the land" clauses) began rapidly absorbing a higher law content. By 1860, spurred by the slavery crisis in which both camps brandished due process arguments in seeking to put the stamp of illegality on opponents, due process as a substantive restriction on government was a major element in the climate of opinion. Far from deriving from professional legal usage, public acceptance, as Howard Jay Graham has shown in a carefully documented study, "preceded, stimulated, and at times unquestionably conditioned use by the Bench and Bar." [68]

When Waite and his associates, men well-versed in the slavery arguments of the 1840's and 1850's, confronted the natural law-due process claims pressed in *Munn*, they were meeting an old friend, not a suspicious stranger. Already it had received almost casual acceptance at the hands of some justices, so casual as to lend support to the explanation that due process as a limitation on government was a widely received idea.[69] Beyond this, the entire "procedural" versus "substantive" dichotomy (a categorization unknown to the law reports of the post-Civil War period) has the air of fiction about it.[70] And, it might be added, of modern value judgments—"procedural" conjures up the

[67] Corwin, *Liberty Against Government*, pp. 92–115; Haines, *Revival of Natural Law Concepts*, ch. iv.; Lowell J. Howe, "The Meaning of 'Due Process of Law' Prior to the Adoption of the Fourteenth Amendment," *California Law Review* XVIII (1930), 583; Mark DeWolfe Howe, "A Footnote to the 'Conspiracy Theory,'" *Yale Law Journal*, XLVIII (1939), 1007.

[68] Graham, "Procedure to Substance—Extra-Judicial Rise of Due Process, 1830–1860," *California Law Review*, XL (1952–1953), 483, 500, and "The Early Antislavery Backgrounds of the Fourteenth Amendment," *Wisconsin Law Review*, Vol. 1950, 479–507, 610–661; Jacobus Ten Broek, *The Antislavery Origins of the Fourteenth Amendment* (Berkeley: University of California Press, 1951).

[69] Baldwin, J., concurring in *Groves* v. *Slaughter*, 15 Peters 449, 515 (1841); Taney, C. J., in *Bloomer* v. *McQuewan*, 14 Howard 539, 553–554 (1853) and *Dred Scott* v. *Sandford*, 19 Howard 393, 450 (1857); Chase, C. J., in *Hepburn* v. *Griswold*, 8 Wallace 603, 624 (1870); Miller, J., in *Bartemeyer* v. *Iowa*, 18 Wallace 129, 133–134 (1874).

[70] A point argued by Walter Berns, *Freedom, Virtue and the First Amendment* (Baton Rouge: Louisiana State University Press, 1957), pp. 95–102; John P. Roche, "American Liberty: An Examination of the 'Tradition of Freedom,'" in Milton R. Konvitz and Clinton Rossiter (Eds.), *Aspects Of Liberty* (Ithaca: Cornell University Press, 1958), pp. 148–149.

niceties of English justice; "substantive" brings to mind visions of robber barons and their bought lawyers sinisterly beguiling the Court into making property its main concern.

A more persuasive explanation of what happened on the postwar Supreme Court would be this: that, from the very beginning, *all* of the justices regarded due process as furnishing protection against any purely arbitrary actions by government, irrespective of whether the arbitrary act occurred in a trial or in a regulation of property. There is then no inconsistency between Bradley's dissent in the *Slaughter-House Cases* (1873) and his position in *Munn* (1877); between Miller's due process-higher law assumptions in *Bartemeyer* v. *Iowa* (1874) and *Loan Association* v. *Topeka* (1875) and his numerous votes upholding economic regulation; between Waite's supposed concessions to "substantive" due process and his repeated affirmations of state regulatory power.[71] To Waite and his associates the notion of "procedural" and "substantive" due process was essentially irrelevant. What divided them was not due process, but their conflicting views of the nature of the judicial function. Activists like Field were far more willing to cry "violation of due process" and rush in with a judicial remedy; while limitationists like Waite and Miller were much less prone to see such violations, trusting the political process to provide its own self-correctives in economic disputes.

Upon this theory, the declaration in *Munn* v. *Illinois*, that "under some circumstances" regulation of property might violate the Fourteenth Amendment, loses the significance with which it has been retrospectively endowed. In its historical context the Chief Justice's words were but a brief reply to the fanciful allegations heard in the case. For the business attorneys had painted a truly bleak picture of what would follow if the Court upheld the Granger laws: new, more tyrannical laws would ultimately put all enterprises and the private fortunes of individual citizens "in the power of a disorderly mob";

[71] Repeated judicial expressions during the period support this interpretation of due process as a generalized safeguard against any flagrantly arbitrary behavior by public authorities, e.g., Bradley, J., dissenting in *Slaughter-House Cases*, 16 Wallace 36, 122 (1873); Field, J., in *Pennoyer* v. *Neff*, 95 U.S. 714, 733 (1878); Miller, J., in *Davidson* v. *New Orleans*, 96 U.S. 97, 101–102 (1878); Matthews, J., in *Hurtado* v. *California*, 110 U.S. 516, 528–536 (1884), an exceptionally good statement of the justices' shared consensus on due process.

warehousemen might be forcibly compelled to store grain without charge; all services and private property would be absorbed into public use.[72] Said one attorney:

> If it [the state] possesses the power at all, it possesses it absolutely and without supervision, and it can reduce compensation to a rate which would barely pay operating expenses. Nay, it might go further, and reduce to a rate which would not pay operating expenses; and then, having compelled the company to cease the performance of its duties, impose penalties for not performing them, and finally manage to take back both franchise and property, for the benefit of the public, but without compensation to the rightful owners.[73]

While these hysterical outbursts failed to sway Waite from his conviction that corporations were subject to regulation, he took note of them, assuring the businessmen that their enterprises were not endangered by arbitrary and unrecompensed confiscation. This assumption that legislative action must not be completely arbitrary still has the Court's support—although the constitutional regulatory problems of yesteryear are today only a memory.[74]

The *Munn* declaration on due process reappeared in subsequent regulation cases, proof, according to many scholars, of the Waite Court's mounting solicitude for the welfare of business. In the *Sinking Fund Cases* (1879) Waite indicated that the Fifth Amendment's due process clause barred unrecompensed federal repossession of its land grants.[75] Much the same thing happened in *Spring Valley Water Works* v. *Schottler* (1884) where the Court sustained a change in the mode of determining the rates charged by a chartered company supplying a municipality with water. The Court's decision turned on contract questions; Waite construed the charter narrowly and supported the municipality's right to alter the rates. As in *Munn*, distinguished

[72] Jewett, Argument, pp. 15–16, 35–36, and Further Argument, p. 20, *Munn* v. *Illinois.*

[73] C. B. Lawrence, Brief and Argument, p. 64, *Winona & St. P. R. Co.* v. *Blake.*

[74] Robert L. Stern, "The Problems of Yesteryear—Commerce and Due Process," *Vanderbilt Law Review,* IV, (1951), 446. Even the reverse of the famed Holmes-Brandeis position—given a state of facts which could lead reasonable men to believe the legislation justified it is presumptively valid—clearly implies this: for if no state of facts exists to support the presumptive validity then, because unreasonable or arbitrary, the legislation may be invalid.

[75] 99 U.S. 700, 718–719.

counsel pressed the due process argument by predicting dire results if the municipality won.[76] Again Waite noted that the basic question was the power to fix prices at all and made the quite unexceptional acknowledgment:

> What may be done if the municipal authorities do not exercise an honest judgment, or if they fix upon a price which is manifestly unreasonable, need not now be considered, for that proposition is not presented by this record.[77]

The most notable of Waite's alleged concessions appears in the *Railroad Commission Cases*.[78] In 1884 Mississippi created a Railroad Commission to supervise and set rates (allowing for a fair and just return) for railroads operating within its borders. Arguing due process grounds, but relying primarily on what they claimed were inalienable charter rights, the companies attacked the regulation. Ignoring the usual exaggerations about communism and the destruction of property —standard fare in these economic cases—the Court, Justices Field and Harlan dissenting, upheld the law. Chief Justice Waite for the majority found no positive grant in the charters which guaranteed an exclusive right to set rates; the power of government, if it can be bargained away at all, "can only be by words of positive grant. . . . If there is reasonable doubt, it must be resolved in favor of the existence of the power." [79]

As the Chief Justice originally prepared the opinion, first in a longhand draft and then in the printed proof sheets for circulation, little was said of due process. He denied that Mississippi's statute violated the Fourteenth Amendment, observing, as in the earlier cases, that general laws setting railroad rates were permissible. Waite's papers show that four other justices besides himself—Miller, Bradley, Matthews, and Gray—voted in conference to uphold the laws. Blatch-

[76] George F. Edmunds, Brief and Oral Arguments, pp. 9–10, p. 19; Francis G. Newlands, Oral Argument, pp. 36–42, *Spring Valley Water Works* v. *Schottler*, 110 U.S. 347 (1884).

[77] 110 U.S. 347, 354; Waite makes a somewhat similar declaration in *Railroad Co.* v. *Richmond*, 96 U.S., 521, 529 (1878).

[78] 116 U.S. 307 (1886). *Santa Clara County* v. *Southern Pacific R. R. Co.*, 188 U.S. 394 (1886), often cited as evidence of the Waite Court's growing concern for corporate property, is considered in ch. xi.

[79] 116 U.S. 307, 325–326.

ford did not participate and Field, Harlan, and Woods dissented. Although Woods may have changed his mind (he did not dissent publicly) the majority in favor of the regulation was a somewhat uncertain five to three. No doubt this was in Waite's mind when he circulated his draft opinion. Bradley and Miller raised no objections, suggesting only a minor change, which Waite adopted.[80] But another member of the majority, Stanley Matthews, after first writing "No objections & no suggestions—S.M." on his copy of the draft, crossed it over and sent the Chief Justice a note:

> In the Embargo cases, it was held that the power of Congress to regulate foreign commerce included the power to destroy: and it was said in Osborne v Bk U.S. by Marshall C.J. that the power to tax, if permitted to the State in respect to agencies of the Federal government would carry with it the power to tax out of existence. But in these cases the powers referred to, were viewed as unlimited by any other principle.[81]
>
> But the power of a State legislature to regulate the charges of Railroad companies or carriers is limited by other principles.
>
> One limitation is, that the regulation shall not be equivalent to confiscation, by requiring property devoted to such a public use to be used by the public or individuals, or part of the public, without just compensation: another limitation is that the regulation shall apply so as not to deprive the party complaining of the equal protection of the laws, by discriminating in favor of some at the expense of others.[82]
>
> S.M.

Stanley Matthews of Ohio was an old acquaintance of the Chief Justice, one of former President Hayes' closest political associates, and a good lawyer, making it more than likely that Waite would weigh his advice seriously. Before coming to the Court in 1881 Matthews served as attorney for some of the nation's most powerful railroads, and in fact his appointment was made for that reason.[83] On the Court he proved himself independent, yet naturally, as his note

[80] Bradley to Waite, probably early Jan. 1886, Legal File, Oct. Term 1885, Docket Book, Oct. Term 1885. Waite Papers.

[81] *United States* v. *The William*, 28 Fed. Cas. 614 (1808); *Gilchrist* v. *Collector*, 10 Fed. Cas. 355 (1808); *Osborne* v. *Bank of the United States*, 9 Wheaton 739 (1824).

[82] Matthews to Waite, probably early Jan. 1886, Legal File, Oct. Term 1885. The initials "SM" are, of course, also Samuel Miller's but the handwriting is Matthews'.

[83] Ch. xii, *infra*.

suggests, he opposed outright confiscation of railroads. For that matter, so did Waite. He promptly accepted Matthews' suggestion—though surely he was not unmindful of the fact that if Matthews changed his mind and joined the dissenters, the five to three vote upholding the regulation would become a four–four vote affirming a lower-court order in favor of the railroads.

Waite therefore composed a qualification indicating that the regulatory power did not extend to confiscation. The first version read:

> From what has thus been said it is not to be inferred that this power of limitation or regulation is itself unlimited. Carriage for hire implies pay, return, reward, for the reasonable expenses and trouble of the carriage. To deprive a carrier of this would be to confiscate not to regulate his charges. Practically, therefore, the power of the state is confined to charges in excess of the reasonableness of the carriage; that is to say to the reasonable profits of the business.

He then revised this into the form in which it appears in the opinion:

> From what has thus been said it is not to be inferred that this power of limitation or regulation is itself without limit. This power to regulate is not a power to destroy; and limitation is not the equivalent of confiscation. Under pretence of regulating fares and freights the state cannot require a railroad corpora[tion] to carry persons or property without reward; neither can it do that which in law amounts to a taking of private property for public use without just compensation,—or without due process of law. What should have this effect we need not now say, because no tariff has yet been fixed by the commission, and the statute of Mississippi expressly provides "that in all trials of cases brought for a violation of any tariff of charges, as fixed by the commission, it may be shown in defence that such tariff so fixed is unjust." [84]

However fuzzy the notion of reasonableness may seem in the light of the Court's later unhappy experiences with the doctrine of reasonable rates,[85] Waite's statement, added as an afterthought to assuage fears that the Court would sanction confiscation, is totally un-

[84] Notes, Legal File, Oct. Term 1885. In the *Railroad Commission Cases* the statement appears at 116 U.S. 307, 331.

[85] Beginning with *Smyth* v. *Ames,* 169 U.S. 466 (1898).

deserving of its reputation as a retreat from *Munn* v. *Illinois* and a leading concession to laissez faire.[86] There would indeed appear to be great wisdom in Professor Frankfurter's warning: "One must be on his guard against recreating history by hindsight and attributing to the language of an early doctrine the implications which the evolution of experience has put into it." [87]

Even aside from the preceding evidence garnered from a detailed look at decisions—an exercise which always smacks a little of pedantic logic-chopping—an impressive case can be made for the proposition that the Waite Court never became, wittingly or unwittingly, a tool of business. Whatever the eventual significance of the *doctrinal statements* appearing in its opinions, the *actual decisions* clearly pointed in the direction of support for public regulation. After all possible interpretations have been canvassed it is well to remember that *Munn* v. *Illinois*, the *Sinking Fund Cases, Spring Valley Water Works* v. *Schottler*, and the *Railroad Commission Cases* were decided in favor of public regulation. In recognition of this stubborn fact, as the following chapters show, the country's business leadership launched a subtle but nonetheless potent attack against the Waite Court. Apparently, Waite's verbal assurances that due process barred arbitrary regulation failed to relieve the businessman's pain at losing specific cases.

On the other side, Populist and working-class interests found relatively little to criticize in the Supreme Court's performance during the seventies and eighties.[88] Only after the changes in its composition that came in the 1890's did the Court arouse Populist wrath by becoming a bastion for the forces of capitalism.[89] With the departure of judges like Waite, Miller, and Bradley and the advent of Fuller,

[86] Thus, McCloskey writes, Waite "seized the occasion" of the *Railroad Commission Cases* to put substantive due process into the Constitution because he believed it "might prove very useful in the cause of righteousness." *American Supreme Court*, pp. 130–131. And see, Corwin, *Liberty Against Government*, p. 131; Haines, "History of Due Process After the Civil War," 276. Cf., Fairman, "Granger Cases," 661–666. Professor Fairman is one of the few scholars to minimize the significance of Waite's statements on due process.

[87] Frankfurter, *Commerce Clause*, p. 60.

[88] A partial exception must be made for the municipal bond cases discussed in ch. xi.

[89] Arnold M. Paul's recent study, *Conservative Crisis and the Rule of Law* (Ithaca: Cornell University Press, 1960), reinforces the proposition that the Court's response to the claims of business remained in doubt until the 1895 term.

Brewer, and Brown came victory for Stephen J. Field. Through more than two decades he had waged a powerful though unsuccessful campaign for his view that the Fourteenth Amendment was the guardian angel of vested property rights. Field scored an important gain in 1890 when a divided Court invalidated the procedure by which the Minnesota Railroad Commission set rates. Dissenting and with undue exaggeration, Bradley claimed the majority had overruled the *Munn* case.[90] Although a most ambiguous decision, its key elements appeared to be that a legislature could not delegate its rate-setting power to a commission which would then set conclusive rates, i.e., rates not open to challenge in the courts.[91] In almost all of the earlier cases the rates, whether set by legislature or commission, were only prima-facie evidence of reasonableness and hence open to challenge in the courts. Whatever the correct interpretation of the case, the pendulum swung back again in *Budd* v. *New York* (1892) and *Brass* v. *Stoeser* (1894) where the principle of regulation won victories.[92]

Ultimately Field enjoyed a satisfaction accorded few prophets: that of seeing his views vindicated during his own lifetime. Four years before his death the Court struck down the federal income tax and gravely weakened the Sherman Anti-Trust Act.[93] The year was 1895 and it serves as a useful, admittedly arbitrary, benchmark to indicate victory for the Fieldian position. In the years following there were, to be sure, exceptions and periods such as the second decade of the twentieth century when regulatory legislation fared comparatively well. In general, however, after that date and until the upheaval of the late 1930's federal regulatory laws were frequently voided by means of constricting interpretations of the commerce and taxing powers. At the same time judicial invalidation of state actions under the Fourteenth Amendment rose dramatically—to cite just one example, of fifty-five rulings in which the Court reversed state actions

[90] *C., M. & St. P. R. Co.* v. *Minnesota*, 134 U.S. 418, 461 (1890).

[91] *M. & St. L. R. Co.* v. *Minnesota*, 186 U.S. 257 (1902), upheld the law in its revamped form which gave the Commission power to set rates that would be prima-facie evidence of reasonableness in the state's courts.

[92] 143 U.S. 517; 153 U.S. 391.

[93] *Pollock* v. *Farmers' Loan & Trust Co.*, 158 U.S. 601 (1895); *United States* v. *E. C. Knight*, 156 U.S. 1 (1895).

under the Amendment during the entire period 1872–1910, forty-six came between 1896 and 1910.[94]

Field marched victorious but the spirit of judicial self-restraint symbolized by Waite's opinion in *Munn* v. *Illinois* was not quite "a'mouldering in the grave." That opinion had applied to state regulation, the most important kind in 1877, but its implications were broad: it denied to vested property interests a preferred position in the American constitutional system, assumed that legislative policy judgments overrode judicial policy judgments, and insisted that factual realities deserved the Court's highest respect: in short, it allowed for power to regulate in the public welfare. In the great twentieth century dissents of Holmes, Brandeis, and Stone these assumptions would remain alive. Oliver Wendell Holmes and Morrison R. Waite were unlike in many ways. Yet in his dissents urging judicial tolerance for the legislative process and a respect for factual realities, the polished intellectual with an articulate judicial philosophy was close in spirit to the unspectacular lawyer from northwest Ohio. With *NLRB* v. *Jones & Laughlin Steel Corporation* (1937), when after a long struggle the Supreme Court finally upheld the economic regulation of the New Deal, that spirit of self-restraint again triumphed.

"The question is one of power, not expediency," Waite once wrote. "We must assume that, if a state of facts could exist that would justify such legislation, it actually did exist." Who can deny that the concept behind Morrison Waite's simple declarations has not been vindicated?

[94] Charles W. Collins, *The Fourteenth Amendment and the States* (Boston: Little, Brown and Company, 1912), Appendix C; Frankfurter, *Mr. Justice Holmes and the Supreme Court* (Cambridge: Harvard University Press, 1938), Appendix 1.

II

ECONOMIC CASES AND CONTROVERSIES

The Justices and the New Industrialism. A Certain Coolness.
The Chief Justice as "Nihilist." Attitudes Toward Regulation.
Waite v. Field. Cases and Controversies.
Municipal and State Bonds. Readjusters and Repudiators.
Commercial Regulations. Capitalists Criticize the Court.
Justice Field, Railroad Lobbyist. California Tax Cases.
Laissez Faire and Legal Trends.

IN ECONOMIC MATTERS THE WAITE COURT DISPLAYED INDIFFERENCE to the claims for special constitutional protection submitted by the nation's economic leaders. For one thing, its judges lacked any real commitment to the immense concentrations of financial and corporate property which appeared after the Civil War. For another, all of the fourteen men who at one time or another made up the Waite Court grew to maturity in Jacksonian America, and most of them retained their democratic faith. As a perceptive student once noted, many of the Waite Court's members

> had been lawyers for great financial interests. But practice had not yet become specialized. They had been lawyers for ordinary men as well. They shared the ordinary man's anxiety as to the effect upon him of industrial expansion and the concentration of wealth. . . . They wanted the great new United States to be rather an enlargement than a subversion of the United States in which they had grown up. . . . Conditions being new, legislation must be experimental. Legislative power must therefore be comparatively free.[1]

Allowing for the gaps left by a generalization, this is an apt characterization of the Waite Court. Almost all of its strongest members, Waite, Miller, Bradley, Harlan, Matthews, and Gray, were political moderates—ex-Whigs and Democrats turned Republican. With the exception of Matthews, they did not owe their appointments to corporate influence. None fits the stereotype of the railroad attorney

[1] Walter Nelles, Book Review of Swisher's *Field, Yale Law Journal,* XL (1931), 999.

of the 1880's and 1890's. Moreover, much of their professional and political experience had been at the state level. They were receptive to local intervention in economic affairs, whose importance during the post-Civil War period far exceeded that of the national government. Only Field falls outside this general pattern. The fervor of his basic commitment to a liberty (which did not, however, embrace the Negro) that included property rights as one of its crucial elements led him to adopt the position that the judiciary was its ultimate preserver.[2] Even with Field generalizations must be tempered: he often voted against the claims of bondholders, on occasion favored railroad regulation, and, with Waite, opposed a rigid application of the harsh fellow-servant rule, which left injured workmen without protection against the consequences of industrial accidents.[3]

The Chief Justice himself best typifies the Court's attitude toward the new industrialism. Morrison Waite moved with ease among the nation's social and economic elite. He often visited New York's very Republican Union League Club, allowed railroads to provide him with special cars, and commonly accepted their passes.[4] (Needless to say, he remained quite uncorrupted—though the railroad leaders may have thought him a bit ungrateful when they read his opinions.) Certainly he was not at war with the main assumptions of American capitalism—that stable property rights are essential in the good society, that individual initiative can be the way to wealth for most men, and that the profit motive is an honorable one. But neither was he slave to the materialistic Gospel of Wealth expounded by William Graham Sumner and practiced by Leland Stanford. With his roots in Old Lyme, his classical education and upbringing in the home of a respected judge, and his later experiences in a close-knit frontier com-

[2] Graham, "Justice Field and the Fourteenth Amendment," discusses Field's motivations. Note should also be taken of Justice Strong. Until his retirement in 1880 he sided with Field on most economic issues. In 1884 Strong commended Field on his dissent in *Spring Valley Water Works* v. *Schottler*, saying, "My opinion of . . . [*Munn*] has not changed." Strong to Field, Feb. 21, 1884. Field Papers.

[3] Representative cases include: (bonds) *County of Warren* v. *Marcy*, 97 U.S. 96 (1878); *Scipio* v. *Wright*, 101 U.S. 665 (1880); *Anthony* v. *County of Jasper*, 101 U.S. 693 (1880); (railroads) *Missouri Pac. R. Co.* v. *Humes*, 115 U.S. 512 (1885); *Georgia R. Co.* v. *Smith*, 128 U.S. 174 (1888); (fellow-servant) *C., M. & St. P. R. Co.* v. *Ross*, 112 U.S. 377 (1884); *Vicksburg & Meridan R. Co.* v. *O'Brien*, 119 U.S. 99 (1886).

[4] Rail passes in Waite Papers; Edward S. Martin, *Joseph H. Choate* (New York: C. Scribner's Sons, 1920), I, 316.

munity where personal honesty and character mattered as much as business acumen, Waite represented the ante-bellum class of professional and mercantile men to whom wealth was not an end in itself.

As with the civil rights question, Waite's outlook paralleled that of Rutherford Hayes. During the 1880's the ex-President, who had been called upon to face the Railroad Strike of 1877—the first nationwide labor disturbance produced by the new industrialism—became increasingly concerned about the power of corporate wealth.[5] At his home in Fremont, Ohio, Hayes read widely, absorbing the ideas of Henry George's *Progress and Poverty* and the vague socialism of William Dean Howells. He condemned the disparity of wealth existing between the industrial plutocracy and the masses and told his confidant, the newspaperman William H. Smith, that even a monopoly such as Standard Oil, which paid good wages, was "offensive." According to Hayes, it destroyed competition, menaced individual liberty, and threatened to "seize political power and usurp the functions of the State." This probably was a harsher judgment than Waite would have made; nevertheless, Hayes was able to quote the Chief Justice as saying "the dollar has too much to say in the affairs of the Republic." In 1886 when he asked Waite's opinion of the New York mayoralty campaign which pitted Henry George against Abram S. Hewitt, Tammany's candidate, and a rising young politician named Theodore Roosevelt, Waite declared his support of "the protest against the dangerous tendencies of the times." "The dollar," he said,

> is too much regarded; character and humanity too little. I will give you an illustration that but recently came to my knowledge. My son [Christopher C. Waite] is President of a railroad [the Cincinnati, Hamilton & Dayton], a corporation so prosperous that its securities have been invested in by guardians and executors for the benefit of children and widows, and by trustees and agents charged with the responsibility of trust funds. One day a lady entered my son's office and said: "A man has been twice to see me and has advised me to sell my stock. He says that new parties are coming into control, and when the change is made the value of the stock will be depressed. What shall [I] do?"

[5] His growing radicalism is recorded in Barnard, *Hayes*, pp. 513–518, and *Hayes Diary*, IV, 348, 354–355, 374, 556, 621, and 637.

> My son replied that he knew nothing of any such movement; that he did not believe it could or would be done, and advised the lady not to sacrifice her investment. Before the day closed two other stockholders made inquiries to the same effect, and within two weeks a new and mischievous power had gained control of this fine property for the purpose of plunder. The wrong was effected through combination and it is through combination and consolidation of wealth in the hands of bad men that evils threaten society. If the Henry George movement only results in compelling discussion, it will accomplish great good.

This answer, the ex-President playfully remarked, showed that the Chief Justice, "the proper representative of things established," was in reality "a nihilist." [6]

The picture ought not to be exaggerated. Waite's condemnation was directed against the speculative manipulations of hucksters and operators like "Jubilee Jim" Fisk and Jay Gould. Honest, conservatively operated businesses, which earned legitimate profits by providing goods and services, had his warm approval. The distinction between the rapacious and exploitative capitalism of the Gilded Age and the commercial enterprises of the ante-bellum period may be subtle and somewhat arbitrary, but it was clearly felt, not only by Waite but by some of his most intelligent colleagues. Samuel Miller denounced "the united, vigorous, and selfish effort of the capitalists," a class "but recently known in this country" who "engage in no commerce, no trade, no manufacturing. They *produce nothing*." Joseph Bradley told Waite of his contempt for the "modern Shylocks and Railroad Smashers" who "wish to grab everything—the fruits of the poor laborer and everything else—and make the courts their servant, or cats paw to pull the chestnuts out of the fire." [7] Given this coolness, this lack of commitment, toward the new capitalism, Waite was able to view legislative economic experimentation with detachment. Moreover, his frontier background in Ohio had left him with a faith that the people know best; he came to the Court favorably disposed

[6] Hayes used "nihilist" as a synonym for "reformer." This account is drawn from a private memorandum prepared by William H. Smith, Dec. 14, 1887. Hayes Papers.

[7] Miller to William P. Ballinger, April 28, 1878, in Fairman, *Miller*, p. 67, pp. 300–302; Bradley to Waite, (n.d.). Bradley Papers. Bradley was referring to a railroad mortgage opinion which Waite was preparing.

to the legislature, the branch of government which stood closest to the mass of men.

Stephen J. Field, Waite's great antagonist, had a totally different conception of his function as a judge. Fearing the collectivism of communism—whose challenge he perceived in such diverse events as the Paris Commune, the Granger movement, and miners' strikes in his native California—and having enjoyed a spectacularly successful career as an individualist, Field came to see the people as a mob of rabble highly susceptible to the suasions of demagogues. He sought therefore to enlarge the judicial function, believing that only the judiciary could save the people from themselves. As he told his fellow judges on the occasion of his retirement in 1897, the Supreme Court "possesses the power of declaring the law, and in that is found the safeguard which keeps the whole mighty fabric of government from rushing to destruction. This negative power is the only safety of a popular government." [8]

Waite conceived of his function as being much narrower. He did not, to paraphrase Justice Harlan F. Stone, assume that courts were the only agency of government with the capacity to govern. And when they did govern, he hoped they would do so modestly. Sending a railroad mortgage opinion to a district judge, Waite commented:

> Perhaps they [sic] settle nothing. Certainly they lay down no inflexible rule. My only object was to begin a foundation on which something might be built. In my judgment the fault of Judges sometimes is to try and make too much law at once. The true rule is to feel the way, and not be afraid to draw back if the ground will not hold you up.[9]

Dislike for the rapaciousness of the new capitalism, confidence in the people's capacity to govern, and a feeling that the function of judges was properly a limited one were, then, the judicial and social attitudes which shaped Morrison Waite's response in economic cases. To a large extent these were also the attitudes of his brethren. As a

[8] Mr. Justice Field to the Chief Justice and the Associate Justices, 168 U.S. 713, 717 (1897).

[9] Waite to Robert W. Hughes, March 25, 1879, Letterbooks. The opinion was *Fosdick* v. *Schall*, 99 U.S. 235 (1879).

result, the Waite Court turned a deaf ear to pleas that it curtail legislative interference in economic affairs by writing constitutional limitations into the law of the land.

There were of course exceptions, the most important involving the municipal bonds issued in aid of railroad construction. Eager for modern transportation, countless midwestern communities—wildly overestimating their economic resources and potentialities—attempted to spur railroad construction in the 1850's and 60's. In return for lavish subsidies in the form of long-term, high-interest bonds, rail and land companies promised to reward the local residents with an economic paradise created through the magic of the railroad. The promoters were often unscrupulous, obtaining issues by fraud, quickly unloading the bonds on unsuspecting creditors in the East, and then disappearing—leaving the hapless community in debt and without a railroad. In many regions the bond subsidies did finally bring the much desired transportation, but even then its cost was an excessive debt that soon proved an intolerable burden. When agricultural depression began gripping the Midwest in the late 1860's, and farmers came to realize that the railroad's presence did not guarantee an economic utopia, they retaliated by defaulting on interest payments and repudiating the legality of the bonds.[10]

State courts in Iowa, Wisconsin, Michigan, and Missouri, whose elected judges were responsive to local opinion, threw their support to the agrarian debtors. But the federal judiciary, led by the Supreme Court, set, as John F. Dillon described it, "a face of flint against repudiation," disallowing the efforts of most counties and municipalities to avoid redeeming their bonds. A long line of cases antedating the Waite period declared that the bonds constituted binding contracts whose impairment by subsequent legislation or constructions of the law violated Article I, section ten of the Constitution. Under Waite the same pattern continued, with the Court deciding for the bondholders in most of the approximately two hundred bond cases it heard between 1874 and 1888.[11] From these decisions Justice Miller

[10] John F. Dillon, *Commentaries on the Law of Municipal Corporations* (Boston: Little, Brown and Company, 1890), I, 227–228; A. M. Hillhouse, *Municipal Bonds* (New York: Prentice-Hall, Inc., 1936), chs. ii, vii.

[11] Warren, *Supreme Court*, II, 678.

furiously dissented, privately accusing the majority of being as much "bigots and fanatics" on the subject as "the most unhesitating Mahemodan in regard to his religion." [12]

For his part, the Chief Justice, believing that the bonds involved "a principle of commercial honor," [13] usually supported the bondholders. Despite Miller's protests, Waite was hardly fanatical in his approach to these cases and often denied the validity of municipal bond issues.[14] On balance, though, the Chief Justice did his share to expand the blanket of protection with which the Court sheltered the bondholders. He joined the majority in an important series of closely divided decisions which held that bona fide bondholders might collect even though the recitals made in the bonds by municipal officers were, in effect, false.[15] In *Douglass* v. *Pike County* Waite broadened the contract clause's protection of bondholders by holding that when a state court reversed its earlier constructions of statutes authorizing bond issues, the new interpretation could apply only prospectively: to allow it to apply retroactively would impair contract rights accrued under the old rulings.[16] Whatever the merits of these decisions, the issues were complex and the equities confused. Not all virtue was with the agrarian communities, nor were the bondholders, many of whom were innocent purchasers, the personification of evil. The Court, for better or worse, tipped the judicial scales in the latter's favor.

If the justices set faces of flint against municipal repudiation, they showed feet of clay when it came to state repudiation. The facts were roughly comparable to those in the municipal bond cases except that

[12] Miller to Ballinger, Feb. 3, 1877, in Fairman, *Miller*, p. 232. Leading pre-Waite Court cases include *Knox County* v. *Aspinwall*, 21 Howard 539 (1859); *Gelpcke* v. *Dubuque*, 1 Wallace 175 (1864); *Olcott* v. *The Supervisors*, 16 Wallace 678 (1873).

[13] Dissenting in *Town of South Ottawa* v. *Perkins*, 94 U.S. 260 (1877).

[14] E.g., Waite, C. J., in *McClure* v. *Township of Oxford*, 94 U.S. 429 (1877); dissenting in *United States* v. *County of Clark*, 96 U.S. 211, 218 (1878); in *United States* v. *County of Macon*, 99 U.S. 582 (1879); in *Anthony* v. *County of Jasper*, 101 U.S. 693 (1880).

[15] Statutory authority existed for the bond issues, but, contrary to the recitals, municipal officers had failed to comply with certain conditions prescribed by state law. *Town of Coloma* v. *Eaves*, 92 U.S. 484 (1876); *Town of Venice* v. *Murdock*, 92 U.S. 494 (1876); *Town of Genoa* v. *Woodruff*, 92 U.S. 502 (1876); *Humboldt Township* v. *Long*, 92 U.S. 642 (1876); Dillon, *Law of Municipal Corporations*, II, 592–599.

[16] 101 U.S. 677 (1888).

the debtors were Southern states bankrupted by the expenses of war and Reconstruction. Faced with public debts of close to $50 million, states such as Virginia and Louisiana sought to ease their financial burdens by reducing the interest and scaling down and postponing the payments. Despite the aggrieved cries of creditors, these actions were not outright repudiation. They had, nonetheless, the characteristics of class legislation, drawing their support from economically depressed farmers, low-income urban groups, and, where they participated in political life, from Negroes. Virginia's colorful General William Mahone led a Readjuster Movement, which combined partial repudiation with a program of corporate taxation, railroad and insurance regulation, higher wages for mechanics, political appointments for Negro supporters, and generous grants to public schools. In South Carolina the Populist leader, Martin Gary, courted popularity by lashing out at "elegant, smooth-mannered, oily-tongued bond holders, bond speculators" and bankers who insisted on "Quixotic schemes of public honesty." [17]

Although creditors won some minor victories,[18] most of their suits came to naught. One court action, the unreported case of *South Carolina, ex. rel. Douglas & Jackson* v. *Gaillard* (1880), is especially noteworthy. It did not technically involve state bonds, but had a direct bearing on the entire relationship between states and their creditors. In 1868 South Carolina passed a law giving holders of bills issued by the defunct State Bank of South Carolina until January 1, 1869, to exchange them for new but devalued state bonds. Since these bank bills previously had been admissible as payment for state taxes, many of the holders refused to turn in their bills, and over $400,000 worth remained outstanding. To prevent their use for tax payments, the state in the late 1870's passed legislation forcing bill holders to go through a cumbersome procedure before they could pay taxes with

[17] Jarrell, *Wade Hampton and the Negro*, p. 126; Charles C. Pearson, *The Readjuster Movement in Virginia* (New Haven: Yale University Press, 1917), pp. 144–147; William L. Royall, *History of the Virginia Debt Controversy* (Richmond: G. M. West, 1897). For a general history of the state debt problem see William A. Scott, *The Repudiation of State Debts* (New York: T. Y. Crowell and Company, 1893).

[18] *Board of Liquidation* v. *McComb*, 92 U.S. 531 (1876); *Hartman* v. *Greenhow*, 103 U.S. 672 (1881).

the old bank bills. Among other things, it prohibited use of the common law mandamus procedure for the purpose of compelling tax collectors to accept the bills. Because mandamus proceedings had been available to the bill holders when the bills were originally issued, they claimed that the state's elimination of this remedy impaired the obligation of its contract. The state disagreed, saying that a remedy such as mandamus was no part of the contract and that the legislature, believing many of the outstanding bills to be fraudulent, had good reason for not wanting its tax collectors to accept them. A defeat in the state courts led the creditors to appeal to the Supreme Court. They retained some well-known lawyers, Roscoe Conkling, Daniel H. Chamberlain, and William B. Hornblower, to handle their case, which was heard in mid-November, 1879.[19]

At the conclusion of argument five justices, Waite, Clifford, Miller, Bradley, and Harlan, voted to support the state; the Chief Justice assigned himself the opinion. On January 3, 1880, however, the Court, Waite and Miller dissenting, ordered a reargument. Clifford then switched his vote, and since Justice Hunt was ill and unable to participate, the state's position was affirmed by an equally divided Court and Waite's opinion never read. It is a strong statement, giving his basic position in these bond cases: that the states enjoyed wide latitude in using their taxing power (important because many of the disputed statutes revoked the admissibility of bonds and interest coupons in payment of taxes) and that changes in remedies for enforcing the bonds' validity did not violate the contract clause. Beyond this, the Chief Justice made clear that the spirit of *Munn* v. *Illinois* dictated a broad view of legislative powers:

> In all cases of this kind . . . the question becomes one of reasonableness, and of that the legislature is primarily the judge. . . . We ought never to overrule the decision of that department of government, unless a palpable error has been committed. In judging of that, we must as far as possible put ourselves in the place of the legislators, and pass upon their actions in the light of the circumstances which

[19] *State* v. *Gaillard*, 11 S.C. 309 (1879); U.S. Supreme Court Records and Briefs. Vol. 101, pp. 407–472.

> surrounded them: for what is reasonable in a particular case depends on its particular facts. If a state of facts could exist which would justify the change in the remedy that was made we must presume it did exist, and that the law was passed on that account.[20]

This reasoning guided the Court in most of the state bond cases decided during the 1880's. In *Antoni* v. *Greenhow* (1883) Waite spoke for the majority in ruling that Virginia's changes in the mode of enforcing its bonds were not a violation of the contract clause.[21] Two years afterwards in the *Virginia Coupon Cases* the bondholders succeeded in getting a bare majority of the Court to draw an artificial line between "state" and "government" and so uphold certain forms of proceedings against tax collectors. Waite, Miller, Bradley, and Gray dissented, charging that the proceedings were really suits in violation of the Eleventh Amendment.[22] *In re Ayres* (1887), however, ruled that the amendment forbade injunctions to stop the enforcement of Virginia's "coupon crusher" act of 1887; the act required the State Attorney General to prosecute taxpayers who tendered coupons in payment of taxes. Prodding by the Court in a subsequent case finally jogged the state and its creditors into reaching a settlement, thus ending a decade of legal maneuvers.[23]

Creditors from other states suffered similar reverses.[24] Waite's declaration in the important case of *Louisiana* v. *Jumel* that mandamus actions to compel the state's officers to honor its bonds could not be maintained because "the political power cannot be . . . ousted of its jurisdiction and the judiciary set in its place" brought an angry protest from Justice Field:

[20] Undelivered opinion of Chief Justice Waite in *State* v. *Gaillard;* Docket Books, Oct. Term 1879; Manuscripts and Proofs of Opinions, Oct. Terms 1874–85. Waite Papers. For contemporary discussion of the case see *American Law Review,* I (1880), 361; N.Y. *Times,* May 7, 1880.

[21] 107 U.S. 769 (1883).

[22] Eight cases reported at 114 U.S. 269 (1885), and the companion case of *Royall* v. *Virginia,* 116 U.S. 572 (1886), in which Waite, Miller, Bradley, and Gray withheld their conference room dissent. Docket Book, Oct. Term 1885. Waite Papers.

[23] *In re Ayres,* 123 U.S. 443 (1887); *McGahey* v. *Virginia,* 135 U.S. 662 (1890), hastened a compromise settlement. Royall, *Virginia Debt Controversy,* pp. 95–96.

[24] *New Hampshire* v. *Louisiana,* 108 U.S. 76 (1883); *Cummingham* v. *Macon & B. R. Co.,* 109 U.S. 446 (1883); *Hagood* v. *Southern,* 117 U.S. 52 (1886).

> Is this inhibition [the contract clause] against the repudiation by the State of her engagements of any efficacy? The majority of the Court answer No. I answer, adhering to the doctrines taught by a long line of illustrious judges preceding me, "Yes, it is. . . ." I dissent from the judgment of my associates, and I shall continue to do so on all proper occasions, until the prohibition inserted in the Constitution as a barrier against the agrarian and despoiling spirit, which both precedes and follows a breach of public faith, is restored to its original vigor.[25]

Besides upholding state power to regulate railroads and alter the rights of creditors, the Waite Court sustained a variety of local regulatory laws despite claims that they violated the Fourteenth Amendment's due process clause, conflicted with the contract clause, or infringed on Congress' power over interstate commerce. Quarantine regulations, wharfage fees for public docks, prohibitions on the sale and manufacture of liquor, and condemnation of businesses that were a public nuisance all won judicial approval.[26] Laws repealing earlier grants of monopolistic privileges were upheld in decisions taking a broad view of the states' police powers. Speaking for the Court in *Stone* v. *Mississippi*, a case which ranks among the leading modifications of the *Dartmouth College* doctrine, Chief Justice Waite laid down the principle that states might repudiate charter rights (in this instance to operate a lottery) deemed harmful to the public welfare. "No legislature can bargain away the public health or the public morals," said Waite, for "the power of governing is a trust committed by the people to the government, no part of which can be granted away." [27]

The Court, however, invalidated a number of state laws for conflicting with the federal commerce clause. It did so selectively, voiding state and local regulations only when they appeared to discriminate against national interests. While there was no wholesale

[25] 107 U.S. 711, 728, 733 (1883).

[26] *Morgan's Steamship Co.* v. *Louisiana*, 118 U.S. 455 (1886); *Transportation Co.* v. *Parkersburg*, 107 U.S. 691 (1883); *Beer Co.* v. *Massachusetts*, 97 U.S. 25 (1878); *Mugler* v. *Kansas*, 123 U.S. 623 (1887); *Fertilizing Co.* v. *Hyde Park*, 97 U.S. 659 (1878).

[27] 101 U.S. 814, 819–820 (1880); also *Butcher's Union Co.* v. *Crescent City Co.*, 111 U.S. 746 (1884).

invalidation of regulation, the justices of the seventies and eighties took a positive stand in favor of national free trade. They wanted commerce to be unhampered by state and local legislation, which was often designed to protect regional interests under the guise of police power regulation. The Court's decisions were not animated by hostility toward public regulation of business; after all, a mass of state commercial regulation had judicial sanction. "With consistent caution," James Willard Hurst has observed, the justices "refused to adopt extreme doctrine as to the 'exclusive' range of national commerce power, in years when it was politically most unlikely that Congress would fill the gap left by the end of state regulations." Laissez faire, to paraphrase Hurst, was apparently not a concealed motive in the Waite Court's commerce clause decisions.[28]

Waite agreed to the invalidation of these regulations much less frequently than the Court majority. Only when convinced that the laws penalized national commerce would he vote to overturn them.[29] On this issue he clashed with Miller, whose view that commercial exchange should be free from state and local restrictions dominated the Court. In a case striking down a Pennsylvania tax on auction sales, which taxed foreign goods at a higher rate than local ones, Waite supported Miller's opinion but thought it too broad. As he told Miller, he would have upheld the constitutionality of the tax if it was not discriminatory:

> Is not the question of tax on imports one of intention, and if there is no discrimination against foreign goods, and the charge is in form upon the business, will it not be presumed that the intention was to tax the business and not the goods. The discriminations prove the intent to place the burden upon the goods and not upon the business.[30]

Miller kept his broad language and Waite acquiesced, but a similar disagreement in *Cannon* v. *New Orleans* ended with Miller modi-

[28] James Willard Hurst, *Law and the Conditions of Freedom* (Madison: University of Wisconsin Press, 1956), pp. 50–51. Waite Court decisions voiding state and local laws on commerce clause grounds include *Welton* v. *Missouri*, 91 U.S. 275 (1876); *Henderson* v. *New York*, 92 U.S. 259 (1876); *Chy Lung* v. *Freeman*, 92 U.S. 275 (1876); *Pensacola Tel. Co.* v. *W. U. Tel. Co.*, 96 U.S. 1 (1878); *Wabash, St. L. & Pac. R. Co.* v. *Illinois*, 118 U.S. 557 (1886).

[29] E.g., *Welton* v. *Missouri; Henderson* v. *New York; Chy Lung* v. *Freeman.*

[30] Waite to Miller, Oct. 30, 1878, Letterbooks; *Cook* v. *Pennsylvania*, 97 U.S. 566 (1878).

fying his language. In conference Waite and Hunt dissented from the majority's determination that a certain tonnage fee, allegedly intended to cover wharfage costs, was in fact an evasion designed to tax out-of-state vessels. Miller wrote an opinion acknowledging that while states might charge for legitimate costs, such charges, because prohibited by the Constitution, might not be in the "particular form" of tonnage fees. The actual prohibition was against "any duty of tonnage" (Article I, section ten), and Waite, a fact-conscious judge, rebelled against Miller's suggestion:

> Whatever is a tax or duty cannot be apportioned according to tonnage. But compensation *for actual service rendered* or facilities afforded by the city or state may be. . . . Such a charge may be made according to the size of the vessel whether by the ton as such or the measurement.[31]

Both judges compromised. Miller removed the offending language, leaving open the question as to the proper form of wharfage charges; Waite (and also Hunt) withheld from dissenting—a good illustration of the interplay that lies behind Court decisions as well as of Waite's dislike for deciding more than the essential minimum.

This split over the extent of state power in interstate commerce deepened in the mid-1880's and forced Waite to dissent from the Court's increasing tendency to limit regulation within state boundaries. By far the most significant of these limitations was Miller's opinion in *Wabash, St. L. & Pac. R. Co.* v. *Illinois* (1886), which prohibited the regulation of long- and short-haul-rate discrimination in interstate commerce and spurred Congress into passing the Interstate Commerce Act of 1887. Waite's dissent from this holding emphasizes his extreme deference to local authority, and, as Professor Frankfurter has remarked, his pragmatic dislike for "the abstraction of 'exclusive' power in Congress in vacuo." [32] But once Congress acted, he took a gen-

[31] Emphasis added to Waite's notation on Miller's draft opinion. Manuscripts of Opinions, Oct. Terms 1874–85. Waite Papers; *Cannon* v. *New Orleans*, 20 Wallace 577 (1874).

[32] Frankfurter, *Commerce Clause*, p. 101. Ch. iii is a brilliant discussion of the commerce clause under Waite. In addition to the *Wabash* case, 118 U.S. 557, (1886) Waite dissented from the limitations on state power contained in *Robbins* v. *Shelby County Taxing District*, 120 U.S. 489 (1887), and *Bowman* v. *C. & N. W. R. Co.*, 125 U.S. 465 (1888).

erous view of its powers. His opinions in *Pensacola Tel. Co.* v. *W. U. Tel. Co.* and *Newport and Cincinnati Bridge Co.* v. *United States*, decisions which Field vigorously opposed, represent notable expansions of federal power. So also did Waite's opinion in the *Sinking Fund Cases*, which gave Congress broad regulatory power over federally chartered corporations.[33] Other Waite Court decisions upheld Congress' power to establish civil service regulations, levy income taxes, and make treasury notes legal tender in time of peace. The legal tender ruling led Justice Field to protest that "what was in 1862 called 'the medicine of the Constitution' has now become its daily bread." And an aroused George Bancroft, who bluntly informed Waite that the Court had made a grievous error, circulated a pamphlet asserting that the Constitution had been "wounded in the House of its Guardians." [34]

Bancroft's indictment reflected the disenchantment with the Waite Court felt by those whom Clinton Rossiter has described as "laissez-faire conservatives"—those who, from whatever motives, emphasized property rights and favored governmental laissez faire in the economic realm.[35] The tender regard displayed by the justices for the rights of municipal bondholders did little to alleviate the pain caused the nation's economic leaders by the Court's decisions allowing states to tamper with their debts, permitting railroad regulation, and sanctioning broad congressional power over federal corporations and interstate commerce. Indeed, if as often charged, the Fieldian position was on the verge of triumph in the 1880's, those most eager for its success lived in complete ignorance of their coming success. Quite the contrary, conservative interests and property-minded publicists were convinced that the Supreme Court had embarked on a revolutionary course dangerous to the security of capitalist property.

Of the economic interests antagonized by the Court, none felt

[33] 96 U.S. 1 (1878); 105 U.S. 470 (1882); 99 U.S. 700 (1879); also, *Head Money Cases*, 112 U.S. 580 (1884). Field's concern over the *Cincinnati Bridge* case is expressed in a letter to Waite, May 21, 1882.

[34] *Ex parte Curtis*, 106 U.S. 371 (1882); *Springer* v. *United States*, 102 U.S. 586 (1881); *Julliard* v. *Greenman*, 110 U.S. 421, 458 (1884); Bancroft to Waite, May 6, 1884, in Mark A. DeWolfe Howe, *The Life and Letters of George Bancroft* (New York: C. Scribner's Sons, 1908), pp. 297–299.

[35] Clinton Rossiter, *Conservatism in America, The Thankless Persuasion* (New York: Vintage Books, 1962), ch. v.

more distressed than the railroads. Because many of the Granger laws upheld in *Munn* were virtually dead letters anyway, the decision did not sting the railroads as much as might have been expected. When the Court continued to sustain federal and state regulations over the vast economic empire that constituted the nation's rail system, the reaction became sharper. "It begins to look Pretty Certain that a RR entering the Supreme Court of the U.S. leaves hope behind," lamented the president of the Illinois Central, though he saw merit in one of Waite's suggestions:

> I am beginning to think that perhaps Mr. Chief Justice Waite was right in his declaration that railroads must look to the polls and not to the Courts, to have their wrongs redressed. There are upwards to 750,000 voters engaged on the Roads in the United States and $50,-000,000 of money added to this, would make a pretty strong party, if concert of action and co-operation were once had.[36]

Discouraging as the Court's rulings were to corporate and financial interests, they had a powerful ally in Justice Field. Both on and off the bench he fought "the agrarian and nihilistic element" in the great contest "between civilization on the one hand and anarchy on the other." [37] He favored enlarging the Supreme Court to twenty-one members, most likely hoping that an infusion of new members would make possible a reversal of the majority's decisions. In 1884 his abortive campaign for the Presidency was motivated in part by his desire, as he said, to "have placed on the Bench able and conservative men and thus have brought back the decisions of the Court to that line from which they should not have departed." [38] Following his defeat in the state bond cases of *Antoni* v. *Greenhow* and *Louisiana* v.

[36] James C. Clarke to Stuyvesant Fish, Jan. 29, 1884; to James Fentress, Feb. 6, 1884, in Cochran, *Railroad Leaders*, p. 191, 297. Besides the *Granger Cases*, numerous rulings in the 1870's and 1880's hurt the railroads in their most sensitive area—the pocketbook. E.g., *Railroad Co.* v. *Richmond*, 96 U.S. 521 (1878); *Sinking Fund Cases*, 99 U.S. 700 (1879); *Ruggles* v. *Illinois*, 108 U.S. 526 (1883); *Missouri Pac. R. Co.* v. *Humes*, 115 U.S. 512 (1885); *Railroad Commission Cases*, 116 U.S. 307 (1886); *Dow* v. *Beidelman*, 125 U.S. 680 (1888).

[37] Field to Deady, April 8, 1885. Deady Papers.

[38] Field to Pomeroy, July 28, 1884. Field Papers. Graham, "Four Letters of Mr. Justice Field," *Yale Law Journal*, XLVII (1938), 1100–1108, is a useful annotation of Field's correspondence with Pomeroy. Field's economic attitudes are explored in Graham's "Justice Field and the Fourteenth Amendment."

Jumel, he arranged for his lawyer friend, John Norton Pomeroy, to write an article for the *American Law Review* "reviewing" the majority's recent decisions. Pomeroy's article, "The Supreme Court and State Repudiation," appeared in the October 1883 issue of the journal and also in pamphlet form where it attracted wide attention. Praising Field's dissenting opinions, it savagely attacked the doctrines of constitutional interpretation which, according to Pomeroy, had been dominant since Waite's appointment. The flavor of his "review" of the Court's work may be judged by his comments on *Munn* v. *Illinois:*

> No other decision has ever been made in the course of our judicial history,—not even excepting the notorious Dred Scott case,—which threatens such disastrous consequences to the future wealth and prosperity of the country. . . . [I]ts doctrine involves the *very essence* of the destructive theories maintained by the socialists and communists of France and Germany. . . . It is relied upon as an authority to sustain and validate the communistic legislation already enacted by several of the States. . . . [T]he step from the property of corporations to that of private persons is a short and easy one; it will soon and certainly be taken, *for it has already been taken by the Supreme Court.* The Dred Scott Case indirectly struck at the stability of our political fabric; the Elevator Case directly strikes at the stability of private property,—at rights which lie in the very foundation of modern society and civilization.[39]

While at the national level Field's eloquent dissents in the *Slaughter-House*, *Granger*, and *Sinking Fund* cases comforted conservatives with the thought that at least one justice spoke for sanity, he also worked hard to make these dissents law in his far western ninth circuit. When California agrarian and working-class groups pushed through laws regulating and steeply increasing the tax liability of the Pacific railroads, Field did his best to thwart the legislation. Unable to convince California courts that the Fourteenth Amendment barred the new tax assessments, the Central Pacific and Southern Pacific Railroads—well aware of Field's sympathies—decided to try the federal courts. The Justice did not disappoint them: he recommended to

[39] *American Law Review*, XVII (1883), 712; Field to Pomeroy, March 28, 1883. Field Papers.

Collis P. Huntington and Leland Stanford that they hire Pomeroy to defend them (they did, for $10,000 a year). Next, Field turned around and heard the San Mateo County tax case. Accepting the arguments of Pomeroy and a bevy of high-priced attorneys, he then delivered an opinion supporting the railroad position. The tax, Field declared, was prohibited by the Fourteenth Amendment which protected all persons, natural and corporate, from being deprived of their life, liberty, and property without due process.[40]

San Mateo County appealed to the Supreme Court in 1883 and so provided the occasion for Roscoe Conkling's historic oration on the meaning of the Fourteenth Amendment. To bolster the railroads' claim that the amendment afforded them comprehensive immunity from state regulation, Conkling relied on his prestige as a former member of the Joint Congressional Committee on Reconstruction which had drafted the amendment. Misquoting from its secret journal, he shrewdly implied that Congress deliberately intended to protect corporations from hostile state actions and intimated that the amendment's framers meant the word "person" to include corporations. Field found the oral argument "great," adding, "The written pages want the fire of the speaker which warmed and illuminated everything that was said." [41] Nothing, however, came of Conkling's argument, except, of course, for the now exploded conspiracy theory of the Fourteenth Amendment. The Court apparently suspected the accuracy of certain statistics submitted by the railroads and postponed decision. In 1885 the railroads, sensing defeat, hastily paid their taxes to the county in order to drop the litigation in favor of a new test case from Santa Clara County.[42]

A side effect of the *San Mateo Case* was the public criticism Field incurred for his close association with the owners of the Pacific railroads, an association which he himself emphasized by the "Chamberlin's dinner incident." Shortly after the completion of argument, Leland Stanford gave a dinner for Conkling, Silas W. Sanderson, and other Southern Pacific attorneys at Chamberlin's, a well-known Wash-

[40] Graham, "An Innocent Abroad: The Constitutional Corporate 'Person,'" *U.C.L.A. Law Review*, II (1955), 175–176, 180–194, cited hereafter as "Constitutional Corporate 'Person'"; *San Mateo County* v. *S. Pac. R. Co.*, 13 Fed. Cas. 722 (1882).

[41] Field to Deady, Feb. 18, 1883. Deady Papers.

[42] Graham, "Constitutional Corporate 'Person,'" 194–205.

ington restaurant. On the evening of the dinner Field went to call on his friend Sanderson, learned he had gone to Chamberlin's, and joined him there for a few hours of pleasant conviviality. The ensuing criticism included a damning cartoon accusing Field of making a mockery of justice. Waite, who valued the judicial proprieties, cut it out and marked it "Judge Field's dinner at Chamberlin's." Field was unperturbed. He wrote Pomeroy—whom he had given private information on the Court's deliberations in the *San Mateo Case*—that "so long as I retain a consciousness of having endeavored to do my duty, I shall not be troubled by what others say of my action." [43]

As with the earlier tax case, the litigation from Santa Clara County came to the Court on the wings of Field's circuit opinion holding for the railroads on the basis of the Fourteenth Amendment.[44] And again, as with the *San Mateo Case*, it failed to reach the constitutional questions. The justices did sustain the railroad but on technical grounds; Field, concurring, would have met the broad issues posed by the Fourteenth Amendment. *Santa Clara County* v. *S. Pac. R. Co.* (1886) has nonetheless been endowed with great constitutional significance because, just prior to oral argument, Chief Justice Waite told the attorneys that the Court was uninterested in a discussion as to whether or not the Fourteenth Amendment's guarantees to persons included corporations. All the justices, he said, agreed that it did.[45] The announcement, coming in 1886, is commonly cited alongside Waite's "concession" in the *Railroad Commission Cases* (1886) as evidence of the Court's growing conservatism.

But corporations had been regarded as natural persons under the common law since Coke's day, and a host of pre-Civil War cases indicated that corporations were either "citizens" or, alternatively, that, because their members were citizens, they could sue in the federal courts.[46] As a natural continuation of this trend, a number of

[43] Cartoon from a California journal, *The Wasp*, in Waite Papers; Field to Pomeroy, March 28, 1883; Swisher, *Field*, p. 257. In fairness it should be said that in the 1880's standards of "judicial morality" were more lax than today. Field, however, was particularly insensitive.

[44] *Santa Clara County* v. *S. Pac. R. Co.*, 18 Fed. Cas. 385 (1883).

[45] 118 U.S. 394, 396.

[46] Graham, "Constitutional Corporate 'Person,'" 159; Gerald C. Henderson, *The Position of Foreign Corporations in American Constitutional Law* (Cambridge: Harvard University Press, 1918), ch. iv.

significant decisions preceding the *Santa Clara* declaration implicitly assumed that corporations were persons.[47] In 1871 Congress itself matter-of-factly passed a routine bill to define words commonly used in legislation and directed that "in all acts hereafter . . . the word 'person' may extend and be applied to bodies politic and corporate." [48] What is significant here is that the assumption of corporate personality by legislators and judges was thoroughly natural. Waite and his associates sensed that corporations stood for powerful economic interests, yet they lived in an age when the full dimensions of corporate power were not well understood. Keep in mind that Berle and Means' pioneering study of the modern corporation was almost half a century away and it may be clearer why to the justices of 1886 corporations were still essentially aggregations of individuals participating in economic enterprises.[49]

Actually the key issue in the two California tax cases was not corporate personality—which the state's counsel largely ignored in the *San Mateo Case*—but the state's general power over railroads. Certainly Waite, who had assumed the existence of corporate personality in the *Granger Railroad Cases* and in his other opinions sustaining corporate regulation, regarded the question with casual concern as this exchange with the Court Reporter, Bancroft Davis, reveals. While preparing the report in the *Santa Clara* case Davis sent the Chief Justice a note:

> I have a memorandum in the California cases
>
> Santa Clara County
> v
> Southern Pacific &c &c
>
> as follows.
>
> In opening the Court stated that it did not wish to hear argu-

[47] E.g., *United States* v. *Insurance Companies*, 22 Wallace 99 (1874); *Peik* v. *C. & N. W. R. Co.*, 94 U.S. 164 (1877); *Railroad Co.* v. *Richmond*, 96 U.S. 521 (1878); *Sinking Fund Cases*, 99 U.S. 700 (1879). And see the discussion in Corwin, *Liberty Against Government*, pp. 193–194; Andrew McLaughlin, "The Court, the Corporation and Conkling," *American Historical Review*, XLVI (1940), 45.

[48] Chap. LXXI, sec. 2 of the Act of Feb. 25, 1871, *Congressional Globe*, 41st Cong., 3rd Sess. 341 (1871), and the discussions of the bill, 775 and 1473–1474. Credit for the discovery of this interesting legislative incident belongs to John P. Roche, and I am indebted to him for bringing it to my attention.

[49] That Waite thought along these lines finds support in a newspaper editorial de-

ment on the question whether the Fourteenth Amendment applies to such corporations as are parties in these suits. All the judges were of opinion that it does.

Please let me know whether I correctly caught your words and oblige.

Waite replied:

I think your mem. in the California Rail Road Tax cases expresses with sufficient accuracy what was said before the argument began. I leave it with you to determine whether anything need be said about it in the report inasmuch as we avoided meeting the constitutional question in the decision.[50]

In other words, to the Reporter fell the decision which enshrined the declaration in the United States Reports. Had Davis left it out, *Santa Clara County* v. *Southern Pac. R. Co.* would have been lost to history among thousands of uninteresting tax cases. With the announcement the case had become an apparently significant indication that the Waite Court was now ready to confer on corporations special immunity from economic regulation.[51] But the very fact that Waite assumed the existence of corporate personality even while sustaining regulatory legislation suggests that the Court did not view it as a bar to governmental exercises of power. Furthermore, Waite's willingness to let the Reporter include or omit the *Santa Clara* announcement, under the assumption that it had little intrinsic interest, strongly supports this explanation. For unless Waite regarded it as a fairly routine instruction given to counsel, it seems almost inconceivable that he would have delegated the announcement of a major constitutional doctrine to the Court Reporter.

The California tax cases were nevertheless victories of a sort for Justice Field. The justices refused to endorse his sweeping circuit opinions, but neither had they overruled them. They remained good

fending Conkling's *San Mateo* argument, which he saved. The editorial contained passages strongly urging that corporations were merely individuals, and Waite—perhaps approvingly—marked them off. Unidentified clipping in envelope labeled "California Tax case." Waite Papers.

[50] Davis to Waite, May 26, 1886. Waite Papers; Waite to Davis, May 31, 1886. Bancroft Davis Papers.

[51] Robert K. Carr, *The Supreme Court and Judicial Review* (New York: Rinehart & Company, Inc., 1942), p. 147; Hacker, *Triumph of American Capitalism*, p. 389; McCloskey, *American Conservatism in the Age of Enterprise*, p. 181.

law in the ninth circuit, increasingly cited by the property-minded judges who more and more were becoming ascendant in state and federal courts.[52] At the same time, conservative spokesmen, legal scholars, and bar associations took sharp exception to the Waite Court's tolerance for legislative decisions. Brooks Adams, in typical Adams' pessimism, wondered if the Court would "ever again act as an effective check upon the popular will." Hamilton Fish, a pillar of conservatism as well as of probity, recoiled from the legal tender ruling which decreed "that 'rags & lamp black' may discharge an obligation to repay a debt contracted in real money. The only sound reasoning," he moaned, "in the opinion of the single *dissenting* Justice—& he a Democrat!!! Oh! shades of Marshall & of Story! how are the mighty fallen." [53]

More consequential than individual expressions of opinion were the activities of the American Bar Association. Formed, appropriately enough, a year after the *Munn* decision, the ABA rapidly assumed leadership in the campaign to infuse American law and legal thought with laissez-faire principles. Two of its most prominent members, jurists Thomas C. Cooley in his *Constitutional Limitations* and Christopher G. Tiedeman in his *Limitations of Police Power* (written to combat the "Socialism, Communism, and Anarchism" he believed "rampant throughout the civilized world") produced influential legal works which roundly condemned the power-granting principle of the *Munn* case.[54] Cooley and Tiedeman did not labor in vain. Scores of lower-court judges in the eighties and nineties followed their line: in 1885 Waite's own friend, William Evarts, who served high in the councils of the ABA, persuaded New York's Court of Appeals to invalidate a state law designed to eliminate sweatshop conditions caused by the manufacture of cigars in tenement houses; in 1886 Pennsylvania's Supreme Court overturned an act requiring that laborers' wages be paid in cash once a month—"vicious and void," it

[52] The cases are cited in Graham, "Constitutional Corporate 'Person,'" 205, note.

[53] Brooks Adams, "The Consolidation of the Colonies," *Atlantic Monthly*, LV (1885), 307; Fish to Davis, Nov. 25, 1885, Dec. 7, 1886. Bancroft Davis Papers.

[54] Twiss, *Lawyers and the Constitution*, pp. 37–38, 122–140. Tiedeman's criticism was especially severe. *Limitations of Police Power*, pp. 233–238. For a thorough discussion of Cooley and Tiedeman see Clyde Jacobs, *Law Writers and the Constitution* (Berkeley: University of California Press, 1954).

said, "an insulting attempt to put the laborer under a legislative tutelage which is not only degrading to his manhood, but subversive of his rights"; and increasingly the states' highest courts voided legislation by citing Field's minority opinion in the *Slaughter-House Cases* as if it were the opinion of the Court.[55]

To these judges almost any form of state interference in economic affairs appeared tyrannical. Thoroughly convinced of the enduring wisdom of laissez faire, they could not swallow their doubts and leave economic policy judgments to the legislature. Nor could they be expected to accept as binding precedent the premises which characterized the Waite Court's approach to regulatory legislation, that the facts, as interpreted and defined by legislatures, deserved its highest respect and that, for most abuses, the proper tribunal of appeal was *vox populi*, not *vox legis*. Rufus W. Peckham, sitting on the New York Court of Appeals in 1889, had called a law regulating grain elevator rates "communistic"; he suggested that the price regulation justified in *De Portibus Maris* was as outmoded as the witchcraft which Lord Hale believed in. Was there any reason to doubt how Peckham would vote when, as a justice of the Supreme Court, he confronted a law regulating working hours in bakeries? Or, could one expect Justice David J. Brewer, who openly proclaimed, "the paternal theory of government is to me odious," and who regarded the *Munn* opinion an introduction to Edward Bellamy's *Looking Backward*, to be guided by the Waite Court's decisions?[56]

So long as Judges Waite, Miller, and Bradley—who most often found allies in Gray, Blatchford, and Woods—lived, there was a majority for legislative supremacy. Only after they departed, and were replaced by judges like Peckham and Brewer, did the people learn that their legislatures lacked power to meet the social and economic problems brought on by the new industrialism. However sincere in their motives and convictions, the judicial attitude symbolized by Peckham and Brewer left the Republic, to use Waite's imagery, de-

[55] *Matter of Jacobs*, 98 N.Y. 98 (1885); *Godcharles and Company* v. *Wigeman*, 113 Pa. St. 431, 437 (1886); *Millet* v. *People*, 117 Ill. 294 (1886); *People* v. *Marx*, 99 N.Y. 377 (1885); Roscoe Pound, "Liberty of Contract," *Selected Essays on Constitutional Law*, II, 222–230.

[56] Peckham, J., dissenting in *People* v. *Budd*, 117 N.Y. 1, 47, 71 (1889); Brewer, J., dissenting in *Budd* v. *New York*, 143 U.S. 517, 551 (1892).

fenseless against the forces of the dollar. In the normal course of events it became almost inevitable that the dollar would receive a more favorable hearing in the Court of the 1890's than it received from the Waite Court. For the cumulative effect of three very property-conscious Presidents between 1884 and 1900—Cleveland, Harrison, and McKinley—was to staff the bench with a new majority, a majority receptive to the idea that to it fell a major role in safeguarding the rights of property. But, as the following pages will show, the forces of the dollar were too impatient to wait upon the normal course of events—and as early as 1880, disturbed by the Waite Court's decisions, took steps to assure a more sympathetic hearing in the Supreme Court.

12

COURT-PACKING IN THE AGE OF ENTERPRISE

Pacific Railroads. Promoters and Profits.

The Sinking Fund Act Resisted. Congress to Court.

Waite's "Revolutionary" Opinion. Business Leaders Retaliate.

Opportunities in the Election of 1880.

"Monied Men" Propose a Bargain. James Abram Garfield "whispering 'I will ne'er consent,' —consented."

Hayes' Disputed Nomination of Stanley Matthews for the Supreme Court. Renomination by Garfield. Mr. Justice Matthews.

The "Great Barbecue" and the Inhospitable Court.

THE WAITE COURT'S RULING IN THE *Granger Cases* (1877) MADE THE nation's corporate and financial leadership uneasy; the decision in the *Sinking Fund Cases* (1879) confirmed their worst fears: the majority had embarked on a revolutionary course "entirely in harmony with a theory of Government which rests its foundations on might and asserts the divine right of Kings." [1] While their fears and lamentations about governmental persecution had the hollow ring of deliberate exaggeration, the stakes were nonetheless high. At issue in the *Sinking Fund Cases* was an important principle, that of federal control over congressionally chartered corporations, and a very practical matter as well, a sum of over $100 million.

The story begins in 1862 when the federal government, anxious for transportation that would span the continent, chartered two corporations, the Union Pacific and the Central Pacific. To speed construction, the government guaranteed the rights of way, extinguished Indian land titles, promised military protection, and donated timber, earth, and stone from the public lands; most valuable of all, it contributed huge land grants and loans which totaled close to $65 million. Such largess had its results, one of them being the transcontinental juncture which the railroads effected in 1869 at Promontory Point, Utah. Other results were less obviously in the public interest although, indisputably, they were in the interest of the railroad promoters. Forming a dummy construction company called Crédit Mobilier, the directors of the Union Pacific granted themselves exorbitant prices

[1] Leland Stanford, quoted in N.Y. *Times,* Jan. 23, 1881.

for construction work and pocketed a small fortune. When Congress, which had donated to the Union Pacific ten million acres of public land, became suspicious, the entrepreneurs hastily distributed Crédit Mobilier shares among influential congressmen. The ensuing scandal implicated people as prominent as Schuyler Colfax, the Vice President of the United States, and, perhaps less justly, James A. Garfield, the virtuous-sounding representative from Ohio. Equally adept at combining railroading with fortune making were the promoters of the Central Pacific, Leland Stanford, Collis Huntington, Mark Hopkins, and Charles Crocker, who, while receiving $121 million for construction, spent but $58 million, the balance going to themselves.[2]

Not content with their immense construction "profits," the promoters determined to extract every possible cent from the railroads' operations. Under the terms of the federal chartering acts of 1862 and 1864, the Pacific Railroads agreed to repay the $65 million bond issue made by the government at six per cent interest within thirty years after completion of the line. Following final completion of the road, all payments by the government for transportation (to carry troops and mail) were to be applied to this debt, as was at least five per cent of the net income. But instead of beginning interest payments once the roads were completed, the directors challenged every aspect of the chartering acts in the courts—disagreeing with such matters as the federal government's interpretation of the date of completion and the time when interest payments fell due.

Meanwhile, the companies were enjoying large earnings, but applying them only to interest payments on their own bonds and to generous dividends among stockholders. Nothing was laid aside to repay their debt to the government which by the end of the century would come to around $116 million.[3] With the railroads thus stalling on repayment, a move began in Congress—its sensitivity to railroad

[2] Cochran and Miller, *The Age of Enterprise*, pp. 132–134; Hacker, *Triumph of American Capitalism*, pp. 370–371. Cf., Robert W. Fogel's interesting study, *The Union Pacific Railroad, A Case in Premature Enterprise* (Baltimore: Johns Hopkins Press, 1960). Fogel argues that, considering the social utility of a transcontinental railroad and the great risks it involved, the promoters' profits were not immense or unjustified. However, he accepts the Crédit Mobilier affair as a corrupt attempt "to seduce public officials," p. 54, 86.

[3] Riegel, *Story of the Western Railroads*, pp. 195–198; *Sinking Fund Cases*, 99 U.S. 700, 724 (1879).

abuses somewhat heightened since the Crédit Mobilier affair—in the mid-1870's to hold the promoters to the terms of the chartering acts. Its principal backer was Senator Allen G. Thurman of Ohio, an incorruptible Democrat of the old states'-rights school known to his generation as "the Old Roman," who sponsored a "Sinking Fund" law requiring the Pacific Railroads to pay 25 per cent of their annual net earnings into the federal treasury. A bitter fight was quickly joined, the railroads denouncing the proposed law as an invasion of their contract rights under the chartering acts. Thurman had powerful support from George F. Edmunds, David Davis, and Augustus H. Garland, three highly capable men who served with him on the Senate Judiciary Committee. He also faced fierce opposition: from within Congress his fellow Ohioan, Senator Stanley Matthews, fought for the railroad position; from without Collis Huntington used a skilled lobbyist, David D. Colton, to resist the measure.

Despite this resistance, on May 7, 1878, the Sinking Fund, or Thurman Act, won congressional approval. If enforced, the Union and Central Pacific Railroads would have to defer approximately $100 million in anticipated profits, a loss the directors were determined to avert. They arranged a test suit to challenge the act's constitutionality, their hopes encouraged by conversations between the incautious Justice Field and Huntington's agent, Colton, who reported that "the hope of the country is in the Supreme Court if the nation is to be saved from disgrace." In September 1878 Colton informed Huntington that "Judge Field will not sit in the Gallatin case [a suit against the Thurman Act begun in California] but will reserve himself for his best effort (I have no doubt) on the final termination of the case at Washington before a full bench." According to Colton, Field's views would have more impact if he reserved them until the final appeal, a strategy with which Huntington agreed.[4]

On appeal to the Supreme Court from the lower tribunals, where the decision went against them, the railroads pulled out all the stops. Their distinguished counsel, among whom were Samuel Shellabarger,

[4] Colton to Huntington, Sept. 20, 1878; Huntington to Colton, Sept. 30, 1878. These letters are quoted in Swisher, *Field*, pp. 247–248, which notes that there is a question as to the authenticity of the references to Field. The assumption here—based on Field's indiscretions in other cases and his well-documented relationship with the Pacific Railroad directors—is that they are accurate.

a former Republican congressman from Ohio, Silas W. Sanderson, a onetime justice of California's Supreme Court and a regular attorney for the Huntington-Stanford interests, and Georgia Senator Benjamin H. Hill, eloquently urged that the funding act infringed the Constitution's contract and due process clauses. It was, they argued, a violation of "every guarantee of property known to this government"; the consequences were frightening:

> It is a matter of universal recognition . . . that when the rights of corporations are selected to be the victims of legislation, then the principles of public morality, of original justice and of common law, too often go down under the combined forces of demagoguery and of perverted ambition, building upon the real or supposed prejudice of populace and of the commune against corporations and capital.[5]

There was, however, force to the contention of former Attorney General Williams, who filed a brief for the United States, that "indefinite and eloquent denunciations of the act will not show its invalidity. . . . Somebody must point out the article, section or clause of the Constitution with which it conflicts." [6] Williams struck at the railroad's softest point. The Constitution's contract clause applied only to the states, not Congress, forcing their attorneys to rely on the "spirit" and "principles" of American government as a supposed limitation on federal impairments of contracts.[7]

This, as Justice Miller implied in sharply questioning Senator Hill, was not good enough: even if the Thurman Act "clearly" impaired the obligation of a contract, "Is it not an incident to the power of the Government to take care of itself—to collect its debts and pay its debts?" [8] Miller's remarks foreshadowed the decision, and on May 6, 1879, Chief Justice Waite announced that the Court, Justices Field, Strong, and Bradley dissenting, had found the act constitutional. Where most cases in the post-Civil War period took three to four years to reach decision, this one came within a year of the act's passage. Beyond doubt, the justices were responding to the parties' intense

[5] Samuel Shellabarger and Jeremiah Wilson, Brief for the Union Pacific R. Co., p. 22, pp. 52–53. *Sinking Fund Cases*, 99 U.S. 700 (1879).
[6] Williams, Brief for the United States, p. 3.
[7] Shellabarger and Wilson, Brief, pp. 32–34.
[8] Hill, Oral Argument for the Central Pacific, pp. 25–26.

concern with the outcome; in fact, the announcement preceded the opinions, which were not delivered until the following fall.[9] Waite assigned himself the opinion of the Court with Miller advising him to prepare it carefully. "Permit me again to suggest," he counseled, "that if I were you I would take the vacation to write the Pacific Rail Road opinions." Field, too, prepared for a summer's work, promising a dissent sure to pin back the errant majority's ears, "better than all the rest" of my opinions, "for, if there is any constitutional law acceptable to the profession generally throughout the country, it will be found there." Clearly, fire-and-brimstone was about to flow from Judge Field's pen.[10]

Waite's opinion, concurred in by Justices Clifford, Miller, Swayne, and Harlan, was delivered on October 20. Relying in part on *Munn* v. *Illinois*, he pointed out that the Pacific Railroads, though private corporations, were "created for public purposes" and hence affected with a public interest. Not only this, but in its incorporation act Congress reserved power to amend the charter. And so, while it might not take away property rights already acquired, "whatever rules Congress might have prescribed in the original charter for the government of the corporation . . . it retained the power to establish by amendment."[11]

Three sharp dissents challenged this conclusion. Justice Strong found the Thurman Act "plainly transgressive of legislative power":

> The contract implied an agreement not to call for payment [of the debt] or additional security before [1897]. . . . There is no technicality about vested rights. Most of them grow out of contracts and . . . are all equally sacred, equally beyond the reach of legislative interference. . . .[12]

Justice Bradley believed it a violation of "at least" the spirit of the due process clause of the Fifth Amendment and the prohibition against

[9] By consent of the parties, who wished to hasten a Supreme Court ruling, the Court of Claims gave judgment for the United States without even hearing the case and without opinion. *Union Pacific R. Co.* v. *United States*, 14 C. Cls. 594 (1879).

[10] Miller to Waite, April 28, 1879. Waite Papers; Field to Deady, May 21, 1879. Deady Papers.

[11] *Sinking Fund Cases*, 99 U.S. 700, 719–721 (1879).

[12] 99 U.S. 700, 731, 733.

taking private property without compensation. He called the Thurman Act a law which "strikes a blow at the public credit" and "saps the foundations of public morality." [13]

It was Field's opinion, however, which caused the excitement. Much of it—his charges that the decision would "create insecurity in the title to corporate property," that if contracts were broken the rights of all persons would be unsafe, and that anarchy and tyranny would follow—was characteristic, typical of Field's passionate concern for the rights of property. But he went further, assailing the Thurman Act as an invasion of states' rights (because one of the railroads was also a California corporation subject to state law) and criticizing the majority for abetting this destruction of local independence.[14] So strong was his language that reports circulated—Field called them "entirely false"—which described the majority as annoyed at their colleague's breach of decorum. In addition, many newspapers saw the dissent as a step toward the fulfillment of Field's scarcely concealed desire to become President. Since Senator Thurman was a leading contender for the Democratic nomination in 1880, Field's intemperate denunciation of the Thurman Act as well as his rousing state-supremacy language bred suspicion. "Simply scandalous," scolded the Chicago *Tribune*. Said the New York *Herald:* "Judge Field is out of place. He should be on the stump." [15]

Field's gloomy predictions were echoed in the severe disappointment felt by the railroads. Their counsel had summoned the Supreme Court to a high duty: that of "the impassable barrier" and "sleepless defender" of the rights of property against invasions "by the hasty, the ignorant, or the depraved action of the legislature." [16] Instead, as a pro-railroad newspaper charged, the majority responded with a "reprehensive" and "barbaric" opinion, which was "the most dangerous ever enunciated by any judicial authority." [17] Collis P. Huntington, endorsed by the New York *Tribune*, which praised him

[13] 99 U.S. 744, 750.
[14] 99 U.S. 700, 750, 766–769.
[15] Field to Deady, Jan. 5, 1880. Deady Papers; Chicago *Tribune*, Oct. 22, 1879; N.Y. *Herald*, Oct. 22, 1879.
[16] Shellabarger and Wilson, Brief, p. 57. *Sinking Fund Cases.*
[17] Unidentified clipping in envelope labeled "Criticism on the Thurman Bill decisions." Waite Papers.

as "the man to whom the country owes the Central and Southern Pacific Railroads," recorded his dismay. Waite's opinion was "but another of a series of steps recently taken calculated to fill the country with alarm." These made it a "guiding principle of jurisprudence" that "neither corporation nor person can acquire any right of ownership or enjoyment in property which the majority of the legislative power cannot at its discretion abridge, annul, or take away under the pretence of giving it to the public." [18] One thing surely was clear: as in the *Granger Cases* of 1877, the corporate interests had tried the Supreme Court; again they had found it wanting.

Whatever the flaws in the character of the Gilded Age's business leaders, lack of determination in attaining their objectives was not among them. Believing themselves responsible for developing the country, the entrepreneurs regarded theirs as the moral side, justifying the use of any means to remove obstacles that stood in the way of maximizing wealth and strengthening business. "We must," as the President of the Chicago, Burlington & Quincy put it, "keep at it and do the best we can to educate honest people, who are greatly in the majority. As to the dishonest ones, of course, there is no way of reaching them except through their pockets." Of course. If legislatures were "venal and corrupt," threatening business regulation and higher taxation, the answer was simple: buy the legislators.[19] If the Supreme Court denied corporations special protection, the answer was equally simple: change its composition.

An opportunity to do so presented itself in a most alluring fashion during the presidential campaign of 1880, since the man who succeeded retiring President Hayes would have two, possibly many more, appointments at his disposal. Justice Ward Hunt was paralyzed, and had not participated in a decision since early 1879. Lacking ten years service (he was appointed in 1872), he was ineligible for a pension and held on to his seat, waiting for Congress to pass a special retirement act. Also ailing was seventy-seven-year-old Justice Nathan

[18] Letter of Huntington to the *Nation*, Oct. 30, 1879; N.Y. *Tribune*, Nov. 1, 1879.

[19] Charles E. Perkins to William W. Baldwin, March 18, 1885; James C. Clarke to Stuyvesant Fish, March 11, 1885, in Cochran, *Railroad Leaders*, p. 299, 440, and Cochran's excellent discussion on p. 200. See also Leland Stanford's statement in the N.Y. *Times*, Jan. 23, 1881.

Clifford, the last of the pre-Civil War judges, and it was commonly known that seventy-six-year-old Justice Noah Swayne intended to resign. In addition, the Waite Court was overburdened with cases, its docket almost four years behind, and a raft of proposals were before Congress that envisaged raising the Court's membership to as high as twenty-one.

Because the *Sinking Fund* decision came on a five to three vote (Hunt not participating), a switch of only two votes could change the result. Even more than the Pacific Railroads' loss of $100 million was involved, for the 1880's were sure to see the large corporations buffeted by regulatory pressures. Encouraged by the ruling in the *Granger Cases* and responding to the demands of agrarian and working-class groups, states such as Mississippi and California were moving toward business regulation. In turn, at the national level a move for federal control over railroads was also gaining strength; a better barrier than the Waite Court's majority would be needed to stem the tide.

The business leadership was quick to see that the election of 1880 offered a marvelous opportunity to remake the Court into a more reliable guardian of its interests. Both parties were almost evenly divided. Republicans controlled the Senate, Democrats, the House, and to many partisans outgoing President Hayes was still "His Fraudulency." At any rate, Samuel J. Tilden had outpolled him by 250,000 votes in 1876, and Republican possession of the Presidency was based on the Electoral Commission's narrow eight-to-seven decision in favor of the Hayes' electors. Since the ill-starred days of President Buchanan no Democrat had sat in the White House, but 1880 looked promising. Thanks to Hayes' policy of reconciliation, the Democracy entered the campaign with a solid block of Southern states; capture of but two or three Northern states would assure victory. To lure one doubtful state, Democrats nominated Indiana Governor William H. English, a banker and "War Democrat" during the Civil War, for the Vice-Presidency. To head the ticket and further attract Northern support, they chose General Winfield S. Hancock, a man with no obvious qualifications for the Presidency but possessed of a somewhat exaggerated reputation for superb generalship in behalf of the Union cause. Here indeed was formidable opposition for the Republicans. Unlike recent campaigns such as that of 1872, when they were burdened with the hopeless candidacy of Horace Greeley, or those of 1864, 1868, and 1876, when their candidates were tainted by equivocal war records, Hancock and English were sure to appeal in the North while holding the South.

The Republicans, though respectably strong throughout the country (except for the South, which by 1880 had already become a Democratic preserve), were plagued by intra-party factionalism. To be sure, the division was largely over spoils—who would occupy the seats of power—but it was nonetheless a very real one. At their Chicago convention Republicans took thirty-six ballots before settling on a representative of the party's Half-Breed wing, the congressional leader and ex-Union officer, General James A. Garfield. Neither of the preconvention favorites, General Grant, whom the Stalwarts—Roscoe Conkling, John A. Logan, and Pennsylvania's Camerons—supported, or the supposedly "magnetic" James G. Blaine, backed by financier William W. Phelps and Whitelaw Reid's New York *Tribune* had had quite enough strength. Unable to nominate their man, the Blaine forces eventually combined with other anti-Grant delegates to nominate Garfield. Then, to appease the powerful Conkling faction, they rather cynically chose Chester A. Arthur, the antireform New York customs collector whom President Hayes had unceremoniously dismissed from office, as the party's candidate for Vice President.

Garfield himself was something of an enigma. Introspective, well educated, and in many ways a brilliant parliamentarian, his character was marred by a certain weakness and indecision as shown by his evasive behavior following the exposure of the Crédit Mobilier scandal and his representation, for a large fee, of a Washington street builder interested in a contract from the District's government. Hayes, who knew him well, probably came closest to characterizing him: a man of "large faculties, memory, analysis, fluency," and a skill for popular debating, but "not executive in his talents, not original, not firm,

—not a moral force"; his course "when trouble came betrayed weakness." [20]

For James Abram Garfield the campaign of 1880 brought much trouble. As the representative of the party which had presided over the birth of industrial capitalism, Garfield might—perhaps—count on the country's financiers and corporation leaders for the financial contributions sorely needed by his campaign managers. He faced stiff competition because the Hancock-English ticket was not the sort to make capitalists tremble for the safety of their property. The Republican Stalwarts, moreover, were undisguisedly cool toward Garfield, not at all appeased by the sop given them in Arthur's nomination for second place. By late July 1880, almost two months after Garfield's nomination, Roscoe Conkling and his New York lieutenants, such as Thomas Collier Platt and Alonzo B. Cornell, gave every indication of sitting out the election. Without the support of their party machine Garfield's chances of carrying New York were dim; without New York he would probably lose. As he prepared for the coming campaign at his home in Mentor, Ohio, no problem troubled him more than that of winning the Stalwarts' cooperation and acquiring financial contributions.[21]

Finally, at the urgent request of his campaign managers, he journeyed East in a bid to restore party unity and gain the backing of the New York Stalwarts. Harmony conferences were held in New York City in early August and all factions pledged to work for the ticket. In return, Garfield agreed to clear all federal appointments in the state with the regular party organization led by Conkling and Platt. Later, as President, he would claim that the promise to "be guided" by them was not a firm contract to turn patronage over to the Stalwarts and, encouraged by Blaine, would defy the Conkling machine. At the moment, though, he had their support and, of particular value,

[20] *Hayes Diary*, IV, 110; Ellis P. Oberholtzer, *A History of the United States* (New York: The Macmillan Company, 1931), IV, 89–91; cf., Theodore C. Smith, *James A. Garfield* (New Haven: Yale University Press, 1925), I, ch. xv, cited hereafter as Smith, *Garfield*.

[21] Unless otherwise indicated, this account of the 1880 campaign draws on Herbert J. Clancy, *The Presidential Election of 1880* (Chicago: Loyola University Press, 1958); George F. Howe, *Chester A. Arthur* (New York: C. Scribner's Sons, 1957), ch. x; Matthew Josephson, *The Politicos 1865–1896* (New York: Harcourt, Brace and Company, 1938), pp. 290–301; Smith, *Garfield*, II, ch. xxvi.

a pledge from Levi P. Morton, a Conkling politician and one of the nation's wealthiest financiers, that he would take charge of campaign finances.

Garfield returned to Mentor feeling he had restored party unity. Yet the problem of adequate financial support remained in doubt. While Morton's pledge was a promising start, Garfield needed, as Whitelaw Reid of the *Tribune* made clear, additional support from New York's business aristocracy.[22] Reid's was a powerful voice in the Republican councils of the late nineteenth century. One of Blaine's closest political associates, he was also an old friend of the candidate. During the campaign he acted as Garfield's personal representative in New York, publicly editorializing in his behalf and, more discreetly, canvassing for monetary contributions. Reid's effort had begun in earnest in the course of the candidate's August visit to New York. "W. W. Phelps of N.Y. met me & drove me to Whitelaw Reid's house—& Jay Gould & we had a conversation on the campaign—I think he will help," Garfield recorded in his diary.[23] William W. Phelps, also a Blaine associate, was a sometime congressman and diplomat, a wealthy New York businessman, and a corporation lawyer. Jay Gould, whom in now forgotten days Congressman Garfield had denounced as "the guilty plotter" of the "Black Friday" gold market scandal,[24] controlled the Union Pacific, the Kansas Pacific, the Denver Pacific, the Missouri Pacific, and the Central Pacific Railroads.

In the Age of Enterprise the support of Jay Gould might prove decisive. It came, however, with a price tag. Gould, after all, was a businessman, and for services rendered he demanded payment: in this case a promise from Garfield that he would reconstitute the Supreme Court with men more friendly to the corporations than the majority led by Chief Justice Waite. On August 31 Reid wrote to Garfield:

> Your visit to my house was good, and at least stopped the headway the other side was making. The real anxiety of these people is with reference to the Supreme Court. The next President will almost certainly have the appointment of three new Judges—even if a great

[22] Reid to Garfield, Aug. 31, 1880, Letterbooks. Whitelaw Reid Papers, L.C.
[23] Garfield's *Journal*, Aug. 6, 1880. Garfield Papers.
[24] In 1869. Smith, *Garfield*, I, 450.

enlargement of the court should not be ordered. All monied men, and especially all corporations, regarded the course of the Supreme Court in the Granger cases and in the Pacific R.R. case as bad law and bad faith. I believe that you sympathize with the general view of the law taken by Judge Field and his associates in the minority. As you doubtless know, the Court [in the *Sinking Fund Cases*] would have stood 5 to 4 except for the illness of Judge Hunt. These people hesitate because they say they are unwilling to elect a President unless they are sure that he disapproves what they call the revolutionary course of the majority of the court. If they could be satisfied on this point, I know we could make a big demonstration at once, and probably settle things beyond a peradventure.[25]

To this quite specific request for a commitment Garfield replied with characteristic vagueness:

I note carefully what you say in reference to the danger to vested rights from impending changes in the Supreme Court. On the suggestion of two or three friends I left out a paragraph from the letter of acceptance, touching that very subject, and this was its purport; that, while in every just way we should promote cheap transportation yet the Government should not only sacredly respect vested rights, but should refrain from adopting any policy which would prevent capitalists from extending our great railroad system. I did not leave this out because of any doubt as to the justice of the sentiment itself, but from motives of campaign discretion.[26]

Reid was not satisfied:

Yours of the *2nd* inst. is at hand. It is scarcely so precise on the point of the decisions of Judge Field as wd. be desired by some of the gentlemen concerned. I feel confident, however, that if you as a lawyer concur in the views of the minority in these cases, the subject is of such importance as to warrant early and very important action.

[25] Reid to Garfield, Aug. 31, 1880, Letterbooks. Reid Papers. Reid devoted other parts of his letter to describing the support Garfield might expect from the New York Stalwarts. The reference to Justice Hunt's voting intentions in the *Sinking Fund Cases* is of doubtful accuracy. Appointed by Grant in 1872 at Conkling's behest, he, presumably, was close to the corporations. There is, however, little in Hunt's brief judicial career to indicate that his votes were dictated; he voted with the majority in the *Granger Cases*.

[26] Garfield to Reid, Sept. 2, 1880, Letterbooks. Garfield Papers.

A week later Reid wrote again, advising him not to "show this letter to a living man—whether National Committee, Senator, or anything" and pressing for a firm answer:

> I send you herewith those Supreme Court decisions. That of Judge Strong is the most important since it covers more ground than the others. What I want to get at is whether as a lawyer you hold the views of Judge Strong & his associates or the opposing view. If the former, then I will go out at once, on the matter we have spoken of, & am sure my visit can do great good. If the latter, I don't see that I can render any other service than to keep pounding away on the paper, as I am now.[27]

Garfield's reply crossed Reid's letter of the fourteenth. He averred his devotion to "good order and public faith" and assailed "the Democracy" for "rapidly drifting, in the wake of the Greenback party, towards communism." Then he turned to the Court's decision in the *Sinking Fund Cases:*

> Thurman's bill of 1878 was a dangerous step in the direction of the repudiation of public obligations. When it came into the House, its Democratic managers would not let it be referred to a committee as I suggested, & with but a very brief debate rushed it through. I was surprised that a majority of the Supreme Court sustained it. As a lawyer I have no doubt that the dissenting opinion of Judge Strong is the sound doctrine of the Constitution.
>
> I believe in protecting the interests of the U.S. and the rights of the people but not in repudiation, nor in violating the plain terms of a contract.[28]

The business leaders were still unsatisfied. On September 23 Reid hurried to Mentor, apparently to extract from Garfield a specific pledge that he clear his Supreme Court appointments with the New York financiers. Much agitated, Garfield refused, but in his very manner of refusing greatly compromised himself. Reid returned to New York that evening and, as soon as he had left, Garfield sat down to write a letter explaining his position:

[27] Reid to Garfield, Sept. 6, 14, 1880, Letterbooks. Reid Papers.
[28] Garfield to Reid, Sept. 15, 1880, Letterbooks. Garfield Papers.

It is due to you, as my trusted friend, that I state the reasons which led me to reject at once the proposition which you brought me in reference to appointments to the Supreme Court. I do not reject it because I differ from your views of the case. But any agreement that should be or appear to be a delegation of the power vested in the Chief Executive, implies such distrust of his faithfulness to his own convictions of duty, as I cannot tolerate with self respect. I have stated to you, fully, my well considered views of the constitution in reference to the sanctity of Contracts and of vested rights—Under no circumstances would I entrust the high functions of a Justice of the Supreme Court, to any person whom I did not believe to be entirely sound on these questions. I should insist upon evidence which would be satisfactory to you as well as to me.[29]

My life has been so earnestly devoted to the defense of the public faith, that I cannot tolerate the suggestion of giving bonds that I will not act otherwise hereafter. I do not care even for the Presidency to assume its functions under any bonds but my convictions of duty. No man will say that I ever betrayed his trust in me—and I will do nothing which implies that I cannot still be trusted. What I have written above implies no disrespect to your friends. With one of them [Phelps?], my relations have been those of intimate friendship, and as to the other [Gould?] I am satisfied not only by my personal knowledge, but by your hearty testimony—I recognize their great ability, & have no doubt of their honorable good faith.

But I make you—my trusted friend for 20 years,—& the friend also of these gentlemen—the sole custodian of this letter.[30]

To which Reid replied: "It has all worked out right." [31]

In this way Garfield retained his "self respect." He also acquired the desired contributions—Jay Gould's reportedly being $150,000.[32] Earlier, he had picked up financial support from John D. Rockefeller

[29] A first draft declared: "Under no circumstances would I entrust the high function of a Justice of the Supreme Court to any person whom I did not believe to be entirely sound on the questions involved in Judge Strong's recent decisions & I shall want evidence which you would agree with me was satisfactory."

[30] Garfield to Reid, Sept. 23, 1880, Letterbooks; Garfield's *Journal*, Sept. 23, 1880. Garfield Papers. Garfield's sympathetic biographer, ignoring Garfield's other correspondence with Reid on the subject of judicial appointments and quoting only selected passages from the letter of September 23, cites it as evidence of Garfield's "executive independence" and "personal record." Smith, *Garfield*, II, 1029.

[31] Reid to Garfield, Sept. 30, 1880, Letterbooks. Reid Papers.

[32] James F. Hudson, *The Railways and the Republic* (New York: Harper & Brothers, 1886), p. 454.

of Standard Oil and Chauncey Depew of the New York Central.[33] With the aid of these sums Garfield's managers eked out a 10,000 vote victory over Winfield S. Hancock. As expected, New York and Indiana proved to be the crucial states; their loss would have meant Hancock's election. Garfield barely carried them, an expenditure of $100,000 in the closing days of the campaign saving Indiana for the Republican Party. At a well-liquored victory dinner at Delmonico's in New York, Vice President-elect Chester Arthur explained:

> Indiana was really, I suppose, a Democratic State. It had been put down on the books always as a State that might be carried by close and perfect organization and a great deal of—(laughter). I see the reporters are present, therefore I will simply say that everybody showed a great deal of interest in the occasion and distributed tracts and political documents all through the State.[34]

Meanwhile, before Garfield's inauguration, the business interests received an unexpected boon quite unrelated to their liberal contributions to the Republican campaign. Without even asking for it, they learned that the Supreme Court was to be adorned by a man who, to all outward appearances, was one of their own: railroad attorney Stanley Matthews of Ohio. Justice Swayne had retired, and on January 26, 1881, President Hayes nominated Matthews to fill the vacancy. There were no disreputable motives behind his nomination. Among the President's personal and political associates few were closer to him than Stanley Matthews. Their friendship dated back to student days at the then wilderness college of Kenyon, and the President's wife, Lucy Webb Hayes, was related to Matthews. They joined the Union Army together in 1861 and afterwards cooperated politically. Matthews played a key part both in Hayes' presidential campaign and in the subsequent maneuvering that surrounded the Disputed Election. After the 1876 election Hayes supported Matthews' bid for a Senate seat by successfully intervening with Ohio

[33] Josephson, *Politicos,* pp. 290–291; Smith, *Garfield,* II, 1025.
[34] N.Y. *Tribune,* Feb. 12, 1881; *Nation,* Feb. 24, 1881.

political leaders, though, he later admitted, "In the Senate a short time, he did not show political wisdom." [35]

Matthews was also a noted corporation lawyer, being Jay Gould's chief midwestern counsel, and while a Senator had vigorously lobbied against the Thurman Act. As a result, the nomination met a storm of disapproval. Cried the Detroit *Free Press:* "Mr. Jay Gould has been appointed to the United States Supreme Court in place of Judge Swayne, resigned." Repeated protests came from the New York *Times,* and Godkin's *Nation* remarked that Matthews' confirmation was one which Hayes had greatly at heart "and which the Pacific Railroad corporations have greatly at heart, too, and cannot bear to give up. In fact, this nomination, which was bad enough on its merits, is growing into a gross scandal through the means employed to push it." Inside the Senate Matthews faced similar opposition. Senators Thurman, Edmunds, Garland, and David Davis, all of whom had crossed swords with him over the Sinking Fund Act, dominated the Judiciary Committee, refusing to report out on the appointment.[36]

The nomination died with the Forty Sixth Congress, apparently ending Matthews' chances of reaching the Supreme Court. There was, certainly, little reason to believe that the incoming President Garfield would resubmit his name. Both Garfield and Matthews were Ohio politicians who had no special love for each other. They had previously clashed over monetary policy and when, in 1877, thanks to Hayes' intervention, Matthews became an Ohio senator, it was at Garfield's expense. He had long coveted a Senate seat, had the votes to win it, and withdrew from the contest only because of Hayes' plea that he remain in the House to lead the Administration's forces. This act of "self-sacrifice," as Garfield described it, had left him feeling "a little bit nettled." [37]

Additional factors militated against a Matthews renomination. It was bound to be unpopular and would only add to Garfield's troubles

[35] *Hayes Diary,* IV, 458–459; Barnard, *Hayes,* p. 498. Hayes' nomination of Matthews had been expected. Fairman, *Miller,* pp. 380–381.

[36] Detroit *Free Press,* quoted in Harold Helfman, "The Contested Confirmation of Stanley Matthews to the United States Supreme Court," *Bulletin of the Historical and Philosophical Society of Ohio,* VIII (1950), 162 and generally 157–163; N.Y. *Times,* Jan. 27, Feb. 2, 9, 10, 1881; *Nation,* Feb. 24, 1881.

[37] Smith, *Garfield,* I, 647–649.

—of which he had plenty during the early months of 1881. By refusing to heed Conkling's wishes in Cabinet appointments, he had set the stage for a major test of the Stalwarts' power in the Republican party; for Garfield personally it meant a life and death struggle over patronage with the New York machine.[38] Under these circumstances there was presumably little likelihood that the sorely beset new President would invite further trouble by renominating Stanley Matthews, a man to whom he had no particular obligations.

Events proved otherwise; on March 14, 1881, less than two weeks after his inauguration, Garfield resubmitted Matthews' name to the Senate. The renomination touched off a new struggle, yet left Whitelaw Reid's *Tribune* strangely silent. Except for one editorial during the first Matthews nomination, which hailed it as the strongest in many years, its sole contribution was brief news notices that ignored the real points of controversy. Nothing appeared on its editorial page, but a background story attributed the unpopular nomination to the President's respect for Matthews "as a jurist." According to a "staff correspondent," Garfield's action showed him to be a man who does not "cherish resentments." The President, after all, "as all men who know Ohio politics are well aware, has no sort of admiration for Matthews as a politician," who, "by the help of Mr. Hayes," was responsible for "pushing him aside" in the senatorial election of 1877.[39]

Apart from this, Reid kept quiet, causing the rival New York *Times* to speculate as to the reason:

> Jay Gould's editorial methods have not hitherto been characterized by this kind of reticence, and we must conclude either he had not time to advise his organs as to the line of comment to be adopted or that he has become more cautious in showing his editorial hand.

More likely, Reid and Gould decided that a blatant *Tribune* campaign on Matthews' behalf would only play into the opposition's hands. For, while nothing could be proved, the nomination aroused great suspicion. Opposing confirmation, the *Albany Law Journal* reported that "powerful corporations with a view to their own pur-

[38] Garfield's feud with Conkling is covered in Smith, *Garfield*, II, chs. xxxvii–xxxviii.
[39] N.Y. *Tribune*, Jan. 27, March 19, 1881.

poses" had dictated the appointment. The *Nation* charged Gould with lobbying in the Senate. The New York *Times*, normally a pro-Garfield newspaper, was even more specific in its accusations. Noting Matthews' hostility to the Thurman Act, it claimed that his confirmation would be the signal for a new suit by the Central Pacific Railroad and described the renomination as "injudicious" and "objectionable." "What motives and considerations," the *Times* speculated, "could have led him into this blunder it is impossible to understand. They are beneath the surface, and cannot by any possibility be creditable." [40] Such influential resistance had an impact, but fell short of success by one vote. On May 12, 1881, a Senate vote of 24 to 23 confirmed Stanley Matthews as an Associate Justice of the Supreme Court.

Years later, ex-President Hayes recorded in his diary that he "held" Garfield to the renomination. Undoubtedly he asked him to resubmit Matthews' name, but it is not clear why Garfield should have followed the advice. Hayes was lukewarm toward Garfield, estranged from the party leadership, and had not even campaigned for the ticket.[41] Indeed, as the Garfield-Reid correspondence suggests, it was Jay Gould, not Rutherford Hayes, who "held" Garfield to Matthews' renomination.[42]

The sequel to the renomination is not without its irony. If, as seems almost certain, Jay Gould enriched Garfield's campaign coffers by $150,000, he got a poor bargain. While the Pacific Railroads used

[40] N.Y. *Times*, Feb. 2, 9, 10, March 16, 30, April 27, May 31, 1881; *Albany Law Journal*, Feb. 5, May 14, 1881; *Nation*, May 19, 1881.

[41] *Hayes Diary*, IV, 458; Barnard, *Hayes*, pp. 492–495. The *Nation*, March 24, 1881, speculated that the nomination was a "gesture" to Hayes. Garfield himself was quoted as saying that he renominated Matthews "through a sense of justice and the conviction that he should have a fair day in Court." Helfman, "Contested Confirmation of Matthews," 166.

[42] In 1885 T. C. Crawford, a correspondent for the New York *World*, published an article entitled "Gould's Supreme Judge." Purportedly based on confidential sources, the article linked Matthews' appointment to a $300,000 sum contributed by Gould and Collis P. Huntington to Garfield's campaign. While the general drift of Crawford's account seems correct (he described the railroaders' chagrin at the *Sinking Fund* decision and named Reid as an intermediary), it probably errs in important details: e.g., in claiming that Senator Thomas Collier Platt and Reid, who were representing Garfield, signed a written pledge that Garfield would appoint Matthews; and in tracing Hayes' nomination of Matthews to a request made by Garfield. N.Y. *World*, March 11, 1885. Writing in his diary, Hayes pointed out that the story did not implicate Matthews. He labeled it as "not true" and "absurd," but conceded that "there is a belief . . . among newspaper men at Washington that the story is founded in fact. . . ." *Hayes Diary*, IV, 220.

a variety of tactics to evade the Thurman Act,[43] no effort was made to again challenge its constitutionality. As for Justice Matthews, in eight years of judicial service he proved himself a capable craftsman, popular with his Chief, who called him "a most valuable judge" and a "splendid" worker.[44] On the important judicial issues of the day he generally sided with the majority, denying the claims of Negroes to federal civil rights protection, tolerating state bond repudiation, and permitting railroad regulation.[45] Attorney Stanley Matthews was a loyal, many said notorious, servant of the large corporations. Justice Stanley Matthews, while sympathetic to property rights, did not—as the business elite had clearly expected—join Justice Field in protest against the majority's "revolutionary course," again demonstrating the lack of causal relationship between a judge's pre-Court career and his judicial voting.

In other respects, too, Gould got a poor return for his money. With Garfield's assassination Chester Alan Arthur, the New York Stalwart under no obligation to Whitelaw Reid or Gould, succeeded to the Presidency. His two appointments to the Court, Samuel Blatchford and Horace Gray, neither of whom fit the railroad attorney model, also aligned themselves with Waite on the major economic issues before the Court.

Although the attempt by business to capture the Waite Court failed, the episode is nonetheless highly instructive. It is, first of all, a case history in the methods and morals of the Age of Enterprise. Everything had its price—judges as well as railroad shares; nothing, it would seem, was exempt from the laws of the marketplace. At the same time, the buyers and the sellers—the business leaders and the politicians—clothed their actions in a garb of morality. Nor was the moralizing purely cynical. Garfield, for one, retained his sense of integrity ("I do not care even for the Presidency to assume its functions under any bonds. . . .") even as he assured the New York

[43] Riegel, *Story of the Western Railroads*, pp. 195–198.

[44] Waite to Amelia Waite, Nov. 7, 1881.

[45] See: (civil rights) *United States* v. *Harris*, 106 U.S. 629 (1883); *Civil Rights Cases*, 109 U.S. 3 (1883); (state bonds) *Antoni* v. *Greenhow*, 107 U.S. 769 (1883); *Louisiana* v. *Jumel*, 107 U.S. 711 (1883); *In re Ayres*, 123 U.S. 443 (1887); (railroads) *Ruggles* v. *Illinois*, 108 U.S. 536 (1883); *Railroad Commission Cases*, 116 U.S. 307 (1886); also, *Julliard* v. *Greenman*, 110 U.S. 421 (1884), the peacetime legal tender case.

financiers that they would find him a worthy investment. In this he resembled the railroad leader who, while abhorring corruption, had, "of course," no choice but to reach dishonest legislators "through their pockets."

Second, the effort to dictate Court appointments emphasizes the extent to which the Waite Court antagonized the nation's business leaders. By and of itself, it is true, the Supreme Court was not much of a threat to the interests of W. W. Phelps, Jay Gould, and Collis P. Huntington. An occasional decision such as the *Sinking Fund Cases* cost the Pacific Railroads in dollars and cents, crystallizing corporate hostility toward the Waite Court, but the real issue went deeper. At stake was the Court's role in the American system of government. Traditionally, that role, surely the great legacy of John Marshall's thirty-four year reign as the Moses of the American Constitution, was one of solicitous concern for vested property rights. Even Taney's Jacksonian Court, if only because property rights faced few serious challenges during his era, did little to destroy the legacy. But during the Waite period—as the Granger movement, the agrarian–working-class rumblings in California, and the increasing calls for federal regulation of monopolies and railroads graphically illustrate—there came the first serious attempts to bring the new industrial capitalism under at least a semblance of public control. When it seemed that governmental intervention might end the "Great Barbecue" (to use Vernon Parrington's imaginative phrase) that made the Gilded Age so splendid a feast for the businessman, he turned, as John Marshall had told him he could, to the Supreme Court.

Instead of finding a warm reception, the businessman was coldly directed by Chief Justice Waite to present his grievances elsewhere —to the people at election time. This he was hardly prepared to do: Jay Gould might have faith in the survival of the fittest in the economic marketplace; he had no such faith as to his success in the political marketplace: for there the unfittest—the agrarian, the laborer, in a word, the mob—might triumph. Accordingly, the business leadership, with an eye to the likely increase of public regulation, strove to remake the Court into a potential barrier against the popular will—speaking bluntly, to pack the Bench. The effort failed. The Waite

Court remained sympathetic to state and federal exercises of regulatory power. Judge Matthews proved himself, as Hayes said, "able, conscientious, firm, and just."[46] And Garfield's death cheated—if that is the word—the Jay Goulds of two additional appointments. The business leadership had to wait yet a little longer before it could hope to remake the Supreme Court into its own image.

[46] *Hayes Diary*, IV, 459.

13

COURT MANAGER

Chief Justice of the Supreme Court. The Power of Personality.
Waite and his Brethren. A Mortifying Experience.
The Hot Temper of Stephen J. Field.
Waite's Assignment of Opinions. Eight Sensitive Men.
The Docket Explosion. Work and Worries. New Judges.
Justice Miller on Waite. "A Sow's Ear"? The Ideal Chief.

BY COURTESY AND TRADITION THE CHIEF JUSTICE REIGNS; HE DOES NOT rule. Apart from his ceremonial status as head of the Court and his right to preside at conferences and assign opinions, he stands on an equal plane with his brethren. One man, one vote is the principle by which the tribunal reaches decisions, and the Chief Justice, as Justice Miller once remarked, exerts additional power only when his character and qualifications "would give him a controlling influence without the position." [1] Yet, while he controls merely his own vote, the position is nonetheless a special one. When Court is in session he sits in the center and is, in fact, the center of popular attention, a symbol of the nation's quest for justice under law. Equally important, the Chief Justice is responsible for the conduct of business and serves as the Court's manager. As such, it is to his distinct advantage to promote good working relationships among the often headstrong and conflicting personalities with whom he works. Not only is harmony essential to the tribunal's inner operation, but a Court that runs smoothly enhances its stature and adds to its prestige—ends which all Chief Justices desire. Success in this, as in all things, undoubtedly depends on a number of factors. Clearly, however, diplomacy—ability to compromise differences, to treat colleagues fairly, and to cultivate a relaxed atmosphere—is a prime ingredient. Moreover, while intellectual power may be of value in shaping decisions, it hardly guarantees a successful chief justiceship. Charles Evans Hughes, the model Chief Justice, owed his success as much to a masterful personality as to his

[1] Miller to Ballinger, July 27, 1873, in Fairman, *Miller*, p. 256.

powerful mind; his successor, Harlan Fiske Stone, while a man of capable intellect, lacked the arts of leadership. By contrast, Melville W. Fuller, though greatly overshadowed by judges such as Holmes and Field, was a highly successful Chief Justice.[2]

In this respect Morrison Waite brought to the Court an ideal personality. While he could be firm, he was by temperament a conciliator, an amiable, easygoing person who liked people and enjoyed their company. Following his death, the parish newspaper of Toledo's Trinity Church, which Waite, an Episcopalian, served as a vestryman for twenty-five years, recalled his reputation as "a peacemaker"—"always opposed to any proposition that tended toward discord, always ready with some calm, fair statement, to appease the ruffled passions of his colleagues." [3] Even apart from his natural temperament, Waite strongly believed in the wisdom of what he called "policy," of moving slowly in seeking to influence men rather "than jumping at once to the lead without having built behind." Perhaps the best statement of this attitude occurs in a letter of advice to his newspaper friend, Clark Waggoner, a combative editor who was involved in a feud with the stockholders of the Toledo *Commercial:*

> There may have been times when you might have been more politic without compromising in any degree your principles. Here I am afraid is the pinch. No one can ask you to yield up any of your honest convictions. What they do ask is that you use a little more tact sometimes in the means by which you give effect to your convictions. You can't always make a man good by telling him he must be so, and fighting him if [he] don't agree with you. Ten to one, in such a contest you will be beaten yourself. When you know you are right, and in a fair contest can make it so appear, is it not sometimes well to lose a "pawn" in order that you may take a "knight". When you are in a fight, and where might alone can win, the powerful blows are those that tell. But when the question is fight or no fight diplomacy is useful.
>
> Think of this a little and see if you can't come to some understanding that will permit of your going on [as editor]. I don't ask you to

[2] Felix Frankfurter, "Chief Justices I Have Known," *Virginia Law Review*, XXXIX (1953), 883–905; King, *Melville W. Fuller*, ch. x, xiii; Alpheus T. Mason, *Harlan Fiske Stone* (New York: The Viking Press, 1956), chs. xxxiv–xxxvii; Merlo J. Pusey, *Charles Evans Hughes* (New York: The Macmillan Company, 1951), II, ch. lxiv.

[3] *The Parish Guide,* April, 1888. Waite Papers.

> yield one iota of principle, but are there not some non essentials which you can lop off to accommodate yourself to the wishes of those you are in conflict with. It has been my fortune to assist in healing differences among newspapermen before. The result has been success.[4]

Unlike many, he followed his own advice. From the moment of his appointment Waite practiced diplomacy. Knowing well that he had been plucked from obscurity to preside over men some of whom felt entitled to his seat, the new Chief Justice shunned elaborate private parties as "undue glorification," made a show of calling upon his colleagues almost immediately after his arrival in Washington, and, to a point at least, good naturedly tolerated Justice Clifford's attempts to direct him in the performance of his duties. The caution was justified. Miller and Swayne were resentful at having been passed over; Field's attitude was disparaging; and Clifford, succumbing to the infirmities of old age, was easily offended. Not surprisingly, Waite's earliest years were the hardest. For he, on his part, had to acquire familiarity with the Court's work and a sense of confidence when presiding from the chair once occupied by John Marshall. And, in turn, his associates needed time to accept the modest Ohioan as their Chief.

An early disappointment, and a revealing illustration of Waite's insecure status, occurred in 1875 during his second year as Chief Justice. As the 1875 term approached, the Court Reporter, John W. Wallace, announced his intention of resigning. In those days the reportership was a coveted position, attracting men of public stature who associated as equals with the justices and paying (through a combination of salary and profits from the sale of the reports) approximately $12,000 a year—a tidy sum compared to the $10,000 earned by the Associate Justices and $10,500 earned by the Chief Justice. Wallace's intentions became known in early September, and soon two men emerged as potential successors. The name of Albert G. Browne, a former reporter for the Supreme Judicial Court of Massachusetts and managing editor of the New York *Evening Post*, was brought forward by Justice Clifford, Chief Justice Gray of Massa-

[4] Waite to Waggoner, Dec. 20, 1875, Letterbooks; Waite to Amelia Waite, May 14, 1882.

chusetts, and Charles O'Conor of the New York bar.[5] Orville H. Browning, supported by Justices Davis and Field, suggested William Tod Otto, a former Indiana judge and Browning's Assistant Secretary of the Interior during the Johnson Administration. A third candidate, William Green, a distinguished Virginia lawyer and legal scholar, failed to receive serious consideration because of his advanced age of almost seventy years.[6]

Meeting in conference on October 16, 1875, the justices set Saturday, October 30, as the day on which they would elect a new reporter. Up until this point Waite had no preference. Then, one week before the election, while dining with Justice Bradley, it occurred to John L. Cadwalader, the Assistant Secretary of State and a good friend of the Chief Justice,[7] that J. C. Bancroft Davis would make an ideal reporter. Davis and Waite had been intimate friends since their service before the Geneva Tribunal; moreover, as Hamilton Fish's former assistant in the State Department and at the time Minister to Germany, Davis was a man of excellent qualifications. Waite, "surprised that he had never thought of it," was immediately enthusiastic and set out to contact his colleagues. Several, he learned, were committed to Judge Otto, but Waite told Cadwalader that he thought he could muster a majority for their mutual friend.[8] Even at best, however, the vote was bound to be close. Clifford was firmly set on Browne;[9] Field and David Davis had promised to vote for Otto; Bradley and Hunt were with Waite in favoring Davis—leaving Swayne, Miller, and Strong as the key figures.

The day prior to the election Waite informed Hunt that "unless some change takes place in the opinion of my brethren, which I can-

[5] Gray to Waite, Oct. 20, 1875; O'Conor to Waite, Oct. 18, 1875.

[6] *Browning Diary*, II, 427–430; Waite to James Lyons, Oct. 25, 1875, Letterbooks. (Lyons, a Richmond attorney had proposed Green.) Waite to Green, Oct. 30, 1875, Letterbooks.

[7] John Lambert Cadwalader was descended from a prominent New Jersey family. Following retirement from public service in 1877 he practiced law in New York. *Lamb's Biographical Dictionary of the United States* (Boston: James H. Lamb Company, 1900), I, 539.

[8] Cadwalader to Davis, Nov. 2, 1875. Bancroft Davis Papers.

[9] Browne's prospects were seriously impaired because, as an editor of the New York *Evening Post*, he had written numerous articles denouncing the New York Court of Appeals for its handling of the Tweed Ring prosecutions. This raised doubts about his ability to abstain from political strife if he were Reporter. Browne to Waite, Oct. 29, 1875; Waite to Browne, Oct. 30, 1875, Letterbooks.

not now expect" he would not nominate Davis.[10] Presumably, Waite believed "some change" had occurred, for on the thirtieth he presented Davis' name—and was solidly defeated. Hunt and Bradley stayed with him in the crucial "informal vote," but Strong, Field, Davis, Miller, and Swayne elected Otto. Clifford stubbornly supported Browne, even refusing to make it unanimous when the justices cast a "formal vote." [11]

Deeply upset, Waite shot off a note to Cadwalader saying he was "profoundly thankful" for his suggesting Davis, "as I know every judge would be if they would consent to give him a trial." Then he added:

> I have learned something in this experience, which has been personally more mortifying than I can express to you. However, it is said a day is not well spent unless it brings some new knowledge. All I can say is that in this case I prefer it should have been something else.

A few hours later he wrote again:

> The thing is "closed out". If I could put faith in anything, I should say that our defeat was due only to the fact that the name was not mentioned until the Judges had become committed to the other party. As it is I have just now no confidence in anything.
>
> Set me down with Davis as easily as you can. It is to me most mortifying that I should have been instrumental in getting him into this position. I was misled by one man, but do not like to believe it was intentional.[12]

Cadwalader cabled Davis, who had been eager for the post, "one vote wanting" and subsequently explained that Waite had "four votes —and wanted five . . . but the fifth man was in doubt and hard to get." Since Cadwalader also noted, "I did not ask and do not definitely know what took place at the actual election—but that Otto was elected," [13] it seems doubtful that Waite ever had four votes for Davis. More likely, Waite believed he could count on four votes, thereby

[10] Waite to Hunt, Oct. 29, 1875, Letterbooks.
[11] Docket Books (Motions), Oct. Term 1875. Waite Papers.
[12] Waite to Cadwalader, two letters dated Oct. 30, 1875, Letterbooks.
[13] Cadwalader to Davis, Oct. 30, 1875 (cable), Nov. 2, 1875. Davis Papers.

creating a deadlock and perhaps attracting Clifford or one of the other judges. Instead, he had only Bradley's and Hunt's besides his own, leaving an interesting question as to which man "misled" him into believing he would support Davis. Because Clifford, Field, and David Davis were committed before the election, the man who deserted him in conference was either Swayne, Miller, or Strong. Strong's relations with Waite were excellent and, unlike the other two, he harbored no resentments against the new Chief—making it probable that either Swayne or Miller was the offending party.

"The C.J.," Cadwalader told Hamilton Fish, "seems to be very sore indeed." [14] Writing to an Ohio friend on the evening of his setback, Waite spoke of the "dragging effect" of his position and wistfully remarked, "Oh! how I long occasionally for one of our old circuit experiences to lift the burden for a moment." [15] But the Chief Justice was not the sort to stay chagrined over failures. Cadwalader invited him to a Sunday dinner, to "drown our sorrows," with William Evarts and Edwards Pierrepont, the Attorney General. Doubtless, a few hours of conviviality with close friends soon restored Waite's lagging spirits.[16]

Judge Otto served eight years as Reporter with mixed results. The influential *American Law Review*, which had welcomed Wallace's departure because it believed him unfit, soon soured on Otto also. It criticized his "lack of neatness" and his tardiness in taking almost a year to produce reports. Later, in fact, it came out that Otto often prepared them from the first proofs of the judges' opinions, not bothering to include their last corrections. Numerous errors were uncovered and Miller concluded that Otto had been "lazy and careless." [17] At any rate, Otto's resignation in 1883 offered a new opportunity for Bancroft Davis, then serving on the Court of Claims. This time Waite won an easy victory, informing his friend that "the vote was a very flattering one in your favor, and I, as you may well

[14] Cadwalader to Fish, Oct. 30, 1875. Fish Papers.

[15] Waite to H. L. Hosmer, Oct. 30, 1875, Letterbooks.

[16] Cadwalader to Waite, Oct. 30, 1875.

[17] *American Law Review*, X (1876), 357–358, XI (1877), 335, XII (1878), 784, XVII (1883), 115; James E. Briggs to Waite, Feb. 7, 1885. Briggs, president of the Lawyers' Co-operative Publishing Company, cited instances of errors in Otto's reports. Miller to Waite, Feb. 1, 1885.

imagine, was much gratified." A further indication that by the early 1880's Waite's authority was secure came in a comment made to his wife. Discussing possible appointments to the Court, Waite said he was somewhat indifferent, "I am besides being chief, among the oldest. Nobody knows as well as I how much that means." [18]

Except for the reportership affair, most of Waite's early difficulties came in his relations with Justices Field and Clifford. Cantankerous and belligerent, Stephen Field was always a problem to his brethren, to the Reporter, and especially to the Chief Justice.[19] Like many belligerent individuals he reveled in a good fight. Field's circuit decisions in favor of railroads and Chinese aliens repeatedly aroused hostility among California farmers and workers, keeping him, as he observed with evident satisfaction, "under constant fire." "I still live and flourish," he declared, and "I do not feel disposed however to put myself out of the way to please those who thus give me the only return I receive for my labors." [20]

Field, however, was not humorless and certainly Court history would have been far duller without him. An element of playfulness emerges in a note to District Judge Deady written from the Bench, "a somewhat dull talker supposing I am taking notes of his arguments. Judge Miller sitting by my side wishes to be remembered to you." [21] On another occasion he wrote Waite asking to be excused from a Saturday consultation because of "frightful" stomach pains:

> Whether these were . . . [due] to terrapin, lobster salad, or brother Harlan's 33 year old whiskey, or to inward cussedness, or both combined I cannot affirm. I know I thought that if Beecher [Henry Ward Beecher, the famous sermonizer] had knocked hell out of the next world he had sent some portion of it into this.

Nor was he unaware of his acrimonious temper. Writing to Waite that he would be late for the opening of a term, he pointed out that, since a quorum was on hand, his absence would be "of no detriment,"

[18] Waite to Bancroft Davis, Oct. 14, 1883; Waite to Amelia Waite, March, 9, 1882.

[19] Fairman, *Miller*, p. 110, pp. 298–299; King, *Melville W. Fuller*, pp. 170–173, 222–227; Alan F. Westin, "Stephen J. Field and the Headnote to O'Neil v. Vermont: A Snapshot of the Fuller Court at Work," *Yale Law Journal*, LXVII (1958), 363–383.

[20] Field to Deady, May 15, 1884. Deady Papers.

[21] Field to Deady, April 7, 1875. Deady Papers.

adding, "Some of the justices might say that it will be of advantage." [22]

From the outset Waite sought to treat Field with "policy." During his first full term, when Waite was preparing the opinion in *Minor* v. *Happersett*, Field provided him with a copy of a California ruling on women's suffrage. Waite immediately sent thanks, using the opportunity to work in a bit of flattery: "What a happy faculty you have of remembering the right thing at the right time. I wish I had it." [23] He also took care to allot Field his share of significant opinions. On the other hand, he refused to let Field's bluster frighten him.

Among the cases up for decision during the 1875 term was *United States* v. *Union Pacific R. Co.*, an action raising the question as to whether, under Congress' chartering acts, the Union Pacific was required to pay the semiannual interest on the government's bonds in advance of their maturity.[24] The case naturally excited interest in financial circles, and the New York *Herald* reported Wall Street rumors—which proved to be correct—that the Court would decide for the railroad. Jay Gould, who controlled large blocks of Union Pacific stock, wrote to Waite, indignantly denying any desire to have advance knowledge of the decision, "because I have a desire to retain a very high respect for the integrity & honor of the exalted tribunal over which you preside"—a "respect," however, which eroded with the *Granger* and *Sinking Fund* decisions.[25]

Even prior to the Wall Street rumors, the Chief Justice had assigned the opinion to David Davis. Since Davis was unquestionably the Court's most "radical" member—the National Labor Reform Party nominated him for President in 1872—Waite's strategy in giving him the prorailroad opinion brings to mind Chief Justice Hughes' practice, whenever possible, of assigning liberal justices to write conservative opinions and conservative justices to write liberal opinions in order to preserve the Court's image of impartiality.[26] Field, however, wanted the opinion for himself. He took grave offense because the Chief Justice gave it to Davis and casually remarked, after a con-

[22] Field to Waite, Feb. 2, 1878, Sept. 21, 1881.

[23] *Minor* v. *Happersett*, 21 Wallace 162 (1875); Waite to Field, March 13, 1875, Letterbooks.

[24] 91 U.S. 72 (1875).

[25] Gould to Waite, Nov. 13, 1875; N.Y. *Herald*, Nov. 12, 13, 1875.

[26] Pusey, *Charles Evans Hughes*, II, 678–679.

ference on November 6, that it was best to let someone not closely identified with the railroads announce the decision. That evening Field fired off an ill-tempered note. Waite answered the next day:

Hon. S. J. Field

Dear Sir,

On my return home last evening I found your note. The direction I gave the case to which you refer, was after mature consideration and most certainly was not influenced by any personal feeling against yourself. I had no idea that you specially desired it, and when the announcement was made, supposed you would not fail to see its propriety. If what I have done is not satisfactory to my brethren, I regret it, but I think if they and you would, as you said the other day, "put your minds alongside of mine" for a little while, it would be seen that my judgment was correct.

Regretting that you entertain the feelings toward me personally that you express

I remain
Truly yrs.
M. R. Waite

Three days later Field responded, still protesting, though retracting some of the harsh language in his first letter. In reply Waite expressed a desire to be friends, but bluntly explained his motives and made it clear that the responsibility for making assignments belonged to the Chief Justice:

Hon. S. J. Field

Dear Sir,

I have just received and read your note of yesterday. I think you must be mistaken in your understanding of the words I used after the consultation. If those you give were the words I did use, certainly they were not used in the offensive sense you appear to have received them.

We cannot conceal from ourselves the fact, that in the excited state of feeling which exists, or has existed, with the public in respect to the connexion of the government with the Union Pacific there may be some feeling of disappointment at the result of this case. It seems to me, therefore, to be specially important that the opinion should come from one who had not only been understood to be watchful of the government purse, but who would not be known as the personal friend of the parties representing these rail road interests. There was no doubt of your intimate personal relations with the managers of the Central Pacific, and naturally you, more than any one else in the court, realise the vast importance of the great work that has been done. To tell the truth also, I knew that you were dissatisfied with the manner of the argument on the part of the government, and was afraid that this might, unconsciously to you, find expression in the opinion. Once in and it would be difficult to get it out. Nothing could be more unfortunate for the court than to have it there.

No one appreciates your vigorous style more than I do, and, but for these considerations, I should have been glad to have had its use in this case— And while I regret that you do not look at the matter as I do, I cannot but think my judgment was for the best interest of us all. As for opinions in important cases, I don't know, but I think you fared better than the Judge [Davis] who has the case did at the last term. Certainly during the present term he has had no advantage over you. I certainly intend to treat all my brethren fairly in this most delicate and at the same time important part of my work. If I do not, it is the fault of the head and not of the heart.

I am glad to know that I misunderstood some of the expressions in your former note, and that I may hope to retain your friendship and respect if my conduct shall be such as to merit it.

Very Respectfully Yrs.
M. R. Waite [27]

The fiery Californian may not have been mollified, but there is no evidence that he again challenged Waite's assignments.

Waite's difficulties with Justice Clifford were of a different order. True, he too could be stubborn. With fellow Democrat Field, he refused for awhile to step into the White House during Hayes' Administration because he felt Tilden had been cheated out of the Presidency. Yet, while not a great mind, he was, as Justice Miller said, "a good man and a true man," who by the time Waite came to know him was near the end of "his days of usefulness." [28] When Waite joined the Court in 1874 Clifford was seventy-one years old and his

[27] Waite to Field, Nov. 7, 10, 1875, Letterbooks.
[28] Miller to Waite, July 24, 1881.

mental powers were rapidly failing—a tragic fact graphically recorded in Miller's correspondence during the period.[29] Clifford's opinions became increasingly diffuse and long. "It will take a good while to find out *all* there is in it," Waite remarked in sending one of them to an inquirer, "Bro. Clifford is never very short." [30]

What was evident to others was not evident to Clifford, who displayed growing sensitivity in all matters affecting his work. He frequently rejected assignments by simply saying he did not care to write the opinion, and he was quick to take offense, forcing the Chief Justice to attempt to pacify him with kind and flattering letters.[31] On one occasion, a clear instance of his mental failure, Clifford returned a case because "I think I did not vote for the judgment. At all events I am not prepared to take the opinion." The docket book, however, shows Clifford voting with the majority; Waite took the case himself.[32] On another occasion, he again felt slighted and curtly informed the Chief, "I am not willing to write an opinion in No. 93 and therefore return it. If you want No. 99 for any of your friends you may have that also." Waite's answer was a model of tact and courtesy:

My dear Judge,

I regret that my assignment of cases to you last evening was not satisfactory. I gave you 93 because you were familiar with the law of copyright, and although the case was a simple one, I thought it might be made the foundation of one of your useful opinions.

In looking over the cases again, since your note came, I can now see where I might have pleased you better, and in respect to one in particular some things have occurred to me that I overlooked before, which make it apparent that there would have been great propriety in giving it to you. I regret that it is now beyond my control.

If you still think you do not want 93, I will keep it and announce the decision stating simply that [*sic*] the grounds on which it is placed without more. I wanted to give you the two important land cases

[29] Fairman, *Miller*, p. 351, 373, 374, 378.

[30] Waite to D. T. Wright, Feb. 22, 1877, Letterbooks.

[31] Clifford to Waite, Dec. 5, 1874, Dec. 31, 1878, Nov. 30, 1879; Waite to Clifford, Dec. 5, 1874, April 5, 1875, Letterbooks.

[32] Docket Books, Oct. Term 1877. Waite Papers; *United States* v. *Morrison*, 96 U.S. 232 (1878); Clifford to Waite, Jan. 27, 1878. Clifford did express a willingness to "write anything else which I did vote for."

which Judge Miller has, but you said expressly in the conference that you did not want them.

Hoping I may be more successful in pleasing you in the future,

I remain very sincerely

Yr. friend

M. R. Waite [33]

As these incidents well illustrate, opinion assignment represents perhaps the greatest test of a Chief Justice's administrative skill—in Justice Frankfurter's words, "his single most influential function." [34] It is to his advantage that he assign opinions to those who can hold the majority together; furthermore, in cases raising important constitutional questions, he will want an opinion writer able to explain the Court's position with precision and clarity. Then too, while the justices are equal within the conference room, reputation and public recognition are acquired by writing opinions. Since men do not forsake their egos by going on the bench, they will be anxious for a fair allotment of significant decisions. Once, when Waite made an unclear assignment, Bradley sought clarification and—half in jest, but half serious too—remarked, "I would have consulted some of our brethren, but I feared that they would have been too grasping, and wd. have taken advantage of the latitude given by the ambiguous assignment." [35]

Even beyond these fairly obvious considerations, a host of personal factors influence assignments. New to the Court and somewhat unsure of himself, Justice Harlan preferred not to take a case because "there is likely to be a dissenting opinion." A few years later Harlan confidentially asked his Chief not to assign him any cases argued by Roscoe Conkling—"I heard last winter that Senator Conkling does not feel altogether *kindly* to me." [36] Asked his preference of assignments, Justice Strong, who had written a great number of municipal bond

[33] Clifford to Waite, Dec. 25, 1878; Waite to Clifford, Dec. 25, 1878, Letterbooks. The opinion in number 93, *Perris* v. *Hexauer,* 99 U.S. 668 (1879), was delivered by Waite; in 99, *Reed* v. *McIntyre,* 98 U.S. 447 (1879), by Harlan. Not long after this incident, however, Clifford volunteered to write an extra opinion and Waite gladly obliged him. Clifford to Waite, Jan. 18, 1879.

[34] Frankfurter, "Chief Justices I Have Known," 894.

[35] Bradley to Waite, April 23, 1876.

[36] Harlan to Waite, Dec. 22, 1877, Nov., 1879.

opinions, wished to be "relieved" from a new load of bond cases. On other occasions justices notified Waite that, while they had voted with the majority, they did not fully agree with the decision, and would find it difficult to prepare the opinion.[37]

Well aware of the delicacy of the assignment function, Waite met the challenge successfully by disposing of cases with care and deliberation: he gave the unpopular *Union Pacific* decision to the "radical" David Davis; handed the opinion in *Kilbourn* v. *Thompson,* limiting the congressional power of investigation, to Justice Miller on account of his "conservative habit of deciding no more than is necessary in any case"; [38] and sent a series of important municipal bond cases to Justice Strong because, Waite explained, he "seems to occupy a sort of middle ground." [39] Especially interesting is the fact that Waite consistently assigned the decisions he believed to be most significant to the Court's strongest members. In seventy-two cases decided between 1874 and 1881, which Waite felt were of constitutional significance, he voted against the majority in only six, thereby giving him the right of assigning the other sixty-six.[40] Of these, the majority went to his Court's leading figures: fourteen to himself, eleven each to Miller and Field, ten to Strong, seven to Bradley, and five to Harlan. Swayne and Davis trailed with four and two respectively; Clifford and Hunt both received only one of these opinions.[41]

Besides attempting to assure a strong voice for major pronouncements, Waite used his assignment power in such a way as to make new justices feel at home—and win their friendship. One of the Chief Justice's techniques was to give them the privilege of choosing for themselves their first opinion. L. Q. C. Lamar came to the Court in 1888, long on political but short on legal experience. To ease the

[37] Strong to Waite, n.d., Oct. Term 1878, Feb. 25, 1878; Harlan to Waite, Jan. 19, 1884, in Legal File.

[38] 103 U.S. 168 (1881); Miller to Ballinger, March 20, 1881, in Fairman, *Miller,* p. 333.

[39] Waite to Clifford, March 6, 1876, Letterbooks. The bond cases were *Venice* v. *Murdock,* 92 U.S. 494 and *Genoa* v. *Woodruff,* 92 U.S. 502 (1876) decided along with three other cases. Justice Strong often spoke for the Court in bond cases.

[40] Waite compiled the list in 1881 at the request of George Bancroft, who asked him to name the most prominent cases involving constitutional questions decided since his appointment. Waite to Bancroft, May 23, 1881. N.Y. Public Library.

[41] Significantly, this pattern applies as well to the period 1874–1878 when there was a full complement of judges. After 1878 Hunt and Clifford were often absent because of illness. It should be noted that Harlan, a strong judge, did not join the Court until December 1877, the year Davis left for the Senate.

burden of transition, Waite gave the newcomer a light work load until he felt more sure of his abilities.[42]

The Chief Justice seized other opportunities to practice the arts of diplomacy. New judges received warm letters of welcome, offers of assistance, and invitations to quickly join the brethren and help with "important" and "interesting" cases.[43] An important announcement such as Justice Gray's opinion in the legal tender case of *Julliard* v. *Greenman*, evoked compliments of "admirable," "a model of style and harmony," and a statement that "my 'judgment' on the assignment of this case will never be reversed." [44] Nor was Justice Field excluded. His acceptance of a compromise amendment in an opinion he was preparing brought hearty thanks and—with some exaggeration—Waite's commendation that "you are always open to reason." Whatever Field's personal evaluation of the Chief Justice, Waite's firm but courteous approach seems to have had its effect. When in 1880 Field wanted to point out an error in one of Waite's opinions, he was anxious to do so "without giving offense." [45]

Justice Harlan came to the Court in 1877, expressing a desire to perform his circuit duties in the southeastern fourth circuit, the circuit then served by the Chief Justice. Waite was willing enough to let him have it and take for himself the vacant midwestern seventh circuit which was closer to his old home. Since, however, the other Court members felt that the Chief Justice should be located in the East (as had been customary from Marshall's day), Waite yielded to their wishes, not that "I could not have made the change if I had insisted upon it, but under all circumstances I thought it better not to insist." As a result, Harlan went to the seventh circuit, preceded by a glowing recommendation from Waite to Circuit Judge Thomas Drummond and with a word of encouragement from his Chief. "You are sure to *capture* the place. So put on a bold face & 'go in.' " [46]

[42] Harlan to Waite, Dec. 15, 1877; Woods to Waite, Jan., 1881; Matthews to Waite, Oct. 15, 1881, in Legal File; Edward Mayes, *Lucius Q. C. Lamar, His Life, Times, and Speeches* (Nashville: Methodist Episcopal Church, 1896), p. 541.

[43] Waite to Lamar, Jan. 17, 1888, in Mayes, *Lamar,* p. 538; Waite to Gray, Dec. 23, 1881. Gray Papers.

[44] Waite to Gray, Feb. 21, 1884. Gray Papers; *Julliard* v. *Greenman,* 110 U.S. 421 (1884).

[45] Waite to Field, April 28, 1882. Field Papers; Field to Deady, Jan. 5, 1880. Deady Papers.

[46] Waite to Drummond, April 25, 1878; to Harlan, April 20, 1878, Letterbooks.

At other times he had to soothe ruffled tempers and seek to avert needless friction. "Judges," Waite commented shortly after entering their circle, "are made of men and men are human. We all have our weaknesses and they will crop out. It is amusing sometimes even though it is amazing to watch the developments" [47]—an observation that the Chief Justice's experiences repeatedly confirmed. Once one of them, probably Bradley, prepared an opinion believing that he had Miller's assent to a certain proposition. Learning he did not, the Justice exploded, scrawling a hasty note to the Chief, "I would be very glad never to write another opinion in the court." [48] That getting the judges to write opinions accurately reflecting the majority consensus could be a delicate business is well brought out in this letter from Waite to Justice Swayne:

> As I said in the consultation room, I am entirely satisfied with your opinion.[49] It expresses the law as I understand it precisely. I think however, Miller had the right to believe from what occurred when the case was decided, that the point which he suggested yesterday was not to go into the opinion. While no formal vote was taken he had good reason to believe his objection was assented to.
>
> I submit to you, therefore, whether, under all the circumstances, that part of the opinion had better not be left out. You know how important it is to avoid, as far as possible, all occasion for unpleasant criticism in our consultations, and if one judge is allowed to write an opinion on a different ground from that on which the decision was placed, it is easy to see how difficult it may sometimes be to enforce the rule as to others.
>
> I hope you will receive this suggestion in the same spirit it is made. I repeat that the opinion is entirely satisfactory to myself, and I should not mention the subject again after what occurred yesterday, except to prevent this case becoming a precedent in case we should think it necessary to apply the rule hereafter.
>
> I leave the matter entirely to your own judgment.

Because Miller held Swayne's judicial abilities in low esteem, Waite had good reason to attempt conciliation without unduly offending

[47] Waite to John T. Wait, May 2, 1876, Letterbooks.

[48] Unsigned note to Waite, Oct. Term 1881. The handwriting resembles Bradley's.

[49] Most likely *Ex parte Reed*, 100 U.S. 13 (1879), a habeas corpus case dealing with the powers of military courts. The opinion, given by Swayne, was approved in conference on November 8 and announced two days later. Docket Books, Oct. Term 1879. Waite Papers.

Swayne. His strategy worked; Swayne "cheerfully" agreed to the suggestion, and some possible unpleasantness was avoided.[50]

To one as conscientious as Morrison Waite the Court's increasingly unmanageable workload left him much troubled. Where the Supreme Court began its 1870 Term with 636 cases on the docket, the 1880 Term opened with 1,202 cases, nearly a twofold increase. Ten years later the backlog stood at 1,816 cases. This steep rise in litigation was in large measure a consequence of the expansion of federal activities in the wake of the Civil War's nationalizing influence and of the vigorous economic life of the postwar period which spurred bankruptcy, patent, and admiralty cases—in short, because of the country's growth. Responding to these forces, Congress deliberately extended the jurisdiction of federal courts.[51] The most significant act was that of March 3, 1875, opening the federal courts to any suits which asserted rights under the Constitution, the laws, and the treaties of the United States, and providing for the removal of such actions to the federal courts. The Supreme Court itself encouraged this trend when it ruled, Waite and Miller dissenting, that because a federal charter of incorporation is a "law of the United States," every action involving federally chartered corporations might be tried in the federal courts.[52]

Waite viewed this development with alarm. Worrisome references to the ever mounting accumulation of Supreme Court cases fill his correspondence. To conserve space in the reports he told the Reporter to severely limit accounts of counsel's arguments, and, without much success, set up a "reporting committee," hoping it could persuade the justices to shorten their opinions.[53] More important, he made sure that, in a discreet way, Congress learned his thoughts as to what legislation should be passed to relieve the Court. In common with

[50] Waite to Swayne, Nov. 8, 1879, Letterbooks; Swayne to Waite, Nov. 10, 1879. On Miller's estimate of Swayne see Fairman, *Miller*, pp. 232–234, 374.

[51] Felix Frankfurter and James M. Landis, *The Business of the Supreme Court* (New York: The Macmillan Company, 1927), pp. 60–61.

[52] *Pacific Railroad Removal Cases*, 115 U.S. 2 (1885). Interestingly, Justices Field and Gray dissented in conference, but acquiesced in the majority's ruling. Docket Books, Oct. Term 1884. Waite Papers. On the effect of the decision see Warren, *Supreme Court*, II, 685–686. Note should be taken of *Ex parte Schollenberger*, 96 U.S. 369 (1877), where Waite, for a unanimous Court, allowed an expansion of federal jurisdiction over suits involving corporations.

[53] Waite to Wallace, May 4, 1875; to Miller, May 15, 1879, Letterbooks.

most of his associates Waite firmly opposed those plans which envisaged dividing the tribunal into two or more divisions. One plan with wide currency proposed, for example, expanding the Supreme Court's membership to twenty-one and dividing this small army of judges into three separate chambers.[54] In place of such a radical change, the Chief Justice favored the bill sponsored by his former colleague, Senator David Davis, which provided for the commissioning of eighteen new circuit judges and the establishment of intermediate circuit courts.

With the situation growing more desperate and the Court almost four years behind in its work, Waite made a public plea for passage of a court bill. Speaking in 1887 at a breakfast given the justices by the Philadelphia bar, he put the issue in its proper perspective. What was needed, he said, was not "relief for the Supreme Court"; there always would be business enough to keep it fully occupied. The need, rather, was for "relief for the people against the tedious and oppressive delays" characteristic of the appellate system. "It is the people that need relief, not the court." [55] But conflicts among backers of widely divergent plans, Southern hostility to any increase in the number of national courts, and the fact that during the 1870's and 1880's Congress and the Presidency were rarely controlled by the same party—making difficult an agreement as to how the patronage plums created by the new judgeships would be divided—all contributed to block passage of a court bill.[56] Not until 1891, after almost two decades of agitation, did Congress finally pass a comprehensive measure, the Circuit Court of Appeals Act, which freed the justices from the archaic necessity of going on circuit, and established an intermediate layer of courts to siphon off cases otherwise destined for the Supreme Court.

If individual zeal alone could have lightened the Court's docket,

[54] Waite to Congressman James Lowndes, Feb. 28, 1878, Letterbooks; Bancroft Davis to Waite, Dec. 24, 1879; Waite to Amelia Waite, May 14, 1882; N.Y. *Tribune*, Dec. 23, 1878; N.Y. *Times*, Sept. 26, 1886.

[55] Remarks of Chief Justice Waite in response to the toast, "The Supreme Court of the United States." Waite Papers. The speech was published in legal journals, e.g., *Albany Law Journal*, Oct. 15, 1887.

[56] *American Law Review, XVII* (1883), 258–259; *Congressional Record*, 47th Cong., 1st Sess. 3504–3506, 3600, 3640–3641 (1881–1882); Frankfurter and Landis, *Business of the Supreme Court*, pp. 77–102.

Waite would soon have reduced it to nothing. So hard did he work that even before the completion of his first term his eldest son was begging him to slow down.[57] Such entreaties were a waste of time. Waite might complain of being on a "treadmill," of "constant and uninterrupted work," and of "vacations" devoted to opinion writing,[58] but he took pride in a job well done and followed a stern inner code which decreed hard work and individual effort. To his wife he once explained:

> You know better than I, that I must have just such work as I do have, or I cannot exist. More than fifty years of life, which has never known a minute that could be devoted to idleness, must be hard worked or it will go off on a switch. I do work all the time, but I am not overworked. I sleep every night when I get tired and go to bed, no matter what the hour. . . . You need not feel afraid. I was never so well in my life, and am taking good care of myself.[59]

Adding to his problems—and work—were illnesses among the brethren. Strengthened by the addition of John Marshall Harlan, who joined the Court in 1877, Waite began the 1878 term full of zest. "The Judges," he announced, "are all in good health prepared to make the attack." [60] Such optimism was premature. Before the term was over Ward Hunt suffered a stroke; the next year the aging Clifford began to give way; and all the while Swayne's mental powers were failing. Despite Waite's gentle hints, Hunt refused to resign, hoping that Congress would vote him a pension (for he was still ineligible). He was obligated, moreover, to Roscoe Conkling for his seat, and Conkling, busily feuding with Hayes because of his reform heresy, wished to deny the President the privilege of filling the vacancy.[61]

Hunt's incapacitation led to a minor crisis in the second circuit where a large number of patent and admiralty cases required disposition by a Supreme Court justice. Duty called, and in the early summer

[57] C. C. Waite to Morrison Waite, Nov. 26, 1874.

[58] Waite to John T. Wait, Oct. 24, 1875; to J. M. Gloyd, Jan. 4, 1878, Letterbooks.

[59] Waite to Amelia Waite, Nov. 13, 1881.

[60] Waite to George S. Bryan, Oct. 11, 1878, Letterbooks.

[61] Waite to Ward Hunt, Jr., Oct. 26, 1879; to Ward Hunt, Oct. 12, 1880, Letterbooks; Fairman, *Miller*, pp. 377–378.

of 1878 and again in 1879 the Chief Justice volunteered to fill the gap by going to New York following the completion of his own circuit work. Hunt expressed heartfelt gratitude and Waite tactfully dismissed the work as "easy and pleasant." But to a man tired out from a year's labors, passing on a batch of admiralty appeals during a New York summer was no pleasure. "You dont know how I am bored here in court, but I must stand it," he complained to his wife. And a few days later:

> I am so glad you are going to Cleveland and only wish I could go too. Confound it, why was I not made of the same kind of selfish material that some other people are. If I had been I should have had my pleasures. True, good Bro. Hunt might have worked himself into his grave. But that's no account. As it is, I am here, well and doing my duty. Likely I shall get no credit for it except from you and myself. You will realise that it is what I ought to do, if I consent to accept the position I have and I know that what I am doing is right.

As the chore drew to a close Waite felt inner satisfaction: "I have stood it first rate so far and if I can accomplish all that I have undertaken shall do a good work for Bro. Hunt." [62] The ethic was high Victorian and it governed Morrison Waite's life.

Although Hunt held on to his seat until January 1882 when, thanks to the efforts of Senator David Davis, Congress passed a special retirement bill, three additional vacancies were filled in the early 1880's. Justice Strong's resignation at the end of 1880 opened the way for President Hayes to appoint Circuit Judge William B. Woods, a former Ohioan who had settled in Alabama after service in the Union Army. While Woods was a man of average capabilities, Waite appreciated his capacity for hard work and told the President, "you have made the best possible choice under the circumstances." [63] The controversial Stanley Matthews, a man of considerable abilities and a good friend of the Chief Justice, joined the Court next. A narrow confirmation victory after his sharply contested second nomination

[62] Hunt to Waite, June 5, 1878; Swayne to Waite, June 5, 1878; Waite to Amelia Waite, June 2, 12, 19, 1878. Waite received some recognition for his labors. The *American Law Review*, XIII (1879), 735, praised "the admirable clearness and conciseness" of his second circuit opinions.

[63] Waite to Hayes, Jan. 4, 1881; to Edward C. Ballinger, January 2, 1881, Letterbooks.

enabled him to fill the vacancy caused by Justice Swayne's long overdue retirement. Nathan Clifford's death in 1881 gave President Arthur his first appointment and he filled it ably, selecting Chief Justice Horace Gray of Massachusetts, a nomination which was cordially endorsed by the justices of the Court.[64]

Arthur's next venture in appointing justices was more troublesome. With Hunt finally retired in January 1882, it seemed at first that his successor would be Senator George F. Edmunds, chairman of the Judiciary Committee and a leading Republican spokesman. "Able and honest" but "dogmatical and contentious" was Miller's judgment of Edmunds, a view probably shared by Waite, who nevertheless favored the appointment because it would add to the Court's stature. "While I confess to not liking Edmunds as well as I used to," he wrote, "his appointment would surely strengthen the court in the estimation of the country." [65] Instead, the President shocked the Chief Justice by turning to an old political ally, Roscoe Conkling, whose reputation for arrogance and vanity would surely not add to the Court's prestige.

Even at this distant date the New York spoilsman seems a singularly inappropriate choice for the Supreme Court; the title, "Mr. Justice Conkling," has a jarring ring. "I feel anxious about you," Amelia Waite inquired of her husband, "knowing the feeling you have about the Supreme Bench. I have been afraid it would get you ill." "I can stand him if necessary," Waite replied, "but it will be a grind unless he changes his manner towards me." [66] Despite recent political reverses which had cost him his Senate seat, Conkling still knew how to act imperiously. He kept Washington in suspense, refusing to say whether he would accept the appointment. Then, winning confirmation, he declined the office—a sequence of events which distressed Waite: "I am more provoked at this than I was about the nomination originally. The President had no right to send the office begging." [67] After next offering the post to Edmunds, who declined for personal

[64] Fairman, *Miller*, p. 384; Harlan to Gray, April 18, 1881. Gray Papers.
[65] Fairman, *Miller*, p. 377; Waite to Amelia Waite, Feb. 19, 1882.
[66] Amelia Waite to Waite, Feb. 26, 1882; Waite to Amelia Waite, Feb. 28, 1882. Waite shared his wife's opinion that Conkling was an unsavory "henchman." Amelia Waite to Waite, Feb. 13, 1882; Waite to Amelia Waite, Feb. 14, 1882.
[67] Waite to Amelia Waite, March 2, 5, 1882.

reasons, Arthur nominated Circuit Judge Samuel Blatchford of New York, a colorless but conscientious individual. Waite felt the appointment to be adequate, if not brilliant, and was soon praising Blatchford as "a good worker" who "will help us amazingly." [68]

Any evaluation of Chief Justice Waite's performance as manager of the Court must reckon with Samuel Miller's disparaging estimate. Feeling a personal responsibility for the Court's successful operation, he believed Waite inadequate to the task:

> I can't make a silk purse out of a sow's ear. I can't make a great Chief Justice out of a small man. I can't make Clifford and Swayne, who are too old resign, nor keep the Chief Justice from giving them cases to write opinions in which their garrulity is often mixed with mischief.

This was in 1875, not long after Waite's appointment, and while the two men always enjoyed a cordial relationship, Miller reiterated his unflattering judgment four years later. As earlier, he was concerned with Swayne's and Clifford's overlong opinions and blamed the Chief Justice for lacking the "firmness and courage" to insist on brevity. Waite, he said, wanted "to be popular as an amiable, kind hearted man" (Miller conceded him these qualities), but was unable to preside over the Supreme Court with competence and dignity: "Of what is due to that court, and what is becoming its character, he has no conception." [69]

Human nature being what it is, Miller's reaction is understandable. Perhaps a bit unpolished in legal training, he nevertheless ranks among the Court's great judges, and had good cause to feel aggrieved when Grant passed him over in favor of the obscure Toledo lawyer. Miller was also endowed with a healthy dose of rugged honesty and, even as he berated his Chief, admitted, "I may be more affected by the fact that I was not [chosen] than I am conscious of." [70] In fact, Samuel Miller was so affected that he was blinded to Waite's substantial achievements. He had come to the Court without public

[68] Waite to Amelia Waite, March 9, May 14, 1882. Edmund's declination is discussed in Waite to Amelia Waite, March 7, 13, 1882.

[69] Miller to Ballinger, Dec. 5, 1875, Oct. 29, 1879, in Fairman, *Miller*, p. 373, 409.

[70] Fairman, *Miller*, p. 373. And see Fairman's comments, pp. 425–426.

stature, called upon to preside over men who at best looked at him with skeptical eyes; some, like Miller, were downright hostile. Not only this, but a group composed of such forceful and brilliant personalities as Stephen J. Field, Joseph P. Bradley, Samuel F. Miller, and later John Marshall Harlan offered limitless opportunities for the sort of disruptive conflict that wracked the Chase Court at the time of the legal tender decisions.[71] Despite these handicaps and potential pitfalls, Waite preserved harmony and strengthened the Court. While he suffered an initial rebuff in the matter of the reportership (in part because he did not begin canvassing for Bancroft Davis until too late),[72] it was his Court and he ran it.

Contrary to Miller's assertion, opinions were carefully assigned with a view to the Court's best interests, and the really significant decisions had a habit of winding up in the hands of the most able judges. Waite, as Miller derisively commented, practiced amiability, deliberately striving for harmony; but he also combined kindness with firmness: the letter to Swayne, asking him to modify an opinion for the sake of peace among the brethren, and the strong reply to Field, refusing to be intimidated by the Californian's arrogance, were not the acts of a man who lacked resolution and courage. Miller's bluntness and forcefulness were useful qualities, yet it is open to serious doubt whether he could have handled the Court as well as Waite. A Chief Justice's powers are strictly limited, and openly telling Noah Swayne that his opinions were a potpourri of "garrulity" would not have made the Court run smoother.

Some test of Miller's ability to preside came in 1885 when years of overwork finally caught up with Waite. Bancroft Davis, the Reporter, had feared as much only a few days before illness forced the Chief Justice to suspend his duties. "Waite is far from well or strong," he wrote to Hamilton Fish, "but wont admit it to himself, and may work on and break down before Spring comes." [73] Soon after, in December 1884, Waite became physically ill, and when he had recovered sufficiently, went to Florida for a period of recuperation. As the

[71] Fairman, *Miller,* ch. vii.

[72] As Hamilton Fish thought. Fish to Davis, Nov. 10, 1875. Davis Papers; also Waite to Cadwalader, Oct. 30, 1875.

[73] Davis to Fish, Nov. 16, 1884. Fish Papers.

senior associate, Justice Miller took over the management of the Court and quickly discovered just how hard the Chief Justice worked. "I always knew that he did a great deal more work than I," he confessed, but "what I had suspected hardly comes up to the draft on his time as he performed these duties"—"disposition of practice motions, motions to dismiss for want of jurisdiction," and instructions to the clerk, all of which were "a heavy load on his time and on his mind." [74]

Miller also learned that the brethren did not pull together automatically. Reporting to Waite on the Court's work, he voiced displeasure at the non-cooperation of Bradley and Field:

> Bradley has not read an opinion (even one) since you were taken ill. Judge Field hasn't done better.
>
> One of our brethren said to me yesterday that Judge Field is lobbying the bill to increase and divide our Court in Congress and I believe it is true. On Saturday he had interviews in the *lobby* of our conference room with a Senator and was in and out presently.[75]
>
> With the advent of a democratic administration we may look for his increased attention to politics and less to his official duties.
>
> I have given Bradley a case at every conference and he said he did not wish his delay in writing up these he has to prevent his being assigned to others.
>
> But if I were permanent C Justice, I would after he had neglected half the term to write up his cases give him no more until that was done.[76]

From his son, who was trying to persuade Waite that upon his return to Washington he should at first confine his activity merely to presiding over conferences, came a further indication that the Chief Justice's absence was being felt:

> The fact is that all is not as harmonious and things do not move as smoothly as when you led them. They miss your tact and they will be glad to have you back and do nothing but preside. They fully

[74] Miller to Ballinger, Jan. 18, 1885, in Fairman, *Miller*, p. 391.

[75] Alone among the justices, Field wanted to solve the docket problem by increasing the Court to twenty-one members who would sit in three separate chambers. Field to Deady, March 16, 1874, Feb. 18, 1883. Deady Papers.

[76] Miller to Waite, Jan. 25, 1885.

appreciate how sick you have been and do not expect or want you to work.[77]

Characteristically, Waite chafed at his enforced idleness, planning such an ambitiously early return that he received an anxious scolding from his son. "You certainly do not realize how sick you have been," Christopher Waite lectured his father and begged him to stay in Florida a little longer:

> Your term will be up, if your health holds out, a year from next November. You cannot possibly see the docket cleaned or an impression made in that time. Neither will you get one particle more credit or honor at that time whether you postpone your coming home now 10 days or not.[78]

Waite relented, postponing his return until early March. His colleagues expressed similar sentiments. Justice Miller, who signed his letters, "your affectionate friend," advised Waite to pace himself and to go about his work slowly. Justices Harlan, Matthews, and Blatchford showed a like concern: "We talked it over & think you should not try to come back & do work the rest of this term." "It would be a sad thing," they said, "to have a new Chief Justice in the next 4 years, and we all feel that it is more desirable for the country & the Court to have you for Chief Justice than that you should do a *little* more work, *too* soon." "I shall take it easy for the rest of the term," Waite promised, "that is to say, as easy as I can." [79] By March the Chief Justice was back on the job, working hard as usual.

As an individual Morrison Waite was not spectacular. He wanted the intellectual brilliance of a Bradley, the boldness of a Field, the wit of a Harlan, and the aggressiveness of a Miller. And yet, perhaps more than any of his talented colleagues, he was the man ideally suited to lead the Court. For Waite had solid abilities as a lawyer and, most important, was a shrewd judge of people, a good amateur psychologist. He understood human nature and through a happy combi-

[77] C. C. Waite to Waite, Feb. 13, 1885. Christopher Waite had just returned from Washington where he had spoken to the justices.

[78] C. C. Waite to Waite, Feb. 5, 1885.

[79] Miller to Waite, Jan. 14, Feb. 18, 1885; Blatchford to Waite, Feb. 15, 1885; Waite to Bancroft Davis, Feb. 12, 1885. Davis Papers.

nation of hard work, tactful firmness, and an easygoing kindness kept a strong-headed team of judges pulling together. "Your brethren alone," he was once told by an associate, "in the intimacy of the conference room, and the privacy of the arcana, know the skill, the patience, the uniform good temper, and the high sense of the dignity of the Court, which have marked the discharge of your duties." [80]

[80] Blatchford to Waite, Nov. 29, 1886.

14

POLITICS AND JUDICIAL PROPRIETIES

A Quest for Impartiality. Waite Suggested for the Presidency.
Uninterested in "A Mere Political Office."
Toledo Editor Clark Waggoner.
President-Making and the High Court. Partisan for Hayes.
The Hayes-Tilden Stalemate. The Electoral Commission.
Waite's Enduring Contribution to Judicial Integrity.

DURING HIS LIFETIME MORRISON WAITE WORKED HARD, FIRST AS A lawyer and later as judge and manager of the Supreme Court, but in nothing did he work harder than in his effort to safeguard the tribunal's reputation for impartiality. It was a labor of love. He regarded the Court as a great political institution, whose function—passing on constitutional questions having political implications—was one of importance and of infinite delicacy. In consequence, Waite believed that the justices should spare no effort both in striving and in appearing to be impartial. And he believed this, not out of any calculating desire to create a mask for judicial legislation by enshrouding the bench in a false aura of disinterestedness, but simply because he revered the Court as an institution. Within proper limits, he felt, it had a significant part to play in governing the nation. Adding intensity to these convictions was a very personal motive, the Chief Justice's determination to prove worthy of the office which, so unexpectedly, had come his way.

An early expression of Waite's concern for the good name of his Court came in November 1874, nine months after his appointment. Britton A. Hill, an attorney who had argued against the Missouri Pacific Railroad in a case that was still pending, became provoked when the St. Louis press published rumors that the Supreme Court had decided for the company.[1] The effect of these rumors, which

[1] The case was *Woodson* v. *Murdock*, 22 Wallace 351 (1874), involving a construction of state law. On November 16, 1874, the Court decided seven to two in favor of the railroad. It ruled that a restriction in the Missouri Constitution, which barred the

boosted the railroad's stock, aggravated Hill and he wrote the Chief Justice to inquire about their accuracy. Waite's answer was tart: "No such announcement has been made in the case" and "it would be highly improper for me to inform you, or any one else whether a decision has yet been reached." The now abashed Hill hastily apologized, explaining that he had not sought to learn the decision. While Waite accepted his apology, the mere suggestion that the Court might have acted improperly annoyed him and prompted a mild lecturing to the unfortunate attorney:

> No one can deprecate more than I do, the idea that the Court, over which I have the honor to preside, can permit its secrets to be divulged. The importance of the cases that come before us, as well as all the proprieties of judicial work, demand that, until our labors as a court are ended, the secrets of the consultation room should be kept inviolate. . . . [T]he implied suspicion of a disregard of this rule, which your letter contained, caused my note in reply.
>
> [W]hile, therefore, I now fully accept your explanation you must permit me to express the hope that, in the future, neither you nor any one will for a moment even, entertain such a suspicion, until we have given better evidence than I think we have already, that we are unmindful of the proprieties of the high position to which we have been called.[2]

Upholding these proprieties was, and remains today, essentially an individual affair. Each judge acts according to his own sense of what is proper, though, as Waite believed, a special responsibility attaches to the Chief Justice, who is the nation's highest judicial officer. Except for his advocacy of federal aid to education, Waite trod the straight and narrow path of judicial decorum. He refused, for instance, to serve as patron of an organization which, not content with the limitless opportunities for promoting Christianity among Christians, dedicated itself to promoting it among Jews. "You cannot but see," he told the sponsoring clergyman, "the absolute necessity there is of my keeping myself impartial as a judge, and not only being in

legislature from releasing liens held by the state upon railroads, did not forbid the legislators from selling the state's claims against the railroads or commuting the debt.

[2] Hill to Waite, Oct. 27, Nov. 2, 1874; Waite to Hill, Oct. 29, Nov. 5, 1874, Letterbooks.

fact, but seeming to be unaffected by any of the influences which in the opinion of any persons may improperly affect the court." Since "the Hebrews are largely a commercial people," who frequently appeared as litigants in the federal courts, some of the "unthinking" might feel his connection with the society affected his judicial conduct. And this would be unfortunate: "The effort of all should be to encourage the respect of every one for the courts of the nation. Anything that can by any possibility have a tendency in the opposite direction should be avoided." [3]

Waite made his major contribution to the cause of true judicial dignity when he was confronted with the problem of the judges' proper relationship to the political arena. The occasion came late in 1875. With a national election approaching, the Republican Party was a party in search of a candidate. Grant's scandal-ridden second term, Democratic election successes the year earlier, and the probability that its rival would be the formidable New York Governor, Samuel J. Tilden, created a severe challenge to continued rule by the Grand Old Party. To be sure, a flock of candidates eagerly waited in the wings. Of these only Benjamin H. Bristow, who, until the men around Grant realized that he *really* was dedicated to honest government, served for awhile as the President's Secretary of the Treasury, could genuinely pass as a reformer. James G. Blaine, Roscoe Conkling, and Oliver P. Morton stood for more of the same: government by spoilsmen. Rutherford B. Hayes, the eventual nominee, had just won the Ohio governorship in an upset victory and was only then beginning to emerge as a serious candidate. As a result, many Republicans were willing to consider any man who could hold the party together, and at the same time, offer hope that he would clean up the mess in Washington.

Morrison Waite's name was soon being bandied about in the press. If his image was hardly a dashing one and his fame but recent, these were also his assets: new to national life, he was not plagued by a record of past commitments; nor, in any way, was he tainted by the scandals which left a cloud of doubt hanging over the careers of so many public men in the 1870's. As early as the summer of 1874, a

[3] Waite to Rev. C. Ellis Stevens, May 29, 1879, Letterbooks.

scant half year after receiving his commission, the St. Louis *Democrat* ran an article, "Shall Toledo Also Furnish the Next President?", suggesting Chief Justice Waite as a presidential possibility. Soon after, admirers began asking the Chief Justice if he would consent to having his name pushed for the Presidency. Waite's reply set the position from which he never deviated:

> I have now no other ambition than to fill worthily the high office to which I have been called. To me it is the most desirable as well as the most honorable position in the government. It suits my taste and education. In it I can labor with some hope of success. . . . I have never looked upon what has been said in the papers upon the subject of the Presidency as anything serious. Certainly they have not as yet assumed a shape to require any action on my part. If and [when that] time should ever come I hope my friends including yourself will not have any reason to find fault with any actions I may take. For me at all times rest assured that at no time shall such a movement receive encouragement from me. I would rather die with a name fit to be associated with those of my great predecessors than be 40 times a President.[4]

Despite Waite's refusal to encourage would-be supporters, his name continued to appear as a possible candidate. In November 1875 the New York *Herald* and certain Ohio papers carried reports that Waite's colleague in the fourth circuit, Judge Hugh L. Bond, was quietly building a political organization favorable to the Chief Justice. Not knowing that the report was false, Waite asked Bond to abandon his plans:

> I am one of those who *know* that a Chief Justice cannot be a candidate for the Presidency, without damaging the office he holds and himself too. It is impossible for a judge to be impartial if he permits himself to *think* of political preferment. He may not be conscious of it, yet his ambitions will influence his judgments, in spite of himself.[5]

[4] St. Louis *Democrat*, July 18, 1874. Waite Papers; Benjamin B. Waite to Waite, Aug. 6, 1874. Waite's statement appears in an incomplete and undated draft of a letter written to answer an inquiry that was dated the twenty-fifth of some unspecified month. The draft is filed in Waite's Aug.–Dec. 1874 correspondence and almost certainly was prepared during the late summer of 1874. See also (draft letter) Waite to Mrs. Sarah Middleton, Jan. 5, 1875.

[5] Waite to Bond, Nov. 7, 1875, Letterbooks; Bond to Waite, Nov. 12, 1875.

The letter to Bond was sent on November 7; that same day he also prepared another statement, one of the strongest ever made by any Supreme Court judge on the subject of presidential politics. Its recipient was his cousin and good friend, John Turner Wait, a Connecticut lawyer prominent in state politics and a Republican Congressman from 1876 to 1887. A few days before, John T. Wait, after analyzing the political situation, had assured his famous kinsman "that you are the only man the Republicans *can* elect." "God bless you old fellow," he concluded, "and dont you fail to take the Presidency, if you have the chance, and I think you will have it." [6] Chief Justice Waite's answer was direct, simple and honest:

> I have yours of the 2d. Sunday is my letter day. Therefore you have had no answer until now. Of course, I am always grateful to my friends for their efforts in my behalf. No one ever had those more faithful or indulgent and no one ever had more cause for gratitude than I. But do you think it quite right for one, who occupies the first judicial position in the land, to permit the use of his name for a mere political office. The Presidency although high is only political. In my judgment, my predecessor [Chase] detracted from his fame by permitting himself to think he wanted the Presidency. Whether true or not it was *said* that he permitted his ambitions in that direction to influence his judicial opinions. . . . I am not one of those who believe he did so consciously, but one who occupies his position, should keep himself above suspicion. There can't be a doubt that in these days of political-judicial questions, it is dangerous to have a judge who thinks beyond the judicial in his personal ambitions.
>
> The Court is now looked upon as the sheet anchor. Will it be so if its Chief Justice is placed in the political whirlpool? The office has come down to me covered with honor. When I accepted it, my duty was not to make it a stepping stone to something else, but to preserve its original purity and make my own name as honorable of posterity as that of any of my predecessors. My whole education and training has been in the line of its requirements. Time & persevering patience added to my habits of work, may give me honor where I am. The other field is altogether untried. If I should fail there, it would to a certain extent drag my present office down with me. No man ought to accept this place unless he takes a vow to leave it as honorable as he

[6] John T. Wait to Waite, Nov. 2, 1875.

> found it. There ought never to be any necessity for rebuilding from below— All additions should be above.
>
> Think of this my friend. I appreciate all the kindness of my friends, but ought not the constitution to have provided that a Chief Justice should not be eligible to the Presidency? If such ought to have been the constitution, can I with propriety permit my name to be used for the formation of political combinations? If I do can I remain at all times and in all cases an unbiased Judge in the estimation of the people? If I am not, shall not I degrade the office? Put these things in your pipe and smoke them and then tell me if you think I ought to permit my name to be used.[7]

Originally, these words were intended solely for private consumption. The less said the better; a public statement, Waite felt, would attract more unwelcome publicity. "It will soon burn out," he wrote Judge Bond. "We can't jump into print." [8] On the thirteenth he sent out another letter, this one to Clark Waggoner, the editor of Toledo's *Commercial*, and repeated the substance of his expressions to Bond and John T. Wait.[9] Meanwhile, however, Waggoner had published an article listing Waite as a possible nominee and then journeyed to Washington to discuss the subject with his old friend. But when Waggoner arrived, Waite showed him his correspondence and again made a positive denial of any interest in the Presidency. Waggoner next proceeded on to New York, surveyed the political situation there, and returned to Washington convinced that public silence only would intensify the boom. Within Ohio the Toledo editor was an influential politician, a battle-scarred veteran of Republican state politics who knew his way around. Waite gave him permission to quote extracts from the letter to John T. Wait for the purpose of preparing an authoritative article that would make clear the Chief Justice's unavailability.[10]

[7] Waite to John T. Wait, Nov., 1875, Letterbooks.

[8] Waite to Bond, Nov. 12, 1875, Letterbooks.

[9] Waite to Waggoner, Nov. 13, 1875, Letterbooks.

[10] Waite to John T. Wait, Nov. 29, 1875, Letterbooks. Clark Waggoner (1820–1903) was a well-known figure in nineteenth century Ohio. A friend of Waite's since the early 1840's, he made his mark as one of northwest Ohio's leading newspaper editors. Great integrity and a willingness to fight for his principles characterized his life: he opposed the Radical Republicans during the Civil War, led a campaign for racially

Waggoner went back to Toledo and on November 27 the *Commercial* published a long editorial, "Chief Justice Waite and the Presidency," intended as a "positive and final" expression of Waite's desire that his name be kept "entirely outside of Presidential and all other combinations." As part of the editorial Waggoner quoted from Waite's letter to his cousin, tactfully deleting all passages which reflected unfavorably on Chief Justice Chase.[11] It appeared none too soon; on the same day that Waggoner ran the editorial *Harper's Weekly* came out with a strong condemnation of all efforts to drag Waite's name into political speculation.[12] Waite's remarks were widely republished and, in most cases, favorably received. The *Nation* lauded Waite's declaration, commenting that public confidence in the Supreme Court would be destroyed if it were searched for candidates every four years.[13] A like sentiment came from the New York *Tribune*, which described the Chief Justice's action as "sensible" and added a thought for the benefit of his colleagues: "We hope this excellent letter will be carefully read by his associates. It will do much to increase the confidence of the country in the Chief-Justice and in his court. Still more would be accomplished in that direction if it were known that all his associates accepted and acted upon his views." [14]

Yet, in an age of political chicanery, some observers remained skeptical. Washington's *National Republican* wondered "what political combination had tendered him the nomination" and declared that the Chief Justice had support among "straightout Republicans because it is known that he is a hard-money man and a firm supporter of the war amendments." Calling his action "uncalled for," it suggested that "the party might go further and fare worse in search

mixed public schools in Toledo, and during the 1890's fought the Standard Oil monopoly. A brief sketch appears in the *National Cyclopedia of American Biography* (New York: J. T. White and Company, 1910), XIV, 243. See also pp. 651–653 of Waggoner's own invaluable *History of Toledo and Lucas County*. His struggle against the Standard Oil interests is described in Chester McArthur Destler, *American Radicalism, 1865–1901* (New London: Connecticut College, 1946), ch. vi.

[11] Toledo *Commercial*, Nov. 27, 1875.

[12] Nov. 27, 1875.

[13] Dec. 2, 1875.

[14] Nov. 29, 1875.

of a candidate." [15] The Washington *Chronicle*, though acknowledging that the letter probably was not intended for publication, found it unsatisfactory as "a positive declination" and hoped for a statement "in plain, unequivocal language." [16] The Cincinnati *Gazette* thought Waite still open to a draft and Toledo's *Sunday Journal* commented:

> The extract only shows that the Chief Justice refuses to go into any combinations to secure the nomination—which is all right, but if the Republicans see fit to call him to higher responsibilities we know he is patriotic enough to respond.[17]

To end all such speculations Waggoner ran a second editorial, quoting this time from a letter Waite had written the editor:

> Everyday I live, I see more and more evidence of the great impropriety there is in forming political combinations around a Chief Justice. He cannot be a candidate for any political office without damaging the place he holds. Even though he should not let his political aspirations affect his judicial action, it would be said he did, and that would be almost as bad as if he did. My only ambition is to make my name honorable among those who have preceded me in the high office I hold.

Moreover, added Waggoner, Waite's private declarations were "even more positive and unequivocal." "These utterances, written and oral, with those acquainted with him," the editorial insisted, "leave no room for doubt as to his design; and to suppose that he contemplates the acceptance of a nomination, is to assume what his whole life utterly forbids." [18] To Rutherford Hayes he wrote: "M R Waite is not the man to say one thing and do another, as suggested by a few would-be friends." [19]

"I disliked exceedingly to get into the prints," Waite confessed, "but now that it is over I am wonderfully relieved." [20] Following Waggoner's second editorial, the Chief Justice thanked his friend:

[15] Nov. 30, 1875.
[16] Dec. 1, 1875.
[17] Quoted in Toledo *Commercial*, Nov. 30, 1875.
[18] Toledo *Commercial*, Nov. 30, 1875. The letter to Waggoner was written on Nov. 13.
[19] Waggoner to Hayes, Nov. 30, 1875. Hayes Papers.
[20] Waite to Waggoner, Nov. 29, 1875, Letterbooks.

Confidential

My dear Waggoner,

You have placed me under renewed obligations. The first publications left a gap that I feared would be seized upon. You will recollect I suggested it. The second, however, has closed the opening. Those that doubt now will say that Gabriel is only "making believe" when he blows his last trumpet.

I have seen very little of what the papers have said. The two leading papers here have rather slurred it. The Republican wondered why some one had not enquired what the political combination was, that had tendered me the candidacy, and the Chronicle thought it a little strange that I would have left it to my "friends" to advise me what to do. There are a great many wheels in this world, and it is not always easy to move one without striking another. If I have done anything which will tend to keep the court out of politics, I am satisfied. In my estimation no Chief Justice of my court can be a candidate for the Presidency without removing at least one stone from the foundations that uphold the government. This, however, is for your private eye and ear.

Tell Hayes to let "lightning strike" if it will. He is right when he says that there must not be too much crowding and pushing. Let things work— Dont force them. He has already a good start. The roots are well in the soil. Let them find the plant in their own way. The people are on the lookout for the man they want, they'll find him, even though he is not always thrust in their faces.

Sincerely Yr. friend,

M. R. Waite [21]

Coming when it did, Chief Justice Waite's renunciation was timely. On the bench Salmon P. Chase may have been, as a Court crier once described him, "dignity personified." [22] But it was a superficial dignity which failed to restrain him from avidly seeking the Democratic presidential nomination in 1868 and 1872. At a time when the *Dred Scott Case* and Radical Republican hostility had already weakened the Court and damaged its reputation, Chase's ambitions only served to weaken it still further. To make matters worse, Justice David Davis joined Chase in maneuvering for the Presidency;

[21] Waite to Waggoner, Dec. 4, 1875, Letterbooks. On Nov. 30, 1875, Waggoner had written Waite to explain his reasons for publishing a second editorial.

[22] Quoted in Fairman, *Miller*, p. 104.

suspected of doing so again in 1876, he elicited one of Waite's rare personal comments about his fellow judges. Davis, he said, had made "the Supreme Court the ante room of the White House." Not long after, Davis escaped to the less restricting confines of the Senate, becoming its President Pro Tem in 1881, and, in the absence of a Vice President, the potential successor to President Arthur. "I suspect," Waite observed, "it is as near to the Presidency as he can get." [23]

The problem of politics on the Bench was of course not new to Waite's period, nor is it likely ever to be completely resolved. The example of Justice John McLean, who spent the better part of thirty years in a vain quest for the Presidency, alternatively courting such diverse groups as the anti-Jacksonians, the Jacksonians, the Anti-Masons, the Whigs, the Free Soilers, the Know-Nothings, and finally the Republicans—probably—and hopefully—will not be repeated.[24] Yet, so long as men of stature sit on the Supreme Court, the names of its judges will at times figure in the great game of President-making that is a staple of American political life. In more recent times Chief Justice Earl Warren and Justice William O. Douglas have found themselves listed in presidential polls, as Waite too would have been had Dr. Gallup's methods existed in his day. Only one justice, however, Charles Evans Hughes in 1916, has received a major party nomination—and then under circumstances which did not discredit the Court.[25]

As with most matters of judicial decorum, the question of a justice's participation in politics is one for individual decision. During Waite's tenure a number of his associates, in addition to Davis, were at least fleetingly tempted by thoughts of moving into the White House. Stephen Field twice indicated a willingness to answer the call of a higher duty, but in both 1880 and 1884 the Democratic Party failed to issue the summons. His colleague, Samuel Miller, with something of a reputation as an agrarian radical, entertained mild hopes for the Republican nomination in 1880 and 1884. Unlike Field,

[23] Waite to Elihu B. Washburne, April 30, 1876, Letterbooks; to Amelia Waite, Oct. 14, 1881.

[24] Francis P. Weisenburger, *The Life of John McLean, A Politician on the United States Supreme Court* (Columbus: Ohio State University Press, 1937).

[25] Pusey, *Charles Evans Hughes,* I, ch. xxxi.

who attracted a good deal of publicity—with a campaign biography, a book of "personal reminiscences" about his early days in California, and, so critics charged, a disposition to turn some of his dissenting opinions into stump speeches—Miller did little to promote his candidacy. If Miller was afflicted with presidential fever, the attack was a mild one and certainly cost him no restless nights. As a sequel to his masterful dissent in the *Civil Rights Cases* of 1883, John Marshall Harlan's name was also briefly brought forward by Republicans still loyal to the Negroes' interests. The flurry ended as quickly as it began when the Justice emphasized that, for him, politics and his judicial duties were "utterly irreconcilable." [26]

Aside from his comment on David Davis, Waite's thoughts on the extra-judicial activities of his brethren are unrecorded. However, in light of his own declarations, they are hardly open to doubt. A glimmer of his feeling is suggested by the fact that the Chief Justice—he was a clipper of articles—saved a number of newspaper stories, some very critical, which discussed brother Field's political efforts. Once, remarking on a certain politician's behavior, he said, "When one gets a Presidential Bee in his ear, he is not to be trusted." [27] But while Waite wisely denied the propriety of political ambition on the Bench, he believed it unrealistic to expect that judges should be opinionless. As he put it in a letter to Dorman B. Eaton, the civil service reformer: "I have for many years believed that a man cannot be both judge & politician. He need not forego his political opinions when he goes on the bench, but he must his political aspirations." [28]

Certainly the Chief Justice did not abandon his own. Throughout his judicial career he remained faithful to the party of Lincoln and, especially when Rutherford Hayes ran for the Presidency in 1876, showed his partisan colors. Waite cheered lustily when his neighbor from northwest Ohio climbed into national prominence by winning the governorship in 1875 and he early favored Hayes' nomination for President. Personally disliking Tilden, whom he con-

[26] Graham, "Four Letters of Mr. Justice Field"; Swisher, *Field*, chs. x–xii; Fairman, *Miller*, ch. xiii; Westin, "John Marshall Harlan and the Constitutional Rights of Negroes," 677.

[27] Waite to John T. Wait, March 27, 1877, Letterbooks.

[28] Waite to Eaton, Nov. 28, 1875, Letterbooks.

sidered to be a grasping lawyer, the Chief Justice—in his private correspondence—could be an unashamed partisan:

> I can't help but feel a trust in Providence. It can't be possible that we are to be turned over to the democracy with Sam Tilden at the head. We have not sinned enough for that yet.[29]

To help Hayes' cause he strongly urged his old Yale classmate, William Evarts, who had cooled on the Republican Party because of his dislike for the Grant Administration, to make some campaign speeches. "You need not be afraid of Hayes," Waite assured him, "He is made of good stuff." Evarts finally came out for Hayes in the campaign's closing days with a rousing speech at New York's Cooper Institute. Although pleased, Waite wondered "why could he not have done this before?" [30]

Since the Chief Justice and his fellow Republicans were all "trembling in our boots a little about the election," Waite had good reason to be annoyed at his friend's indecisiveness.[31] Their concern was well justified. Tilden edged Hayes in popular votes and the tally in the electoral college was the closest in history. Both sides, with justice, charged the other with vote frauds and both claimed victory. Democrats allotted themselves upwards of 185 electoral votes; Republicans claimed to have won by one vote—185 to 184. The outcome depended on whether twenty disputed electoral votes were to be counted for Hayes or Tilden. Four states, Oregon, South Carolina, Florida, and Louisiana, filed contested returns, a possibility to which the Constitution does not address itself. It merely directs that electoral votes are to be sent to the President of the Senate, who, "in the presence of the Senate and House of Representatives," is to "open all the certificates and the votes shall then be counted." This might have worked,

[29] Waite to J. A. Hart, Oct. 15, 1876, Letterbooks. On Waite's dislike for Tilden see *Hayes Diary*, III, 362. He did, however, as "a very proper thing to do," favor Yale's granting Tilden an honorary LLD. Waite to Benjamin Silliman, July 2, 1875, Letterbooks. His support for Hayes is recorded in D. W. Rhodes to Hayes, Nov. 5, 1875, April 14, 1876. Hayes Papers; Waite to Hayes, June 5, 1875, Letterbooks.

[30] Waite to Evarts, Sept. 11, 1876, in Brainerd Dyer, *The Public Career of William M. Evarts* (Berkeley: University of California Press, 1933), p. 169; Waite to Pierrepont, Oct. 29, 1876, Letterbooks. Evarts' speech is reported in the N.Y. *Times,* Nov. 2, 1876. Subsequently, Evarts served as Hayes' Secretary of State.

[31] Waite to Pierrepont, Oct. 29, 1876, Letterbooks.

but the Senate and its President were Republican; the House was Democratic. The Democracy, sixteen years in the political wilderness, was not disposed to let its foes install a minority President in the White House.[32]

It was, as Waite called it, a "great trial." [33] Only a few short years removed from a bloody Civil War, the nation again faced a breakdown of its constitutional machinery. And, as had been the case in the 1850's, the opposing sides turned a political controversy into a legal battle. Again substantiating Tocqueville's observation that Americans resolve almost all political questions into judicial questions, the citizens of 1876 couched their arguments in the rarefied language of constitutional law. Democrats argued that the Republican-dominated returning boards (especially in Louisiana) had acted fraudulently. With little noticeable discomfort, they abandoned their customary states'-rights stance and insisted that the Constitution gave Congress power to examine the correctness of the results certified by the state returning boards. In turn, Republicans posed as stalwart defenders of local authority, contending that the federal government lacked control over a state's method of choosing its electors.

Almost inevitably the Supreme Court became involved. At first Waite succeeded in keeping the Court out of the raging controversy. Because of the inflammatory situation, he declined to call a special term of the circuit court in South Carolina to try the indictments resulting from the pre-election Ellenton Race Riot. Nor, despite the earnest pleas of Democratic party leaders, would he consent to go to South Carolina in order to pass on a conflict surrounding that state's returning board.[34] Finally, however, and despite their reluctance, the justices found themselves in the very center of the dispute. After weeks of negotiation enough Republican congressmen joined with the Democrats to enact an Electoral Commission bill designed to

[32] By far the best modern account of the crisis appears in Woodward's *Reunion and Reaction.* Still useful, though superseded by the former, is Paul L. Haworth, *The Hayes-Tilden Disputed Election of 1876* (Cleveland: The Burrows Brothers Company, 1906).

[33] Waite to Bond, Nov. 25, 1876, Letterbooks.

[34] The *Ellenton Cases* are discussed in ch. ix. The dispute involving the South Carolina returning board can be traced in the Washington *National Republican,* Nov. 22–Dec. 12, 1876; also, Bond to Waite, Nov. 22, 1876; three cables from Democratic officials to Waite dated Nov. 27, 1876. Waite Papers.

end the crisis. Passed in mid-January 1877, the bill created a special commission whose function was to examine the disputed returns and recommend to Congress which electors should be recognized.

Central to the Electoral Commission compromise was its composition. The bill provided for fifteen members, ten congressmen divided between the two parties and five Supreme Court justices—the really crucial participants since no one even remotely expected the five Senators and five Representatives to deviate from party loyalty. Some of the Democrats on the special House and Senate committees which drafted the bill made it clear that because of his reputed personal hostility to Tilden, Chief Justice Waite would not be an acceptable member. Waite himself wanted no part of the commission. Through Democratic Senator Allen G. Thurman he conveyed his emphatic desire that he be excluded from its membership.[35] Strongly committed to Hayes, Waite knew that he could not approach the controversy with any semblance of objectivity. Consider, for example, a letter sent to his wife on November 16, 1876. It is one of his few extended written commentaries on the crisis and a good illustration of his devotion to the Republican Party:

> I am more anxious now about election than ever. I think the returns in South Carolina & Florida will show a majority for Hayes, but I am doubtful if they do in Louisiana. The frauds there have been too great. The evidence of this to my mind is that Tilden's men all or nearly all go to Louisiana.[36] He pays but little more than nominal attention to the other states. This troubles me, and I fear there may be indiscreet things done there. However, we must wait and see. If the returning board attempts to throw out any of the returns for fraud, no matter how glaring the case may be, these men whom Tilden has sent there will surely make trouble.
>
> They were sent there for that purpose and their own bread and butter is dependent upon obeying orders. I am afraid my old friend Trumbull wont be the most conservative of the party either. When a

[35] Samuel S. Cox, *Three Decades of Federal Legislation* (Providence: J. A. & R. A. Reid, 1888), p. 638; Milton H. Northrup, "The Inner History of the Origin and Formation of the Electoral Commission of 1877," *Century Magazine*, LXII (1901), 926, 930.

[36] To assure an honest count the Democratic National Committee sent delegations of prominent Democrats to the capitals of the disputed Southern states; Republicans countered by sending their own committees of "visiting statesmen."

man gets to "lying around loose" as he has done, it wont do to bet on him. . . .[37]

I have not seen the President [Grant] since he was in Philadelphia.[38] I understand he takes it all coolly and says it will come out right. At Philadelphia he didn't move a muscle of his face and was as great and [illegible] as ever, but he was all the time issuing his orders for the movement of troops, and did not know but a conflict might come on at any time. I am inclined to think, though I don't know, that his famous order which has been so simply complimented by all parties was written while we were waiting for him to come to the closing ceremonies. He will go down to history as a really great man—and he deserves to do so.[39]

Subsequent letters revealed the Chief Justice's belief "that the Hayes electors are without doubt elected in S. Carolina & Florida," his hope that "all will come out right" in Louisiana, and a conviction that the Democratic Party's managers (their campaign motto had been "Tilden and Reform") were more interested in grabbing power than in reform.[40] Despite exaggerated fears of a new Civil War and some wild talk that 100,000 armed Democrats would converge on the capital to guarantee Tilden's installation, Waite saw little cause for panic. An early foreboding about "gloomy" political skies soon gave way to his usual optimism and faith in popular government. "The great good sense of the people," he asserted two weeks before the Electoral Commission bill passed Congress, "is exerting its influence upon the leaders of the democracy here as elsewhere." [41] Whatever his initial doubts about the legality of the returns submitted by Louisiana's Republican-controlled returning board, there is little doubt that out of the confusion of claims and counterclaims Waite would have found those of the Republicans more meritorious.

[37] Lyman Trumbull, the well-known lawyer, was one of those who went to Louisiana to look after Tilden's interests. A former Illinois Senator, he began his political career as a Democrat, later joined the Radical Republicans, then became an Independent, and eventually wound up as a Democrat again.

[38] On November 10, 1876, President Grant and some of the justices attended the closing ceremonies of the Philadelphia Centennial Exhibition. While there, Grant ordered General William T. Sherman to send federal troops into Louisiana and Florida to ensure an honest and peaceful count of ballots.

[39] Waite to Amelia Waite, Nov. 16, 1876.

[40] Waite to Amelia Waite, Nov. 23, 1876; to Waggoner, Jan. 8, 1877, Letterbooks.

[41] Waite to John T. Wait, Nov. 22, 1876; to Edward Browne, Jan. 15, 1877, Letterbooks.

Significantly, on January 20 Republican William Dennison, a former Ohio governor who played an important part in the Compromise of 1877, sent this report to Fremont, Ohio, where Hayes patiently awaited developments:

> My instincts are all opposed to the [Electoral Commission] measure. I have not however examined it carefully. Waite, [Senator John] Sherman, [Attorney General Alphonso] Taft & I talked it over last night at the Chief Justice's house. Sherman is opposed to it. [S]o Taft & the CJ listened attentively to all that was said. I have had several conversations with him on the general subject & am very sorry he is not to be on the Commission, if the Compromise be adopted. I dont mean that the two republican Judges selected are not reliable, but I have not talked with either of them. It looks as if Davis may be the fifth Judge, & as to him I will say, that I have more confidence in him than our friends here generally have. I cant well explain on paper. Still, I would feel easier as to him, if he had had less to do with the democracy than he has had. I have no authority to say what he will probably do, if on the Commission. My opinion is personal on what I have heard he has said generally on the presidential question.[42]

Dennison's comments illustrate some of the salient facts about the Electoral Commission bill. It was not, first of all, a Republican plan. For as things stood, all the cards were in Republican hands: they controlled the Senate and, at least nominally, held the reins of power in the key disputed states; most important, Grant still sat in the White House with the federal armies at his disposal. A Hayes-Tilden showdown would have almost surely ended in victory for the Republicans, a state of affairs that Dennison recognized when he opened his letter by castigating the bill as amounting "to the giving a certainty for an uncertainty." Second, the five justices were not expected to judge, but to cast their votes as partisans—hence the great concern over who would be the fifth, and deciding, judge. With Waite eliminated, Congress agreed on Democrats Clifford and Field and Republicans Miller and Strong as the four to be designated by the bill. They were then to choose one of their brethren as the commission's fifteenth member, which, according to a gentleman's agreement, every-

[42] Dennison to Hayes, Jan. 20, 1877. Hayes Papers. On Dennison's part in the Compromise see Woodward, *Reunion and Reaction*, p. 24, pp. 211–213.

one expected would be David Davis. Presumably, his reputation as a political maverick qualified him to balance the scales of justice in a fashion denied those more sure of their partisan affiliation.

Such were the contours of the Electoral Commission compromise. Carefully as it had been planned, the scheme went awry the very day that Congress passed the bill. For on January 25 the Illinois legislature, which had been deadlocked for a number of days, suddenly elected Davis to the United States Senate. The legislature's Democratic members unexpectedly joined a small Greenbacker group to give Davis a bare majority, thus releasing the irrepressible politician from the inhibiting atmosphere of the Supreme Court. Even though Davis (whom the Democrats had expected to support Tilden) immediately announced his inability to serve on the commission, it was too late for the Democratic Party to back down and the bill became law on January 29. Later, some Democrats attributed Davis' election to Republican machinations in Illinois, but evidence of this is lacking. More likely than not, Davis' sudden elimination was the consequence of miscalculation, not calculation.[43]

With Davis out of the picture, the four judges, after "a long struggle" according to Congressman Garfield, selected Justice Bradley to be the fifteenth member. Garfield also quoted Justice Strong as saying, "All the Judges, *save one*, were very sorry to be called to this commission." [44] Their hesitancy, subsequent events showed, was well-founded. While the Democrats were plainly discomfited by Davis' unforeseen absence from the commission, some of them acknowledged Bradley as a tolerable substitute. He was not a militant party man and had pleased the Democracy with his circuit opinion in the *Cruikshank* case against the validity of the Enforcement Act. But Democratic tolerance for Bradley was short lived. On all key issues the Justice sided with the commission's seven other Republicans to decide in favor of the Hayes electors under the theory that Congress

[43] Democratic National Chairman Hewitt subsequently expressed suspicions. Allan Nevins, *Abram S. Hewitt* (New York: Harper and Brothers, 1935), pp. 365–367. But there is evidence that Tilden's supporters arranged Davis' election in the hope that he would then favor their cause. King, *David Davis*, pp. 289–292; Woodward, *Reunion and Reaction*, p. 165.

[44] Garfield's *Journal*, Jan. 31, 1877. Garfield Papers. The willing judge was undoubtedly Field. Swisher, *Field*, p. 272.

lacked constitutional power to examine the disputed returns for possible fraud. Congress still had to complete the formal count, but the Republican electors now wore the mantle of legality, a tenuous eight-to-seven legality, yet it practically assured the seating of Rutherford Hayes.

Outraged at their narrow defeat, the Democrats descended on Joseph Bradley with all their fury. Democratic National Chairman Abram S. Hewitt and the staunch Tilden paper, the New York *Sun*, openly accused him of having changed an earlier decision in favor of the Tilden electors. The brunt of their charges, never proven and convincingly denied by Bradley, was that at the last moment he yielded to the dictation of the Republican leadership and certain railroad interests to whom he was supposedly beholden.[45] In truth, the question of the disputed returns was essentially political; no man, judge or otherwise, could have written a legal decision satisfactory to both sides. Ample precedents supported Bradley's decision against going behind the returns, and, clearly, his votes were no more biased than those of the commission's seven Democrats who consistently voted for Tilden. As Chief Justice Waite dryly commented: "Just at present our judges are severely criticized, but I feel quite sure time will bring us out all right. Wonderful partisans our Republicans are. Strange that no one ever thought such a thing of a Democrat." [46]

Time proved Waite's estimate to be correct. Bradley's reputation suffered from unjust criticism, but the Court as a whole came through the Disputed Election crisis comparatively unscathed. The worst charge was that the judges behaved as Republicans and Democrats—which is what virtually everyone else in the country did. Furthermore, their role on the commission had been unsolicited, reluctantly acceded to because a refusal would have upset an artfully contrived compromise and plunged the country into deeper trouble. Under these circumstances the Court was not very vulnerable to charges of having debased itself during the crisis of 1876. Quite the contrary,

[45] The charges and Bradley's denials may be pursued in Charles Bradley (Ed.), *Miscellaneous Writings of Joseph P. Bradley* (Newark: L. J. Hardham, 1902), pp. 8–11, 220–223; Fairman, "Joseph P. Bradley," in Allison Dunham and Philip B. Kurland (Eds.), *Mr. Justice* (Chicago: University of Chicago Press, 1956), pp. 83–84; Nevins, *Abram S. Hewitt*, pp. 372–373; Woodward, *Reunion and Reaction*, pp. 165–174.

[46] Waite to Pierrepont, Feb. 27, 1877, Letterbooks.

by doing its best with an unusual and nasty chore it assisted in ending one of the Republic's few really serious political crises.

On his part, Chief Justice Waite made a lasting contribution to the Supreme Court's tradition during the politically turbulent years of 1875 and 1876. His honesty characteristically forced him to decline service on a commission he could not serve objectively. More important were his actions in the closing days of 1875, which set an enduring example of judicial propriety and of sensitivity for the nature of the Court. By removing his name from political speculation, as well as by the reasons he gave, Waite revealed an instinctive appreciation for its peculiar nature as both a legal and a political tribunal. He understood well—as well he might, with the *Reese* and *Cruikshank* cases at that very moment being considered in conference—that the Court's decisions involved "political-judicial questions." Because this was so, it was all the more essential that a justice shun "the political whirlpool" and not think "beyond the judicial in his personal ambitions." How else could his decisions escape the suspicion that they were not self-serving? Finally, and perhaps most meaningfully, Morrison Waite revealed his own integrity, his inner sense of balance. A man who had climbed so rapidly from obscurity to national fame was all the more prone to find power exhilarating and succumb to its tempting siren song. But the steady Ohioan found challenge enough in filling his office with honor and in striving to preserve the Supreme Court as a "sheet anchor" of the American system.

15

''MOTT WAITE''

A Genial Host. 1415 I Street. Working Habits.
The Judges at Play. Whist and Brother Harlan's Whiskey.
Waite's Financial Embarrassments. Kindness to Others.
His Character and Common Sense. Vacation Pleasures.
Overwork Takes Its Toll. Final Days. The Beloved Man.

TO HIS FRIENDS CHIEF JUSTICE WAITE NEVER CHANGED FROM THE genial and unaffected person he had been as an attorney in Toledo. You invariably saw, one of them said, "the same Mott Waite, unspoiled by the dignity of office. The same pure, fresh, manly spirit lived within him and looked joyously out at you from his eyes."[1] Old friends and acquaintances, especially those from the circuit days —days nostalgically remembered as having "heaps of enjoyment covered up in them"[2]—were always welcome in the Waite household. "I hope," he would say, "I am no more inaccessible to my friends than I used to be. Officially I must surround myself with somewhat of etiquette, but otherwise I am always glad to see and meet my friends and their friends without form or ceremony."[3] So cordial a host was Morrison Waite that his grandson recalls the Chief Justice's home as rarely being without informal guests; the dinner table was good-sized, ever ready to accommodate the visitors who made mealtimes an occasion for pleasant relaxation and easy conversation.[4]

During his first year in Washington the Chief Justice lived on H Street next door to George Bancroft, staying in the house of his friend Bancroft Davis. From there he moved to Rhode Island Avenue, renting a house that belonged to the son of Edwin M. Stanton, and finally, in the late 1870's, he bought his own property at 1415 I Street. In the

[1] Thomas Dunlap, "Chief Justice Waite," p. 27.

[2] Waite to Dunlap, Aug. 4, 1881. Toledo Public Library.

[3] Waite to James French, Nov. 9, 1879, Letterbooks.

[4] Conversations with Mr. Morison R. Waite of Cincinnati, Sept. 19, 1960, May 12, 1961; Cincinnati *Commercial Gazette*, March 24, 1888. Waite Papers.

style of the day, it was a fashionable brownstone, comfortable and spacious enough to take care of the guests who crowded his home. Covered by vines on its two sides, the I Street home had bay windows in front which looked out on a street shaded by leafy trees. The historian Martha Lamb, a frequent visitor to the Waite home, described it as "a veritable home, roomy, restful, with an air of substantial personal comfort, its appointments so tastefully blended that no one feature fixed itself upon the mind; a home in the highest degree interesting from the fact that it seems in its refined simplicity to reflect the character of its distinguished occupant." [5]

On the second floor in the rear of the house was the Chief Justice's study, a large cluttered room whose central feature was a long library table piled high with papers. Bookcases rimmed the walls; above them hung engravings and pictures of the public men he admired—Webster, Clay, Marshall, Lincoln, Grant, and Hayes.[6] This room Waite regarded as sacrosanct; in it he did most of his work. To the young nephews, nieces, and grandchildren who periodically filled his home the study was forbidden territory. He made one exception, for a favored granddaughter who used to slip into the room, sit in a rocking chair, and quietly rock her doll. Waite customarily rose early, and fortified by some black coffee, would put in at least two hours work before the family's nine o'clock breakfast. After breakfast he returned to the study for perhaps another hour's labor before, weather permitting, setting out on foot in time to reach the Court for its eleven o'clock opening. Unless some social duty interfered, he went back to the study following dinner and spent his evenings working on opinions and the business of the Court. He always worked alone, writing opinions longhand and reading them aloud to himself before delivery: modern aids such as secretaries and dictation of letters were spurned because, said the Chief Justice, he was too "old-fashioned" to change his habits.[7]

In his judicial work he collaborated most often with Justice Brad-

[5] Martha Lamb, "Chief Justice Morrison Remick Waite," *Magazine of American History*, XX (1888), 4.

[6] Lamb, "Chief Justice Waite," 4; N.Y. *Times*, Dec. 22, 1880.

[7] Conversations with Mr. Morison R. Waite, Sept. 19, 1960, May 12, 1961, and his sketch, "Morrison R. Waite."

ley, a good choice since Bradley outshone many of his brethren in intellectual power and legal ability. Waite once said that he respected his advice above all others, and particularly during the trying early years, found Judge Bradley a valuable ally.[8] When Bradley praised one of Waite's first opinions as accurate, "clearly expressed," and "exactly right," the Chief Justice must have felt encouraged.[9] And, as this note about an opinion they were interested in indicates, he was more than willing to be generous in acknowledging Bradley's help:

> I will take the credit, and you shall do the work, as usual. But . . . we are on the right track, and the principles we enunciate will stand. As soon as I get in my proof we will have a conference. I am sure, if we put our shoulders to the wheel, our work, which in this case will apparently be mine, cannot be successfully attacked.[10]

Lest it be thought that Chief Justice Waite lacked his own powers of persuasion, here is an extract from a letter he sent his wife near the close of the 1877 term:

> My last proof went to the printer yesterday and as I am inclined to think the opinion is one of the best I have ever written, I will send a copy which you can read or not as you like. It is a sort of supplement to my Geneva "coal" argument. My brethren have complimented me more upon it, than any other I have ever written. Judge Bradley tore up his dissent which he wrote and had printed so that I might see it and became contented. Judge Field wrote a dissent, but backed out from making it in open court, after I read mine, though he recorded a dissent. Whether he will file his or not I don't know. He did say to me though after we left court, that mine was able. Judge Clifford voted against the decision in conference, but did not dissent publicly. He simply asked me to change a single expression, which of course I did.[11]

[8] Waite to Bradley, Dec. 11, 1883.

[9] Bradley to Waite, Dec. 21, 1875. He referred to Waite's opinion in *Rubber Tip Pencil Co.* v. *Howard*, 20 Wallace 498 (1876), a patent case.

[10] Waite to Bradley, May 14, 1878, Letterbooks.

[11] Waite to Amelia Waite, May 19, 1878. The case was *Young* v. *United States*, 97 U.S. 39 (1878), a suit for the recovery of the value of cotton seized by the federal government during the Civil War under the Captured and Abandoned Property Act of 1863. Waite, for the Court, held that an Englishman, who had gone out of his way to assist the Confederacy, might not recover nearly one million dollars worth of his

The letter also reveals Waite's inward enjoyment of his work, his overcoming of the initial fears that he felt when first appointed. What Justice Harlan, in his inimitable way, called "*Judicial Worms*"—"that kind of worms which produce doubt and hesitation, and which do not permit the mind to rest in certainty, until a decision of some Master of the Rolls is found," no longer troubled the Chief Justice.[12] As he wrote his wife in 1878, "I thrive under hard work, if there is nothing to fret me. I am long past thinking of a case after I have decided it."[13]

Among the justices his closest social friends were John Marshall Harlan and, after they came to the Court in the 1880's, Stanley Matthews and Horace Gray. All the brethren joined in the whist parties which, enlivened by a few rounds of bourbon, were a favored recreation. Writing to the Chief Justice just before the opening of a new term, Judge Harlan showed that he was not solely preoccupied with weighty legal matters: "I wish to give notice that the experience of this Summer has improved my knowledge of whist. So next winter, when opportunity arises, I will not be so modest when Bro. Miller is discoursing upon the fundamental rules of that game."[14] Waite must have enjoyed Harlan immensely. While they frequently disagreed in civil rights and state bond cases, the Kentuckian was blessed with wit and humor and a knack for leaving his differences in the conference room. When Waite sent Harlan a photograph, the Judge promptly responded, commending it as "absolutely perfect," typically adding, "You look natural and life-like as you would look if I were to say that a gallon of old Bourbon was on the way from Kentucky for you."[15]

Near the end of one delightfully irreverent letter asking Waite to help him with a difficult case Harlan feared that "you may come to the conclusion that my mind has become confused by reading the decisions of our court" on municipal bond cases, "or that I have

cotton which fell into federal hands in the war's closing days. Justices Clifford, Field, and Bradley voted against the majority in conference, but withheld a public dissent. Docket Books, Oct. Term 1877. Waite Papers.

[12] Harlan to Waite, June 17, 1885.

[13] Waite to Amelia Waite, May 3, 1878.

[14] Harlan to Waite, Sept. 8, 1884; also, Harlan to Waite, n.d., 1880, n.d., 1883.

[15] Harlan to Waite, n.d., 1883.

seen Ben Butler on his Yacht & tasted some of his New England rum." Neither supposition, he assured the Chief, would be correct. He closed by ordering Waite to "put this letter into the fire" so that his biographer would not know he corresponded with a man capable of writing such undignified letters. The Chief Justice fortunately ignored the request, preserving Harlan's witty sketch on the vacation activities of some of the brethren:

> The last I heard from Bro Woods he was at Newark. Bros Matthews and Blatchford will, I fear, get such lofty ideas in the Mountains that there will be no holding them down to mother Earth when they return to Washington. Bro Bradley, I take it, is somewhere studying the philosophy of the Northern Lights, while Gray is, at this time, examining into the Precedents in British Columbia. Field, I suppose has his face towards the setting sun, wondering, perhaps, whether the Munn case or the essential principles or right and justice will ultimately prevail.[16]

Less enjoyable than whist parties, Kentucky bourbon, and Harlan's anecdotes was the strain of living on a restricted income. Where his legal work in the early 1870's earned him about $25,000 a year, as the nation's highest judicial officer his fee slipped to $10,500. By contrast, an accomplished lawyer like Philip Phillips of the Supreme Court bar made almost $35,000 in 1876. Phillips averaged between $300 to $500 per case; in an important bond case, for instance, *Town of South Ottawa* v. *Perkins*, he commanded as much as $2,700.[17] Waite, of course, knew his income would decrease. This did not bother him—he had no interest in accumulating a fortune—but he hoped to live graciously and make ends meet. Writing to Amelia Waite shortly after his appointment about an old and now well-to-do acquaintance, he put it this way:

> How things change. He is now "out of business," that means "seeing his money grow." You & I never will and I am glad of it. What can be worse? All I ask now is to make what I have and the salary that I earn, keep me from being actually pinched. All the rest

[16] Harlan to Waite, July 31, 1888.
[17] 94 U.S. 260 (1877); Account Book, 1876–1877. Phillips Papers.

may take care of itself. We shall have to pull in the purse strings somewhat, but I hope they will leave a little play. . . .[18]

Instead, the Chief Justice soon found himself severely pinched. For one thing, his wife was recurringly troubled by illnesses, and this meant unexpected medical expenses. For another, the cost of living was higher in Washington than in Toledo, and his expenses soared simply because he was Chief Justice. Almost every year he went on circuit to the southeastern states, an item that alone cost him around $400 each time. A degree of style was appropriate to his position and he could not escape certain social obligations. When Lord Coleridge, the Chief Justice of England, came on a visit to the United States, Waite gave him a lavish dinner and followed it with a reception for two hundred people. "I suppose," he commented, "that is one of my extra honors as Chief," hopefully adding that the expenses of the reception "will not probably be so very much more than a dinner." [19]

As a result, Waite soon found, as he graphically told the accountant in his old law firm, that "the cost of living here is eating up my very vitals." [20] To another he complained, "For the first time in my life I really have been made to feel that I must count the cost of everything." [21] Worst of all, he had to go into debt, borrowing money from his first law partner, Samuel M. Young, who had since become a prosperous Toledo banker and businessman. Embarrassing as this was, Young proved to be a true friend, gladly loaning the Chief Justice nearly $3,000 between 1876 and 1877. By selling his few stock holdings and some real estate he owned in Toledo, Waite repaid the debt but never again attained financial security. So small were his savings that after he died little was left for his wife, and to support her remaining years friends and bar associations throughout the country subscribed a fund.[22] The federal judiciary during the nineteenth century received a thoroughly inadequate compensation and it led to some ironical situations: attorneys like Conkling or Evarts,

[18] Waite to Amelia Waite, July 14, 1874.

[19] Waite to Amelia Waite, Oct. 8, 1883. An account of the dinner and reception appears in the Washington *National Republican.*

[20] Waite to J. M. Gloyd, May 6, 1876, Letterbooks.

[21] Waite to Dr. R. F. Bissel, March 4, 1878, Letterbooks.

[22] Waite to Young, Dec. 25, 1876, June 20, Nov. 14, 1876, Letterbooks; conversation with Mr. Morison R. Waite, Sept. 19, 1960.

with annual incomes of $100,000, would appear in cases involving huge sums; the judges who passed on the arguments had an income equal to perhaps one-tenth of the counsels' earnings.

Despite these financial embarrassments, Waite never for a moment contemplated resigning. His sense of duty and reverence for an office "covered with honor" forbade any such thoughts. "I would rather be Chief J. than President," he told Bradley in 1877. When a college classmate, having just presented Yale with a bust of its former president, Theodore Woolsey, suggested that if he resigned and gave him the chief justiceship, he would also erect a statue in his honor, Waite shot back: Woolsey "is worthy of all that can be done for him, but I wont surrender my place to you even for a bust." [23]

Even though his resources were limited, Waite managed to fulfill the impulses of a generous nature. For many years he helped subsidize the musical education of a young lady named Nancy Hart, the daughter of a boyhood friend whom illness had made a permanent invalid. In addition, he often dipped into his own pocket to make "loans" to one Mrs. Lizzie K. Sherman, of whom a few words should be said. Lizzie Sherman was one of three children descended from John Poag of Toledo, a close friend and a former client of Waite's law firm. A man of considerable wealth, he became insane in middle life, subsequently dying and leaving three children, Lizzie, Emily, and John Poag, Jr. M. R. & R. Waite took over execution of Poag's trust and Waite himself accepted the boy as his ward.

Long after he became Chief Justice and after his legal connection with the Poag trust had been severed, Waite continued to assume personal interest in the children's welfare. He treated young Poag as a son, taking him into his home. "None of my children ever received more consideration," he once told him, for "we all felt that you were alone and became much attached to you." [24] Regrettably, Poag was an unstable lad, quite ungrateful and anxious only to inherit the money that he could claim at the age of twenty-one. Eventually he ran away, making his way to Europe. From there he wrote the Chief Justice an abusive letter, claiming that because "my father liked me

[23] Waite to Bradley, Feb. 25, 1877, Letterbooks; Pierrepont to Waite, March 13, 1877; Waite to Pierrepont, June 16, 1877, Letterbooks.

[24] Waite to John Poag, Jr., Nov. 15, 1875, Letterbooks.

best of all," he deserved more money than his sisters, and denouncing his guardian for never treating "me as a gentleman's son." Waite replied mildly, "I am very glad to learn from you in what ways I have offended." He realized that the son, like his father, was not quite responsible for his actions. All the while, he also kept a lively, time-consuming interest in the fate of Lizzie and Emily. Lizzie constantly troubled him for loans, advances on her trust allowance, and interminable letters about her marital difficulties—induced in part by the fact that she too was ill, being an opium addict who died at a young age. More stable was Emily, but she also had problems; her husband was an army officer whose alcoholism caused repeated troubles, and again Waite gave his time and help.[25] During 1874, Waite's first and most demanding year on the bench, letters concerning the Poag children dominated his correspondence. All were thoughtfully answered.

This kindness, a major element in Morrison Waite's character, finds expression in every aspect of his life. Robert B. Warden, a former Ohio judge, who at times practiced before the Supreme Court, published a controversial biography of Salmon P. Chase. Critics felt it libeled the deceased Chief Justice, and Judge Warden heard that some of the justices shared "a deep prejudice" against the book and its author. In a mood of dejection and extreme self-pity he wrote Waite, saying he feared "to present myself before you and your brethren as an advocate." The Chief Justice promptly disabused him of this notion—"come to us with all the cases you can get" and you will have "no occasion to find fault with your reception"—and offered some encouraging advice. "My friend," he told him, "come down from your high horse or else come up from your low one. You ought not to have so discouraged yourself. Don't get moody. Step up your professional powers and make yourself the lawyer your friends know you can be." And reassuringly, "Come up and see me." [26]

Other attorneys also felt the Chief Justice's kindness. When an octogenarian, "one of father's contemporaries at the bar," had a case in Washington, Waite noticed that the old man had "been in court

[25] Waite to Amelia Waite, Sept. 22, 1874; to Morton Rose & Co., Oct. 5, 1874; to John Poag, Jr., Nov. 15, 1874, Letterbooks; numerous letters to and from the Poag children.

[26] Warden to Waite, Oct. 19, 1874; Waite to Warden, Oct. 19, 1874, Letterbooks.

nearly every day for a week waiting for his case to come on." By the time his argument came due, "he was so excited that I adjourned court until Monday so that he might [get] cooled down." Both in Washington and on circuit Waite was especially popular with younger members of the bar. An Alabama lawyer, nervous over his first appearance before the Supreme Court, wrote later to thank Waite for the "courteous and considerate thought" which made it possible for him to present his case. Another inexperienced young lawyer, arguing his first Supreme Court case and on the verge of collapse, was carefully led back to the right track by the Chief, who perhaps recalled his own near breakdown when he began practicing half a century earlier in northwest Ohio.[27]

Morrison Waite's character was that of a simple man—not simple in a naive, uninformed way, but in the fashion of an honest and unaffected man. He was, also, a man with a common-sense cast of mind. One sees these qualities most at the important moments of Waite's life, as when, with tact and humility, he took his seat as the new Chief Justice; or again a year later, when he vowed not to besmirch the Supreme Court in politics. They are evident at lesser moments as well. One of Waite's minor duties, a statutory responsibility conferred by Congress, was to serve as chancellor of the Smithsonian Institution's Board of Regents. Until 1874 the Smithsonian's museum had been closed on Sundays, but that year a movement began to open it to the public on Sunday afternoon. Its secretary and first director, Joseph Henry, one of the nineteenth century's foremost scientists, strongly opposed this, feeling it would be irreverent. He sent the Chief Justice an emphatic protest against the Regents' considering a Sunday opening. Waite's reply reveals a man of great practicality:

My dear Prof.

I have your note of today. There was no necessity for it. I will

[27] Waite to Amelia Waite, March 29, 1874; Thomas Jones to Waite, Nov. 23, 1876. Statements of Waite's kindness to young attorneys appear in "Supreme Court Proceedings in Memoriam of Morrison R. Waite," 126 U.S. 585 (1888); "Proceedings in Memoriam of Morrison R. Waite," United States Circuit Court for the Fourth Circuit (1888). Waite Papers. See also, recollections of Judge John Doyle, Toledo *Blade*, March 24, 1888.

go as far as anyone to promote the observance of the Sabbath, and to make it a day of holy thoughts, but I am by no means certain that the opening of the rooms of the Smithsonian under proper rules and regulations may not conduce to that end. All people will not attend church, and as Sunday is a day of rest, they are very likely to go to some other place. That place will probably be worse than the Smithsonian.

My idea is, if you cant make people as good as you wish, make them as good as you can. Education at the Smithsonian may send some to Church. At any rate it is not likely to make anyone who wont go there worse.

So I shant vote against opening the doors on the afternoon of Sunday, if anyone wishes it.

Yrs. very truly
M. R. Waite [28]

If dogmatism was alien to Waite's thinking, he never wavered in his personal religious commitment. Throughout his life a low-church Episcopalian, he was always extremely active in church affairs. During his years in Toledo he faithfully attended the meetings of his church vestry. In Washington he served as a vestryman of the Church of the Epiphany and represented his diocese at general convention. On Sundays, from religious motives as well as from necessity, he believed in resting thoroughly; yet he did not wear his religion on his sleeve: "he was a religious man, a true christian, not ostentatiously, but quietly, deeply and sincerely." [29]

In common with most humans, Morrison Waite liked to live in comfortable style. He had his expensive tastes—oysters, clams, and lobsters were lifelong favorites, and New York's Park & Tilford received regular orders for sherry, claret, and sauterne. Still, he was scarcely the sort to care for a fancy life, and the artificial formalities of Washington society annoyed him. "Pure etiquette," he once snorted, is "a humbug." [30] When Grant's Administration was shaken by the scandalous revelations involving War Secretary W. W. Bel-

[28] Henry to Waite, Oct. 26, 1874; Waite to Henry, Oct. 26, 1874, Letterbooks.
[29] Morison R. Waite, "Morrison R. Waite," 98.
[30] Waite to Amelia Waite, Nov. 20, 1876.

knap, Waite characteristically felt that "some good" would come out of the disgrace: "It will for a moment at least put a stop in part to the reckless extravagance of living that prevails here."[31]

His greatest pleasures came in spending time with close friends—people such as Samuel Young, his old law partner, William Evarts and Edwards Pierrepont, who graduated with him from Yale in 1837, or Rutherford Hayes, to whom he grew close in the years between 1877 and 1881. Nothing, however, pleased him more than to revisit among the old "Maumee pioneers." "As I get farther and farther away from our early years on the Maumee," he would say, "the pleasures of meeting with those I knew increase. Aside from that too it is pleasant to hear the stories of the old times repeated and to live over in imagination the life we there led."[32]

Summer vacations were normally spent at his boyhood home of Lyme, Connecticut. Following the annual circuit swing down South, Waite would join his family in Lyme; though, when possible, he would first try to go to Toledo for a few days among his friends there. Vacation time was a chance to catch up on opinion writing, but there was also opportunity for relaxation amidst a lovely New England setting. One summer he went on a "stag" trip West with Judge Horace Gray and General William Tecumseh Sherman. The spectacle of the soft-spoken and peaceful Chief Justice in company with the warlike conqueror of Georgia and one of America's great military minds seems perhaps incongruous, but Judge Waite and General Sherman were fast friends. Waite had long looked forward to the trip. It was to be made with a small party, following military supply routes and traveling largely in mule trains and by horseback. "Some parts of it will be 'camping out' and horse back travel, but it seems to me nothing could be better," Waite informed Gray, whom he urged to make the journey.[33] Armed with a special memorandum of instructions from General Sherman on what to bring, Waite eagerly set out for

[31] Waite to John T. Wait, March 7, 1876, Letterbooks.

[32] Waite to Thomas Dunlap, Aug. 24, 1882. Toledo Public Library. Dunlap's address on "Chief Justice Waite" gives an excellent picture of how Waite enjoyed himself at one such meeting of the Maumee Valley Pioneer Association.

[33] Waite to Gray, June 3, 1882. Gray Papers. The trip was, however, postponed until 1883.

a summer of "roughing it" in Montana, Yellowstone Park, and other places in the western states.[34]

Back in more sedate Old Lyme his wife received long and enthusiastic letters. The western railroad systems, the mining in Montana, the natural wonders at Yellowstone, and the life of pioneers, all caught his interest and were the subjects of detailed descriptions. One wonderfully human letter, datelined "Tom Miner's Creek, Montana," bears quoting:

> After pitching camp at 5350 feet above the sea we sat around, hungry until dinner was cooked. At McIntyre's [ranch] we tried for fish but they would not come. I ate raw onions on the steak & liked them. Then came a beefsteak, potatoes, (which [I] also ate), ham and eggs &c. They all tasted good. Soon after supper was over a camp fire was built and we all sat around until the rain came again, when Gray and I went to bed—a little after eight. As the men were tired out the tents were not all put up, and Gray and I slept in one on the ground. Bedsteads have been discarded. The thermometer went down below freezing, but it did not disturb me, for I slept straight through. At four we were up, and I washed outdoors where the thermometer stood a[t] freezing, dressed myself and had breakfast at five, which tasted good, bacon & eggs and lambchops the fare. It was a most superb morning—Not a cloud to be seen, but all the overcoats were in demand. . . .

A few paragraphs below he commented:

> I am sitting on the bank of the stream under a tree, and writing this on my knee. The mosquitoes are as thick as they can be, but fortunately dont sting, and as soon as they begin to bite they submit, without any attempt at escape, to being killed. The mark [on the paper] was caused by my efforts in that direction which were successful.[35]

Unfortunately, the trip ended for Waite a few days later. A horse threw him, and, since broken ribs do not make "agreeable travelling companions," he reluctantly returned to Lyme.[36] His next excursions,

[34] Sherman to Waite, April 20, 1883.
[35] Waite to Amelia Waite, July 6, 1883.
[36] Waite to Mrs. Bryan, Oct. 11, 1883. Chicago Historical Society.

to England in 1885 and to California and Alaska in 1886, were made by more conventional means of travel. At the age of sixty-seven, he had learned, it was best to relive the rough experiences of the old circuit days in memory only.

As a matter of fact, the Chief Justice was aging rapidly. "We cannot help it, darling," he told his wife in 1887 after hearing of the illness of a beloved friend, "age has got hold of us all." [37] They were an exceptionally devoted couple and had long looked forward to 1890, the fiftieth anniversary of their marriage. Amelia Waite herself was often ill during the seventies and eighties and caused Waite great concern. He would beg her to be careful, saying he did not want to miss the pleasure of a golden wedding anniversary. Instead he was the first to go.

Years of overwork began to take their toll in 1885. That year he suffered the breakdown which kept him briefly out of his seat, but not until March 1888 did he suffer a final collapse. For months Waite had been preparing the Court's opinion in the *Bell Telephone Cases*, an extremely complicated suit involving the validity of the patents owned by the American Bell Telephone Company.[38] With a sigh of relief—the opinion occupies an entire volume of the United States Reports—he wrote the Reporter on March 5, 1888, "I have at last finished the opinion." [39]

It was scheduled for public announcement two weeks later, and meanwhile the Chief Justice became sick. On Saturday the eighteenth he attended a Senator's evening reception, walking both ways because of his coachman's illness. The next day he came down with a chill. Physicians were called in; nevertheless, Waite insisted on going to Court on Monday to read the opinion. His wife was then on a visit to California and he told friends that his absence from Court would appear in the press dispatches and make her worry needlessly. But once there he lacked strength to read the lengthy opinion, which was announced by Judge Blatchford. Attorney General Garland later recalled it as a sad and painful sight, "It was evident to the observer

[37] Waite to Amelia Waite, Aug. 10, 1887.

[38] 126 U.S. 1 (1888). A useful account of the controversy surrounding the Bell patents is in Cummings and McFarland, *Federal Justice*, ch. xv.

[39] Waite to Bancroft Davis, March 5, 1888. Davis Papers.

death had almost placed its hand upon him." [40] Returning home, he was put in bed and his sickness diagnosed as a severe case of pneumonia. The end came in the early morning of March 23. Awakening after a peaceful night's sleep, he asked his nurse to help him turn over. As she did, he remarked, "I feel better," and immediately thereafter stopped breathing. He was buried in Toledo, vast crowds assembling to observe the arrival of his body from Washington and a memorial procession in his honor—testifying, a local paper commented, "if testimony was wanted, of the respect and esteem in which the dead citizen was held by his fellow citizens." [41]

The personality of a man long dead is not easily captured by the printed word. A man is so much more than the official acts, the private statements, the major events which make up his formal "life" that his true essence—as a warm and living human being—becomes elusive and distorted, as distant as the bygone days in which he lived and breathed. But a glimmer of what Morrison Waite was to those who knew him survives in two radically different expressions, complementary only because both were unsolicited and are free from cant. One, rough and half-illiterate, comes from an obscure settler in northwest Ohio. He had written Rutherford Hayes, asking if he would attend a Maumee Valley pioneer meeting, and praising him for not having "got away" from the people. To which he added: "It is also felt to be preeminently so with M. R. Waite C.J. U.S.A. his greeting is as corteous his hand shake as cordial his eye glance as honest as of yore & Sir the people *love him*." [42] The second, more polished, more refined, comes from the former President. Set down by Hayes in his private diary a few scant hours after the Chief Justice's death, it exudes freshness and spontaneity:

> He was of large and strong intellect. He was great-hearted, warm-hearted, and of generous, just and noble sentiments and feelings. He was thoroughly trained and schooled from his youth up. He was in the best sense a learned and a well educated man. He had saving

[40] Augustus H. Garland, *Experience in the Supreme Court of the United States* (Washington: J. Byrne and Company, 1898), pp. 35–36.
[41] Washington *Post*, March 24, 1888; Toledo *News Bee*, March 29, 1888.
[42] Ruel Alden to Hayes, Aug. 17, 1887. Hayes Papers.

common sense, untiring industry, and great energy. He was always cheerful, easily made happy by others, and with amazing powers and a never-failing disposition to make others happy. He was the best beloved man that ever lived in this part of the United States.[43]

[43] *Hayes Diary*, IV, 380 (March 23, 1888).

16

THE WAITE PERIOD: CONSOLIDATION AND CONCILIATION

The Unheroic Era. The Supreme Court Under Chief Justice Waite.

Cautious Conservatism. Rulings for Reunion.

Judicial Opinions and Public Opinions.

Capitalism and the Court.

Morrison R. Waite: the Judge and the Man.

WHEN MORRISON WAITE WAS NOMINATED AS CHIEF JUSTICE, CHARLES Sumner is reported to have said:

> I hesitate; I fear. We stand at an epoch in the country's life, in the midst of revolution in its constitutional progress, at a nascent stage in the development of some of its institutions; and I long for a Chief Justice like John Marshall, who shall pilot the country through the rocks and rapids in which we are.[1]

Although Waite was no Marshall, it is doubtful whether any other Chief Justice ever can be "like John Marshall." Only Marshall was in the unique position that permitted him to combine brilliance and determination with a long tenure and so interpret a comparatively new constitution in his own image. Sumner, moreover, misread the spirit of the times. The Civil War may have been "the second American Revolution" and the war amendments "the second American Constitution," but by 1874, the year Waite took his seat, the revolution was over. Whatever the opportunities for new constitutional departures, they simply were not seized in the years between 1870 and 1890; they were allowed to pass and few people seemed to mind. Anxious to concentrate on business, eager to leave sectional strife behind, and convinced that the Negro was inferior to the white man, most Americans had little interest in heroic ventures and radical constitutional experiments.

[1] Quoted by Samuel Shellabarger, "Supreme Court Proceedings in Memoriam of Morrison R. Waite," 126 U.S. 585, 599–600 (1888).

In any event, the Supreme Court under Morrison Waite trod a constitutional path best described as one of consolidation and conciliation. It eschewed radical interpretations, instead absorbing the war amendments into the framework of traditional constitutional constructions. Decisions such as those in *Munn* v. *Illinois* and the *Sinking Fund Cases* in the area of economic regulation, and *United States* v. *Cruikshank* and *United States* v. *Reese* in the civil rights field stood for the proposition that the turmoil of the sixties had not changed the basic nature of the Union. Secession was a dead doctrine, but otherwise the relationship between the states and the federal government remained much as it had been before the firing on Fort Sumter. States retained primary jurisdiction over the behavior of their citizens, and, as had been the case since the days of Marshall and Hamilton, the nation's public authorities were guaranteed power to govern economic relationships.

This path of consolidation was a natural consequence of the essential conservatism of the Waite Court's majority—conservative in the sense that its constitutional interpretation was characterized by caution and a respect for precedent. Nothing better illustrates this than the contrast between Stephen Field and Morrison Waite. "The period of Waite's Chief Justiceship," Professor Frankfurter observed, "is in large measure the history of a duel between him and Field." [2] Despite Field's outraged protests that the majority was forsaking the Constitution known to the fathers, it was he who was the revolutionary, the innovator of new constitutional departures. A master of rhetoric and invective, Field accused the majority of having embarked on a subversive course because of its decisions upholding rate regulation, federal control over corporations, state bond repudiation, and issuance of paper money as legal tender. Quite the contrary, was it not he and his corporation friends who were the real revolutionaries? Even as they applauded Field's dissents, the business leaders were busily initiating radical changes in the American economy; and at the same time, the Justice's bold dissents sought to fashion a judicial policy capable of serving the new capitalism.

Field agreed with the majority in seeing little power in the war

[2] Frankfurter, *Commerce Clause*, p. 110.

amendments with which to safeguard civil rights, yet insisted that the Fourteenth Amendment gave the Court power to sit as a board of review over state regulatory legislation. But the *Munn* case, the landmark case of the Waite period and the great object of Field's ire, was a consolidating, not a revolutionizing decision. Although it is rather futile to search the Constitution for guidance as to whether warehouses and railroads may be regulated, the English Common Law and American experience in the eighteenth and nineteenth centuries reveals a history of regulation. True, the scope of the post-Civil War regulation was much greater. Waite and his colleagues nonetheless decided as they did with the firm conviction—and with ample precedents in law and in traditional canons of constitutional interpretation to support their conviction—that economic regulation was within American experience and law. The Chief Justice who normally allowed legislatures wide discretion in making policy choices and who believed that judges should not "make too much law at once," but should feel their way "and not be afraid to draw back if the ground will not hold you up," was no revolutionary.

Waite, of course, voted to void legislation in the civil rights cases, abandoning his otherwise almost habitual deference to legislative power. Inconsistent in this respect, the Chief Justice's civil rights decisions accorded with the large role he customarily reserved the states. And they were of a piece with his overall conservative view, adhered to in numerous economic cases, that the new amendments had not drastically altered the American political system.[3]

In their broad implications the civil rights decisions suggest that if the Waite period was one of consolidation rather than innovation, it was even more obviously a period of conciliation. The rulings in the *Reese*, *Cruikshank*, and *Civil Rights Cases* harmonized neatly with the specific political acts known as the Compromise of 1877. They harmonized as well with a vague attitude shared by a majority of Americans, who, in place of radical crusades, wanted the Negro question returned to the control of the Southern states. By restricting the Fourteenth and Fifteenth Amendments so that in general they

[3] It should be recalled that, except in the area of civil rights, Waite was as sympathetic to federal power—once it was exercised—as he was to state power.

applied only to state action, and by insisting on carefully drawn indictments in civil rights prosecutions, the Court simultaneously encouraged and sanctioned national reconciliation. Waite, Bradley, and Miller, the judges most influential in these cases, decided according to their own lights, interpreting the war amendments as they understood them. While it is inaccurate to say that they deliberately fashioned a policy of conciliation, the justices, no less than the President, the congressmen, and the varied bargainers who helped arrange the Compromise, were prominent actors in the drama that marked the return of American union. Their civil rights decisions serve as a reminder that while the Court may occasionally deviate from dominant national attitudes, the more normal pattern sees it in step with the country's mood.

The Waite Court, in fact, successfully avoided running afoul of national popular opinion—an unusual achievement in view of the significance of its decisions affecting civil rights, corporations, and bondholders. Where decisions in other eras provoked full-blown assaults—the Jacksonians, the Populist-Progressives, and later the New Dealers all waged war against "judicial usurpation"—the Waite Court's potentially controversial opinions largely balanced each other out, muting popular hostility. Except among the politically powerless Negroes, the civil rights rulings won praise throughout the nation and created a reservoir of good will in the South. The municipal bond cases antagonized midwestern communities, but in the face of decisions upholding railroad regulation and partial repudiation of state bonds there was little impetus for an anti-Court crusade. Nor did Congress have cause for disaffection. Its powers to regulate interstate commerce and federally chartered corporations, to levy income taxes, and to decree legal tender were all broadened; the one exception to this, the limitation on federal civil rights power, was greeted with indifference.

One interest, the corporate, found itself severely alienated by the Waite Court. The decisions sanctioning Granger rate regulation, permitting congressional control over the Pacific railroads, and allowing Virginia's despised Readjusters to tamper with the state's debt convinced many railroad and financial leaders that the spectre of communism had cast its spell on the United States Supreme Court. American businessmen, never timid in the use of power, applied intense pressure to change the majority's course. By its very nature the pressure was not in the form of a great popular protest. Many, no doubt, shared the values glorified by the social Darwinists. But even in the Age of Enterprise the American people were far from denouncing the justices because some of their decisions harmed the interests of Leland Stanford or Jay Gould. Farmers, working-class groups, and small businessmen provided just enough opposition to make the corporation's position unpopular, eliminating the threat of any broadly based assault upon the Court. The business leaders themselves preferred to make their influence felt by indirect means. While they occasionally fired at the Court in pro-corporation journals, their main attack was far more subtle: cooperation with sympathetic judges such as Field, employment of brilliant attorneys and skillful manipulation of cases, education through the medium of bar associations, and attempts to control the President's judicial appointments.

Despite the pressure, the Waite Court stuck to its independent course. In refusing to give corporations special constitutional protection, it created a situation rich in irony. Since Marshall's day Americans of property and substance had regarded the Supreme Court as their special preserve, a tribunal sure to protect them against popular majorities. When the *Granger* and *Sinking Fund Cases* arose, business leaders awaited the results with confidence. They received a rude shock: decisions that were considered by "all monied men," Whitelaw Reid had informed Garfield, as "revolutionary" and as "bad law and bad faith." The justices may have acted as they did out of their old Whiggish faith, which taught the primacy of legislative rule, and because they were uncommitted to the new industrial order. Still, it is remarkable that during America's most capitalistic phase, the Supreme Court—which textbook history, describing the years before 1937, commonly labels a bulwark of private property—should align itself with what Justice Field furiously charged was "the agrarian and despoiling spirit."

The Waite period is, finally, the history of the man himself: Chief Justice Morrison R. Waite. He was at the time of his death a subject of conflicting evaluations. No one denied his personal qualities as an individual, what Attorney General Garland called his "beautifully rounded" character.[4] Judge Miller paid tribute to his "practical tact" and declared that as an individual he combined "steadiness and firmness in action" with "courtesy and consideration" towards all with whom he came into contact.[5] But many of the estimates were tinged with depreciation, which in some cases shaded into outright disparagement. Roscoe Conkling, in an address prepared for the New York bar but undelivered because of his sudden death, could say no better than that Waite survived "the ordeal" of succeeding to a position once filled by men such as Taney and Chase. "Not to have been seriously disparaged by comparison with the men he met as his associates," Conkling patronizingly said of the man who became Chief Justice after he had spurned the office, was "itself ground for eulogy." [6] The Washington *Post* described Waite as lacking "those characteristics which excite ardent admiration," and the New York *Times* thought it not improper to hope for a "return to the early standard of choice" by the selection of a successor "who has already exhibited the qualities and acquirements that give assurance of judicial greatness." [7] The *American Law Review* was even more derogatory. All that could be said for Waite was that he "did nothing to lower the dignity" of the office. He "left no great memorials of his strength as a judge," though, fortunately, "he was able to avoid the display of any great deficiencies as a lawyer." [8]

On the other hand, many of the judgments, such as this one from the Chicago *Tribune*, were highly complimentary:

> In freedom from prejudice, justness of decision, as well as in the personal dignity with which he presided, and in his courtesy to practitioners, he was the peer of any one of his six predecessors in his exalted office if not the equal of some of them in ability. Those who doubted his ability when first appointed have since promptly con-

[4] Garland, *Experience in the Supreme Court*, p. 35.
[5] "Supreme Court Memoriam," 126 U.S. 610–611.
[6] "Memorial Before the Association of the Bar of the City of New York," (specially printed in 1890). Waite Papers.
[7] Both papers dated March 24, 1888.
[8] XXII (1888), 303.

> ceded it, and no lawyer, however eminent he might be, has had cause to complain either of his lack of it or of judicial partiality.[9]

New York's *Herald* hailed him for giving "dignity and elevation" to the Supreme Court's judgments;[10] the *Central Law Journal* described Waite as an "eminent jurist" who "held the high position which he adorned for a period far too short for the benefit of his country."[11] *Harper's Weekly* found that "the atmosphere of the judicial chamber was never more free from party passions and influences than during Chief Justice Waite's term."[12] The *Albany Law Journal* praised him as a wise man of "large sagacity and sound common sense." "He was not so great a judge as Marshall—but who save Mansfield ever was?" Neither was he "so learned a lawyer as Taney; but in both respects we deem him superior to Chase." Beyond this, "He also put the right value on his place. No presidential bee ever buzzed in his bonnet. . . . He knew that he had the highest post on earth, dispensing justice rather than dividing offices, the oracle of litigants rather than the prey or plaything of politicians."[13]

With the perspective of the years certain things now stand out—none more clearly than that Morrison Waite has been a vastly underrated figure in American constitutional history. As many have observed, he was no John Marshall. But, then, Rutherford Hayes was not Andrew Jackson; Roscoe Conkling was not Daniel Webster; and the able Hamilton Fish was not John Quincy Adams. The Gilded Age had its giants—John D. Rockefeller, Collis P. Huntington, and Andrew Carnegie—but their talents were finding expression in endeavors other than public service: building railroads, exploiting natural resources, creating mammoth industries, and, most of all, acquiring immense fortunes.

As a judge, Waite, unlike Marshall and Taney, did not act self-consciously as a statesman.[14] He was, and considered himself to be,

[9] March 24, 1888.
[10] March 24, 1888.
[11] XXVI (1888), 309.
[12] April 7, 1888.
[13] March 31, 1888.
[14] The point is suggested by Frankfurter in his *Commerce Clause*, p. 82.

primarily a lawyer to whom there was "no better fun" than to fight cases in court.[15] His opinions clearly show his bent as a lawyer, a good lawyer. They are concise, logically constructed, and emphasize factual realities. Their greatest weakness is stylistic; Waite's prose is rarely inspired. But this flaw, perhaps the major reason for his underrated status, reflects lack of artistic ability, not intellectual shallowness. While he could never match Bradley in legal learning, it is doubtful whether Field, Miller, or Harlan surpassed Waite in anything but rhetorical ability. Intellectually, he matched them all in consistency and he was as tenacious as they in standing by his convictions. Then too, Waite had a judicial philosophy, which however inelegantly he expressed it, is one of continuing vitality. He held to a simple—but never disproven—faith that the people, acting through legislatures, know their own best interest. Because of this and because he trusted the legislative process to provide its own self-correctives, Waite believed that judges ought to be chary about upsetting legislative decisions. Moreover, in performing his function as judge, Waite displayed a receptivity for realities dictated by facts, a fact-consciousness, that in the hands of articulate judicial craftsmen such as Oliver Wendell Holmes and Louis D. Brandeis has become a characteristic of the best in the modern Supreme Court's decisions.

He was also a most successful Chief Justice. Not only was the Court managed with skill and a wise understanding of human nature, but the years of Waite's chief justiceship saw it strengthened as an institution. Coming to Washington in 1874 as Grant's fifth, possibly his seventh, choice and with barely any national reputation, he took his seat among associates who were leading public figures and who had jockeyed for the position he now held. The Court itself had labored under a cloud of suspicion for nearly two decades. The *Dred Scott Case*, the Radical Republican attack, the reversal in the *Legal Tender Cases* of 1871, which left the suspicion of Court-packing, the unseemly political maneuvering of Chief Justice Chase and Justice David Davis, not to mention Grant's fumbling efforts to find a Chief Justice, had combined to blur the image of a lofty tribunal impartially devoted to the public interest. Yet, by the time he died in

[15] Waite to George Willey, Nov. 11, 1874, April 14, 1875, Letterbooks.

1888, Waite, like his friend Rutherford Hayes in the Presidency, had restored respectability to the Supreme Court. His manner may have been unspectacular and his personality less than scintillating. But by his quiet dignity and careful observance of the judicial proprieties he did much to add new luster to the Court's tarnished reputation.

Waite's major achievement, however, was personal. Convinced that the Chief Justice had a position of profound honor and that the tribunal over which he presided was one of the nation's great political institutions, he came to the Supreme Court fired with a determination to prove himself a worthy successor to Marshall and Taney. He succeeded. That he did was undoubtedly due to many things; certainly his legal ability and sensitive appreciation for the judicial function played an important part. Above all, though, his success was due to his character. Engaging modesty, genuine kindness, unquestioned integrity, and willingness to work long and hard—in a word, character of the highest sort, assured Morrison Waite's triumph.

Often, when pressed as to why he worked so hard, he would say simply that he was doing it "for the honor of my grandchildren." The ambition was fulfilled; the post which he described as coming to him "covered with honor" is an even more honored one because Morrison R. Waite occupied it during the difficult years from 1874 to 1888.

A BIBLIOGRAPHICAL NOTE

THE PRIMARY SOURCE FOR THIS STUDY IS THE APPROXIMATELY 20,000 items contained in the Morrison R. Waite Papers stored at the Library of Congress. Unless it is otherwise indicated, all citations in the narrative of correspondence to and from Waite refer to letters in the Waite Papers. In addition to this main collection, the following persons and libraries made available some small, but highly useful, collections of Waite's papers: the late Mr. Morrison R. Waite of Cincinnati, Professor and Mrs. John B. Waite of Ann Arbor, Michigan, the Toledo Public Library, the New York Public Library, and the Chicago Historical Society.

A second source of great importance was provided by the manuscript collections which are listed below. Numerous collections which were searched and yielded no significant information are omitted; the list includes only those papers quoted or cited in the book.

Adams, Charles Francis, MSS., Massachusetts Historical Society.

Bancroft, George, MSS., *ibid.*

Barlow, Samuel L. M., MSS., Henry E. Huntington Library, San Marino, California.

Bradley, Joseph P., MSS., New Jersey Historical Society.

Butler, Benjamin F., MSS., Library of Congress.

Chase, Salmon P., MSS., *ibid.*

Davis, J. C. Bancroft, MSS., *ibid.*

Deady, Matthew P., MSS., Oregon Historical Society.

Field, Stephen J., MSS., Berkeley Library, University of California.

Fish, Hamilton, MSS., Library of Congress.

Garfield, James A., MSS., *ibid.*

Gray, Horace, MSS., Library of the Supreme Court of the United States.

Hayes, Rutherford B., MSS., Rutherford B. Hayes Library, Fremont, Ohio.

Lane, Ebenezer, MSS., Chicago Historical Society.

———, MSS., Yale University Library.

Phillips, Philip, MSS., Library of Congress.

Reid, Whitelaw, MSS., *ibid.*

Sherman, John, MSS., *ibid.*

Washburne, Elihu B., MSS., *ibid.*

Welles, Gideon, MSS., *ibid.*

Wells, David A., MSS., New York Public Library.

In quoting from manuscript sources I have done some editing of a very minor nature. Where dash marks were obviously intended to serve as periods (rather than for purposes of emphasis) the substitution has been made. With brief one-sentence quotations I have dispensed with ellipses at the opening and closing; with the longer quotations I have eliminated the opening and closing ellipses. I have also freely transposed upper case letters into lower case and *vice versa* when running quotations into my textual commentary. All such changes have been made for ease of reading; in no instance have I deliberately tampered with the meaning of quoted materials.

Besides the manuscript collections I have drawn upon a number of other original sources. These include nineteenth century newspapers, the Congressional *Globe* and *Record*, and the official reports of the United States and the Ohio Supreme Court, all of which are fully identified in the footnotes. The Records and Briefs of United States Supreme Court Cases, which I consulted at the Library of Congress and the Supreme Court Library, were useful in preparing my detailed discussion of certain cases. They are frequently cited throughout the book. Finally, I uncovered valuable material from among the multitudinous collections of the National Archives. The Source Chronological File (Mississippi and South Carolina) of the Department of Justice, Record Group 60, was especially helpful. I also profited by sampling selected portions of the Archive's Supreme Court Collection, an enormous body of papers and records covering the period from 1790 to 1909, which undoubtedly will be intensively mined by students of the Court in years to come.

I have not felt it necessary to prepare a bibliography of my secondary sources. These are identified in the footnotes and should provide ample guidance to interested scholars. However, two legal historians on whose work I have often relied deserve special mention. Ever since his now classic "The 'Conspiracy Theory' of the Fourteenth Amendment" was first published in 1938, Howard Jay Graham has been turning out stimulating articles which can only be described by that much abused but, in this case, appropriate phrase—"path breaking." Another trustworthy guide for the study of the post-Civil War Court is Charles Fairman. Professor Fairman's biography, *Mr. Justice Miller and the Supreme Court 1862–1890*, and his other writings on the judges of that fascinating period in Court history are models of careful and conscientious scholarship.

INDEX

INDEX